The Kurdish Conflict

This book is highly topical considering the recent resurgence of violence by the PKK, the incursions into Northern Iraq by the Turkish army and security forces and Turkey's EU accession negotiations. Turkey has become an increasingly important player in Middle Eastern geopolitics. More than two decades of serious conflict in Turkey are proving to be a barrier to improved relations between Turkey and the EU. This book is the first study to address fully the legal and political dimensions of the conflict, and their impact on mechanisms for conflict resolution in the region, offering a scholarly exploration of a debate that is often politically and emotionally highly charged.

Kerim Yildiz and Susan Breau look at the practical application of the law of armed conflicts to the ongoing situation in Turkey and Northern Iraq. The application of the law in this region also means addressing larger questions in international law, global politics and conflict resolution. Examples include belligerency in international law, whether the 'war on terror' has resulted in changes to the law of armed conflict and terrorism and conflict resolution.

The Kurdish Conflict explores the practical possibilities of conflict resolution in the region, examining the political dynamics of the region, and suggesting where lessons can be drawn from other peace processes, such as in Northern Ireland.

This book will be of great value to policy-makers, regional experts, and others interested in international humanitarian law and conflict resolution.

Kerim Yildiz is the founder and Executive Director of the Kurdish Human Rights Project (KHRP) and is a recognised expert on the Kurdish regions.

Susan Breau is Professor of International Law at Flinders University, Adelaide, Australia and is well-regarded for her work in the field of the law of armed conflict and international human rights law.

The Kurdish Conflict

International Humanitarian Law and
Post-Conflict Mechanisms

**Kerim Yildiz
and Susan Breau**

Routledge
Taylor & Francis Group

LONDON AND NEW YORK

First published 2010 by Routledge
2 Park Square, Milton Park, Abingdon, Oxon, OX14 4RN

Simultaneously published in the USA and Canada
by Routledge
270 Madison Avenue, New York, NY 10016

Routledge is an imprint of the Taylor & Francis Group, an informa business

© 2010 Kerim Yildiz and Susan Breau

Typeset in Baskerville by Taylor & Francis Books
Printed and bound in Great Britain by CPI Antony Rowe,
Chippenham, Wiltshire

British Library Cataloguing in Publication Data
A catalogue record for this book is available from the British Library

Library of Congress Cataloging in Publication Data
The Kurdish conflict : international humanitarian law and post-conflict
mechanisms / Kerim Yildiz and Susan Breau.
     p. cm.
   Includes bibliographical references.
   ISBN 978-0-415-56270-6 – ISBN 978-0-415-56273-7 –
ISBN 978-0-203-84933-0 1. Self-determination, National – Kurdistan.
2. Humanitarian law – Kurdistan. 3. Kurds – Legal status, laws, etc.
4. Kurdistan – International status. 5. Kurds – Legal status, laws, etc. –
Turkey. I. Breau, Susan Carolyn, 1955-II. Title.
   KZ4272.Y55 2010
   341.6'709566'7 – dc22
                              2009051457

ISBN10: 0-415-56270-8 (hbk)
ISBN13: 978-0-415-56270-6 (hbk)

ISBN10: 0-415-56273-2 (pbk)
ISBN13: 978-0-415-56273-7 (pbk)

ISBN10: 0-203-84933-7 (ebk)
ISBN13: 978-0-203-84933-0 (ebk)

To Bridget and Dara

To my dear friends and inspirational colleagues Indira Carr, Agnieszka Jachec-Neale and Amrita Mukherjee

Contents

Table of cases

International Court of Justice

European Court of Justice

Court of First Instance of the European Communities

Inter-American Court of Human Rights

Domestic courts

Table of treaties

Domestic laws

Foreword

Professor Kader Asmal

Conflict in today's world can no longer genuinely be solely a domestic affair as hostilities and confrontations often have both anticipated and unforeseeable consequences for regional and the international affairs as well as for individual states. While not all conflicts garner the media's or public's attention, for people living in areas affected by unrest and conflict, life can be extraordinarily difficult with their livelihood, security and fundamental of human needs at risk daily.

As threats to security increase, the resulting transgressions of humanitarian protection and human rights weaken the international norms that protect us all.

The Kurdish Conflict aims to provide a thorough and thoughtful account of the ongoing conflict in southeast Turkey and northern Iraq. As history, politics, law and culture have all played a part in fomenting the conflict; the authors contend they must be central to the Turkish state's and the international community's approach in seeking a peaceful and sustainable resolution to the conflict. Combining Kurdish Human Rights Project Chief Executive Kerim Yildiz's deep understanding of local history, politics and culture and his experience in international human rights law with humanitarian law expert Dr. Susan Breau's expertise in the international legal framework, *The Kurdish Conflict* is distinctive in its comprehensive understanding of the conflict in Turkey, its effects on northern Iraq and conflict-resolution. The arguments put forward in this book will, I hope, encourage further studies along these lines.

I have been privileged to work with a great number of people, in South Africa and around the world, who have dedicated themselves to ending conflict and fostering the conditions for peace and justice to prevail. It is my sincere hope that this book will enhance interest in this area and by contributing to the resolution of the dreadful situation in southeast Turkey and northern Iraq and by providing the parties and negotiators with the international legal and political framework in which to work towards a lasting peace.

In a world where an individual state's security is increasingly related to events occurring outside its borders and a greater emphasis on humanitarian law will be essential, *The Kurdish Conflict* contains important insights for us all.

I strongly commend this book to everyone interested or involved in the protection of national rights and international peace.

Professor Kader Asmal
Hon. Professor of Law, University of the Western Cape and
University of Cape Town, former Minister of Education in South Africa

Foreword

Helena Kennedy and Mark Muller

In today's world, conflict in any part of the world is the responsibility of the international community as a whole. As threats to security increasingly permeate national borders, and each transgression of humanitarian protection, human rights, and international cooperation weakens the system that protects us all, this responsibility grows even more pressing.

There are a number of conflicts across the world today that remain largely unreported, as the gaze of media headlines and key political actors is focused elsewhere. Yet for people living in regions of conflict, life is a daily struggle for their and their families' security and welfare, the most fundamental of human needs. This book affords their plight with the seriousness it deserves, by giving a thorough and thoughtful account of the situation of the Kurdish people living amongst ongoing conflict in southeast Turkey and northern Iraq. Combining a deep understanding of local history, politics and culture with expertise in international legal frameworks, this book is distinctive in its holistic understanding of conflict and conflict-resolution. Law, politics, culture and history can all play roles in fomenting conflict; they must therefore be central to approaches seeking peaceful resolution of conflict. The collaboration between Kurdish Human Rights Project Executive Director Kerim Yildiz and humanitarian law expert Dr Susan Breau in writing this book will, we hope, encourage further studies along these lines.

It is our sincere hope that this book will contribute to the resolution of the conflict in southeast Turkey and northern Iraq, by providing the parties and negotiators with the international legal and political framework in which to work towards a lasting peace.

In a world of inter-dependent security, ongoing conflict, and developing humanitarian law, this book contains important insights for us all. The pursuit of peace and the rule of law can be a difficult path, but the authors' accomplishment here is to illuminate our way along it.

Helena Kennedy QC
Chair of Justice and Former Chair of the British Council
Mark Muller QC
Chair of the Bar Human Rights Committee of England & Wales and
Founding Trustee of the Delfina Foundation

Acknowledgements

This major project would not have been possible without the conscientious and expert research assistance of Ommera Ahmed, Alexandra Bamban, Rachel Bernu, Narin Demircioglu, Loye Jide Olufemi, Antoine Martin, Estella Schmid, Timothy Thrower and Catriona Vine.

A particular mention must be made of the outstanding contribution of Janna Mancini whose tireless efforts ensured the emergence of this project and its completion.

The authors would also extend their gratitude to Katherine Carpenter and Khanam Virjee of Routledge and to the anonymous reviewers of the book proposal.

The authors of the book would like to express their sincere appreciation of the book's research assistant Charlotte Alfred for the work she carried out and upon which this project is based.

Introduction

Although southeast Turkey has seen serious conflict for over 20 years, no exhaustive study has been conducted on the international law and international relations ramifications of the conflict. It is crucial to carry out a comprehensive analysis of this ongoing armed conflict at a time when Turkey not only continues to engage in European Union accession negotiations and cross-border military operations in Kurdistan, Iraq, but is also taking tentative steps towards a political solution to the situation of the Kurdish people in Turkey. This book provides a legal analysis of, and suggests a possible 'roadmap' for resolution of, the conflict, thus filling the crucial gap in academic literature on the topic.

The two authors of this book bring a unique multi-disciplinary perspective to this conflict. Kerim Yildiz, the Director of the Kurdish Human Rights Project (KHRP), has extensive experience in international law and armed conflict and offers unique insight into the political causes of, and ultimate solutions to, this conflict. Since the founding of KHRP, he has been involved in the preparation of many books and reports on the situation of the Kurdish people of the region and has been instrumental in the bringing of cases to the European Court of Human Rights. Dr Susan Breau is an academic international lawyer with particular expertise in examining the laws governing armed conflict, both *jus ad bellum* and *jus in bello* and has also engaged in extensive research on the human rights consequences of movements for self-determination. This book is structured in such a way as to give the reader a comprehensive view – both legal and political – of the conflict in southeast Turkey.

The study commences in Chapter 1 with a brief history of the Kurdish people across Turkey, Iraq, Iran and Syria as well as a brief background to the conflict in the predominantly Kurdish southeast region of Turkey, and the area in the north of Iraq over which the Kurdistan Regional Government has authority (forthwith referred to as southeast Turkey and Kurdistan, Iraq respectively). This background chapter helps to provide readers with sufficient knowledge of the topic and prepares the ground for the analysis in the following chapters.

Part 1 of the book concentrates on the law of armed conflict as directly applied to the situation in southeast Turkey and Kurdistan, Iraq. Chapter 2 deals generally with the international legal regime concerning armed conflict and is also designed to serve an introductory purpose. The first task is to review the definition of 'armed conflict' within international humanitarian law and to apply that definition to discuss whether the situation in southeast Turkey rises to the level of an armed conflict. After examination of the relevant treaties and academic literature, it is determined that this conflict does indeed rise to the level of an armed conflict. Following this determination, the chapter reviews the various types of armed conflict that could exist and, on balance, concludes that a non-international armed conflict exists in southeast Turkey and spills over into Kurdistan, Iraq. It also, importantly, introduces the law within armed conflict, the *jus in bello*, which includes the Hague Regulations and the Geneva Conventions of 1949 with the provision applicable in non-international armed conflict, Geneva Convention, Common Article 3. The chapter concludes with a discussion of the relationship between the protections afforded by international human rights law and the legal obligation under international humanitarian law.

Chapter 3 is crucial to the study of the armed conflict in southeast Turkey and looks in detail at the international humanitarian law standards applicable to a non-international armed conflict including Common Article 3 to the Geneva Conventions of 1949, Customary Humanitarian Law and Minimum Humanitarian Standards. The chapter reviews the legal obligations within non-international armed conflict for both the Turkish military and the fighters of the insurgency within southeast Turkey. It also engages in a specific analysis of the jurisprudence of the European Court of Human Rights and the applicability of those cases in clarifying not only the obligations under the *jus in bello* but also those under international human rights law. The analysis gives particular focus to the civilians in the area who have been caught up in this long-standing war and who have seen their lives and property destroyed.

Chapter 4 moves into a review of the legal regime concerning the distinction between combatants and civilians and the classification of belligerents with reference to the Kurdistan Workers Party (PKK). It discusses the Geneva Conventions' criteria of belligerents and the relevance of customary humanitarian law to this debate. It also reviews the various protections afforded to belligerents within international and non-international armed conflict, describing the extensive protections available to prisoners of war under Geneva Convention III and contrasting that with the limited protections available to detainees in internal armed conflict. The chapter introduces some of the extensive jurisprudence of the European Court of Human Rights which has reviewed conditions of detention within the conflict in southeast Turkey as well as the treatment of the fighters within this conflict.

An issue that is crucial in this examination is the lawfulness of the continued incursions into Kurdistan, Iraq by the Turkish armed and security forces. Chapter 5 introduces and reviews the *jus ad bellum* concerning the lawfulness of both the rebel groups and the Turkish use of force within the context of the United Nations Charter and customary international law. This chapter discusses the various justifications that have been or could be advanced for the Turkish intervention into another sovereign state and assesses the legality of these reasons. Due to the fact that there has been a violation of the prohibition on the use of force, the issue of state responsibility as well as the responsibility of international actors to respond to the threat to international peace and security that results from this intervention is engaged.

Chapter 6 discusses the international legal framework of terrorism. Members of the PKK have been categorised as terrorists and the armed clashes as a series of terrorist attacks. It reviews the legal consequences of defining the insurgency as terrorist attacks and the participants as terrorists. The main area of analysis is whether or not the 'war on terror' has resulted in changes to the law of armed conflict. It also reviews international developments and the recent case law in both the Supreme Court of the United States and the House of Lords in the United Kingdom, discussing the human rights and humanitarian law protections afforded to alleged terrorists and applying these rules to the situation in southeast Turkey.

Part 2 of the book reviews the possible legal and political solutions to the conflict and in two pivotal chapters examines in depth the international relations consequences of the two competing concepts of terrorism and self-determination. These chapters examine the feasibility of conducting constructive dialogue both backchannel and public on the basis of resolving the ongoing armed conflict. The prospects of creating a new common ground for a political solution are explored. Chapter 7 reviews the role of international actors in contributing to, or undermining prospects for, a political solution, and looks at the impact the 'global war on terror' has had on the international community's actions in regards to the conflict. By making some comparative analysis of international engagement in different situations regarding 'terrorists', the chapter suggests some modes of best practise for contributing to peace building. Chapter 8 introduces the legal debate surrounding the principle of self-determination and the consequences to claims of self-determination which are the key political models of federalism and secession, both which involve separate legal structures. Finally, Chapter 9 reviews the current political platform in Turkey with recommendations for the development of a long-term post-conflict environment, with particular reference to the Northern Ireland peace negotiations introducing possible political solutions to the crisis in southeast Turkey, as well as a cessation of cross-border military operations into Kurdistan, Iraq.

In conclusion, the study emphasises the importance and relevance of having the situation in the southeast covered, as comprehensively as possible, by compliance with international law. This is of enormous significance, not only from the human rights perspective regarding the Kurdish civilian populations in Turkey and Iraq, but also from the perspective of finding a long-term solution to the prevailing dispute. It further highlights that analysis of the law regarding armed conflict is highly appropriate in relation to the conflict and should not be undermined. Definition of the situation in Turkey and Iraq according to the law of armed conflict would radically transform the nature and scope of the debate concerning the Kurdish conflict and open up new avenues in the wider discussion about conflict resolution, global politics and international law.

1 Historical background

Introduction

The Kurdish regions of Turkey and Iraq have seen more than 20 years of serious conflict, with severe human cost for its people. So that the reader may tackle the legislative and humanitarian dimension of the conflict in the following chapters, this first chapter provides a brief history of the people living in the region and the circumstances of the conflict. Key demographic, historical and political contexts will be introduced, and the main actors in the conflict analysed. It then examines some of the features of the last two decades of violence in the region, providing the factual resources to engage with the legal and political issues that follow.

1.1 The Kurds

The Kurdish people are believed to number between 30 and 40 million[1] and are widely considered to be the largest group of stateless people in the world. Despite this, they have maintained a strong ethnic identity for over 2,000 years. As an ethnic group, Kurds are the product of years of expansion stemming from tribes such as the Guti, Kurti, Mede, Mard, Carduchi, Gordyene, Adianbene, Zila and Khaldi,[2] and the migration of Indo-European tribes to the Zagros Mountains some 4,000 years ago.[3] The Kurds have a clan history, with over 800 tribes in the Kurdish regions.[4] The Kurds have traditionally inhabited rural districts herding shepherds or goats, with some keeping a nomadic or semi-nomadic lifestyle.

There are a number of dialects in the Kurdish language, but the most widely spoken are Kurmanji and Sorani. Kurmanji is spoken predominantly in Turkey, Syria and Europe, as well as by some Iranian Kurds.[5] Sorani is spoken by Iraqi Kurds south of the Greater Zab, and by Iranian Kurds in the province of Kordestan. The Kurdish language belongs to the Indo-European language family. Its dialects have been influenced by contact with surrounding modern languages and at times have evolved accordingly.[6] For example, most Kurds in Turkey speak Kurmanji, but in the northwest of the Kurdish-dominated area (for example the provinces of Tunceli and Elazig) Zaza is also spoken.[7]

The majority of Kurds are Sunni Muslims who converted between the twelfth and sixteenth centuries and adhere to the Shafi'i school of Islam. However, many

Kurds living in the Iranian province of Kermanshah are Shi'ite. Other Kurds follow Alevism, an unorthodox form of Shi'ite Islam, as well as the indigenous Kurdish faith of Yezidism. There are smaller communities of Kurdish Jews, Christians and Baha'is.

The use of the name 'Kurd' dates back to the seventh century AD, and 'Kurdistan', or the land of the Kurds, was a term that first appeared in the 12th century when the Turkish Seljuk prince Saandjar created a province of that name in what is today modern-day Iran.[8] In the 16th century the term came to refer to a system of fiefs generally.[9] The borders of Kurdistan have fluctuated over time, and the Kurds are now spread through Turkey and the Middle East with smaller populations to be found in the former Soviet Caucasus. The heart of the Kurdish-dominated regions is the Zagros mountain chain which lies in the border area between Iraq, Iran, Syria and Turkey, as well as the eastern extension of the Taurus Mountains. It extends in the south across the Mesopotamian plain and includes the upper reaches of the Tigris and Euphrates rivers. In recent decades, many Kurds have fled the brutality of regimes governing the Kurdish regions to seek refuge in Western Europe, where they form a sizeable and influential diaspora, particularly in Germany, France, Sweden, Belgium and the United Kingdom.

The term 'Kurdistan', however, refers to more than merely a geographical area. It also denotes the culture of the people who inhabit the lands. As successive regimes in Turkey, Iran and Iraq have been extremely reluctant to acknowledge the presence of the Kurds within their borders, and Syria has denied that Kurdistan stretches across its boundaries at all, drawing a map of Kurdistan is always contentious. However, there is no doubt that there exists a large, contiguous area of predominantly Kurdish-inhabited lands, or that the idea of Kurdistan has real meaning to the people who live there, as well as to Kurds living in the diaspora community in Europe and across the world.

Despite the lack of precise figures, largely due to state denial or undercounting for political reasons by countries with Kurdish minorities, the regional spread of Kurdish populations can only be estimated.[10] Kurds in Turkey form the largest population, both numerically and as a percentage of the national population. They currently number approximately 15 to 20 million, making up around 23 per cent of Turkey's population of 69 million. The Kurdish population in Iraq is estimated to be over 5 million, making up 20 per cent of the population; in Syria 1 million and 9 per cent, and in Iran between 7 and 9 million and 15 per cent.

The Kurds in Turkey are concentrated into the south and east of the country, and form a majority of the population in a number of provinces including Mardin, Siirt, Hakkari, Diyarbakir, Bitlis, Mus, Van and Agri.[11] The provinces of Urfa, Adiyaman, Malatya, Elazig, Tunceli, Erzincan, Bingol and Kars have also been traditionally dominated by Kurdish populations. In Iraq today, Kurds predominantly live in the northern governates of Erbil, Dohuk and Sulaimaniya, over which the Kurdistan Regional Government (KRG) has federal jurisdiction.[12]

1.2 History of the Republic of Turkey

Modern Turkey emerged in 1923 from the break-up of the Ottoman Empire in the wake of the First World War. Beginning in 1920, nationalists had begun to defy the authority of the Ottoman Sultan. When Turkey was declared a new republic in 1923, it was fronted by nationalist leader, Mustafa Kemal Atatürk. As modern Turkey's first president, Atatürk formed a government from the members of his Ankara-based revolutionary group, and secured the passage of the new Turkish Constitution in 1924. He remained President until his death in 1939.

The 1924 Constitution set out the new ideological premises from which Turkey would be governed. Spurred by the perceived humiliation of the 1920 Treaty of Sèvres, which divided Ottoman territory, Atatürk and his followers asserted a new, 'Europeanised' Turkish nationalism based on a vision of the unified, centralised and ethnically homogeneous nation state. They sought to enforce a single Turkish identity, introducing dramatic reforms aimed at displacing the importance of Islam in society, placing the military at the core of the state and looking to the secular, industrial West for inspiration.[13] Accordingly, the Caliphate was abolished in 1924, the wearing of the traditional fez was forbidden and the Turkish language was Westernised. Atatürk effectively ruled as a dictator, with his Republican People's Party being the only legal political party.[14]

As the largest and most prominent non-Turkish people in Turkey, the Kurds had much to lose from Atatürk's vision. A necessary tenet of the ambition to achieve an all-Turkish national identity was the destruction of alternative identities through assimilation. This was demonstrated in the failure to recognise the Kurds as a minority in need of protection or to acknowledge their language and culture under the Treaty of Lausanne.[15] Frustration among the Kurds with Turkey's repressive policies towards them spilled over into a number of revolts, and Turkey's army became increasingly active in the Kurdish regions. The very existence of the Kurds within Turkey's borders soon came to be seen in the eyes of the state as synonymous with national disunity, and ultimately, with separatism. The concentration of Turkey's sizeable Kurdish community along the sensitive frontier with Syria, Iran and Iraq, and the presence of frustrated Kurdish communities in these countries, further fuelled Turkey's desire to subjugate the Kurds and neutralise their regional dominance. Throughout the 1920s and 1930s, during which time Atatürk's government ruled Turkey along autocratic lines, a programme of 'Turkification' was introduced aimed at eradicating non-Turkish allegiances and suppressing non-Turkish culture and expression. The Kurds were to become its primary target, as the organs of the state sought to break up the Kurdish community in the southeast through restrictive legislation and state-sponsored violence.

Following the advent of multi-party democracy in 1945, the presiding government was voted out of office and a more liberal government, formed by the Democratic Party, was elected in 1950. This period saw the re-emergence of Islamic influence in Turkey's governing regime. This new political era ended in a military coup in 1960, which infamously resulted in several state executions, including that of the Prime Minister Adnan Menderes and a number of other high-ranking officials. Political instability following the coup combined with economic recession in the late 1960s sparked a wave of unrest and social chaos.[16] The military responded with the 1971 'coup by memorandum', threatening to 'exercise its constitutional duty' and seize power if its demand of the 'restoration of law and order' was not met.[17] The military-backed regime imposed martial law and initiated a widespread crackdown on groups regarded as 'leftist' or 'separatist'. Then, in 1980, the military carried out the third coup in the history of the Republic. Martial law was extended throughout the country, Parliament was abolished and the country ruled through the National Security Council (NSC). A committee appointed by the military drafted a new Constitution, which came into force in 1982.[18] Thus followed a decade of one-party rule under Turgut Ozal's Motherland Party. Ozal's death in 1993 led to the second democratic Presidential elections in Turkey's history.

In 1997 the military again asserted their position within Turkish politics, and forced Prime Minister Necmettin Erbakan's Islamist-led coalition government to resign. The secular military alleged that Erbakan was trying to change the basic nature of Turkish politics and government and turn Turkey into an Islamic-led theocracy like neighbouring Iran. After forcing Erbakan from power, the army turned the government over to more secular politicians in what is called Turkey's 'post-modern coup'. However, in 2002 the Justice and Development Party (AKP), regarded as a successor to Erbakan's party, won parliamentary elections, and in 2007 AKP politician Abdullah Gül was elected President of the Republic.

1.2.1 Political structure

Turkey's Parliament, known as the Grand National Assembly (GNA), is composed of 550 members elected for a 5-year term. The Prime Minister, who is appointed from amongst the members of the GNA by the President, nominates the Cabinet and together they form the Council of Ministers. All laws are introduced into the GNA by the Council of Ministers and the deputies. Once legislative bills are passed, they require the ratification of the President, who may refer the proposed laws (except the budget) back to the GNA for further consideration. The GNA may also empower the Council of Ministers to issue decrees, except during a state of emergency and martial law.

The President is the Head of State and is elected for a 5-year term (renewable once) by the GNA, requiring a two-thirds majority (or an absolute majority in a third round of voting). Turkey's President is not simply a titular or symbolic head of the state. The President has substantial powers mandated by Turkey's Constitution, including the appointment of top military and judicial figures.

Turkey's history of *coups d'état* sheds light on the role that the military, led by stringent Kemalists, has played in modern Turkey. The military is considered by many, and not least its own members, as the guardian of Kemalism, and plays a prominent role in the Republic, exercising both formal and informal power.

One key institution is the NSC, which was set up following the 1960 military coup to oversee security issues in Turkey. The NSC comprises political and military leaders who meet every 2 months to discuss national security. Since the 1960s, and particularly in the aftermath of the 1980 military coup, the role of the NSC has been further strengthened and militarised. While the 1982 Constitution formally states the role of the NSC as advising the government with 'regard to the formulation, establishment and implementation of the national security policy of the State',[19] in reality due to the political weight of the members of NSC, and the institutionalisation of the armed forces within the civilian administration, it appears to have a significant effect on all government decision-making. Although there have been continuous calls, domestically and internationally, for Turkey to reduce the power of, or completely abolish, the NSC, the institution is deeply embedded in the state. While the government of Turkey may wish to alter the role of the NSC, such changes are difficult without comprehensive constitutional reform. as of yet, no meaningful reform regarding the role of the NSC has been forthcoming.

Further complicating the political system, and its reform, in Turkey is the existence of the 'deep state', which is known to be a top-secret network of criminal elements, political figures and members of the military. Due to the work of both domestic and international human rights organisations, much has been learned in recent years regarding the actions of the 'deep state' and the network's relationship to Turkish politics.[20] The discovery of mass graves and evidence of top military personnel's involvement have done much to verify the claims that regional and international non-governmental organisations (NGOs) have been making for years. While all the activities and inner workings of the 'deep state' have not yet been made clear, more information is regularly coming to light. Turkey's government, to its credit, has done much to acknowledge and, where possible, prosecute the activities of the 'deep state'.

Turkey has been, throughout modern history, constantly pulled between the secularist and ethnically homogenous founding vision of Atatürk, and the reality of having a population of which the majority is Muslim and nearly a quarter Kurdish. This legacy has lived on through a string of fractured and unstable governments during over the proceeding three decades, many of whom have sought to preserve Turkey's secular vision by imposing repressive measures such as the 1950 Press Law and the 2006 Anti Terror Law.[21]

The parliamentary and presidential elections in 2007 highlighted these persistent tensions in Turkey's political structure. In April 2007 the ruling AKP nominated former Foreign Minister Abdullah Gül, as a presidential candidate. Gül's previous association with the Islamist movement and the fact that his wife chose to wear a headscarf provoked intense debate regarding his candidacy bid. The military published a memorandum blaming the government for stimulating religious sentiment in society, and the first round of the presidential elections was later cancelled after a decision by the Constitutional Court.[22] The AKP government therefore decided to hold early parliamentary elections on 22 July 2007, resulting in a landslide victory. With this large majority in Parliament, and a clear mandate from the electorate, Gül was again nominated, and on 28 August was elected by the Parliament as President. The July elections also saw 24 deputies stand as independent candidates, most from the Kurdish region, only to later form the pro-Kurdish Democratic Society Party (DTP) in Parliament, thereby circumventing the required 10 per cent threshold for political parties.[23] In November 2007 the Chief Public Prosecutor of Turkey's Constitutional Court filed a case of party closure against the DTP, followed in March 2008 by a case to close the ruling AKP.[24]

These cases follow a long legacy of restrictions on political parties in Turkey, particularly targeting parties with a platform that is politically left-wing or addresses Kurdish issues. Such parties have faced closure proceedings, the removal of parliamentary immunity, and other forms of harassment.[25] National parties that advocated for the cultural and linguistic rights of minorities have been repeatedly closed down.[26] For instance, HEP (*Halkın Emek Partisi*, People's Labour Party),[27] widely regarded as the first political party with an openly Kurdish platform, was closed and its parliamentarians imprisoned in 1994. In the case of *Sadak and Others v Turkey*,[28] which was brought to the European Court of Human Rights by the London-based NGO Kurdish Human Rights Project, the Court found that Turkey had violated Article 3 to Protocol No 1 (right to free elections) when it moved to dissolve the Democracy Party (DEP or *Demokrasi partisi*) only months after its formation in 1993. The 13 applicants were charged by the Turkish state with making statements undermined the integrity of the state and the unity of the nation. Some were charged under anti-terrorism legislation with charges ranging from aiding and abetting an armed gang to distribution of separatist propaganda. While the Court eventually found in favour of the applicants, successive pro-Kurdish parties have accordingly been forced to form and re-form. The exclusion of such parties from democratic processes in Turkey has impeded opportunities to establish a democratic outlet for Kurdish demands.[29]

1.3 Historical background to the conflict

There is a long history of conflict and persecution in the Kurdish regions. Continual repression from external authorities has been met with resistance by the Kurdish people. While a full account of this history is beyond the scope of the book, an overview of some key events will demonstrate the historical influence on the recent conflict.

From the Seljuk Turks in the 11th century, to the Mongols from the 13th to the 15th centuries, and later the Safavid and Ottoman Empires, the Kurdish region has been governed by a succession of rulers, and its population vulnerable to their dispositions. Under the Safavids, hundreds of thousands of Kurds were forcibly removed from the Kurdish regions, and old Kurdish cities and countryside were systematically destroyed. Then, in the 16th century the Ottomans divided Kurdish territory into districts and installed local Kurdish chiefs as governors, allowing Kurdish society considerable freedom to manage their own affairs.[30] But by the beginning of the 19th century the Ottomans sought to again subjugate the Kurdish principalities in order to centralise the decaying Empire.[31] These encroachments were met with a series of revolts led by Kurdish chiefs in 1826, 1834, between 1853 and 1855, and 1880.[32]

When the Ottoman Empire was carved up in the aftermath of the First World War, the Kurds were divided between modern-day Iraq, Iran, Syria and Turkey. At first, Kurdish autonomy had been a strategic concern of the Great Powers. US President Woodrow Wilson's Fourteen Point Programme for World Peace (1918) asserted that the non-Turkish minorities of the Ottoman Empire should be 'assured of an absolute unmolested opportunity of autonomous development'.[33] Under Article 64 of the 1920 Treaty of Sèvres, signed by the Allied Powers and the Constantinople government, the Kurds would be granted independence within a year.[34] However, European fears over the possibility of Soviet influence over newly formed states, and concerns regarding Kurdish representation, combined with historical events to preclude Kurdish independence.[35] As the mandate power over Mesopotamia from 1920, Britain at first seemed committed to the principle of keeping the Kurdish areas separate, but subsequently submitted to mounting pressure to incorporate the area of Mosul into a new Iraqi state. The aftermath of the Turkish War of Independence saw Sèvres superseded by a new accord in 1923, the Treaty of Lausanne, which restored Turkish sovereignty over the Kurdish-dominated area accorded independence at Sèvres. The remaining Kurdish-dominated lands were divided between Iran, Syria and Iraq, with the Allied powers drawing up new national boundaries giving more heed to the allocation of oil resources and rewarding friendly Arab leaders than to the ethnic distribution of the Kurds and their right to self-rule. The Kurds were not given real voice in the discussions over the future of their lands.

The end of empire and the establishment of nation states ended any relative autonomy which the Kurds had enjoyed and Kurdish communities were widely treated with distrust. As a large, non-Arab population inhabiting an area of significant strategic importance, the regimes governing the Kurdish regions founded their policies towards the Kurds on suspicion and hostility. At the same time, these newly emerging and vulnerable nation states were keen to preserve their new found independence by fostering strong national unity and overcoming perceived threats to their territorial integrity.

In Turkey, the post-independence programme of 'Turkification' in the southeast began by filling senior administrative appointments in the Kurdish region with ethnic Turks, and all references to Kurdistan were excised from official materials.[36] In 1924, the use of the Kurdish language in official domains, including in schools, and traditional Kurdish clothing and music were banned. Two major Kurdish rebellions in 1925 and 1930, directed at the 'Turkification' programme, were brutally suppressed. Martial law was imposed in the Kurdish region, and 52,000 Turkish forces were deployed in the region,[37] Kurds were subjected to systematic destruction of their villages, forced displacement and mass killings. In 1934 a new Turkish law divided Turkey into three zones, and the state was vested with the power to compulsorily transfer those from the third 'zone' deemed to 'require assimilation'.[38] The aim of the law was to disperse the Kurdish population and thus break down the Kurdish identity. The advent of multi-party democracy in 1945 saw a challenge to the Kemalist vision with the re-emergence of Islamic influence in Turkey's governing regime, but this failed to herald an end to repressive measures towards Kurds, as evidenced by the restrictive 1950 Press Law.[39]

The succession of *coups d'état* in 1960, 1971 and 1980 renewed the power of military Kemalism to suppress 'other' identities. On the day of the 1971 coup, the public prosecutor opened a case against the Workers' Party of Turkey for carrying out communist propaganda and supporting Kurdish separatism.[40] Soon, youth organisations were banned, union meetings prohibited, leftist publications proscribed and strikes declared illegal. Hundreds of students, young academics, writers, trade unionists and Workers' Party activists were detained and tortured.[41] Martial law was declared in 11 provinces, including major urban areas and Kurdish regions, and renewed every 2 months.[42] Constitutional reforms repealed some of the essential liberal fragments of 1961. Special courts set up to deal with all forms of dissent quickly and ruthlessly, tried over 3,000 people before their abolition in 1976. In an atmosphere conducive to extremism and violence, over 100 people were killed in a massacre incited by the Grey Wolves, the unofficial militant arm of the National Movement Party (MHP), in the southeast Anatolian town of Kahramanmaraş in 1978.[43] Following the 1980 *coup d'état*, martial law was extended throughout the country. Parliament was abolished and the government suspended the Constitution and banned all political parties, trade unions, and most other forms of organisation. For the next 3 years, the Turkish armed forces ruled the country through the NSC, appealing to the unity of the nation and the Kemalist tradition of state secularism as justification. It is estimated that over 500,000 people were detained in the wake of the 1980 coup,[44] only half of which were formally arrested, and almost all were tortured.[45]

The Kurdish population of Turkey were a particular target of state oppression throughout this period, as they were portrayed as a collective threat to state unity. The use of the term 'Kurdish' was totally banned in 1983, as were the use of the Kurdish language, Kurdish folk songs and giving children Kurdish names.[46] Villages were renamed with non-Kurdish words. Exemplary sentences designed to enforce these provisions were periodically meted out.[47] As the Kurdistan Workers Party (PKK) began armed struggle in 1984, the presence of the Turkish army increased in the southeast.[48] Few escaped the trauma of frequent village security sweeps in which villagers were arbitrarily arrested and beaten until confessing involvement with the PKK.

It is difficult to overstate the importance of the influence of these events on the course of Kurdish history over the following decades. From the start, expressions of Kurdish identity were discouraged and the Kurds were compelled to conform to the norms of the countries in which they now found themselves. In time, military incursions into Kurdish regions became common occurrences, with comprehensive attempts made to forcibly dissipate Kurdish communities in border areas and stamp out the notion of a Kurdish identity.[49]

1.4 The conflict in southeast Turkey

This section of the chapter looks at the conflict in the Kurdish regions of Turkey beginning from 1984 and examines the structure of the two main bodies engaged in the conflict: the Turkish state security forces and the PKK, before chronicling the main developments of the conflict up to the present day.

1.4.1 The Turkish armed forces in the conflict

Turkish state policy has been based on the denial of the existence of the Kurds; therefore the state has narrowly viewed the Kurdish problem as a security problem disregarding its broader social and legal foundations. Throughout the last 25 years, the military-dominated NSC has continued to advocate for a solely military solution to the Kurdish issue and ignored other dimensions to the conflict, such as the state's historical repression of Kurdish cultural expression and forced relocation.[50] Claiming that Turkey is faced with the threat of division, the state has targeted the region with emergency laws[51] and established a penetrating military presence throughout the Kurdish region, comprising the Army, Air Force, gendarmerie, national police and paramilitary village guards. At the height of the conflict in 1995, approximately 300,000 Turkish forces were serving in the southeast.[52] According to press reports, 240,000 additional troops were dispatched to southeast Turkey in April 2006 by the government.[53] Today it is estimated that current troop levels number between 125,000 and 130,000.[54]

The Turkish Constitution mandates that the head of the armed forces is the Chief of General Staff, who is appointed by the President of the Republic upon nomination by the Council of Ministers.[55] Three branches of the armed forces – land, sea and air – report directly to the Chief of the Turkish General Staff and not to the Ministry of Defence authority. Although the General Staff and the Ministry of National Defence work in close coordination and cooperation, it is the General Staff who is responsible to the prime minister and is charged with overall command and control of the Turkish armed forces. The Turkish armed forces consists of five branches, the land, naval and air forces working under the General Staff and the gendarmerie forces and the coast guard working under land and naval forces. The General Command of the Gendarmerie is subordinate to the General Staff of the Armed Forces in matters relating to training and education in connection with the armed forces. However, in matters relating to the safety and public order duties, the General Commander of Gendarmerie is subordinate to the Ministry of Internal Affairs.[56] The Chief of General Staff and the General Commander of the Gendarmerie, as well as, the Commanders of the army, navy and air forces, sit on the NSC, which advises the President and the Council of the Ministers on the formulation, establishment, and implementation of the national security policy of the nation.[57]

The Republic of Turkey has a compulsory military service system under article 72 of the 1982 Turkish constitution.[58] Under the Law on Military Service (No 1111), all males of Turkish nationality are eligible for military service from

January of the year they turn 20 and until January of the year they reach turn 41[59] with a provision to recruit from the age of 19 during mobilisation or states of emergency.[60] The standard duration of military service is 18 months although the Council of Ministers can reduce this period to 15 or 12 months according to the needs of the forces.[61] University graduates also have an option to serve a shorter period.

The Military Penal Code[62] does not recognise the right to conscientious objection for conscripts.[63] Although the United Nations has affirmed that the right to conscientious objection is a legitimate exercise of the freedom of thought, conscience and religion,[64] the European Court of Human Rights has been more muted on the subject. The Turkish Constitutional Court has explicitly ruled that the freedom of conscience stated in article 24 of the 1982 constitution does not include the right to conscientious objection to military service.[65] Article 45 of the Military Penal Code states that individuals may not avoid military service for religious or moral reasons[66] and evasion and desertion are punishable by up to 3 years' imprisonment under article 63.[67] Completing a prison sentence does not remove the obligation to perform military service and 'persistent disobedience'[68] leads to recurring prosecutions with jail terms of up to 2 years.[69] Military registration numbers are included on identity documents prohibiting those avoiding military service from leaving the country, and they are pursued by the police and gendarmerie who are able to conduct house searches and routine checks in order to arrest them.[70] The exact number of conscientious objectors is not known, but the military courts are believed to deal with around 60,000 cases per year that are connected to draft evasion, although about half of these cases reportedly deal with cases of conscripts who have not reported themselves back in time after a period of leave and have been absent for less than a week.[71] Further, article 318 of the Penal code[72] criminalises 'alienating the public from military service' and stipulates up to 3 years' imprisonment as a penalty.[73] Thus, any person who speaks out against military service is liable to the same treatment as a person who himself refuses to undertake it.

In addition to the armed forces, the state tasks other agencies with security operations in Turkey. The principal agencies charged with internal security and law enforcement are the national police and the gendarmerie. Both fall under the Ministry of the Interior, however the gendarmerie is under the command of the army. The gendarmerie maintains law and order in rural areas, guards against illegal smuggling and illegal border crossing and provides security on the outer perimeters of prisons. In each province the gendarmerie commander advises the governor on matters of security. In areas where a state of emergency is declared, gendarmes play a more significant role than the police or any other civil authority.

The paramilitary village guard system, in which the state funds and equips local civilians to protect their towns and villages, was implemented as a temporary measure in 1985.[74] The rationale behind the system was to take advantage of local knowledge in security operations. Yet the scope and regulation of their activities has not been clearly set out by the state, and in the 1980s and 1990s the guards became notorious as a result of accusations of theft, beatings and rape.[75] Despite an official halt on recruitment in 2000, the total number of village guards stands at 70,000 according to a 2008 report published by the Turkish Economic and Social Studies Foundation (TESEV), of which 57,174 are temporary and 12,279 are volunteers.[76]

The Interior Minister in 2003 stated that 4,804 village guards were involved in criminal activities and they were the target of over 5,200 criminal investigations.[77] Though the government pledged to abolish the village guard system in the short term it has made no effort to phase out the system and in May 2007 amended the Village Law to employ up to 60,000 additional village guards according the TESEV report.[78] Although calls to abolish the village guard have been ongoing, the attack on 5 May 2009 in Bilge Köyü, in Mardin province, in which masked gunmen attacked a wedding party killing 45, including six children and 16 women further increased demands that the Turkish government disband the system.[79]

1.4.2 The PKK in the conflict

The PKK (*Partiya Karkerên Kurdistan*) was founded in 1978 by Abdullah Öcalan. The first PKK members came from radical political student circles in urban centres. Initially the organisation held a Marxist-Leninist political ideology, emphasising the need for a radical transformation of the social and political organisation of Kurdish society. It sought the establishment of an independent Kurdistan, uniting Kurds across several borders. Amongst the number of Kurdish political movements that appeared in the 1970s, the PKK established its position as foremost in appeal and notoriety. On the eve of the 1980 coup, some PKK leaders fled to Syria and Lebanon. The rise in the awareness of Kurdish identity in Turkey, coupled with the narrow political space that resulted from the 1980 military coup, substantially increased the number of people who became actively involved with the PKK in the 1980s.[80] Open conflict between the PKK and the security forces in Turkey started in 1984. Since then the PKK has combined attention-grabbing attacks in urban centres, and guerrilla-style operations against the Turkish state in the southeast.[81]

By the early 1990s, the PKK had abandoned the references to independent Kurdistan in its manifesto, and was concentrating on the idea of a 'democratic republic'. The organisation has always classified itself as a political party that uses military means to achieve political goals. By the mid-1990s, the PKK had virtual control over large parts of southeast Turkey and at its peak, the group had nearly 15,000 operatives.[82] The main target of PKK military activity has always been the Turkish military presence in southeast of Turkey. However, from 1985 the PKK also targeted the village guards[83] and in the 1990s began to target economic and social assets in Turkey such as railroads, bridges and tourist sites.[84] Between 1996 and 1999, PKK members (mainly female) conducted 16 suicide attacks.[85] In tandem with its military operations, the PKK pressed forward on the political front and in 1994 called for a dialogue. The organisation encouraged supporters to take part in civil disobedience campaigns, such as sit-ins and protest marches. In January 1995, the PKK communicated to the Swiss government their commitment to observe the Geneva Conventions and Protocol 1 of 1977 in its conduct of hostilities, listing its understanding of legitimate targets under the conventions as being restricted to the Turkish armed forces, contra-guerrilla forces, intelligence services, gendarmerie, and village guards, and stating that captured forces would be treated as prisoners of war. Accepting the principle of command responsibility, the PKK stated its adoption of a system of discipline to ensure respect for these rules and punish their violation.

In February 1999, while in Kenya Abdullah Öcalan was handed over to Turkish security personnel. Convicted of treason, he received a death sentence that was later commuted to a life sentence.[86] Öcalan now remains the sole inmate in a specially configured jail on İmralı Island. In August 1999 Öcalan issued a public statement calling on the PKK to issue a unilateral ceasefire and pursue a democratic solution to the conflict, which was accepted by the PKK's decision-making and armed sections shortly after, but reserving the right to self-defence in the event of military attack.[87] In 2000 the word 'Kurdistan' was dropped from PKK's name in recognition of it's abandoning of its former demands for Kurdish independence.[88] In 2002 the PKK announced its dissolution and formation as a new group, the Kurdistan Freedom and Democracy Congress (KADEK) to pursue the political aims of the Kurdish people through democratic means.[89] However, in June 2004 the PKK ended the ceasefire, citing ongoing Turkish military operations, though it was reported that there were splits within the organisation over the use of armed violence.[90] Since 2004 PKK military activity has predominantly consisted of small ambushes, including use of mines, snipers and long-range strafing of military outposts, rather than direct combat with the Turkish military.[91]

1.4.2.1 Structure of the PKK

The PKK has a central committee for organisational decision-making and regional preparations committees across the region of Turkey to oversee local actions.[92] After Öcalan fled to Syria, the Presidential Council was established to coordinate the implementation of Öcalan's decisions.[93] The combatants, who wear uniforms, are organised into guerrilla units under the command of a hierarchy of commanders.[94] All these bodies have varied in size over the years, depending on strategic objectives and operating context. Women have traditionally played a significant role in the PKK, and comprised approximately a third of PKK armed forces in the early 1990s.[95] The PKK has a strict system of internal discipline, and transgressors have been executed[96] or imprisoned in the camps.[97] It holds an Annual Congress which, as far as possible, gathers together members from across the regions to share information and decide future strategy. New recruits conduct a programme of military training and graduate in a formal ceremony.[98]

1.4.3 Chronology of the conflict

Rooted in the long history of discord and persecution in the Kurdish regions that is detailed earlier in this chapter, the conflict in the southeast of Turkey has continued to rise to new levels since its start in 1984. The political situation in Turkey following the 1980 military coup as well as the instigation of an armed campaign by the PKK in 1984 opened a new chapter of violence in the region. Since 1984 it is estimated that close to 40,000 people have been killed,[99] 3 million have been displaced[100] and over 3,000 villages have been destroyed in the Kurdish region.[101] This section will examine how the conflict has evolved since 1984, looking at both its causes and its impact.

Decades of state policy that denied the existence of a distinctive Kurdish identity in Turkey, combined with the limitations political participation and a crackdown on freedom of association following the 1971 and 1980 military coups, lead a number of political groups, including those on the extreme left and right, to advocate the use of violence to achieve political objectives.[102] By mid-1979, there were nearly 20 political murders a day.[103] In this atmosphere, a number of Kurdish political organisations appeared, including the PKK, which in 1984 began to engage in open confrontation with the Turkish state.

On 15 August 1984 the PKK attacked military barracks in the towns of Eruh and Semdinli simultaneously.[104] The group followed up these first attacks by killing three members of a unit responsible for guarding President Evren at Yuksekova, and then ambushing and killing eight soldiers in Çukurca, Hakkari in October 1984.[105]

Initially, the state did not take the PKK attacks seriously. However, by April 1985 the military general who became President of Turkey in the 1980 coup, Kenan Evren, amended the Village Law to allow for the maintenance and arming of village guards at the government's expense.[106] By 1987, Turkey had recruited 70,000 village guards. As a state-mandated but largely unregulated armed force, the village guard system exacerbated lawless violence in the region, in particular against civilians.[107] Rural Kurdish communities were obliged by the Turkish state to prove their loyalty by joining the Village Guard system. If villages failed to put forward volunteers for the Guard, they would be placed in the dangerous position of being viewed as PKK sympathisers, and thus liable to attack by Turkish security forces. However, those who did sign up were deemed traitors by the PKK. Kurdish villagers faced a stark choice: they could become village guards and chance being attacked by the PKK, or refuse and risk becoming victims of a state security operation. Village guards became a target of the PKK, while villagers who refused to join the guard often faced reprisals such as forcible displacement by Turkish security forces.

On 19 July 1987, the Turkish Parliament declared a civil state of emergency in 10 provinces in southeast Turkey, later extending the state of emergency to 14 provinces.[108] The state of emergency legislation granted exceptional powers to state security forces, which led to a heavy military presence, martial law and severe restrictions on civil and political rights enforced by a special governor.

Decree 285[109] granted the Governor General power to evacuate villages on a temporary or permanent basis. Officially sanctioned village evacuations were accompanied by violent state security operations against Kurdish villages considered unsupportive of the government's agenda. When the Turkish soldiers were unable to distinguish between rural civilian populations and armed insurgents, it was reported that they drove the villagers off their land, burned down their homes, and destroyed their crops, orchards and livestock.[110] This has been corroborated by judgments of the European Court of Human Rights, which found Turkish security forces responsible for torturing civilians, extra-judicial killings of non-combatants, abductions and disappearances and the destruction of Kurdish villages, property and crops.[111]

An atmosphere of intimidation and violence prevailed. State security forces targeted the PKK, although Kurdish rural communities were often caught in the crossfire. Security operations in Kurdish villages were accompanied by arbitrary arrests, looting of moveable property, beatings, torture and 'disappearances'.[112] Few Kurds escaped the trauma of the actions of state security forces. In detention, Kurds were frequently subject to extra-judicial execution, ill-treatment and torture, including *falaka* (beating the soles of the feet), electric shock treatment and rape. This was facilitated by the relative ease with which public authorities could subject Kurds to prolonged, incommunicado detention and a climate of impunity among the police and gendarmerie in which convictions for such acts were rare and sentences, when imposed, were light.[113] The ensuing terror caused thousands to flee their homes. Mass internal displacement was compounded by a deliberate policy of village evacuation by the government.[114] Between 3 and 4 million villagers were forced from their homes throughout this period.[115] Reports of mass graves where the bodies of the disappeared had been dumped by security forces started to appear as early as the late 1980s.[116] However, it was not until the opening of the Ergenekon case in 2008[117] that excavations of the mass graves began to reveal the extent of extrajudicial executions during this period.[118]

During the 1980s, the army assigned a steadily increasing number of troops to the Kurdish regions in the southeast. By the early 1990s the number had reached 200,000.[119] Expressions of dissent were brutally put down. On 20 March 1990, 10,000 Kurds demonstrated in the town of Cizre in a mass protest against the security forces, who subsequently imposed a curfew on 11 towns in Mardin and Siirt provinces. The death toll of the civilians who were shot by the security forces at the demonstration exceeded 100.[120]

In November 1991, Prime Minister Süleyman Demirel took office, stating his commitment to human rights reforms and ending the village guard system. However, despite Demirel's assurances the conflict markedly intensified in 1992. Government reports of PKK attacks were used as justification for the security forces' retaliation against the civilian population. The PKK attacked security forces deployed in towns in the Kurdish region, and the state security forces retaliated with such ferocity that the town's inhabitants were killed, wounded or forced to flee in terror. State security forces opened fire and shot randomly at houses, shops and vehicles, and fired on civilian residential areas with panzers and other tanks and heavy artillery. During security operations the offices of human rights defenders, journalists and lawyers were raiding and destroyed, and forces waged house-to-house campaigns to root out members of the PKK.[121] In 1992 alone, 2,000 were killed in the southeast, including many unarmed civilians.[122] 1992 also saw a substantial increase in targeted assassinations by unknown assailants, including high profile doctors, lawyers, teachers, political leaders, journalists, human rights activists, and business people. The then Minister of the Interior reported 881 casualties that year in the 13 provinces under emergency rule in southeast Turkey where the victims' attacker was unknown.[123]

The London-based NGO the Kurdish Human Rights Project (KHRP) was established in 1992, laboured to assist victims of such violation seek redress in the European Court of Human Rights. KHRP was one of the first organisations to use the individual right of petition to the European Court of Human Rights, accepted by Turkey in 1987, to promote and protect the rights of all people in the Kurdish regions and beyond. Its work with the European Court and other human rights bodies has been ground breaking in helping to establish an objective record of systematic human rights violations in the Kurdish regions. KHRP cases, for example, have played a crucial role in the use of fact-finding missions by the European Commission.[124] Additionally, KHRP cases have brought international attention to the human rights violations that have occurred as a result of Turkey's conflict with the PKK being viewed as purely military.

The PKK announced a unilateral ceasefire in 1993, after the Democratic Party government signalled a willingness to examine the situation in the southeast and broke significant taboos by openly naming the Kurdish issue. Yet that same year, then President of Turkey Turgut Özal outlined a programme of forced migration of Kurds from the southeast to western parts of the country, and suggested building a large number damns to prevent the locals returning to the region.[125] These actions and the government's unwillingness to exert any real control over the army's activities in the southeast led to a resumption of violence by the PKK within months.[126] Given the ongoing climate of impunity, it took judgments of the European Court many years later to establish the activities of the security forces at this time. For example, a military operation carried out by gendarme soldiers of the Bolu Commando Brigade in October 1993 led to the 'disappearance' of 11 Kurdish men following their detention during the operation,[127] which was brought before the European Court by KHRP. Another case detailed the 'disappearance' of three men from the village of Çağlayan in Diyarbakir.[128] The men were detained and taken away by security forces follow-ing the forced evacuation and deliberate destruction of the village by the security forces of the villagers' homes and properties.[129] Turkey was found to have violated the right to life in both cases. During this time the PKK witnessed a steady rise in the number of members. According to one estimate membership grew from a few hundred army fighters in the early 1980s to between 15,000 to 20,000 in 1994.[130]

Records of Turkish military operations, submitted by the Turkish Government to the European Court in *Orhan v Turkey*, indicate that 30 operations took place in the province of Diyarbakir from 2 to 31 May 1994.[131] Although there were no records of troop numbers, the Court noted evidence that large numbers of military units took part in military operations in Diyarbakir.[132] Reports detailed helicopters and jets bombing Kurdish villages in 1994, resulting in 26 civilians being killed, including at least 17 children. Witnesses reported that in the days leading up to the attack, gendarmes had subjected the villagers to death threats for having refused to join the village guard corps.[133]

European Court judgments also established a pattern of abductions and extrajudicial killings by state agents or people acting on behalf of the state authorities at this time.[134] The European Court of Human Rights in its judgment found a large number of cases found where Turkey had violated the right to life, liberty and an effective remedy in this regard.[135] A report of the Turkish Parliamentary Commission on Unsolved Political Killings, leaked to the press in 1995, confirmed that the village guards were involved in extrajudicial killings, amongst a wide range of other such illegal activities such as extortion.[136]

In addition to extrajudicial killings, cases before the European Court of Human Rights also highlighted the systematic nature of the destruction of villages in the southeast, including the burning of houses, destruction of crops, and the killing of livestock.[137] Following its fact-finding investigation, the European Commission on Human Rights in *Mentes and others* described the officially sanctioned lawlessness in southeast Turkey in the 1990s:

> The Commission considered that the burning of the first three applicants' homes constituted an act of violence and deliberate destruction in utter disregard of the safety and welfare of the applicants and their children who were left without shelter and assistance and in circumstances which caused them anguish and suffering. It noted in particular the traumatic circumstances in which the applicants were prevented from saving their personal belongings and the dire personal situation in which they subsequently found themselves, being deprived of their own homes in their village and the livelihood which they had been able to derive from their gardens and fields.[138]

The capture of PKK leader Abdullah Öcalan in June 1999, and his subsequent announcement of a unilateral cessation of armed activities by Kurdish armed groups marked a turning point in the conflict. Öcalan called upon PKK fighters to withdraw from the southeast,[139] and made a statement to reporters via his lawyer to stating that 'a ceasefire would ease the deadlock over the Kurdish question and open the way to dialogue in a democratic solution'.[140] Despite Öcalan's call, however, his arrest and conviction was accompanied by a wave of terror, including the assassination of a regional governor and a firebombing that killed 13 people.[141] Recently, Öcalan has once again called for a ceasefire and urged the Turkish state to act in kind. The action is ostensibly aimed at working towards a political solution to Turkey's Kurdish issue. The effects of Öcalan's latest pronouncement are yet to be seen.

Excessive use of force and extrajudicial killings by Turkish security forces became a particular issue for Kurdish detainees during the conflict. On 19 December 2000, for example, a security forces operation to transfer prisoners in 20 prisons to new 'F-type prisons', holding one to three occupants, resulted in the death of 30 inmates and two gendarmes. This was followed a hunger-strike by more than 1,000 inmates across Turkey lasting for 61 days to protest the planned transfer of prisoners. The inmates maintained that the new institutions would lead to increased isolation of prisoners and expose them to abuse and torture. The declared rationale behind the government's decision to replace the ward-based prison system with F-type cells was to end the collective ward life of political organisations, which had reportedly become uncontrollable.[142]

The security forces' use of excessive force during these operations is well-documented by human rights groups. Testimonies of former prisoners to the KHRP during its mission to Ankara in 2001, reveal that the security forces used excessive force, including indiscriminate gunfire, gas, stun and incendiary grenades as well as other explosives, in order to gain access to the prison wards or when rounding up prisoners for transfer.[143] The UN Special Rapporteur on extrajudicial, summary or arbitrary executions during her visit to Turkey noted that during prison operations the prisoners were beaten and in some instances tortured, both during and after the transfer operation. The report also noted that most of the inmates killed appeared to have been shot dead by security forces, or burned to death either by incendiary grenades or self-immolation.[144]

In September 2000, a PKK Congress called for an end to the armed conflict with Turkey,[145] and in April 2002 the PKK relaunched itself as the KADEK.[146] A few months later, Turkey lifted the state of emergency in the southeast, and, as a result of European Court of Human Rights judgments against Turkey, from this point to June 2004 the conflict remained at a lower level. Violence had already been waning since the PKK's unilateral ceasefire in 1999. While 194 police and gendarmes were reported killed in 1999, the corresponding figure for the year 2000 was 27. The same figures for suspected PKK militants were 1,202 and 365, respectively. The number of deaths of unarmed civilians was 64 in 1999 and 43 in 2000. Over the next few years, killings continued to decline. It was reported that between January 2000 and July 2003, 161 PKK members and 39 Turkish soldiers were killed in operations in the southeast.[147] The number of incidents of extrajudicial killings also fell sharply, but the phenomenon by no means disappeared. Village evacuations slowed in pace, and what is often referred to by international bodies as a process of 'normalisation' began. Turkey believed that the capture and conviction of Öcalan would effectively put an end to the Kurdish conflict, as the PKK would fade in importance without its leader. This belief, however, was based on the state's policy of denial of the Kurds and, although violence ebbed in the short term, ignored the real, political issues that remained unresolved.

However, a low intensity conflict continued. Reports by Turkey's Human Rights Association referred to around 100 deaths per year resulting from armed conflict during this period.[148] Citing ongoing state military operations against the organisation's fighters, the PKK announced that it was calling off its unilateral ceasefire in June 2004. Over 50 clashes between PKK's fighters and Turkish security forces were reported between 1 June 2004 and 13 August 2004.[149] By the end of August 2004, the PKK said it would be prepared to halt attacks if Turkey's government agreed to a truce.[150] But in September 2004 a major outbreak of violence in Pervari, Siirt Province was reported, with government forces announcing that they were expanding their operations in order to target PKK forces in the region. Sporadic clashes followed in October,[151] November[152] and December.[153] Some 166 battle-related deaths were reported in 2004, with fighting mainly being focused in the Tunceli, Bingol, Batman, Diyarbakir, Van and Mardin provinces. Figures issued by the Turkish government report that 2,100 people have died in the conflict since this period, including 172 civilians, 556 Turkish forces, and 1,380 members of the PKK.

In 2005, the Turkish state began to pay close attention to the formation of the Iraqi government over fears of Kurdish autonomy in the north, particularly with the nomination of Kurdish leader Jalal Talabani as Iraqi president. Fears over empowering Kurdish nationalism led the military to escalate the number of clashes and operations carried out in the southeast near the Iraqi border.[154] This escalation led to the Turkish army launching a major security operation in May 2005 in the Dersim region involving as many as 10,000 troops pursuing 350 members of the PKK.[155] The sixth anniversary of former PKK leader Öcalan's arrest also led to protests and violence in the southeast.[156] June 2005 saw a series of major security sweeps by the army in the Dersim province, involving 2,000 to 3,000 troops.[157] The PKK rejected a plea from Turkish intellectuals to end the violence and increased its attacks with bombings in Kusadasi and Cesme resorts.[158] In the second major operation of the year, 10,000 troops in the southeast were deployed in October 2005 to combat the PKK. At this point, Ankara adopted new state security measures and the military defined terrorism as the number one threat.[159] Conflict continued to mar the region, with clashes in the southeast provinces of Mardin[160] and Van[161] with security rapidly deteriorating in the southeastern cities of Diyarbakir and Batman. Protests at the 28 March 2006 funeral of four PKK members, who were among the 14 killed in a military operation in Mus province, sparked 4 days of rioting in which seven casualties were reported.[162]

The PKK again proclaimed a unilateral ceasefire in October 2006, following calls from Abdullah Öcalan. The ceasefire was rejected by then Turkish Chief of Staff Büyükanit who demanded that the group must lay down arms unconditionally.[163] Violence in the southeast and east of Turkey thus continued, including a bomb attack in Diyarbakir, which killed 10 people, mostly children, and a grenade attack on a café in the southwest city of Izmir.[164] In December 2006 at least four soldiers and two civilians were killed in mine explosions, and one soldier was killed when a helicopter was bombed in Bingol.[165] The beginning of 2007 saw further unrest in the southeast, partly triggered by the assassination of journalist and Armenian community leader Hrant Dink, who had been an outspoken proponent of human and minority rights in Turkey, on 19 January 2007.[166]

During this period, the Turkish state continued to escalate troop levels along the border with Kurdistan, Iraq. By the first week of July 2007, Turkey had deployed an estimated 140,000 troops to the Turkish-Iraqi border. The government also declared 'temporary security zones' between the provinces of Sirnak, Siirt and Hakkari in southeast Turkey close to the Iraqi border in June 2007, which effectively returned the region to a state of emergency.[167] As the military presence intensified in the region, prominent acts of violence attributed to the PKK resumed and the security situation in the southeast further deteriorated[168] as increased PKK attacks saw over 50 killed, including seven soldiers killed during a rocket and grenade attack on 4 June 2007 at a military base in Dersimand and a bomb explosion in Istanbul on 10 June 2007.[169]

On 8 July 2008, the PKK seized three German tourists while they were climbing Mount Ararat in east Turkey. The PKK stated that the three climbers would be held until Germany abandoned its 'hostile policies towards the PKK'.[170] A spokesperson for the German Foreign Minister Frank-Walter Steinmeier demanded the 'immediate and unconditional' release of the climbers and said that Germany would not respond to blackmail by the PKK.[171] German Chancellor Angela Merkel was also quoted as saying that Germany would not negotiate with the PKK, however, there were reports that the German government had communicated with the hostages. The PKK requested that the Red Cross become involved in helping to secure the release of the hostages. The hostages were released without warning after 2 weeks in captivity on 20 July 2008.[172]

In October of 2008, reports that Abdullah Öcalan had been ill-treated in prison led to demonstrations across the Kurdish regions, in which one protestor was killed and many injured.[173] The PKK has often used such reports and similar incidents to call upon its supporters to demonstrate against the Turkish state. As such the violence continued with the killing of six Turkish soldiers on 27 May 2009 when their vehicle struck a remotely controlled PKK landmine in Çukurca district of Hakkari province. The PKK described the attack as a defensive action. Following the blast Turkish troops launched an offensive near the Iraqi border. This incident, as well as the many that have preceded it and the many that have since occurred, act as evidence that the Turkish military approach to its Kurdish issue is not effective. Constructive dialogue and democratic solutions are called for in order to reach a sustainable peace and move the state beyond the conflict.

1.5 The conflict in Kurdistan, Iraq

Turkish military activities and diplomatic efforts focused in the Kurdish regions beyond its own borders have been primarily motivated by Ankara's obsession to dissipate the perceived 'threat' of Kurdish autonomy through military means.[174] The creation of a safe haven in the wake of the first Gulf War, following Turkey's refusal to accept hundreds of thousands of Iraqi Kurds fleeing a brutal Ba'athist crackdown, intensified Turkey's deep-seated paranoia that moves towards Kurdish autonomy in Iraq could spill over into southeastern Turkey.[175]

The following section of the chapter focuses on the Turkish armed forces bombardments and incursions into Kurdistan, Iraq as well as the PKK activities that have caused the Turkish state to conclude, and defend, such military operations as necessary to state security.

1.5.1 The conflict

The ongoing conflict between the PKK and Turkey has had a destabilising effect not only on Turkey but has carried over into Kurdistan, Iraq and contributed to the high number of internally displaced peoples.[176] Due to the security vacuum in the border areas, precipitated by the establishment of the semi-autonomous Kurdish region in 1991 and coupled with the emergence of factions within the leadership of this area, the PKK was able to establish *de facto* control over the Qandil mountain area bordering Turkey and Iran. This provided the PKK with a location for operating bases that was not only strategically close to the Turkish border, but also represented a source for affordable weapons and a launch pad for attacks on Turkish soil.[177]

The intensification of violence in the southeast in the 1990s prompted the Turkish government to respond with increasingly intense and large-scale incursions into Kurdistan, Iraq. Backed by the presence of a 'hot-pursuit' agreement with Iraq, Turkey carried out operations across the border throughout the 1990s.[178] Major raids into Kurdistan, Iraq by Turkey occurred in 1992, 1993 and 1995, ostensibly with the aim of ousting PKK bases in the area.[179] During this period, indiscriminate bombing and shelling by the Turkish air force lead to civilian deaths and injuries.[180] These raids, as well as increasingly common interventions by Iran using intelligence from Turkey, caused many Kurds living in the area to be displaced in an effort to escape the region's growing insecurity and instability.[181]

The first major Turkish incursion occurred in August 1992 as a joint operation with the Patriotic Union of Kurdistan (PUK), and succeeded in flushing 5,000 PKK members out of the mountains in Kurdistan, Iraq.[182] PUK support for the operation stemmed from the organisation's frustration with the continued presence of the PKK, with whom it had stormy relations, in Kurdistan, Iraq. It also arose from pressure from the United States to oust the PKK, and the PUK's dependence upon Turkey to effectively conduct its operations.[183] At the end of 1992, Turkey decided to change its operational functionality of hot pursuits, to take action against the organisation's camps, launching major air operations.

Although, the PKK announced a unilateral ceasefire on 17 March 1993, the PKK resumed military hostilities against the government on 25 May 1993. A 1993 Human Rights Watch (HRW) report gives accounts of indiscriminate shelling, bombing and strafing in Kurdistan, Iraq in 1993 and 1994.[184] For example, the Turkish air force's raid on the village of Zahko in Dohuk governorate in August 1993 killed three, injured 12, and destroyed civilian property.[185] Another operation by Turkey in August 1994 led to the injury of eight civilians and the destruction of civilian property. An HRW witness from the Bagdowan village in the Koysanjaq district in northern Iraq saw 32 Turkish airplanes bomb his village for nearly an hour and 20 minutes.[186]

In 1995 Turkey waged another large-scale operation, sending 35,000 troops into Kurdistan, Iraq in order to overcome approximately 2,500 members of the PKK believed to be based there.[187] This was ostensibly on the basis that a power struggle between the Kurdish organisations in Iraq had led to a breakdown in the previously effective system whereby the PUK and Kurdistan Democratic Party (KDP) had 'policed' the PKK in Iraq, preventing it from launching attacks across the border into Turkey. Turkey thus argued the need to protect Turkish citizens from such attacks.[188] In May of that year, the then Turkish President Süleyman Demirel briefly went so far as to propose a change in Turkey's border with Iraq, potentially granting Turkey swathes of territory in Kurdistan, Iraq.[189]

It was during these 1995 operations that Turkish soldiers detained seven Kurdish shepherds near the village of Azadi, and reportedly kicked, slapped and beat them with riffle butts before taking them away. Their families tried to find them, but the Turkish military in the area provided no information about their whereabouts. When the Turkish army withdrew some days later, villagers found the shepherds' bodies riddled with bullet wounds and grossly mutilated.[190]

A further significant incursion took place over a 2-week period in May 1997 with the backing of the KDP.[191] This was the fourth spring season in a row that Turkey had sent troops into Kurdistan, Iraq to attack the PKK. With the deployment of an estimated 50,000 troops, backed by tanks and warplanes, the incursion was no shorter in time or scope than the three previous operations. From 1997, Turkey announced the establishment of a 15-kilometre 'security zone' within Kurdistan, Iraq that would be patrolled and extensively monitored by 5,000 troops. The security zone was officially aimed at protecting Turkey's people against the PKK.[192]

Following the capture of Abdullah Öcalan in 1999, the PKK retained bases in Kurdistan, Iraq, despite the declaration of a ceasefire. It was reported that, in dismissing the PKK ceasefire, Turkish forces provided assistance to both the PUK and KDP in their fight against PKK.[193]

In 2000 Turkey again launched another incursion to support the PUK against the PKK.[194] In August 2000, 38 civilians, including women and children, were killed when Turkish jets bombed a group of pastoralists near Kendaxor in Kurdistan, Iraq.[195] A foreign ministry spokesperson confirmed that Turkish forces had carried out airborne operations on that day, and that they would investigate claims of civilian casualties.[196] In October of that year, news reports indicated that the Turkish government had paid an undisclosed sum of money to the leader of the KDP, Masoud Barzani, to be forwarded as compensation to relatives of civilians killed in the Kendaxor bombing.[197]

Since the collapse of the Ba'ath regime in Iraq, the autonomy exercised by the Kurds since 1991 increased significantly. The Kurdistan region has been pro-gressing, albeit unevenly, in economic development, security and infrastructure. These gains are viewed as a threat by neighbouring states like Turkey and Iran as they believe that this progress will motivate the Kurds living in these states to seek greater autonomy, or even independence, themselves.[198] In March 2003, more than 60,000 Turkish troops and heavy artillery were deployed near the border with Iraq to discourage Iraqi Kurds from securing additional territory and power along the Iraqi-Turkish border.[199]

It should be noted that Turkey is a very important player militarily within the region with the second largest army in NATO after the United States.[200] Particularly in the run up to the US invasion of Iraq, Turkey had a great deal of influence on the US-led coalition as its location and cooperation were viewed as vital to the invasion plans. For this reason the United States agreed to supply the Turkish military with intelligence on the location of PKK bases, which in turn Turkey shared with Iran with whom they coordinated cross-border operations.

In April 2006 continued clashes in southeast Turkey resulted in major Turkish military build-up in areas bordering Iran and Iraq. At the time, both the United States and Iraq warned Turkey against conducting cross-border operations aimed at PKK. Turkey called on both to curb PKK activities in Kurdistan, Iraq, denying its troops had crossed Iraqi border.[201] In July 2006, a state terror summit was convened after a wave of soldier deaths in the southeast. The Turkish government again called on the United States and Iraq to crack down on PKK bases and activities in Kurdistan, Iraq, signalling that it would otherwise mount cross-border operations to halt PKK incursions.[202] After a decline in operations aimed at the PKK in Kurdistan, Iraq, Turkey resumed cross-border operations, confirming that in August 2006 Turkish planes targeted PKK positions along border with Iraq.[203]

A resurgence of violence in the beginning of 2007 motivated the Turkish army to launch a series of military strikes in Kurdistan, Iraq, directed at PKK insurgents believed to be in the mountains. With continued clashes in southeast Turkey, Prime Minister Erdogan called for concrete measures against PKK in Kurdistan, Iraq, and again asserted Turkey's right to combat terrorism.[204] In February 2007, during a visit to Washington, the Chief-of-Staff of the Turkish military, General Yaşar Büyükanıt, underlined the resolve of the military to protect Turkey's territorial integrity, directed at separatist Kurds on both sides of the Turkish-Iraqi border as well as Kurdish leaders in northern Iraq. The military, spearheaded by Büyükanıt, had long been advocating an invasion into northern Iraq in order to root out what the military refers to as 'Kurdish terrorist camps'.

In May 2007, Turkish Prime Minister Erdogan signalled that Parliament was ready to support any decision by the military to launch cross-border attacks on the PKK in Kurdistan, Iraq.[205] In June the three provinces of Hakkari, Siirt and Sirnak located along the Iraqi border were declared 'security zones', a measure tantamount to declaring a state of emergency. These three provinces comprised the region where Turkish military build-up had been taking place, and from where an invasion into Kurdistan, Iraq was most likely be launched. Land forces Chief General İlker Başbuğ stated that Turkey had the legal right to protect itself and to act against PKK in Kurdistan, Iraq.[206]

A new Turkish Parliament was sworn in on 4 August 2007 and 3 days later, Iraqi Prime Minister Maliki visited Ankara to sign a memorandum of understanding in regards to ending PKK access to their Kurdistan, Iraq mountain bases.[207] However, by October 2007 Ankara had further stepped up threats to launch a major anti-PKK offensive into Iraq unless action was taken against the group by Iraqi regional and national authorities and the United States. The Turkish Prime Minister Recep Tayyip Erdogan went to the GNA and requested authorisation to undertake military incursions into Kurdistan, Iraq. The lawmakers voted 507 to 19 to give Erdogan permission to order strategic strikes and large-scale invasions of Iraq for a one-year period.[208] This was followed with a call from mainstream politicians for greater powers to be granted to the security forces and for a buffer zone to be established along the Iraqi border. Some went so far as to argue in favour of the re-establishing emergency rule in parts of southeast Turkey as it had been in the 1980s and 1990s when millions of people were forcibly displaced and arbitrary detention and torture were commonplace.[209]

Then on 21 October in the south east province of Hakkari, 12 soldiers were killed, and eight abducted by the PKK. Tensions rose as mass protests against Kurdish separatism were held throughout the country and in the Turkish nationalist movements in the diaspora. Public anger and Turkish society's lack of appetite for pursing a political solution following the incident, gave the state *carte blanche* to begin cross-border military operations. The army massed troops in the border region and stepped up operations, shelling Kurdish villages in Iraq and mounting air strikes on border mountain passes.[210] The incident in the Hakkari province allowed Turkey to present the resumption of operations as a defensive response to PKK activity, which threatened to undermine the sovereignty of the Turkish state. However, given that Turkish operations in Iraq had been ongoing and that the incident in Hakkari did not represent a substantial escalation in the conflict, this explanation was lacking.[211]

In November 2007, shelling by the Turkish armed forces of areas located between Duhok and the border with Turkey resulted in the displacement of tens of families, who were sheltered by local communities in Zakho.[212] The same month Turkish threats of a major military incursion into Kurdistan, Iraq declined after having received assurances from US civilian and military leadership on intelligence sharing and pressure on north Iraqi leadership.[213] On 16 December 2007, Turkey launched air strikes against PKK rebels in northern Iraq. It was reported that over 50 Turkish fighter jets hit PKK positions in Zap, Hakurk and Avasin. The Turkish military stated that only 'terrorist' targets were hit, however the PKK said five of their fighters and two civilians were killed, while local Iraqi officials said 10 villages were attacked and one woman killed.[214] In another December attack, meant to target the PKK, it was reported the operations had hit eight villages, killing at least two civilians.[215] Since the first major strikes of 16 December, Turkish warplanes have conducted a number of air strikes and led ground troops into northern Iraq, Kurdistan.[216]

In a fourth wave of cross border aerial attacks, Turkish warplanes bombed PKK bases in Kurdistan, Iraq on 15 January 2008.[217] Turkey's government argued that the recent escalation of violence in the southeast and increased clashes between Turkish armed forces and the PKK stemmed from PKK members operating in northern Iraq and infiltration of PKK members from across the Iraqi border.[218] The army and government reiterated threats of major military operations into Kurdistan, Iraq, while NATO and the European Union called for restraint.[219] However, despite some calls for Turkey to suspend its cross-border bombardments, the international community gave tacit, if not explicit, approval to the ongoing ground and air operations. As is discussed in later chapters, these operations represented a violation of Turkey's obligations under international law and should have elicited a much more forceful condemnation from the international community.

On 22 February 2008, Turkish military vehicles and thousands of troops crossed the border into northern Iraq.[220] The incursion and subsequent armed clashes were confirmed by both the Turkish authorities and KRG. It was reported that ground troops began to pull out of Kurdistan, Iraq one week later.[221] The Turkish general staff announced that the ground offensive was completed and that troops had returned from Iraq after achieving their objectives. The Turkish armed forces denied any foreign influence on the decision of withdrawal from Kurdistan. However, the PKK claimed that the troops withdrew after meeting fierce resistance.[222] However, the international community, particularly the United States, has increased pressure on Turkey to withdraw its troops and to show some restraint in its pursuit of the PKK in the interest of preserving the fragile stability the exists in Kurdistan, Iraq and the region. At the same, the United States has provided Turkey with intelligence on PKK locations and publicly supported its portrayal of the conflict as being part of the larger fight against terrorism in the region.

On 25 and 26 April 2008, the Turkish Air Force was again conducting air strikes in northern Iraq, ostensibly against the PKK. The strikes targeted PKK guerrillas based in the Zap, Avasin-Basyan and Hakurk regions, who were trying to launch operations against Turkey, according to Turkish intelligence.[223] A second wave of air strikes came on 1 and 2 May, which were carried out in the Qandil Mountains in northern Iraq. The PKK denied claims made by the Turkish military that more than 150 of their fighters had been killed in the air strikes and would confirmed that only six rebels had died and they belonged to a faction fighting against Iran.[224] Along with Turkey, Iran has for years conducted ongoing shelling in the Kurdistan region under the pretext of targeting members of the Free Life Party of Kurdistan (PJAK).[225] The deputy head of Turkey's armed forces General İlker Başbuğ has stated that Turkish forces have collaborated with Iran in attacking bases of the PKK in northern Iraq.[226]

According to witness reports, Turkish and Iranian attacks have remained more or less constant and since March 2009 there has been non-stop aggression in the region.[227] Due to the ongoing Turkish military cross-border raids into Northern Iraq and the air strikes mounted in that region, government forces claim to have killed hundreds of PKK militants while taking far fewer casualties themselves. The number of deaths caused by the armed conflict, as presented by the government, includes 49 civilians, 143 members of security forces, and 657 militants, giving a total of 849.[228]

Conclusion

Far from being isolated cases of belligerence, the military incursions into northern Iraq should be understood in the broader context of Turkey's long-standing strategic goal in countering a strong regional Kurdish autonomy. As witnessed by the authors in the course of their research, as well as by various human rights organisations operating in the region, the ongoing and frequent shelling and bombing by Turkish, as well as Iranian, forces causes extreme distress and suffering to the civilian populations who live in the affected areas. Turkey's cross-border operations violate the basic human rights of civilians living in the region and constitute a contravention of the Geneva Conventions to which the state is a signatory. These actions are also a clear violation of Iraqi sovereignty, often carried out with minimal regard for the rights of the civilian population.[229] Additionally, on a macro level, these military interventions have a detrimental effect on the wider development and stability of Kurdistan, Iraq by entrenching existing problems such as the chronic infrastructural under-development and lack of self-sufficiency, and contribute to the authorities' strong emphasis on security at the expense of human rights issues. Due to the level and intensity of violence taking place in southeast Turkey and Kurdistan, Iraq over the last two decades, a review of the conflict in the context of international law is now imperative. The ongoing destruction of the lives and livelihoods of the people living in these regions gives this project a particular urgency.

Part 1

2 The international law of armed conflict

Introduction

As is outlined in Chapter 1, the history of the clash between the Turkish government and the Kurdish people in southeast Turkey is a long and complex one and has escalated again in recent years. The analysis in this chapter discusses the legal framework surrounding the military clashes between the Turkish army (together with Turkish security forces) and the Kurdish insurgents, particularly the Kurdistan Workers Party (PKK), which has been ongoing since 1984. The international treaties and customs governing armed conflict will be discussed with respect to the classification of an armed conflict and conduct of the use of force – in traditional international law terms – the *jus in bello*. First and foremost, this chapter examines the key threshold question – has the long-standing insurgency in southeast Turkey risen to the level of an armed conflict? This discussion will involve an examination of the rather limited treaty law in this area and the more extensive international law literature debating this important topic. Classification of an insurgency as an armed conflict is not only a politically charged topic, but a major unresolved controversy in public international law. It is by no means clear how an insurgency crystallizes into armed conflict. However, once a situation becomes an armed conflict a host of legal questions emerge, and these are also introduced in this chapter.

Second, once the threshold of armed conflict has been reached, the next critical issue is the classification of the armed conflict. It is essential that the armed conflict be classified as either an international or non-international armed conflict as each attracts different international treaty regimes. In these circumstances there may be three different types of armed conflict that could be taking place separately or in tandem. One choice is that the long-standing insurgency in southeast Turkey with the involvement of Turkish security and armed forces and the PKK (and other groups including the Kurdistan Freedom Falcons), could be categorised as a non-international armed conflict. However, it must be noted that there is the contrasting Turkish position that the PKK and other insurgent groups are terrorists engaged in criminal behaviour and therefore are to be dealt with by domestic criminal law. At the other end of the spectrum, there is a possible international armed conflict taking place sporadically in Kurdistan, Iraq between the PKK and the Turkish armed forces with the *jus ad bellum* issue of legality of an invasion of another sovereign state involved, which is discussed in Chapter 5. Furthermore, in Additional Protocol 1 to the Geneva Conventions of 1977, the applicability of this convention protecting victims of international armed conflicts includes wars of national liberation.[1] Even though the provision is not applicable to this situation as Turkey is not a party to the Additional Protocols, it is necessary to consider whether this provision could be customary international law.

There is a half way position of an internationalised armed conflict where an internal armed conflict spills over into the territory of another state but with an additional requirement that another state becomes involved in the internal conflict by such methods as supplying military aid, or in this case supplying intelligence information for targeting. This chapter surveys the applicable laws of armed conflict for each scenario. A common factor between both the situation in southeast Turkey and Kurdistan, Iraq is the denial by the Turkish government of the existence of an armed conflict. However, any such denial is not in itself determinative of the situation and this chapter discusses the ongoing debate as to criteria for armed conflict.

As a third task in this chapter, there is a brief introduction to the discussion of the large body of law that will govern the conduct of any armed conflict found to exist – the *jus in bello* known as international humanitarian law. The problem is that there are two separate legal regimes governing international and non-international armed conflict although there is a live debate that the two types of conflict should be merged and governed by the same international humanitarian rules.[2] After the introduction of this important topic, Chapters 3 and 4 deal in more detail with the most important aspects of international humanitarian law applicable to this conflict; the minimum humanitarian guarantees primarily incorporated into Common Article 3 of the Geneva Conventions of 1949 if this is a non-international armed conflict and the specific treatment of belligerents which is one of the most controversial issues in armed conflict.[3]

2.1 The existence of an armed conflict in international law

Although this area of law might well intersect with the lawfulness of the use of force, known in international law as the *jus ad bellum*, traditionally the classification of a situation as an armed conflict falls within the *jus in bello*. This is because the debate within this area focuses on the applicability of the treaty and customary rules of international humanitarian law[4] and not on such issues as self-defence or collective security which are exceptions to the prohibition on the use of force.[5] Therefore, deciding on the existence of an armed conflict is the essential first step before any other legal issues can be considered.

Since the advent of the United Nations Charter in 1945 by far the most numerous incidents of the use of armed force has been in the context of civil wars or disturbances.[6] This is particularly problematic as the Charter collective security regime was designed as a response to major international armed conflicts that had resulted in two world wars. Since the end of the Cold War simmering ethnic conflicts erupted in many parts of the world resulting in the loss of millions of lives. It has become a major concern for the international community as represented by the United Nations.

One of the most controversial areas in international humanitarian law is whether or not a civil disturbance or insurgency can rise to the level of an armed conflict. The other major legal difficulty is that there is not *per se* a prohibition on civil wars within *jus ad bellum*. The tragedy of civil conflict is the large loss of civilian life and the concurrent refugee crises which often spills over into other territories – destabilising whole regions. In fact a civil conflict can escalate to an international armed conflict as it did in Yugoslavia and in the Great Lakes region of Africa. If the situation between the Kurdish insurgents and the Turkish army rises to the level of an armed conflict, the consequence is that neither Turkey or the Kurdish fighters can legitimately refuse to be bound by international humanitarian law and if it is a non-international armed conflict they are all bound by Common Article 3 to the four Geneva Conventions (this is discussed in Chapter 3). This means that the Turkish regime cannot simply treat the PKK as a terrorist group and permit torture and other inhumane acts to take place as a means of combating enemies. (It is noted in subsequent chapters that these activities would also be unlawful in the jurisprudence of human rights within the context of terrorism.) The characterisation of the situation in the southeast as an armed conflict and the PKK as lawful belligerents would not only bring the situation under the international treaty protection of the Geneva Conventions but put further pressure on the international community and Turkey to find a political solution to the problem.

There are two main legal difficulties with respect to actually classifying an armed conflict. First, due to disagreement among states, there was the deliberate absence in the 1949 Geneva Conventions of a definition of what constitutes an armed conflict, as the provision for non-international armed conflict, Common Article 3 states simply that it applies to 'an armed conflict not of an international character occurring in the territory of one of the High Contracting Parties'.[7] Second, there is also no definition of armed conflict that might constitute customary international law.[8] States express positions on whether situations of violence in other countries amounts to armed conflict in UN General Assembly or UN Security Council Resolutions but the particular states involved in this type of insurgency rarely agree with the classification and tend to argue that actions of their military or security forces are for the purposes of law enforcement or counter-terrorism operations. Rather, it is left to the international community and often civil society to argue that the situation has escalated to that extent. A pertinent example given by Peijić is the ongoing conflict between Russia and the break-away province of Chechnya. The Russian Constitutional Court in 1995 indicated that Additional Protocol II (which Russia was a party to) was applicable to the fighting in Chechnya at that time, but when hostilities resumed in 1999 the Russian executive referred to their response to the situation as a counter-terrorist action.[9]

Given the lack of treaty provisions, distinguishing between situations of non-international armed conflict which will trigger the operation of Common Article 3 to the Geneva Conventions and Additional Protocol II of 1979 (if applicable), and situations of internal disturbance or tension is a very difficult task. The result of this lack of definition is that a series of criteria have been developed in the practice of states and in the legal literature even though they might not be accepted as customary.[10] The first and primary criterion is the existence of parties to the conflict. Common Article 3 is applicable to 'each Party to the conflict' and so there must be in existence at least two parties. It is not difficult to determine the existence of the armed forces of one of the parties – the state but the non-state armed group is more difficult. It is widely recognised that an armed group must have a 'certain level of organisation and command structure, as well as the ability to implement international humanitarian law'.[11] This rules out armed attacks by unorganised individuals as their actions would be classified as criminal.

There are other important criteria mentioned in the literature: whether the government is obliged to use military force; the number of victims; the means used to deal with the opposing side; and the duration and level of violence involved.[12] In his lectures to The Hague Academy of International Law, Schindler came up with the following definition which seems most apt for the purpose of examining the Kurdish conflict in southeast Turkey. He stated:

> Practice has set up the following criteria to delimit non-international armed conflicts from internal disturbances. In the first place, the hostilities have to be conducted by force of arms and exhibit such intensity that, as a rule, the government is compelled to employ its armed forces against the insurgents instead of mere police forces. Secondly, as to the insurgents, the hostilities are meant to be of a collective character, that is, they have to be carried out not only by single groups. In addition, the insurgents have to exhibit a minimum amount of organisation. Their armed forces should be under a responsible command and be capable of meeting minimal humanitarian requirements. Accordingly, the conflict must show certain similarities to a war, without fulfilling all conditions necessary for the recognition of belligerency.[13]

The intensity of the violence is also relied upon in the jurisprudence of the International Criminal Tribunal for the Former Yugoslavia. In *Prosecutor v Tadić*, the Appeals Chamber held that 'an armed conflict exists whenever there is resort to armed force between states or protected armed violence between governmental authorities and organised armed groups or between such groups within a state'.[14]

If a state is a party to the Additional Protocol II of 1977 to the Geneva Conventions of 1949 the test for an internal armed conflict alters and is much more stringent. The criteria set out in Article 1 are:

1. This Protocol, which develops and supplements Article 3 common to the Geneva Conventions of 12 August 1949 without modifying its

existing conditions of application, shall apply to all armed conflicts which are not covered by Article 1 of the Protocol Additional to the Geneva Conventions of 12 August 1949, and relating to the Protection of Victims of International Armed Conflicts (Protocol I) and which take place in the territory of a High Contracting Party between its armed forces and dissident armed forces or other organized armed groups which, under responsible command, exercise such control over a part of its territory as to enable them to carry out sustained and concerted military operations and to implement this Protocol.

2. This Protocol shall not apply to situations of internal disturbances and tensions, such as riots, isolated and sporadic acts of violence and other acts of a similar nature, as not being armed conflicts.[15]

The two key additional factors are the necessity of territorial control and the ability to carry out sustained and concerted military operations. An explanation is that Additional Protocol II was negotiated in an atmosphere of determining the lowest common denominator in a situation of infringement of state sovereignty.[16] Therefore, the scope of application is much narrower than Common Article 3 but the Protocol specifically states that it develops and supplements Common Article 3 without modifying its existing conditions of application. The Geneva Conventions are now universally ratified Conventions whereas many countries, including Turkey, are not party to Additional Protocol II. The International Court of Justice has declared that Common Article 3 represents customary international law in both international and non-international armed conflict.[17] This means that it is Schindler's interpretation of Common Article 3 which is persuasive.

There is further international jurisprudence on the issue of classification. One case that has considered this issue is the *Abella* case in the Inter-American Commission on Human Rights. In the view of the commissioners a conflict lasting 30 hours between a group of dissident officers and the Argentine military at the Tabalda military base qualified as an armed conflict and Common Article 3 was held to be applicable.[18]

One cannot leave this issue within mentioning that the Rome Statute of the International Criminal Court which provides yet another definition of a non-international armed conflict. Article 8 2(f) provides a definition that is not as stringent as Additional Protocol II but not as general as Common Article 3. It states:

Paragraph 2 (e) applies to armed conflicts not of an international character and thus does not apply to situations of internal disturbances and tensions, such as riots, isolated and sporadic acts of violence or other acts of a similar nature. It applies to armed conflicts that take place in the territory of a State when there is protracted armed conflict between governmental authorities and organized armed groups or between such groups.[19]

This provision is indeed very close to the definition provided by Schindler and does not insist on territorial control. Peijić summarises the serious legal problem of the threshold for armed conflict by stating:

> Political considerations aside, there remains the difficulty of determining and analysing the various factual criteria to which legal conclusions can be pinned. Based on the facts, it can legitimately, if only hypothetically, be asked whether, for example, the situations in Northern Ireland, Turkey and Algeria, constituted internal disturbances or tensions or internal armed conflicts. The general conclusion to be drawn is not that a definition of internal armed conflict would solve the problem – the examples provided above would attest to the contrary – only that knowledge of the facts, careful analysis and a bona fide approach to the habitual criteria for assessment are required.[20]

It is necessary then to follow Peijić's methodology and Schindler's definition to review the situation in southeast Turkey. If one carefully analyses the facts in southeast Turkey as is set out in Chapter 1 and assesses the history of the conflict, it is evident that there has been sustained violence between the military and security forces of Turkey and an organised group, the PKK, since 1984. In accordance with Common Article 3 there are at least two parties to the conflict. This conflict in accordance with the Schindler definition has been conducted by force of arms and has exhibited such intensity that the government of Turkey has been compelled to employ members of its armed forces against the insurgents and not just security or police forces. In this case there has been the involvement of thousands of members of its military forces.[21] The violence takes place within a sovereign state – Turkey – and it is indeed a protracted conflict at this point lasting almost 25 years, as is outlined in detail in Chapter 1. Turning again to the Schindler definition, the PKK has the level of organisation required and the hostilities have had a collective character. The PKK is organised into a military structure, and it has expressed its agreement to abide by the laws of armed conflict. This was confirmed by a statement to the United Nations delivered in Geneva on 24 January 1995 which states:

> In its conflict with the Turkish state forces, the PKK undertakes to respect the Geneva Conventions of 1949 and the First Protocol of 1977 regarding the conduct of hostilities and the protection of the victims of war and to treat those obligations as having the force of law within its own forces and the areas within its control.[22]

Another important supporting aspect is the several cease fires declared by the PKK, emphasising the collective character of the conflict. Therefore, to summarise with Schindler's final statement, this conflict has all the appearance of an armed conflict and has had such for many years.

Regardless of this careful analysis and in accordance with the other examples given by Peijić, it is clear that Turkey does not agree with this assessment and categorises this conflict as terrorist insurgency and denies the applicability of Common Article 3 to the conflict.[23] Nevertheless, Turkey may have engaged in negotiations with the PKK. It is therefore imperative that this conflict be examined by the rest of the international community in light of these well established criteria. States who are members of the United Nations should not ignore their obligations under international law to respond to situations of armed conflict including non-international armed conflicts as threats to international peace and security. Yet the armed conflict questions resulting from this situation become even more complex than the threshold issue as the conflict from southeast Turkey has spilled over into Kurdistan, Iraq. Therefore, if the fact of the existence of an armed conflict is accepted, we must also consider the issue of the classification of this armed conflict which on several occasions has spilled over into the territory of Iraq.

2.2 Classification of the type of armed conflict

As with the issue of the threshold between armed conflict and civil disturbance, the treaty law is of little assistance in the classification issues as there has been no attempt in treaty law to provide criteria to distinguish between international and non-international armed conflict. Furthermore, when one reviews the conflicts in Yugoslavia or the conflict in Central America leading to the *Nicaragua* decision,[24] it is clear that often non-international armed conflicts become internationalised. As with the analysis above, the focus has to be on the academic interpretation of the classification issue. Again, as with the threshold debate, customary international law has not evolved to an agreed definition of international, non-international or internationalised armed conflict.

2.2.1 Internal or non-international armed conflict

Non-international armed conflicts are often labelled 'civil wars'. A simplistic analysis would be that these conflicts take place within the territory of a sovereign state. However, there has recently emerged a definition that is of great assistance and it is included in the first section of 'The Manual on Non-International Armed Conflict' ('The Manual'), a set of standards, definitions and rules drafted by experts in the law of armed conflict:

1.1.1   Non-international armed conflict

a.   Non-international armed conflicts are armed confrontations occurring within the territory of a single State and in which the armed forces of no other State are engaged against the central government.
b.   Internal disturbances and tensions (such as riots, isolated and sporadic acts of violence, or other acts of a similar nature) do not amount to a non-international armed conflict.[25]

This is supported by the International Committee of the Red Cross (ICRC) March 2008 opinion paper where it states:

> 2. **Non-international armed conflicts** are *protracted armed confrontations* occurring between governmental armed forces and the forces of one or more armed groups, or between such groups arising on the territory of a State [party to the Geneva Conventions]. The armed confrontation must reach *a minimum level of intensity* and the parties involved in the conflict must show *a minimum of organisation.*[26]

We have discussed above the distinction between internal disturbances and internal armed conflict but it also important to discuss the definition of the internal armed conflict as one not involving other states. 'The Manual' goes on to declare:

> Non-international armed conflicts do not include conflicts in which two or more States are engaged against each other. Nor do they encompass conflicts extending to the territory of two or more States.

These definitions seem to encompass what is obvious within a civil war situation and should indeed be accepted as a customary definition given the research that went into determining this definition by an examination of practice of states and *opinio juris.*[27] The key factor is the fact that the conflict is conducted within the frontiers of one sovereign state and has no involvement of other parties.

When one examines the conflict in southeast Turkey there is already a problem with this definition due to the undisputed fact that the conflict has spilled over into Kurdistan, Iraq on several occasions, as is detailed in Chapter 1. Given these events it is necessary to examine whether or not this is an international armed conflict.

2.2.2 International armed conflict

As stated above, there is also no agreed customary law formula as to how to classify a conflict as international or non-international.[28] The traditional definition of an international armed conflict is a conflict between the armed forces of at least two sovereign states. The ICRC released an opinion paper in March 2008 providing treaty law, jurisprudence and academic opinion on the definition of an international armed conflict.[29] The first part of this definition is found in Common Article 2 to the four Geneva Conventions of 1949 which states that:

> In addition to the provisions which shall be implemented in peacetime, the present Convention shall apply to all cases of declared war or of any other armed conflict which may arise between two or more of the High Contracting Parties, even if the state of war is not recognized by one of them.

The Convention shall also apply to all cases of partial or total occupation of the territory of a High Contracting Party, even if the said occupation meets with no armed resistance.[30]

'High Contracting Parties' mean states and so an international armed conflict occurs when one or more states have recourse to armed force again another states. As the ICRC argues, there is no necessity for a formal declaration of war or recognition of the situation. The existence of the international armed conflict depends on what actually occurs on the group and is based on factual conditions even if one of the belligerents does not recognise the government of the adverse party. The Pictet Commentary to Geneva Convention I of 1949 states that:

any difference arising between two States and leading to the intervention of armed forces is an armed conflict within the meaning of Article 2, even if one of the Parties denies the existence of a state of war. It makes no difference how long the conflict lasts, or how much slaughter takes place.[31]

This definition is also supported in the literature. Schindler also discussed the definition of international armed conflict in his Hague Academy lectures. He stated that:

the existence of an armed conflict within the meaning of Article 2 common to the Geneva Conventions can always be assumed when parts of the armed forces of two States clash with each other. [...] Any kind of use of arms between two States brings the Conventions into effect.[32]

H-P Gasser argues that:

any use of armed force by one State against the territory of another, triggers the applicability of the Geneva Conventions between the two States. [...] It is also of no concern whether or not the party attacked resists. [...] As soon as the armed forces of one State find themselves with wounded or surrendering members of the armed forces or civilians of another State on their hands, as soon as they detain prisoners or have actual control over a part of the territory of the enemy State, then they must comply with the relevant convention.[33]

This definition has been extended in the jurisprudence of the International Court of Justice and international criminal tribunals. The first major consideration of this issue was in the *Nicaragua* decision, where the issue before the Court was whether the United States by financing, organising, training, equipping and planning the operations of the paramilitary groups in Nicaragua (the Contras), was responsible for violations of international humanitarian law committed by those rebels. The Court held that: (i) a party should not only be in effective control of a military or paramilitary group, but that (ii) the control should be exercised with respect to the specific operation in the course of which breaches may have been committed. It was necessary to prove that the United States had specifically 'directed or enforced' the perpetration of those acts.[34] By logical extension, made in subsequent tribunals, that meant that another state was involved in an armed conflict, thereby rendering it international. As the *Tadić* Appeal Judgment states:

> what was at stake was not the criminal culpability of the *contras* for serious violations of international humanitarian law, but rather the question of whether or not the *contras* had acted as *de facto* organs of the United States on its request, thus generating the international responsibility of that State.[35]

One of the major issues for the Judges of the International Criminal Tribunal for the Former Yugoslavia was to determine the character of the conflict in Yugoslavia.[36] The Judges in the Appeals Chamber disagreed with the *Nicaragua* 'effective control' test and after an analysis of case law and the law of state responsibility proposed:

> 131. In order to attribute the acts of a military or paramilitary group to a State, it must be proved that the State wields overall control over the group, not only by equipping and financing the group, but also by coordinating or helping in the general planning of its military activity. Only then can the State be held internationally accountable for any misconduct of the group. However, it is not necessary that, in addition, the State should also issue, either to the head or to members of the group, instructions for the commission of specific acts contrary to international law.[37]

Based on this test the Appeals Chamber held that in 1992 the relevant period for the criminal charges against Tadić, the armed forces of the Republika Srpska were to be regarded as acting under the overall control of and on behalf of the Federal Republic of Yugoslavia (FRY) and that therefore the armed conflict in Bosnia and Herzegovina was classified as an international armed conflict.[38] This expanded the definition to not only those conflicts between two states, but conflicts involving paramilitary groups which have a substantial degree of foreign state control.

The definition of an international armed conflict has also been discussed in the jurisprudence of the International Criminal Court in the context of the conflict in the Democratic Republic of Congo (DRC). In the pre-trial phases of *Prosecutor v Thomas Lubanga Dyilo*[39] and *Prosecutor v Germain Katanga and Mathieu Ngudjolo Chui*,[40] the Pre-Trial Chamber held that there were substantial grounds to believe that the Ituri conflict in northeast DRC was international. The reasons given was the direct participation in the conflict of the Ugandan People's Armed Forces and Uganda's 'substantial contribution' of weapons and ammunition to armed groups in DRC.[41] The Chamber in *Lubanga* ruled that international armed conflict can exists alongside an internal armed conflict in these circumstances: '(i) another State intervenes in that conflict through its troops (direct intervention), or if (ii) some of the participants in the internal armed conflict act on behalf of that other State (indirect intervention)'.[42] This opinion was also upheld by the International Court of Justice in *Case Concerning Armed Activities on the Territory of the Congo (Democratic Republic of the Congo v Uganda).*[43]

There is one other degree of international armed conflict that is very controversial. Apart from regular, inter-state armed conflicts, the ICRC opinion paper argues that Additional Protocol I extends the definition of international armed conflict to include armed conflicts in which peoples are fighting against colonial domination, alien occupation or racist regimes in the exercise of their right to self-determination (wars of national liberation).[44] Clearly within a state's domestic law system to attempt to overthrow a government by force is illegal and criminal often governed by the domestic crimes of sedition or treason. However, there has been a long-standing debate on the international law exception to that illegality – wars of national liberation. This is a very controversial area but the widely accepted UN General Assembly Declaration on the Principles of International Law concerning Friendly Relations and Cooperation among States contains a specific exception for this type of armed conflict:

> The establishment of a sovereign and independent State, the free association or integration with an independent State or the emergence into any other political status freely determined by a people constitute modes of implementing the right of self-determination by that people.
>
> Every State has the duty to refrain from any forcible action which deprives peoples referred to above in the elaboration of the present principle of their right to self-determination and freedom and independence. In their actions against, and resistance to, such forcible action in pursuit of the exercise of their right to self-determination, such peoples are entitled to seek and to receive support in accordance with the purposes and principles of the Charter.[45]

This exception is later supported in the Consensus Definition on Aggression. Article 7 contains a specific exception given on the prohibition against the use of force for the exercise of self-determination:

> Nothing in this Definition, and in particular article 3, could in any way prejudice the right to self-determination, freedom and independence, as derived from the Charter, of peoples forcibly deprived of that right and referred to in the Declaration on Principles of International Law concerning Friendly Relations and Cooperation among States in accordance with the Charter of the United Nations, particularly peoples under colonial and racist regimes or other forms of alien domination: nor the right of these peoples to struggle to that end and to seek and receive support, in accordance with the

principles of the Charter and in conformity with the above-mentioned Declaration.[46]

Notwithstanding these declarations, it is the general practice of sovereign states not to admit the existence of internal armed conflicts or to acknowledge that any such conflicts are an exercise of a right of self-determination. Those who wish to secure a new political arrangement are classified as rebels, terrorists or insurgents – or as Margaret Thatcher famously said with respect to the IRA captives during the Northern Ireland troubles – criminals.[47] The denial of the right to self-determination can be argued in the context of the Kurdish people and their struggle in southeast Turkey. This is discussed in more detail in Chapter 5. Based on these declarations, if peoples are denied the right to self-determination, it could conceivably be argued that they might be legally entitled to use force.

The only clear treaty provision that incorporates wars of self-determination as international armed conflict is Additional Protocol I of 1977 to the 1949 Geneva Conventions. Lootsteen discusses the effect of the Provision in Article 1(4) by stating:

> As has been demonstrated, Article 1(4) of Protocol I sets a low bar for the application of the full body of the laws of war – any armed conflict waged to achieve national self-determination ... Even today, in the post-colonial era, wars of national liberation are not uncommon and Article 1(1) of Protocol I could serve to protect the victims of these conflicts.[48]

Additional Protocol 1 (4) states:

> The situations referred to in the preceding paragraph include armed conflicts in which peoples are fighting against colonial domination and alien occupation and against racist regimes in the exercise of their right of self-determination, as enshrined in the Charter of the United Nations and the Declaration on Principles of International Law concerning Friendly Relations and Co-operation among States in accordance with the Charter of the United Nations.

Therefore, international armed conflicts could conceivably include peoples fighting against colonial domination, alien occupation or racist regimes in their exercise of their right to self-determination. However, this definition only applies to those who are states parties to Additional Protocol I and Turkey is not such a party. The only question would be whether this definition because of the Declarations on Friendly Relations and Declaration on Aggression set out above is now part of customary international law. If so, the definition would be applicable to Turkey and it could be argued that the conflict in southeast Turkey is an international armed conflict and therefore a full range of humanitarian protections apply. This provision is discussed in greater detail in Chapter 8, but it can be summarised here by saying there seems to be no academic or state consensus that a war of liberation is an international conflict within customary international law. This is particularly the case for conflicts arising after the end of the decolonization period.[49]

If it is not a war of self-determination then the problem is that although the conflict has spilled over into the territory of Kurdistan, Iraq, it does not involve the army of another sovereign state as it has not engaged either the fledgling army of Iraq, or the United States army which is still involved in military operations in Iraq. The definition of an international armed conflict clearly contemplates conflict between sovereign states, and the Turkish authorities have been clear that they do not intend a conflict with Iraq and rather are pursuing the Kurdish forces into their hiding places in Kurdistan, Iraq. There is another type of armed conflict that might be applicable and that is internationalised armed conflict.

2.2.3 Internationalised armed conflict

Internationalised armed conflict is a controversial third type of armed conflict that at first glance might be apt in these circumstances but on closer analysis is fraught with difficulty. It is defined by Stewart in an article for the *International Review of the Red Cross*:

> The term 'internationalized armed conflict' describes internal hostilities that are rendered international. The factual circumstances that can achieve that internationalization are numerous and often complex: the term internationalized armed conflict includes war between two internal factions both of which are backed by different States; direct hostilities between two foreign States that militarily intervene in an internal armed conflict in support of opposing sides; and war involving a foreign intervention in support of an insurgent group fighting against an established government. The most transparent internationalized internal armed conflicts in recent history include NATO's intervention in the armed conflict between the Federal Republic of Yugoslavia (FRY) and the Kosovo Liberation Army (KLA) in 1999 and the intervention undertaken by Rwanda, Angola, Zimbabwe, Uganda and others, in support of opposing sides of the internal armed conflict in the Democratic Republic of Congo (DRC) since August 1998.[50]

The activities that result in this controversial label are also discussed in 'The Manual' but the authors do not accept that there is this third type of conflict:

> When a foreign State extends its military support to the government of a State within which a non-international armed conflict is taking place, the conflict remains non-international in character. Conversely, should a foreign State extend military support to an armed group acting against the

government, the conflict will become international in character. Admittedly, it is sometimes difficult to determine in the circumstances of a protracted non-international armed conflict whether there exists a government.[51]

These fact situations do not seem to apply to the situation in southeast Turkey and Kurdistan, Iraq as there does not seem to be military support to an armed group acting against the government by Iraq nor is there any evidence of two armies at conflict, but at closer examination it is necessary to examine this possible classification based on an argument of foreign assistance to the Turkish army in this internal conflict. The reason for this review is the tacit and perhaps overt assistance of the United States identifying the targets within Kurdistan, Iraq. As with the *Nicaragua* case,[52] this assistance if extensive could constitute participation in the armed conflict. It may well be that the tacit consent and assistance allowing Turkey to take its conflict into another sovereign state has internationalised the conflict. Yet it has to be noted that 'The Manual' defines this type of conflict with assistance given to a government rather than rebel group, as an internal armed conflict. Furthermore, there is not the level of assistance that was alleged in the *Nicaragua* case as there is no evidence of actual American participation in training or providing assistance in providing weapons and material.

Stewart supports the argument of the ICRC that these classifications are not helpful and that the full spectrum of international humanitarian law rules should apply regardless of the classification.[53] Nevertheless, it is important to embark on this classification exercise due to the lack of acceptance by sovereign states of that insightful position. Yet the aspect of internationalised armed conflict is the least studied and it is by no means clear that this classification adds anything to the classification issue. It is rather a half way point between an internal conflict and an international armed conflict.[54] There is a need for further study of the classification of armed conflict but at this point the term 'internationalised armed conflict' remains controversial and will not be utilised in this book as a category.

Conclusion on classification

It seems clear that the conflict in southeast Turkey rises to the level of an armed conflict and that it might just be an international armed conflict war of national liberation. There is another reason for the situation to have risen to an international armed conflict, which is the invasion of thousands of Turkish troops into Kurdistan, Iraq. Nevertheless, the prudent position is, and will probably remain, that the conflict in southeast Turkey is an non-international armed conflict as both wars of national liberation and internationalised armed conflict are not accepted as part of customary international law. Currently in London, under the auspices of the international law programme at the Royal Institute of International Affairs (Chatham House) a study on the classification of armed conflict is being conducted by a group of humanitarian law experts but the results of this study are not available at present.

Yet there is another debate on armed conflict that although fallen into disuse might be relevant in these circumstances and that is the traditional debate over the classification of a situation of conflict as belligerency. It is to this debate we now turn.

2.3 Belligerency

A long-standing debate in customary international law with respect to the classification of armed conflict is to confer on a situation of insurgency the status of belligerency. It is an important debate – as the status of belligerency bestows on the participants the full spectrum of humanitarian law guarantees available in international armed conflict. This is important as the rights of a belligerent or in the more modern term, combatant, is very much dependent on the classification of the armed conflict, with only very limited protections available in non-international armed conflict. For the belligerent, the conferral of the status of belligerency could be a critical development. Therefore, the focus of this chapter is to review of the legal regime concerning lawful belligerency. This part of the chapter discusses the academic literature that proposes criteria for belligerency that could constitute customary international law. Although the conferral of belligerency has fallen into disuse its revival could be critical to the conflict in southeast Turkey.

2.3.1 Definition of belligerency

Belligerency is defined by Moir as the 'declaration by the recognising party that the conflict had attained such a sustained level that both sides are entitled to be treated in the same way as belligerents in an international armed conflict'.[55] He views this as the third and ultimate level in intensity on a continuum from rebellion (modest, sporadic challenge by a section of a population), insurgency (substantial attack against the legitimate order of the state) to belligerency where there is both internal and international recognition of a sustained internal armed conflict.[56] This does not move the conflict to an international armed conflict but rather the status of belligerency applies to an internal armed conflict. This is a complex distinction as it seems that belligerency grants all the protections of international armed conflict, without the actual label.

It can also be asserted there may be no real distinction between insurgency and belligerency except for the fact of recognition. This was discussed in the *Tadić* interlocutory decision on jurisdiction in which the court argued that the dichotomy between belligerency and insurgence was sovereignty-oriented, based on states looking after their own interests rather than community concerns or humanitarian demands.[57] This means that insurgency and belligerency are factually similar but the key distinction seems to be the recognition of belligerency by the state in whose territory the conflict exists and by third parties who can then assume the obligation of neutrality regarding the conflict.[58] Importantly, this case supported the fact that belligerency might exist as a concept. Facts supporting belligerency according to the academic literature are ' … the existence of civil war within a state, beyond the scope of mere local unrest; occupation by insurgents of a substantial part of a territory of the state; a measure of orderly administration by that group in the area it controls; and observance of the laws of war by the rebel forces, acting under responsible authority'.[59]

The benefits and responsibilities of belligerency are: the captured members of both sides of the conflict were entitled to prisoner of war status (see discussion of belligerents in Chapter 4); insurgent ships were admitted into the ports of other states who recognised the belligerency; the ships also had the right to visit and search at sea; contraband could be confiscated; and the ports of both parties to the conflict could be blockaded.[60] In sum, what the recognition of belligerency meant is that the conflict is viewed in a similar way to an international armed conflict and all of the laws of the *jus in bello* both customary and treaty law are applicable to the conflict.[61] Moir, in his analysis of the major internal conflicts of the 19th and early 20th centuries, states that in those cases where the laws of war were accepted and applied by opposing forces, some form of recognition of belligerency had taken place; if not, there was barbaric conduct on both sides.[62] The examples given by Moir where some form of belligerency recognition occurred were the American War of Independence (1774–83), the Wars of Independence by the Spanish American Colonies (1810–24), the American Civil War (1861–65) and the Greek insurrection (1946–49).[63] Examples where recognition did not occur were the Greek revolt against the Ottoman Empire (1821–29), the Hungarian Civil War (1848–49), the Cuban Wars of Liberation against Spain (1868–78 and 1895–98) and, the Spanish Civil War (1936–39).[64] It was the British that first recognised the situation of belligerency in the American Civil War which enabled them to maintain neutrality in that conflict.[65]

Importantly, it was the Lieber Code developed during the American Civil War that did much to clarify the rules of international humanitarian law and yet was developed in the context of a civil war.[66] This Code recognised Confederate soldiers as prisoners of war, even though this was clearly an internal armed conflict. In contrast to this situation, it seems that although that the Spanish Civil War met the four criteria of belligerency it was political factors that led other European nations not to recognise the situation as belligerency.[67]

It is essential to note that Moir and other academic commentators acknowledge that the doctrine of belligerency has fallen into disuse. Cullen argues that the non-recognition of the Spanish Civil War as a situation of belligerency by neighbouring states 'demonstrated the demise of the concept in traditional international law'.[68] As we have seen earlier, the discussion since has been about the threshold and then classification of armed conflict, rather than recognition of belligerency. Nevertheless, it could be argued that recognition of belligerency could still be relevant in public international law even though the concept has fallen into disuse. Lootsteen, in his persuasive article, argues that the concept could still be used in the future. It is important as the full range of protections of humanitarian law would be available rather than the limited protections offered in Common Article 3 or Additional Protocol II. He does not accept that fact that these treaties have nullified the traditional international law doctrine of recognition of belligerency. This position of applicability would also seem to accord with the argument concerning the progressive elimination of the distinction between internal and international armed conflict. Recognition of belligerency implies recognition of the fact of armed conflict and that both sides of that conflict are entitled to the protection of the laws of war. However, sadly recognition of a state of belligerency in history as the Spanish Civil War clearly demonstrates, has not just based on the four factual criteria but political factors that do not relate to international law issues.[69]

Lootsteen concludes that for belligerency to occur a set of objective facts must be present but also there must be recognition by third party states, by the belligerents or by international organisations. Most importantly, the situation must be recognised by the *de jure* government for the protections of the laws of war to apply. Although it might be rare for a government to recognise a situation as belligerency there might be good reasons to do so. The reason would be that the soldiers of the government would also be entitled to the full respect for the laws of war on the part of the belligerents.[70]

Another argument for the demise of belligerency other than disuse is the idea that Common Article 3 with its guarantees constitutes a complete code for the conduct of an internal armed conflict.[71] As we see below, and in Chapter 3, that cannot be the case as it only provides protection for those who are wounded, sick, civilians or *hors de combat*, not those who are involved in the conflict itself. In fact, it could be argued that the drafters of Common Article 3 recognised the existence of belligerency and that this article was intended to apply to internal armed conflict not reaching the threshold of the belligerency criteria.[72] Lootsteen gives two arguments for the continuation of belligerency in spite of the adoption of Common Article 3. First, the preamble to the provision states that it will apply to armed conflicts not of an international character. If the conflict meets the four criteria of belligerency it is '*ex definitio* an armed conflict of an international character'.[73] Second, the preamble indicates that the provision applies 'as a minimum' and so higher standards of protection can apply. When a civil war reaches the intensity of belligerency the parties might want the full spectrum of protection. An example of this might be that a government might feel it impracticable to prosecute and execute all the insurgents and it would also be of benefit to the government soldiers to be treated with dignity and respect.[74] The Pictet commentary states:

> Care has been taken to state, in Article 3, that the applicable provisions represent a compulsory minimum. The words 'as a minimum' must be understood in that sense. At the same time they are an invitation to exceed that minimum. The time may come when, in accordance with the law of nations, the adversary may be bound by humanitarian obligations which go farther than the minimum requirement stated in Article 3. For instance, if one Party to a conflict is recognized by third parties as being a belligerent, that Party would then have to respect the Hague rules.[75]

Although Additional Protocol II to the Geneva Conventions of 1977 (discussed in more detail below and in Chapter 3) is not applicable in the context of our review, it is important to examine whether this Protocol finally put an end to any discussion of belligerency. Lootsteen first argues that Additional Protocol II, even though its criteria for applicability are almost identical to the criteria for belligerency, this treaty may not yet constitute customary international law. Furthermore, the criteria for belligerency are more stringent as they require occupation by insurgents of a substantial part of the state and a measure of orderly administration over the territory they control and therefore, the criteria are not identical and the customary law concept of belligerency has not been subsumed.[76] Therefore, to Lootsteen, there could be situations of belligerency in the following:

1. The four criteria: a) a civil war within a state, beyond the scope of mere local unrest; b) occupation by the insurgents of a substantial part of the territory of the state; c) a measure of orderly administration by that group in the area it controls; d) observance of the rules of the laws of war by the rebel forces, acting under responsible authority.[77]
2. Tacit or explicit recognition by the *de jure* government of the insurgents' belligerency.
3. The armed conflict is not one in which people are fighting against colonial domination, alien occupation or a racist regime, in the exercise of their right to self determination (this is due to the fact that these wars are international armed conflicts according to Protocol 1, as is argued in Chapter 2).[78]

These criteria might also be too stringent. One could take issue with the tacit or explicit recognition by the *de jure* government. Pictet argued that third parties could recognise belligerency, but one must take into consideration Lootsteen's view that the third party recognition would not guarantee compliance with the rules of war.[79] To Lootsteen the whole notion of belligerency depends on recognition of the four criteria by the *de jure* government. It seems that historically the Pictet view is sounder as Lootsteen is not persuasive in his argument that recognition of belligerence has to take place by the *de jure* government. He may be right that, in effect, the only way belligerency can take effect is if it is respected by the *de jure* government but historically it has been third parties who were influential. In the American Civil War it was a neutral party, the British, that first recognised the belligerency and only reluctantly did the Union government follow suit. In the Spanish Civil War division in the international community prevented the recognition of belligerency. Therefore, in spite of its disuse in recent times, third parties could agree to argue the recognition of belligerency; this could include states and international and regional organisations. For example, the European Union members might be persuaded to accept the facts of belligerency in the long-standing conflict between the Turkish army and the PKK. A powerful more recent precedent exists in the Yugoslav wars of the 1990s. Before the states of Bosnia, Croatia or Slovenia were recognised the country had erupted into a civil war. Nevertheless, states, the European Union and the United Nations called upon the parties to respect the rules of war and one might argue that there was a tacit recognition of the state of belligerency.

2.3.2 Application of belligerency to the conflict of southeast Turkey

Even if belligerency is still relevant and third parties could be urged to call on Turkey to recognise this status, it does not seem that at this point the conflict has risen to this level. The PKK certainly has a level of military organisation, there is sustained violence but it does not have administrative or government control over a substantial part of the territory. The notion should not be dismissed out of hand as it could well be that this conflict could deepen into a type of belligerency. Lootsteen argues that the recent conflicts in Chechnya, Kosovo, East Timor and the Kurdish conflict do not reach the threshold of belligerency. First, these could be conflicts for self-determination but if not none of the *de jure* governments have recognised the condition of belligerency.[80] We do know that in spite of non-recognition of belligerency by Indonesia or Yugoslavia, the conflicts in Kosovo and East Timor resulted in substantial international intervention. The situation remains open in Chechnya and southeast Turkey.

The criteria may not yet be satisfied for belligerency in the case of the Kurdish insurgency in southeast Turkey but a persuasive argument could be made on the basis of this war for self-determination that belligerency ought to be recognised as this is clearly a major armed conflict which fulfils most of the criteria. There might not at this point be administrative control over Kurdish territory in southeast Turkey but there are certainly 'no go' areas for the Turkish army. The remaining three criteria are certainly fulfilled in this case.

If belligerency were to be recognised in this conflict, this would result in the combatants who are members of the PKK being treated not as common criminals or terrorists but as prisoners of war being entitled to all the protections of the third Geneva Convention of 1949 Relative to the Treatment of Prisoners of War.[81] It could not be brought into effect without the cooperation of Turkey, but there might be self-interest involved as it would mandate similar protection of Turkish soldiers and security forces. The whole basis of international humanitarian law is this doctrine of reciprocity and it may well be in the interest of Turkey to acknowledge the fact of belligerency. If this is not the case, as we see in Chapter 4, the protection for combatants (known as fighters) of both sides in internal armed conflict is limited.

2.4 International humanitarian law – the Hague Regulations and Geneva Conventions

Unlike civil strife which engages a domestic criminal law regime, a classification of armed conflict of whatever classification engages international legal regulation.

The current legal regime governing the conduct of armed conflict, the *jus in bello* developed in the Hague Regulations and the Geneva Conventions applies in both international and non-international armed conflict. However, most of the conflicts in the current era are domestic ones and Geneva and Hague law is primarily designed for international armed conflict. However, there are important developments in customary humanitarian law that extend the legal protections in international armed conflict to internal or non-international armed conflict.

2.4.1 International humanitarian law – applicable in international armed conflict

If indeed the argument is accepted that the situation of the Turkish invasion into Kurdistan, Iraq constitutes an international armed conflict, it is important to discuss the international law implications of such a classification as it engages a whole range of treaty and customary rules of international humanitarian law.

The Martens Clause has formed a part of the laws of armed conflict since its first appearance in the preamble to the 1899 Hague Convention (II) with respect to the laws and customs of war on land. It states:

> Until a more complete code of the laws of war is issued, the High Contracting Parties think it right to declare that in cases not included in the Regulations adopted by them, populations and belligerents remain under the protection and empire of the principles of international law, as they result from the usages established between civilized nations, from the laws of humanity and the requirements of the public conscience.[82]

Notions of the 'laws of humanity' and 'the requirements of public conscience' have led to the development of a series of international humanitarian law instruments with a primary focus to prevent human suffering for persons who were '*hors de combat*'[83] and civilians. There were two Hague Conventions negotiated in 1899 and 1907 and there is one part of the 1907 Hague Convention dealing with laws of occupation that still apply to this day. The Hague Regulations of 1907 also introduced a number of rules that showed concern for the civilian population, namely:

Article 23 (1) (g) – prohibition on the destruction of enemy's property unless 'imperatively demanded by the necessities of war'.

Article 25 – prohibition of attack of towns and villages etc that are 'undefended'.

Article 26 – duty of attacking army to warn of forthcoming bombardment when this is possible.

Article 27 – requirement that all necessary steps be taken to spare certain civilian buildings.

Article 28 – prohibition of pillage once the city has fallen.

An attempt was made after the First World War to formally regulate the use of air power in the 1923 Draft Rules on Aerial Warfare. The Rules included the following provisions:

Article 22

Aerial bombardment for the purpose of terrorizing the civilian population, of destroying or damaging private property not of military character, or of injuring non-combatants is prohibited.

Article 24

(1) Aerial bombardment is legitimate only when directed at a military objective, that is to say, an object of which the destruction or injury would constitute a distinct military advantage to the belligerent.

(2) Such bombardment is legitimate only when directed exclusively at the following objectives: military forces; military works; military establishments or depots; factories constituting important and well-known centres engaged in the manufacture of arms, ammunition or distinctively military supplies; lines of communication or transportation used for military purposes.

(3) The bombardment of cities, towns, villages, dwellings or buildings not in the immediate neighborhood of the operations of land forces is prohibited. In cases where the objectives specified in paragraph 2 are so situated, that they cannot be bombarded without the indiscriminate bombardment of the civilian population, the aircraft must abstain from bombardment.

(4) In the immediate neighborhood of the operations of land forces, the bombardment of cities, towns, villages, dwellings or buildings is legitimate provided that there exists a reasonable presumption that the military concentration is sufficiently important to justify such bombardment, having regard to the danger thus posed to the civilian population.

(5) A belligerent state is liable to pay compensation for injuries to person or to property caused by violation by any of its officers or forces of the provisions of this article.

Article 25

In bombardment by aircraft, all necessary steps must be taken by the commander to spare as far as possible buildings dedicated to public worship, art, science, or charitable purposes, historic monuments, hospital ships, hospitals and other places where the sick and wounded are collected, provided such buildings, objects, or places are not at the time used for military purposes. Such buildings, objects, and places must by day be indicated by marks visible to aircraft. The use of marks to indicate other buildings, objects, or places than those specified above is to be deemed an act of perfidy. The marks used as aforesaid shall be in the case of buildings protected under the Geneva Convention the Red Cross on a white background, and in the case of other protected buildings a large rectangular panel divided diagonally into two pointed triangular portions, one black and the other white.

A belligerent who desires to secure by night the protection for the hospitals and other privileged buildings above mentioned must take the necessary measures to render the special signs referred to sufficiently visible.[84]

These rules were not codified until 54 years later in the Additional Protocol I to the 1949 Geneva Conventions but the provisions with respect to aerial bombardment are arguably part of customary international law due to the early efforts to set out these rules and are thus binding on Turkey, not a party to Additional Protocol I.

The most extensive codification of international humanitarian law took place as a reaction to the abuses that took place during the Second World War. In 1949 states parties agreed to a set of four conventions. Geneva Convention I was for the purpose of the amelioration of the condition of the wounded and sick in armed forces in the field and continued the work of Henri Dunant and the first Geneva Convention of 1864. Geneva Convention II was for the amelioration of the condition of the wounded sick and shipwrecked members of the armed forces at sea and was in part response to the merciless killing of sailors on the seas by members of the German Navy. Geneva Convention III concerned the treatment of prisoners of war and sought to expand the protection of the Geneva Convention of 1929 and again was in part response to the appalling treatment of the allied prisoners of the Japanese. Finally, an innovative Geneva Convention IV concerned the protection of civilian persons in time of war. One of the most significant features of the Second World War was the targeting of civilian populations for deportation and extermination. This convention introduced the concept of 'protected persons' which are civilians under the control of the enemy. Article 4 states:

> Persons protected by the Convention are those who, at a given moment and in any manner whatsoever, find themselves, in case of a conflict or occupation, in the hands of a Party to the conflict or Occupying Power of which they are not nationals.[85]

Although most of the provisions in these four treaties are to deal with the consequences of an international armed conflict an active debate is now raging as to whether these guarantees are also to be extended to internal armed conflict. As part of four universally ratified treaties, the Geneva Conventions of 1949 can also constitute customary international law. Thus the provisions are binding on the Turkish government and also binding by its own agreement, on the PKK. We discuss below the customary applicability of some of the provisions to an internal armed conflict.

There was of course a further important codification of international humanitarian law in the Additional Protocols I and II to the Geneva Conventions of 1977. The Turkish government has not ratified either protocol and they are not applicable to this conflict. Many of these rules concern the primary rules of distinction, proportionality and necessity which are arguably also part of customary international law. Within an international armed conflict, it is accepted that the rule is that only military targets which advance the cause of the enemy are to be attacked and within that attack a proportionality calculation must be conducted to ensure that civilian casualties or what is called 'collateral damage' is acceptable.[86] States such as Turkey that are not bound by Additional Protocol I are still bound by these rules as they are customary and accepted in military manuals the world over, such as the manuals of the United States and Israel.[87]

There are a range of other applicable treaties such as the 1954 Hague Cultural Convention,[88] many weapons conventions and the ENMOD Convention[89] that govern international armed conflict and do not apply in non-international armed conflict. However, once again some of these provisions could be customary particularly such items as the prohibition against the use of gas, accepted as unlawful since the First World War.[90]

2.4.2 Non-international armed conflict

Although the Geneva Conventions of 1949 were to deal with any possible violations of the laws of armed conflict in international wars, there was a critical provision with respect to all other conflicts and this was a common article to all four Geneva Conventions which applies to any armed conflict. This is Common Article 3 to the Geneva Conventions which is discussed in detail in Chapter 3. Furthermore, there is an argument that many of the international humanitarian law guarantees in international armed conflict apply on the basis of customary international law to non-international armed conflict. This is also discussed in Chapter 3.

Additional Protocol I closes the gaps left by the Geneva Conventions in the laws of international armed conflict, whereas Additional Protocol II is to say the least disappointing with respect to non-international armed conflict. Its few articles do little to advance the clarification of the rules of non-international armed conflict and it is left to customary international law to provide detail to any rules. On the other hand Additional Protocol I's most valuable contribution is the codification of the cardinal principle of distinction between civilians and combatants during the conduct of hostilities. Although in the context of the conflict in southeast Turkey neither Protocol is applicable, many of the provisions are also reflective of customary international law as is discussed in Chapter 3.

A key factor in non-international armed conflict, which is discussed in Chapter 4, is that belligerents are not entitled to prisoner of war status. This means that even if fighters are legitimately engaged in a non-international armed conflict they are subject to domestic conditions of detention, however, in Chapters 3 and 4 we discuss the efforts to protect these detainees by minimum humanitarian guarantees.

2.5 The relationship between international humanitarian law and international or regional human rights law[91]

It might at first glance be surprising that a chapter on armed conflict discusses human rights law but in recent years these two regimes have become closely intertwined in international and domestic litigations. As we see in Chapter 3, a great deal of litigation has commenced in the European Court of Human Rights against Turkey for human rights violations with respect to the conflict in southeast Turkey.[92] The violations of human rights alleged also involve violations of international humanitarian law. There is a very close relationship between the protections offered to combatants and civilians in international humanitarian law and the protections afforded under international human rights law. Both legal regimes are applicable in the non-international armed conflict in the Kurdish areas of Turkey and Iraq but there are complicated jurisdictional issues particularly with regard to the extraterritorial enforcement of human rights obligations with regard to the intervention in Kurdistan, Iraq (obviously not a party to the European Convention on Human Rights). The International Covenant on Civil and Political Rights[93] is therefore applicable to the conflict as Turkey is a party to this important human rights Covenant. The rights contained within the Covenant include: the right to life (Article 7), a prohibition against torture (Article 7), freedom from arbitrary arrest and detention (Article 9), freedom of movement and a right to choose a residence (Article 12), a right to a fair trial (Article 14), freedom from arbitrary interference with privacy, family or correspondence (Article 17), freedom of religion (Article 18) and freedom of assembly and association (Articles 21 and 22). Turkey is not a party to the enforcement mechanism of the Covenant which is the Optional Protocol allowing individuals to file complaints to the Human Rights Committee, the result of which is that the Committee issues non-binding views.

However, there is a treaty that Turkey is a party to that provides similar rights but also offers binding enforcement, the European Convention of Human Rights and its institutional arm the European Court of Human Rights. The relevant articles are set out here in detail as they are considered in many of the cases involved in this conflict. The most relevant are:

Article 2

1. Everyone's right to life shall be protected by law. No one shall be deprived of his life intentionally save in the execution of a sentence of a court following his conviction of a crime for which this penalty is provided by law.
2. Deprivation of life shall not be regarded as inflicted in contravention of this article when it results from the use of force which is no more than absolutely necessary:

    a) in defence of any person from unlawful violence;

b) in order to effect a lawful arrest or to prevent the escape of a person lawfully detained;

c) in action lawfully taken for the purpose of quelling a riot or insurrection.

Article 3

No one shall be subjected to torture or to inhuman or degrading treatment or punishment.

Article 5

1. Everyone has the right to liberty and security of person. No one shall be deprived of his liberty save in the following cases and in accordance with a procedure prescribed by law:

    a) the lawful detention of a person after conviction by a competent court;

    b) the lawful arrest or detention of a person for non-compliance with the lawful order of a court or in order to secure the fulfillment of any obligation prescribed by law;

    c) the lawful arrest or detention of a person effected for the purpose of bringing him before the competent legal authority on reasonable suspicion of having committed an offence or when it is reasonably considered necessary to prevent his committing an offence or fleeing after having done so;

    d) the detention of a minor by lawful order for the purpose of educational supervision or his lawful detention for the purpose of bringing him before the competent legal authority;

    e) the lawful detention of persons for the prevention of the spreading of infectious diseases, of persons of unsound mind, alcoholics or drug addicts or vagrants;

    f) the lawful arrest or detention of a person to prevent his effecting an unauthorised entry into the country or of a person against whom action is being taken with a view to deportation or extradition.

2. Everyone who is arrested shall be informed promptly, in a language which he understands, of the reasons for his arrest and of any charge against him.

3. Everyone arrested or detained in accordance with the provisions of paragraph 1.c of this article shall be brought promptly before a judge or other officer authorised by law to exercise judicial power and shall be entitled to trial within a reasonable time or to release pending trial. Release may be conditioned by guarantees to appear for trial.

4. Everyone who is deprived of his liberty by arrest or detention shall be entitled to take proceedings by which the lawfulness of his detention shall be decided speedily by a court and his release ordered if the detention is not lawful.

5. Everyone who has been the victim of arrest or detention in contravention of the provisions of this article shall have an enforceable right to compensation.

Article 6

1. In the determination of his civil rights and obligations or of any criminal charge against him, everyone is entitled to a fair and public hearing within a reasonable time by an independent and impartial tribunal established by law. Judgment shall be pronounced publicly but the press and public may be excluded from all or part of the trial in the interests of morals, public order or national security in a democratic society, where the interests of juveniles or the protection of the private life of the parties so require, or to the extent strictly necessary in the opinion of the court in special circumstances where publicity would prejudice the interests of justice.
2. Everyone charged with a criminal offence shall be presumed innocent until proved guilty according to law.
3. Everyone charged with a criminal offence has the following minimum rights:

    a) to be informed promptly, in a language which he understands and in detail, of the nature and cause of the accusation against him;
    b) to have adequate time and facilities for the preparation of his defence;
    c) to defend himself in person or through legal assistance of his own choosing or, if he has not sufficient means to pay for legal assistance, to be given it free when the interests of justice so require;
    d) to examine or have examined witnesses against him and to obtain the attendance and examination of witnesses on his behalf under the same conditions as witnesses against him;
    e) to have the free assistance of an interpreter if he cannot understand or speak the language used in court.

It is evident that these rights are very similar to the fundamental guarantees is Common Article 3. There is another set of rights pertinent to the fundamental guarantees and that is the right to family life and the right to property as follows: Article 8 within the Convention specifies that 'Everyone has the right to respect for his private and family life, his home and his correspondence'. Protocol 1, Article 1 states:

> Every natural or legal person is entitled to the peaceful enjoyment of his possessions. No one shall be deprived of his possessions except in the public interest and subject to the conditions provided for by law and by the general principles of international law.[94]

Due to the close connection between international humanitarian law and international human rights law, it is possible at least to view a large body of litigation concerning the situation in southeast Turkey, as is outlined in Chapter 1 and further discussed in Chapter 3. The limitation on this type of legal regime is that the jurisdiction is limited to the state actors, not the non-state actors. A further problem is that the complex relationship between the two bodies of law is sometimes not properly explored in the human rights litigation, a fact we discuss in Chapter 3.

The International Court of Justice in the 1996 Nuclear Weapons Advisory Opinion considered the interrelationship between human rights law and humanitarian law:

> The Court observes that the protection of the International Covenant of Civil and Political Rights does not cease in times of war, except by operation of Article 4 of the Covenant whereby certain provisions may be derogated from in a time of national emergency. In principle, the right not arbitrarily to be deprived of one's life applies also in hostilities.[95]

The case goes on to discuss how that relationship between the two regimes might be accomplished. In discussing the right to life the court states:

> The test of what is an arbitrary deprivation of life, however, then falls to be determined by the applicable *lex specialis*, namely, the law applicable in armed conflict which is designed to regulate the conduct of hostilities. Thus whether a particular loss of life, through the use of a certain weapon in warfare, is to be considered an arbitrary deprivation of life contrary to Article 6 of the Covenant, can only be decided by reference to the law applicable in armed conflict and not deduced from the terms of the Covenant itself.[96]

This issue of the relationship between the two legal regimes is considered in even more detail in the more recent Advisory Opinion the *Legal Consequences of the Construction of a Wall in the Occupied Palestinian Territory*. The court held:

> More generally, the Court considers that the protection offered by human rights conventions does not cease in case of armed conflict, save through the effect of provisions for derogation of the kind to be found in Article 4 of the International Covenant on Civil and Political Rights. As regards the relationship between international humanitarian law and human rights law, there are thus three possible situations: some rights may be exclusively matters of international humanitarian law; others may be exclusively matters of human rights law; yet others may be matters of both these branches of international law. In order to answer the question put to it, the Court will have to take into consideration both these branches of international law, namely human rights law and, as *lex specialis*, international humanitarian law.[97]

This is, therefore, a complex relationship requiring application in the context of a conflict of the general right in human rights with the specific tests for legality as set out in international humanitarian law. Human rights courts, to say the least, have found this difficult.[98] However, the large body of case law from the Turkish/Kurdish conflict will allow more extensive analysis.

Conclusion

This chapter introduces the general rules of armed conflict in both international humanitarian law and international human rights law that can be applied in the very complex situation in southeast Turkey and Kurdistan, Iraq. The first threshold condition of an armed conflict certainly seems to be satisfied on a factual basis in spite of the denial of Turkey. The second question that results for finding the existence of an armed conflict is the classification of the armed conflict. It may well be that the conflict has evolved from a non-international armed conflict to an international armed conflict with its extensive regime of legal protection. This is particularly the case if the definition of an international armed conflict includes struggles for self-determination. This will remain a controversial question subject to much debate but due to the lack of certainty of the customary nature of wars of national liberation or belligerency there seems clear reason to argue that this conflict is a non-international armed conflict.

The rules of international humanitarian law also depend on that classification. If indeed this is an international armed conflict, the full range of treaty and customary international humanitarian law protections apply. This includes the cardinal rules of distinction, proportionality and necessity. Yet given that classifying this conflict as international would be very controversial it is important to examine in detail the protections offered in a non-international armed conflict. Classifying this situation as an internal armed conflict will also be controversial but the facts on the ground seem to support the fact that the threshold has been reached even without the agreement of Turkey or the European Union. Therefore, Chapter 3 discusses and defines the two most important of the guarantees, the minimum humanitarian guarantees set out in Common Article 3 and the customary international law protections. Furthermore, the existence of any type of armed conflict does not preclude the continued applicability of human rights law, although the standard of protection might become rather complex. We now turn to the specific guarantees applicable in the conflict in southeast Turkey.

3 Common Article 3, customary international humanitarian law, and human rights law applicable to the conflict in southeast Turkey

Introduction

In this chapter the main focus of analysis is a non-international armed conflict, even if an argument could be made, as is discussed in Chapter 2, that this conflict could be classified as an international armed conflict. As is evident from Chapter 2, international humanitarian law as codified in treaties provides basic guarantees to both civilians and combatants embroiled in non-international armed conflict, but no more than that. Regrettably, the development of the law in this area has been constrained by the reluctance of states to limit their sovereignty, particularly when an armed conflict is internal.[1] There is no more obvious an example of this reluctance, than the disappointing Additional Protocol II to the Geneva Conventions of 1977 which provides only a small number of guarantees. In the case of the conflict in the southeast, Turkey is not even a party to this minimal convention. However, Turkey, with the rest of the international community, is a party to the four Geneva Conventions of 1949 with its Common Article 3 applicable to non-international armed conflict. However, due to the development in case law and state practice since the Second World War there are a number of customary humanitarian law rules that apply to both international and non-international armed conflict. As a result there are extensive international treaty and customary law obligations binding the government of Turkey and the fighters of the Kurdistan Workers Party (PKK) even if this conflict does not rise to the level of an international armed conflict.

The purpose of this chapter is to discuss in more detail the applicability of Common Article 3 of the Geneva Conventions, customary international humanitarian law, and human rights law to the armed conflict in the southeast of Turkey. The first part of the chapter comprehensively discusses the protections afforded by Common Article 3. It describes the historical development of this article and defines the various terms within the article, including the issue of its applicability to which participants in the conflict. It also assesses the limitations of this article as it does not provide the detailed protections available in remaining provisions of the four Geneva Conventions of 1949. It also discusses the criminalisation of violations of Common Article 3. Finally, the alleged violations of the provisions by both the Turkish army and the PKK are reviewed.

The second part of the chapter contends that there are also a series of customary international law obligations that apply both to international and non-international armed conflict. This analysis is assisted by the International Committee of the Red Cross (ICRC) Customary International Humanitarian Law Study (ICRC Customary International Law Study) and 'The Manual on Non-International Armed Conflict' ('The Manual') drafted by Schmitt, Garraway and Dinstein.[2] Both of these publications set out customary guarantees for both the participants and the civilians who become embroiled in a non-international armed conflict. Both studies illustrate that international humanitarian law protections are far more extensive than those set out in Common Article 3. Once again the violations of customary international law by both parties to the conflict are assessed.

As can be seen from Chapter 2, it may well be that the whole range of international humanitarian law might well be applicable to this conflict if it is given the status of belligerency but in case it does not, it is important to those rules that will apply regardless, if this conflict is determined to be a non-international armed conflict. However, in the unlikely scenario that the insurgency does not rise to the level of an armed conflict, the third part of this analysis reviews the minimum humanitarian standards proposed by the international community to apply in any situation of rebellion, civil strife or insurgency. Although this book argues for the existence of an armed conflict, the minimum humanitarian guarantees proposed are very similar to those within Common Article 3 and once again many of these could be argued to be customary – especially with the developments in international human rights law. These too must be viewed in light of the compliance or non-compliance by the parties in this conflict to these standards.

Finally, this chapter reviews this conflict through the lens of the violations of human rights law established in the extensive jurisprudence of the European Court of Human Rights. It is evident that the human rights violations will more often than not be violations of Common Article 3 to the Geneva Conventions or other customary humanitarian law rules. A noteworthy limitation of the jurisprudence is that it is only applicable to Turkey as the PKK authorities cannot be brought to the European Court of Human Rights for their infringement of the human rights of the Turkish security forces of armed forces.

3.1 Common Article 3 to all the Geneva Conventions

As is discussed in Chapter 2, this article provides minimum protection in all non-international armed conflicts and if this conflict is classified as such, is applicable to the situation in southeast Turkey. Due to the universal nature of the ratifications and accession to the Geneva Conventions, this article is now also part of customary international law.[3] This is affirmed by the International Court of Justice which stated in the *Nicaragua* decision:

Article 3 which is common to all four Geneva Conventions of 12 August 1949 defines certain rules to be applied in the armed conflict of a non-international armed conflict. There is no doubt that ... these rules also constitute a minimum yardstick ... and they are rules which, in the Court's opinion, reflect what the Court in 1949 called 'elementary considerations of humanity'.[4]

This has been affirmed in the jurisprudence of the International Criminal Tribunal for the Former Yugoslavia. The Appeals Chamber in the influential *Tadić* case states that the common article contained 'certain minimum mandatory rules' which reflects 'elementary considerations of humanity'. The Appeals Chamber also confirms that customary international law imposes criminal responsibility for serious violations of Common Article 3.[5] This criminal liability can be on the representatives of the state but also on leaders of rebel factions, a fact confirmed in arrest warrants issued by the International Criminal Court.[6] This has also been confirmed in the International Criminal Tribunal for Rwanda in its major case *Akayesu* where the court stated:

> It is today clear that the norms of Common Article 3 have acquired the status of customary law in that most States, by their domestic penal codes, have criminalized acts which if committed during internal armed conflict, would constitute violations of Common Article 3.[7]

The history of the development of this article leads to an understanding of its significance in non-international armed conflict. Until 1949 the Geneva Conventions were only applicable to military personnel involved in international armed conflict. After the Second World War with its massive loss of civilian life, the protection of civilians was also incorporated into the treaty regime. Geneva Convention IV Relative to the Protection of Civilian Persons in Time of War applies in international armed conflict and in situations of occupation.[8] However, the drafting process of the four Geneva Conventions revealed that the ICRC had long been concerned with the victims of internal armed conflict. A draft Convention on the role of the Red Cross in civil wars or insurrections was submitted, for the first time, to the International Red Cross Conference in 1912 but the subject was not even discussed.[9] The question was again placed on the agenda of the 10th International Red Cross Conference in 1921, and a Resolution was passed affirming the right to relief of all victims of civil wars or social or revolutionary disturbances in accordance with the general principles of the Red Cross. The Resolution, as such, had not the force of a Convention, but it enabled the ICRC in at least two cases – the civil war in the plebiscite area of Upper Silesia in 1921, and the civil war in Spain in the mid 1930s – to induce both sides to undertake more or less to respect the principles of the 1906 Geneva Convention.[10] This Resolution was also incorporated in the 1928 revision of the Statute of the ICRC which stated 'The Special Role of the ICRC shall be to ... (d) to take action in its capacity as a neutral institution, especially the in case of war, civil war or internal strife'.[11] The 16th International Red Cross

Conference in 1938 passed a Resolution which strengthened the 1921 resolution. It stated:

> The Conference having taken cognizance with keen interest of the Report presented by the International Committee of the Red Cross on the role and activity of the Red Cross in time of civil war, recalling the Resolution relating to civil war adopted by the Xth Conference in 1921, pays tribute to the work spontaneously undertaken by the International Committee of the Red Cross in hostilities of the nature of civil war, and relies on the Committee to continue its activity in this connection with the co-operation of the National Societies, with a view to ensuring on such occasions respect for the high principles which are at the basis of the Red Cross movement, requests the International Committee and the National Red Cross Societies to endeavour to obtain:
>
> (a) the application of the humanitarian principles which were formulated in the Geneva Convention of 1929 and the Tenth Hague Convention of 1907, especially as regards the treatment of the wounded, the sick, and prisoners of war, and the safety of medical personnel and medical stores;
> (b) humane treatment for all political prisoners, their exchange and, so far as possible their release;
> (c) respect of the life and liberty of non-combatants;
> (d) facilities for the transmission of news of a personal nature and for the reunion of families;
> (e) effective measures for the protection of children; requests the International Committee, making use of its practical experience, to continue the general study of the problems raised by civil war as regards the Red Cross, and to submit the results of its study to the next International Red Cross Conference.[12]

This resolution together with the positive results of compliance achieved in the Spain and Upper Silesia conflicts, encouraged the ICRC to propose that provisions relating to civil war be inserted into the Geneva Conventions to be adopted after the war.[13] Initially at the Preliminary Conference of the National Red Cross Societies in 1946 the ICRC attempted to have all of the provisions of the Geneva Conventions applicable to all cases of armed conflict not of an international character provided the adverse party acted in adherence to the conventions.[14] The final draft by the ICRC and proposed to the XVIIth International Red Cross Conference at Stockholm stated:

> In all cases of armed conflict which are not of an international character, especially cases of civil war, colonial conflicts, or wars of religion, which may occur in the territory of one or more of the High Contracting Parties, the implementing of the principles of the present Convention shall be obligatory on the adversaries. The application of the Convention in these circumstances

shall in no way depend on the legal status of the Parties to the conflict and shall have no effect on those states.[15]

This was the high water mark of an attempt to make all the rules applicable to international or non-international armed conflict. This position was largely accepted at the Stockholm conference and proposed as part of the First and Second Geneva Conventions and in the case of the Third and Fourth Conventions made the application of the Convention subject to the proviso that the adverse party (not the state party) should also comply with it.[16]

This draft provision was discussed at the Diplomatic Conference charged with drafting the Geneva Conventions of 1949. However, it became clear that many states opposed such a wide ranging protection. Two working parties were established to attempt to re-draft this provision. The final drafts based on ideas from the Italians, French and Soviets proposed to limit the applicable provisions to non-international armed conflict as they did not provide for all of the provisions of the Geneva Conventions to apply. After much discussion and debate Common Article 3 was adopted by the conference and regrettably the humanitarian law protections in non-international armed conflict were very limited and thus signalled a victory for those who wished to preserve sovereignty over internal armed conflicts. The first difficulty as is discussed in Chapter 2 would be to decide to which conflicts this article was applicable as it failed to provide the specificity of the proposed article. However, it represented at least some protection to those embroiled in civil wars. The text agreed upon was:

In the case of armed conflict not of an international character occurring in the territory of one of the High Contracting Parties, each Party to the conflict shall be bound to apply, as a minimum, the following provisions:

(1) Persons taking no active part in the hostilities, including members of armed forces who have laid down their arms and those placed 'hors de combat' by sickness, wounds, detention, or any other cause, shall in all circumstances be treated humanely, without any adverse distinction founded on race, colour, religion or faith, sex, birth or wealth, or any other similar criteria.

To this end, the following acts are and shall remain prohibited at any time and in any place whatsoever with respect to the above-mentioned persons:

(a) violence to life and person, in particular murder of all kinds, mutilation, cruel treatment and torture;
(b) taking of hostages;
(c) outrages upon personal dignity, in particular humiliating and degrading treatment;
(d) the passing of sentences and the carrying out of executions without previous judgment pronounced by a regularly constituted court

affording all the judicial guarantees which are recognized as indispensable by civilized peoples.

(2)   The wounded and sick shall be collected and cared for.

An impartial humanitarian body, such as the International Committee of the Red Cross may offer its services to the Parties to the conflict. The Parties to the conflict shall further endeavour to bring into force, by means of special agreements, all or part of the other provisions of the present Convention. The application of the preceding provisions shall not affect the legal status of the Parties to the conflict.[17]

To borrow the phrase of one of the delegates to the 1949 conference, Article 3 is like a 'Convention in miniature'.[18] In the situation of non-international armed conflict, according to the Pictet commentary, it ensures the application of the rules of humanity which are recognised as essential by civilized nations and provides a legal basis for intervention by the ICRC or any other impartial humanitarian organisations. An important aspect of the article is that it is not conditioned on reciprocity, it applies automatically and its observance does not depend on discussion of which clauses are to be respects, they are all to be observed.[19] Pictet in his authoritative commentaries on the four Geneva Conventions has provided detailed definitions of the various phrases in the article which are applicable to the Kurdish conflict. These can be updated by the influential study on internal armed conflict by Lindsay Moir who gives actual case studies of the application of the article. Both provide the content to the article by which the actions of the Turkish army and the PKK can be assessed.

We discuss in Chapter 2 the nature of an armed conflict not of an international character and the conditions placed for the application of this article, and that discussion is not repeated in this chapter, but it is an important first step in assessing the application of this article. It is the task of this chapter to discuss the obligations of the parties in the event this article is applicable.

The first part of the article discusses the binding nature of the obligation to 'each Party to the conflict'. It is not controversial to regard the government party as bound, as it chooses to become a party to the Convention and is bound by its terms.[20] However, according to the Pictet commentary this obligation is not just on the part of the government involved in the internal conflict but on the insurgent party. Pictet acknowledges that the insurgent party may choose not to apply the article but if it does so it will 'prove that those who regard its actions as mere acts of anarchy or brigandage are right'.[21] Moir does not accept it, as a given, that insurgents would be bound and discusses the international law basis for such an argument. He examines Articles 34–36 of the 1969 Vienna Convention on the Law of Treaties,[22] which established that treaties can impose rights and obligations upon third parties provided that is was the intention of the parties to the treaty to do so and the third parties consent to be bound.[23] Moir poses the question of what would happen to those parties who refuse to be bound and he introduces the doctrine of legislative jurisdiction. This would mean that insurgents would be bound as a result of the parent state's ratification or accession to the treaty as a legally constituted government has the capacity to legislate for all nationals.[24] Yet the controversy may not end there, as a rebel group may assume control over part of a territory and suspend domestic law, if indeed the treaty obligations have been incorporated into domestic law. Therefore, another explanation is necessary.

Another possible explanation also does not stand up under scrutiny. This holds that if an insurgency takes over territory it may assume the international law obligations of the previous state as set out in the Articles of State Responsibility.[25] This would only apply if the insurgency is victorious and becomes the successor government. Therefore, it would not apply during the conflict which would defeat the whole purpose of the article and would not apply if the insurgency continues for decades without a victor which is the situation in southeast Turkey. Therefore, none of these explanations above can stand up to legal analysis.

The final and more plausible explanation is that insurgents are bound by Common Article 3 as individuals under international law. This would accord with other developments in international law, particularly international criminal law and international human rights law where individuals become the subjects of international rights and duties.[26] However, Moir argues that this argument will have force if it is shown that the article is binding directly through customary international law and removed from the domestic law sphere. Based on the discussion in the various international tribunals quoted above, the article is clearly customary and contains international law obligations for individuals.[27] One other strong factor in support of this position is that violations of this article are criminalised and individuals held responsible. There is a strong argument upheld in international criminal jurisprudence from the Nuremburg tribunals and the following International Military Tribunals subsequent to the Second World War that customary international law is binding upon individuals as well as states.[28]

Accepting the position that both military/security forces and insurgents are bound by Common Article 3, it is necessary to examine what members of these groups are actually being protected. The article specifies that it applies to '[p]ersons taking no active part in the hostilities, including members of armed forces who have laid down their arms and those placed "hors de combat" by sickness, wounds, detention, or any other cause'. It is uncontroversial to assert that civilians are to receive the full protection of the article, provided, that they take no part in the hostilities. However, as Moir and Schmitt point out, this can be a difficult distinction.[29] Due to the asymmetry between state forces and insurgent forces, rebels depend on the civilian population in terms of food, shelter and concealment. It is therefore difficult to distinguish between civilians and guerrilla fighters.[30] We discuss the debate concerning direct participation in the definition of belligerents in Chapter 4.

Once you leave the realm of civilian and are involved in active participation, Moir poses the question of what degree of protection is afforded to rebels or civilians who directly participate in the action. He states that once rebel soldiers are captured, or otherwise are unable to continue fighting, they become *hors de combat* and are entitled to the full level of protection. But the legal status and recognition of these individuals as lawful or unlawful combatant remains domestically unchanged. These accordingly remain subject to the full force of the state's criminal law rather than to the limited protections of Common Article 3.[31] As a consequence, it is clear that active participants in the conflict, are liable to be killed, wounded and captured. We discuss in Chapter 4 the specific problem of detainees as clearly Common Article 3 does not provide prisoner of war status and detainees find themselves at great risk of further harm or death even if they are *hors de combat*.

Once the scope of applicability is determined the next step is to review the actual obligations of Common Article 3. The first and primary obligation is *'humane treatment'*. Whatever the broadness of the term implies, the ICRC finds that this represents the fundamental principle underlying the four Geneva Conventions.[32] Pictet argues that it represents the minium which must be applied in the least determinate of conflicts.[33] If defining humane treatment constitutes a difficult task, it is easier to list activities that are incompatible with the standard. Article 3 does just that, and indicates a list of acts that, according to the ICRC commentary, world public opinion[34] finds particularly revolting, so that these are therefore absolutely prohibited. These acts are:

(a)   violence to life and person, in particular murder of all kinds, mutilation, cruel treatment and torture;
(b)   taking of hostages;
(c)   outrages upon personal dignity, in particular humiliating and degrading treatment;
(d)   the passing of sentences and the carrying out of executions without previous judgment pronounced by a regularly constituted court affording all the judicial guarantees which are recognized as indispensable by civilized peoples.[35]

The form of wording of these prohibitions is broad enough to cover almost all of the possible range of abuses to be inflicted on persons and is very similar to the prohibitions within later human rights conventions such as the 1966 International Covenant on Civil and Political Rights (ICCPR) and the 1950 European Convention on Human Rights.[36] These are absolute non-derogable rights and it could be argued that Common Article 3 is a human rights convention in miniature. Moir argues that the concept of humane treatment will not always be objective and might vary according to the circumstances such as the climate and the level of treatment practically feasible.[37] This position could be challenged in light of agreed definitions of such prohibitions included in the General Comments to the ICCPR that could be applicable in these contexts. There could be argued to be an international minimum standard as reflected in developments in the case law of human rights which could be transferable to international humanitarian law.[38]

Pictet in his commentary concentrated on whether there was a legal basis to argue that the taking of hostages and the sentences and execution without proper trial were prohibited. He acknowledged that these practices were fairly general in wartime but even though they were common practice they were nevertheless shocking to the civilized mind.[39] This opinion finds further support in the International Military Tribunal trials following the Second World War that confirmed the unacceptability of summary justice and reprisal killings.[40] In fact, it is clear in the 21st century that these activities are prohibited in customary law.

The second critical element of the Article is '*Care of the wounded and sick*'. Common Article 3 thus reaffirms the fundamental principle underlying the original Geneva Convention of 1864 and the concern of the founder of the ICRC, Henri Dunant, that the wounded and sick on the battlefield should be collected and cared for. The Pictet commentary argues that this clause expresses a categorical imperative which cannot be restricted and needs no explanation.[41] However, the ICRC commentary also poses the question of why Article 3 does not add that the wounded and sick are to be 'respected and protected', using the expression which has been accepted since the 1929 Convention.[42] The answer from the ICRC is that if Article 3 was to be adopted at all, it had to be short – no more than a statement of principle, together with a few rules regarded as a minimum acceptable to all, even when dealing with rebels.[43] What had to be carefully avoided – and this was the main difficulty throughout the discussions at the Diplomatic Conference – was anything which might appear, even in the slightest degree, either to limit the right of the state to put down a rebellion, or to encourage discontented elements, or even common bandits, to rise in revolt against the state in the fallacious belief that the Conventions would 'protect' them, or in other words, save them from being duly punished for their misdoings. It was therefore necessary to avoid using an expression about whose meaning there might be some doubt, particularly as it was not in any way essential. In the same way, since the obligation to collect and care for the wounded and sick is absolute and unconditional, any act incompatible with the duty imposed by that obligation is prohibited. Moreover, the obligation in question is reinforced by the general obligation under sub-paragraph (1) (humane treatment) and by the prohibitions which result from it. In actual fact, therefore, the ICRC argues and this author agrees that the Article certainly provides the wounded and sick with 'respect and protection'.[44]

A third element is '*An impartial humanitarian body, such as the International Committee of the Red Cross, may offer its services to the Parties to the conflict*'. At first this paragraph may seem self-evident as it is clear that any governmental or non-governmental organization can 'offer its services' to the parties to the conflict at any time, just as any individual can. The ICRC historically has offered its services for humanitarian purposes during many civil wars, just as it has offered them when any international conflict has broken out. According to Pictet this paragraph may therefore appear at first sight to be merely decorative and without any real significance. Nevertheless, it is of great moral and practical value.[45] Although the ICRC has been able to do a considerable amount of humanitarian work in certain civil wars, in others the sovereign state has refused the ICRC entry, as the offer of its services has been regarded as an unfriendly act – an inadmissible attempt to interfere in the internal affairs of the state. What is significant is that the adoption of Article 3 means that an impartial humanitarian organization is now being legally entitled to offer its services. The parties to the conflict can, of course, decline the offer if they can do without it. But they can no longer look upon it as an unfriendly act, nor resent the fact that the organisation making the offer has tried to come to the aid of the victims of the conflict.[46] The ICRC argues that it is mentioned here for two reasons – first, on its own account, as an organisation called, by its statutes and traditions, to intervene in cases of conflict, and, second, as an example of what is meant by a humanitarian and impartial organisation. Pictet emphasised that the organisation involved must be both *humanitarian* and *impartial* and the ICRC fulfils those criteria.[47]

The fourth element is '*special agreements*', whereby parties can agree to all of the humanitarian guarantees in the remainder of the four Geneva Conventions. The ICRC argues that legally, the parties to the conflict are only bound to observe Article 3 and may ignore all the other articles. It is obvious, however, that each one of them is completely free – and should be encouraged – to declare its intention of applying all or part of the remaining provisions. It is certainly desirable to settle in detail the treatment victims of the conflict are to receive, the relief which is to be brought to them, and other matters as well. The provision points out a duty: 'The Parties to the conflict should further endeavour ... ' Although the only provisions which the individual Parties are bound to apply unilaterally are those contained in Article 3, they are nevertheless under an obligation to try to bring about a fuller application of the Convention by means of a bilateral agreement. In spite of the plea by the ICRC it is the practice of states not to agree to extend the protections beyond Article 3 as it provides legitimacy to the rebel groups and to the conflict itself.[48]

The final element of Common Article 3 is '*Lack of effect on the legal status of the parties to the conflict*'. According to Pictet this clause is essential.[49] Without it neither Article 3, nor any other article in its place, would ever have been adopted. It meets the fear – always the same one – that the application of the Convention, even to a very limited extent, in cases of civil war may interfere with the *de jure* government's lawful suppression of the revolt, or that it may confer belligerent status, and consequently increased authority, upon the adverse party. The provision was first suggested at the Conference of Government Experts convened by the ICRC in 1947 was reintroduced with very little change in all the succeeding drafts. It makes it absolutely clear that the object of the Convention is a purely humanitarian one, that it is in no way concerned with the internal affairs of states, and that it merely ensures respect for the few essential rules of humanity which all civilized nations consider as valid everywhere and under all circumstances and as being above and outside war itself.[50]

Consequently, the fact of parties to a conflict applying Article 3 does not constitute any recognition by the government of a state embroiled in civil war that the adverse party has authority of any kind; it does not limit in any way the government's right to suppress a rebellion using all the means – including arms – provided for under its own laws; it does not in any way affect its right to prosecute, try and sentence its adversaries for their crimes, according to its own laws.[51]

In the same way, the fact of the adverse party applying the article does not give it any right to special protection or any immunity from domestic law. Article 3 resembles the rest of the Convention in that it is only concerned with the individual and the physical treatment to which he or she is entitled as a human being without regard to his or her affiliation. It does not affect the legal or political treatment which he may receive as a result of his behaviour. Furthermore, the discussions at the Diplomatic Conference brought out clearly that it is not necessary for an armed force as a whole to have laid down its arms, for its members to be entitled to protection under the article. The Convention refers to individuals and not to bodies of troops, and a man who has surrendered individually is entitled to the same humane treatment that he would receive if the whole army to which he belongs had capitulated. The important thing is that the man in question will be taking no further part in the fighting.[52]

In spite of the rather optimistic discussion in the Pictet commentary, there is a question of the non-applicability of certain protections as outlined by Farer:

(i)   Although torture is prohibited nothing in article 3 prevents the rebels being hung for treason.
(ii) Civilians who inhabit areas where insurgents are active are also subject to forms of detention normally garbed in euphemistic vestments, such as 'relocation centers' or 'fortified hamlets', with respect to which article 3 contains no specific safeguards.
(iii) Civilians may also be compelled by the rebellions to serve in effect as slave labourers and subjected to the process of conflict.
(iv) There is no reference in the Convention prohibiting the requisition/ destruction of food and other essential goods with a view to prevent them from falling into the hands of other party.[53]

Farer may be correct that there is no specific outlawing of the above behaviour but they may well be prohibited under the general ambit of humane treatment. Starving or enslaving a civilian population surely cannot be considered humane and the use of the death penalty must be in accordance with due process and humanitarian guarantees.

3.1.1 Consequences of violations of Common Article 3

There is a serious problem with the Geneva Conventions as violations of Common Article 3 are not considered 'grave breaches' in the Conventions and therefore there is no obligation for states parties to pass laws criminalising violations of this article.[54] There is not a supervisory body existing to oversee its implementation. National courts in Europe, however, have criminalised conduct that violate the rules of humanitarian law applicable in internal conflict and the ad hoc International Criminal Tribunals for Yugoslavia and Rwanda have also done so.

Importantly, in spite of the violations not being grave breaches, the Statute of the International Criminal Court does provide for criminal consequences for violation of Common Article 3 and 106 countries are now parties to the Statute including most of the countries in Europe but not Turkey. Paragraph 8 (2) (c) specifies these offences as war crimes:

(c) In the case of an armed conflict not of an international character, serious violations of article 3 common to the four Geneva Conventions of 12 August 1949, namely, any of the following acts committed against persons taking no active part in the hostilities, including members of armed forces who have laid down their arms and those placed *hors de combat* by sickness, wounds, detention or any other cause:

   (i) Violence to life and person, in particular murder of all kinds, mutilation, cruel treatment and torture;
   (ii) Committing outrages upon personal dignity, in particular humiliating and degrading treatment;
   (iii) Taking of hostages;
   (iv) The passing of sentences and the carrying out of executions without previous judgement pronounced by a regularly constituted court, affording all judicial guarantees which are generally recognized as indispensable.[55]

These international provisions and the case law of the ad hoc tribunals confirm the obligation on sovereign states to criminalise breaches of Common Article 3 and this could well be developing into a customary obligation. Rule 156 in the ICRC Customary International Law Study states that 'Serious violations of international humanitarian law constitute war crimes'.[56] Included in the commentary are violations of Common Article 3 and the authors of the study argue that as Common Article 3 has crystallised into customary international law and that breaches have been recognised as war crimes in the Statutes of the International Criminal Tribunals for Yugoslavia and Rwanda, the Special Court for Sierra Leone and the International Criminal Court.[57] Although there is no rule specifically calling for domestic implementation, treaty obligations themselves mean that countries have an obligation to criminalise violations of Common Article 3.

3.1.2 Applicability of Common Article 3 to conflict in southeast Turkey

Once the scope of application has been determined as binding on both the Turkish forces and the insurgents, mostly members of the PKK, it is important to discuss the allegations on both sides of continual violation of Common Article 3. These can be listed under each one of the specific guarantees. The European Court of Human Rights has considered many of these violations, which are discussed in our final section on human rights but these cases also consider violations of international humanitarian law.

(a) Violence to life and person, in particular murder of all kinds, mutilation, cruel treatment and torture

It has been continually argued by Kurdish groups and non-governmental organisations including Amnesty International (AI) and the Kurdish Human Rights Project (KHRP) in London, that there have been many deaths and incidents of torture in Turkish custody of those suspected of being members of or support the PKK. This contention is supported by jurisprudence from the European Court of Human Rights, which has found violations of the right to life and prohibition against torture. Examples are discussed in the final part of this chapter. The violation by the Turkish authorities of the right to life, disappearances and torture are also supported in an influential AI report released in 1996.[58] The report specifically alleges that torture is widespread and systematic in Turkey.[59] This statement is supported by the UN Committee Against Torture (CAT) and the European Committee for the Prevention of Torture (ECPT).[60] According to the US Department of State's March 2009 report on Human Rights in Turkey, during 2008 'Human rights organizations reported a rise in cases of torture and abuse during the year'. In a 5 July report, AI noted that a 'culture of impunity' allowed police and Jandarma[61] to escape accountability for torture and enabled courts to disregard medical evidence of torture and accept as evidence statements allegedly extracted under torture.[62] The report gives specific incidents many of whom were Kurdish persons in custody, including reports of death in custody due to ill treatment.[63] The Kurdish Human Rights Project has in its database hundreds of files of allegations of unlawful killings and torture.[64]

There are also allegations of the same behaviour on the part of the PKK. AI alleged in 1996 that the PKK had attacked and killed civilians.[65] The report alleges that since 1984 the PKK have frequently killed Kurdish villagers taking no part in the conflict as well as civil servants, most particularly targeting teachers, 90 of whom were killed between 1984 and the writing of the report in 1996.[66] There are also allegations that the PKK has utilised torture.[67]

(b) Committing outrages upon personal dignity, in particular humiliating and degrading treatment

In most human rights treaties, this provision is part and parcel of the description of torture, but it also can encompass sexual assault. This again has been a continual charge against the Turkish security forces when they take women suspected of supporting the PKK into custody. The case of *Aydin v Turkey* is very pertinent and is discussed below.[68] The ECPT also found incidents of sexual assaults of males (squeezing of genitals) during one of their visits to detention centres.[69] AI in 2003 reported that it had documented numerous cases of women being sexually tortured while in police and gendarmarie custody in Turkey.[70] The KHRP has also documented cases of systematic sexual assault of Kurdish women while in custody.[71]

(c) Taking of hostages

Once again there are allegations of the violation this prohibition on both sides of this armed conflict. Media reports confirm that the PKK have taken hostages of Turkish soldiers and security forces in this conflict.[72] The Turkish forces have also launched operations into Kurdish villages, whereupon certain persons have disappeared and one could assume that these persons were hostages prior to their deaths. For example in the March 2008 State Department report, 11 corpses were discovered near the town of Kulp, Diyarbakir Province, in late 2004 which were identified in February 2006 by DNA matching as belonging to villagers who disappeared after detention in 1993.[73]

(d) The passing of sentences and the carrying out of executions without previous judgement pronounced by a regularly constituted court affording all the judicial guarantees which are recognized as indispensable by civilized peoples

There have also been allegations of summary executions without trial by the Turkish security forces.[74] Furthermore, there have been serious criticisms of the Turkish judicial system with respect to terrorist offences, which is discussed below with respect to the trial of Öcalan.[75] Once again the allegations can also be made with respect to the PKK in its murders of civilians for being collaborators with the Turkish forces, without any due process involved.[76]

The difficulty with the situation in southeast Turkey is that there is no independent body investigating war crimes and prosecutions are not taking place domestically or internationally for violations of international humanitarian law.[77] There are of course trials and hearings for human rights violations but no acknowledgement that these violations are also crimes within international humanitarian law. This is a situation that cries out for an independent assessment of the alleged violations but certainly the course of this conflict seems to suggest that those who are captured or wounded or *hors de combat* on both sides of this conflict are not treated according to treaty and customary standards of Common Article 3.

3.2 Customary international humanitarian law applicable in non-international armed conflict

There are other rules of international humanitarian law that are critical to this and any other armed conflict. There are customary international humanitarian law protections available in both non-international and international armed conflict, particularly the cardinal rules of distinction, necessity and proportionality applicable in any decision by an armed force to launch a military attack. The ICRC, in 2005, released its influential and substantial customary international humanitarian law study co-authored by Jean-Marie Henkaerts and Louise Doswald-Beck.[78] This three-volume study contains rules of international humanitarian law argued to be customary in both international and internal armed conflict. These rules are important as many of the provisions are only codified in Additional Protocol I of 1977 to the Geneva Conventions of 1949 which Turkey among other states including the United States are not yet states parties. However, in an extensive analysis of the practice of states including *opinio juris* (the subjective element of belief that the practice is lawful), many of the rules of international humanitarian law codified in that protocol are argued to be customary in both international and non-international armed conflict. This assertion is not without controversy, but in an extensive analysis of these rules a group of expert scholars were prepared to accept the customary nature of the vast majority of the rules.[79]

The rules of *jus in bello* with respect to targeting decisions have evolved into three primary rules: necessity, distinction and proportionality. It is possible to identify these principles in the rules in the customary law study, which are discussed in detail. To summarise these principles, first, it is accepted that human lives will be lost in an armed conflict but the primary goal is to limit the casualties to the actual belligerents. Armed conflict is to be directed against a state's military not its civilians. Attacks are to be against military targets not civilian ones such as hospitals, schools and churches and for that matter, villages, as has been the alleged practice by the Turkish forces in the course of this conflict, particularly in the village clearances in the mid-1990s where over 3,000 villages had been 'virtually wiped from the map'.[80] The military includes by customary practice, paramilitary groups such as the PKK. These rules do much to clarify the simple proposition that to wage war against a civilian population is unlawful.

In the ICRC Customary International Law Study, the first part of the rules set out these cardinal rules surrounding the three principles of distinction, proportionality and necessity:[81]

Rule 1

The parties to the conflict must at all times distinguish between civilians and combatants. Attacks may only be directed against combatants. Attacks must not be directed against civilians.

This Rule 'unquestionably represents accepted customary law'.[82] This is supported by the International Court of Justice which labelled distinction as a 'cardinal principle' of international law in its *Nuclear Weapons* advisory opinion.[83] Part of the rules of distinction as reflected in Additional Protocol I is the concept of military objectives. The customary international study attempts to define these objectives:

Rule 8

In so far as objects are concerned, military objectives are limited to those objects which by their nature, location, purpose or use make an effective contribution to military action and whose partial or total destruction, capture or neutralization, in the circumstances ruling at the time, offers a definite military advantage.

Again Schmitt argues that '[t]he formula set forth in Rule 8 is universally accepted, a fact aptly demonstrated in the Rule's commentary and the Practice Volume (II)'.[84] It is important to note however, in the context of an armed conflict in civilian areas, such as southeast Turkey, civilians can be targeted if civilian structures are turned into military command or supply centres, a village home full of arms is a lawful target.

The next set of rules, however, further limit choices of targets:

Rule 11
    Indiscriminate attacks are prohibited.

Rule 12
    Indiscriminate attacks are those:

(a)   which are not directed at a specific military objective;
(b)   which employ a method or means of combat which cannot be directed at a specific military objective; or
(c)   which employ a method or means of combat the effects of which cannot be limited as required by international humanitarian law; and consequently, in each such case, are of a nature to strike military objectives and civilians or civilian objects without distinction.

Rule 13
    Attacks by bombardment by any method or means which treats as a single military objective a number of clearly separated and distinct military objectives located in a city, town, village or other area containing a similar concentration of civilians or civilian objects are prohibited.

These rules specify the content of the rule of distinction and again are customary.[85] Therefore, to turn to our earlier example of the village house turned into an armoury, it is not lawful to destroy the whole village to eliminate this one house. The next rule provides even further refinement:

Rule 14
    Launching an attack which may be expected to cause incidental loss of civilian life, injury to civilians, damage to civilian objects, or a combination thereof, which would be excessive in relation to the concrete and direct military advantage anticipated, is prohibited.

Rule 15
    In the conduct of military operations, constant care must be taken to spare the civilian population, civilians and civilian objects. All feasible precautions

must be taken to avoid, and in any event to minimize, incidental loss of civilian life, injury to civilians and damage to civilian objects.

These rules relate to the principle of proportionality, in many ways one of the most difficult of international humanitarian law rules to grasp. With respect to our village house, a military commander would have to establish the necessity of destroying that house and potentially the neighbours' houses as a concrete and direct military advantage resulting in the loss of civilian life which is not excessive: an extremely difficult calculation, which is discussed further below.

With respect to classification of armed conflict this study contends that all these rules are applicable in internal armed conflict even though they are not specifically mentioned in either Common Article 3 or Additional Protocol II to the Geneva Conventions of 1977 and are only mentioned in the provisions in Additional Protocol I.

There are other customary rules that further extend the protections guarantees in Common Article 3 particularly rules of respect for civilian establishments such as hospitals, churches and environmentally hazardous locations. Critical as well is the obligation to respect prisoners of war. In internal armed conflict the classification of combatants is particularly difficult. Guantanamo Bay is an example of what can happen when the rules of armed conflict are not respected. The PKK like the IRA would argue that they are combatants entitled to prisoner of war status. No such facilities exist and PKK rebels are tried and convicted as criminals. Although the United States argues for a status of unlawful combatant that status does not exist in international humanitarian law. The rules respecting prisoner of war in part, can extend to internal armed conflict.

However, there is another source that importantly supports these rules customary status in non-international armed conflict and that is the International Institute of Humanitarian Law's 'The Manual'. The drafting committee which concluded this manual in Sanremo in 2006 was composed of leading scholars in international humanitarian law.[86] This committee drafted rules with slightly different wording to apply to the participants in non-international armed conflict but accepted the legally binding nature of the rules of distinction, necessity and proportionality. The first rule sets out the general principle:

1.2.1 Introduction

a.   All military operations must comply with the principles of distinction, prohibition of unnecessary suffering, and humane treatment.
b.   Military necessity has already been taken into account in the formulation of these rules. Therefore, where not mentioned explicitly as an exception in the rules, military necessity cannot serve as a justification for their violation.[87]

The commentary states that these principles are based on customary law dating from the expression in the 1874 Brussels Declaration and the 1880 Oxford

Manual and as codified in the 1899 and 1907 Hague Regulations. Support for this principle could also be found in international tribunals such as the Nuremberg Tribunal holding that the rules included in the 1907 Hague regulations 'were recognized by all civilized nations and were regarded as being declaratory of the laws and customs of law'.[88] It was the *Tadić* decision that confirmed the applicability of the principle to non-international armed conflict and the appellate chamber held that the customary rules had developed to govern 'internal strife', covering 'such areas as protection of civilians from hostilities, in particular from indiscriminate attacks, protection of civilian objects, in particular cultural property, protection of all those who do not (or no longer) take active part in hostilities, as well as prohibition of means of warfare proscribed in international armed conflicts and ban of certain methods of conducting hostilities'.[89]

The next rule is of equal importance:

1.2.2 Distinction

A distinction must always be made in the conduct of military operations between fighters and civilians. A distinction must also always be made between military objectives and civilian objects.[90]

The commentary argues that the principle of distinction is the 'foundation on which the codification of the laws and customs of war rests'.[91] Importantly, the commentary argues that 'it is indisputable that the principle of distinction is customary international law for both international and non-international armed conflict'.[92] It was also confirmed in *Tadić* to be customary law in non-international armed conflict.[93]

'The Manual' then embarks on a discussion of specific rules of targeting in Chapter 2, Conduct of Military Operations. These rules are:

2.1 Targeting

2.1.1 General rule

Attacks must be directed only against fighters or military objectives.

The commentary refers this rule back to the principle of distinction (Rule 1.2.2 discussed). The next rule provides further specificity.

2.1.1.1 *Attacking civilians and civilian objects*

Attacking the civilian population as such, as well as individual civilians, is forbidden. It is also forbidden to attack civilian objects, unless they become military objectives. Certain categories of individuals and objects are subject to special rules of protection.[94]

The commentary indicates that this provision is directly from Article 13.2 of Additional Protocol II and has also been included in Article 8 2 (e) (i) of the ICC Statute. The commentary also argues the customary nature of the provision by again relying on the *Tadić* decision but also the fact that Common Article 3 (1) (a) of the Geneva Convention requires humane treatment of those taking no active part in hostilities and includes the prohibition on violence to life and person. There is an important limitation to this protection: if the civilian object becomes a military objective within the definition of Rule 1.1.4, it loses its protection and also civilians lose their protection if they take an active/direct part in hostilities (Rule 2.1.1.2).[95]

The next rule gives great specificity to the rules of necessity and distinction:

2.1.1.3 Indiscriminate attacks
Indiscriminate attacks are forbidden. Indiscriminate attacks are those that are not specifically directed against fighters or military objectives.

The commentary states that indiscriminate attacks are those that are of a nature to strike military objective and civilians and civilian objects without distinction. This is particularly set out in Articles 51.4 and 51.5 of Additional Protocol I but is argued to be equally applicable to non-international armed conflict. There are two types of indiscriminate methods of combat described. The first is carrying out an attack where no attempt is made to identify specific military objectives. The second method is an attack which treats separate and distinct military objectives collocated with civilians or civilian objects as a single entity, such as carpet-bombing an entire urban area. Again, *Tadić* is used to support the proposition that this prohibition is a customary rule of international law applicable to non-international armed conflict. 'The Manual' does argue that the full specificity of the Additional Protocols might not be applicable to non-international armed conflict which is probably why these and the ICRC rules are more general than the treaty provisions.[96]

Finally, there are the complex rules on proportionality with its calculation of military advantage:

2.1.1.4 Proportionality
An attack is forbidden if it may be expected to cause incidental loss to civilian life, injury to civilians, damage to civilian objects, or a combination thereof, which would be excessive in relation to the concrete and direct military advantage anticipated. It is recognised that incidental injury to civilians and collateral damage to civilian objects may occur as a result of a lawful attack against fighters or military objectives.

The commentary states that the rule of proportionality was first codified in Additional Protocol I, Articles 51 and 57. 'The Manual' justifies its customary status in non-international armed conflict by discussing its inclusion in a number of instruments. For example, the Conventional Weapons Convention cites proportionality in relation to the indiscriminate placement of weapons in both the original 1980 Protocol II on the Use of Mines, Booby Traps and Other Devices (Article 3.3(c)) and in the 1996 Amended Protocol II on the same subjects (Article 3.8(c)). By these documents, a placement that causes excessive incidental injury or collateral damage is forbidden. Also cited is Article 7(c) of the 1999 Second Hague Protocol for the Protection of Cultural Property in the Event of

Armed Conflict, which forbids attacks that may cause incidental damage to cultural property protected under the Convention that would be excessive in relation to the concrete and direct military advantage anticipated.[97]

The commentary argues that the absence of proportionality in instruments governing non-international armed conflict should not be construed as meaning it is inapplicable in those conflicts as the ICRC commentary to Additional Protocol II labelled proportionality as one of 'the general principles relating to the protection of the civilian population which apply irrespective of whether the conflict is an international or internal one'.[98]

It is important to describe the content of this complex rule and the commentary does just that. First of all there is the notion of 'collateral damage'. It is part of the rule that those who plan attacks against fighters or military objections must take into account the principle of proportionality that collateral damage to civilian objects and injury to civilians 'must not be excessive in relation to the concrete and direct military advantage anticipated'.[99] This also introduces the second critical concept 'military advantage', both the customary rules by the ICRC and 'The Manual' support a customary rule that any attack but be established to be for a 'military advantage' not to terrorise or dislocate or injure civilians. This is assessed with reference to the attack as a whole not from isolated portions of the attack. It is defined broadly as extending from force protection to diverting the enemy from an intended site of invasion.[100] A major debate in targeting is the attack of 'dual use' objects such as the national electricity grid. 'The Manual' argues that the military advantage from such an attack has to be weighted against effects of causing injury or death to civilians or damage or destruction to civilian objects. This has to be done on a case-by-case basis taking into account all the surrounding circumstances.[101]

The authors of 'The Manual' also argue that another key word is 'excessive'. This means unreasonable conduct in light of the circumstances prevailing at the time.[102] Importantly, the test involved to determine whether the attacker knew or should have known that civilian damage or injury would be excessive is an objective one.[103] As with violations of Common Article 3, this cries out for an independent assessment or inquiry of alleged violations.

The next rule is part and parcel of the rules on targeting:

2.1.2 Precautions in planning and carrying out attacks

a) All feasible precautions must be taken by all parties to minimise both injuries to civilians and damage to civilian objects.
b) When a reasonable choice between methods or means used in an attack exists for obtaining a similar military advantage, the methods or means expected to minimise the danger to civilians and civilian objects must be selected.
c) An attack must be cancelled or suspended if it becomes apparent that the target is not a fighter or military objective or is subject to special protection, or if the expected injury to civilians and/or the expected

damage to civilian objects would be excessive in relation to the concrete and direct military advantage anticipated.

d) When a reasonable choice is available between several military objectives for obtaining a similar military advantage, the objective expected to minimise the danger to civilians and civilian objects must be selected.

Again, 'The Manual' argues that neither Common Article 3 nor Additional Protocol II set forth any requirements for precautions in the planning or carrying out attacks. One possible source is the general statement in Article 13.1. of Additional Protocol II, that 'the civilian population and individual civilians shall enjoy general protection against the dangers arising from military operations'. 'The Manual' argues that this was already recognised by customary international law at the time the Additional Protocols were drafted. Further support is argued to be in the *Tadić* judgment, where the International Criminal Tribunal for the Former Yugoslavia's appellate chamber cited with approval UN General Assembly Resolution 2675 which contained a clause that 'in the conduct of military operations, every effort should be made to spare civilian populations from the ravages of war and all necessary precautions should be taken to avoid injury, loss or damage to civilian populations' and stated that it was 'declaratory of the principles of customary international law … in armed conflicts of any kind'.[104]

The commentary to this rule in 'The Manual' defines feasible precautions as 'those precautions which are practicable or practically possible taking into account all circumstances ruling at the time, including humanitarian and military considerations'.[105] Importantly, the authors assert that when there is a choice of methods and means for conducting an attack, those that minimise civilian danger must be selected. This could involve planning attacks at night when civilians are not likely to present, or using precision weapons in an urban area.[106]

The rules and commentary in 'The Manual' do much to support the customary status of the primary rules of necessity, distinction and proportionality which further supports the ICRC Customary International Law Study. Even though 'The Manual' has not been accepted as a definitive source of customary international law, it is likely to be very influential on the development of standards of humanity in non-international armed conflict. It is also further support to the argument contained in the Customary International Humanitarian Law Study that most of the customary rules apply to non-international armed conflict. 'The Manual' also contains important provisions on protections for belligerents, which are discussed in Chapter 4.

3.2.1 Applicability of customary law to the conflict in southeast Turkey

The targeting decisions by the Turkish military both in southeast Turkey and northern Iraq seem to concentrate on civilian objects and there is credible evidence of the systematic destruction of villages and farms.[107] What has to be established is whether or not there are a number of PKK fighters sheltering within these targets. These are targets destroyed primarily by setting fire to houses and property but nevertheless this in international humanitarian law terms is a targeting decision to attack a civilian target.[108] The onus is on the Turkish army to establish that these targets are a military necessity, that they distinguish between civilians and fighters and that the proportionality calculation of acceptable civilian casualties is completed. The evidence must be objectively verified that all due precautions were taken in planning the attack to minimise the damage to civilians and their property. At this point this evidence has not been made available to the international community. Furthermore, human rights consideration of the right to property discussed below has found violations of this right in the conduct of the Turkish forces in southeast Turkey.[109] A recent investigation of the KHRP in northern Iraq has documented the targeting of civilian objects in the recent military campaigns by Turkish forces.[110]

3.3 Minimum humanitarian standards applicable to any internal conflict

There is an interesting 'soft law' instrument to be reviewed in the context of the conflict in southeast Turkey. This is the Declaration of Minimum Humanitarian Standards negotiated at Turku.[111] These standards merit examination in the context of any type of internal disturbance which might not rise to the level of armed conflict as they mirror the guarantees contained in Common Article 3 to the Geneva Conventions. In this case it is important to set these out in light of the Turkish objection to this conflict being classified as an armed conflict.

Efforts to develop minimum humanitarian standards which would apply to all situations of internal strife and tensions have been ongoing. The Moscow Declaration of 1991 and the Budapest Summit in 1994 stressed the importance of a declaration setting out the minimum standards applicable to all situations. These were developed in Turku and reprinted in the report of the Sub-Commission on Prevention of Discrimination and Protection of Minorities in their 46th session in 1995.[112] This declaration in Article 1 affirmed that minimum humanitarian standards were applicable in all situations, including internal violence, disturbances, tensions and public emergency and could not be derogated from in any circumstances. Article 2 specified that these standards would apply to all persons irrespective of their legal status and without any adverse discrimination.

The core guarantees in the remaining articles are very similar to those guarantees contained in Common Article 3, discussed above. These include in Article 3, the right to be recognised as a person before the law and to respect for their person, honour and convictions, freedom of thought, conscience and religious practices. They shall in all circumstances be treated humanely, without any adverse distinction. In the same article the following acts were prohibited:

a) violence to the life, health and physical or mental well-being of persons, in particular murder, torture, mutilation, rape, as well as cruel, inhuman or degrading treatment or punishment and other outrages upon personal dignity;

b)   collective punishments against persons and their property;

c)   the taking of hostages;

d)   practising, permitting or tolerating the involuntary disappearance of individuals, including their abduction or unacknowledged detention;

e)   pillage;

f)   deliberate deprivation of access to necessary food, drinking water and medicine;

g)   threats or incitement to commit any of the foregoing acts.

The rights upon detention are more detailed than those in Common Article 3, Article 4 specifies that persons deprived of their liberty shall be held in recognised places of detention and accurate information on their detention and whereabouts should be made promptly available to family members. Persons detained shall be allowed to communicate with counsel and have a right to an effective remedy including habeas corpus and to embark on legal proceedings to challenge their detention. These rights also include the right to be treated humanely with adequate food and drinking water, decent accommodation and clothing and be afforded safeguards as regards health, hygiene and working and social conditions. These conditions are reminiscent of the Geneva Prisoner of War Convention. Other human rights guarantees including the right to life (Article 8), the right to a fair trial (Article 9) and rights to review of detention (Article 11) are specified in detail.

The minimum guarantees in Article 5 also include basic international humanitarian law rules including the rule of distinction, in that attacks against persons not taking part in acts of violence shall be prohibited in all circumstances. It also includes the rule of proportionality in its statement that '[w]henever the use of force is unavoidable, it shall be in proportion to the seriousness of the offence or the objective to be achieved'. Finally, it specifies that any weapons or other material or methods prohibited in international armed conflicts must not be employed in any circumstances.

Other humanitarian law guarantees include the prohibition against displacement of population unless safety or imperative security reasons so demand (Article 7), the special measures of protection of children including a prohibition against recruitment of child soldiers (Article 10), care and collection and humane treatment of the wounded and sick (Articles 12 and 13), special measure of protection for medical and religious personnel (Article 14) and special arrangements for humanitarian organisations (Article 15). As we have seen these protections are customary in international humanitarian law but these standards attempt to widen their ambit to non-armed conflict situations.

Finally and interestingly there is a prohibition against terrorism in Article 6 which states: 'Acts or threats of violence the primary purpose of foreseeable effect of which is to spread terror among the population are prohibited'.

Once again it could be argued that these standards are a convention in miniature. The standards incorporate both human rights and humanitarian law guarantees. It is clear, however, that these standards are a very recent development and they cannot be argued to be part of customary international law. Rather they may be 'soft law' standards that the conduct of two opposing parties can be measured against.

3.3.1 Applicability of the standards to conflict in southeast Turkey

These standards have not met with the approval of states but we argue that they are applicable to the situation in southeast Turkey. The reason for this is that these standards simply reflect customary human rights and international humanitarian law and should be available in situations of war and peace. Once again the violations outlined earlier in the chapter are clearly violations of these minimum standards. Incidents such as hostage takings, deaths in custody, torture and sexual violence all fall foul of these standards. Both parties can be accused of violating these rules for minimum human decency. However, this is not an enforceable legal regime but the human rights standards contained within these guarantees certainly are, as seen from the final part of the chapter.

3.4 Applicability of international human rights law to the conflict in southeast Turkey

In Chapter 2 we introduce the concept of competing regimes within non-international armed conflict, international humanitarian law and human rights law. This section of the chapter discusses the numerous cases in the European Court of Human Rights that have considered violations of human rights obligations within the context of the international armed conflict, and discusses how the violations may also be violations of international humanitarian law. Although there are many violations of human rights that could be discussed, in this section we discuss those human rights most similar to the guarantees provided in Common Article 3 with reference to those not participating in the armed conflict by virtue of being civilians or *hors de combat*. The European Court of Human Rights has been called upon to decide literally thousands of cases from this conflict and some of the leading decisions are outlined here. The difficulty is that the lens of review has been human rights rather than humanitarian law, which in this circumstance should be the *lex specialis*, nevertheless the findings are pertinent and must be addressed in any process of peace and reconciliation, which is discussed later in the book.

In this chapter we discuss the violations of rights of persons who clearly are not participating in the armed conflict. In Chapter 4 we discuss human rights of belligerents, particularly the right to life, prohibition against torture and fair trial provisions as these rights are closely related to the rights of belligerents. This is by necessity a false division as in many of these cases it is uncertain whether we are speaking of belligerents or civilians because the human rights cases do not discuss the distinction between civilians and combatants (or fighters as labelled in 'The Manual'). Many of those killed were suspected of some involvement with the PKK but it is unclear if they were direct participants in the armed conflict.

3.4.1 Right to life

Many of the right to life cases, although they do not discuss the issue, seem to deal with the deprivation of life of those suspected of being fighters with the PKK. However, there are judgments (although they deal with events in the early 1990s) which clearly involve the death of civilians in this conflict, as is discussed in Chapter 1. However, there are examples to be reviewed that relate to the operation of the non-international armed conflict.

A prominent case of deaths caused in some type of fighting is *Seyfettin Acar and others v Turkey* and its predecessor case *Acar and Others v Turkey*.[113] The *Seyfettin Acar* case was brought by six relatives of two killed and two wounded civilians and it was alleged that on 20 April 1992 a number of villagers from Çalpınar village were travelling in two vehicles. Some time after they left their village the vehicles were stopped by a group of village guards. As is discussed in Chapter 1, village guards were authorised by the Turkish government to keep order in the villages in southeast Turkey. On this occasion, the village guards then opened fire on the villagers and killed six of them, including the first applicant's brother and the sixth applicant's husband, Mr Süleyman Acar. A number of other villagers were injured. Two of the injured persons, including the second applicant's brother and the fifth applicant's husband, Mr Sabri Acar, died the following day in hospital. The third and the fourth applicants were among those injured in the incident. The third applicant, Yusuf Acar, was shot in the leg and his injuries required a month to heal. The fourth applicant, Süleyman Acar, had broken bones and a bullet had split in his body.[114]

In both cases the Court ruled that the killings and the injuries caused to the two applicants had been in breach of Article 2 of the Convention in its substantive aspect. It also reached the conclusion that the investigation and the trial had been ineffective and that the applicants had thus been deprived of an effective remedy, in breach of Articles 2 (in its procedural aspect) and 13 of the Convention.[115] The Court expressed in these cases its misgivings as regards the use of civilian volunteers such as village guards in a 'quasi-police function' due to the fact that 'the village guards operated outside the normal structure of discipline and training'.[116] Importantly, the Court found that the village guards were employed and armed by the state and that the state 'must bear responsibility' for the killing of the relatives and the attempt to kill the other applicants.[117] Although it is outside of the remit of the European Court of Human Rights, one could examine this case in light of the clear prohibition of killing civilians during armed conflict unless the rules of military necessity and proportionality are adhered to. In this case there was no suggestion these civilians were near a military objective of any kind, in that these persons were travelling from a village in a minibus and truck.[118]

There are also cases that deal with deaths resulting from violations of the rules of targeting. *Ergi v Turkey* concerned the killing of an uninvolved woman in military operations.[119] The European Court of Human Rights held that in the planning and execution of a military operation care must be taken where the use of force is envisaged in the vicinity of civilian populations, to avoid incidental loss of life and injury to others.[120] The Court held that the State of Turkey had failed to take all feasible precaution in the choice of means and methods of a security operation mounted against an opposing group with a view to avoiding, at least minimising incidental loss of civilian life.[121] Analysing these decisions, Heintze argues that the European Court of Human Rights resorts directly to international humanitarian law, in that it elaborates on the lawfulness of the target, on the proportionality of the attack and on whether the foreseeable risk regarding civilian victims was proportionate to the military advantage.[122]

This type of reasoning was confirmed in *Gülec v Turkey* which concerned an incident in which shots were fired from a tank at demonstrators and the main complainant's son was killed.[123] Again, the Court held that the use of force must be proportionate to the aim and means used. In this case the armed forces had used battlefield weapons for the fighting of demonstrators in the southeast Turkey province of Sirnak. Although this case held a violation of the right to life in Article 2, Heintze argues that it is the method of finding the violation that shows parallels with humanitarian law especially in that area of Turkey where a state of emergency was declared. Interestingly, the Court held that insufficient 'rules of engagement' and lack of education of the armed forces. Although the security situation resulted in frequent 'violent armed clashes' this did not release the state from observance of Article 2 of the European Convention on Human Rights.

A more recent case continuing consideration of targeting principles is the case of *İpek v Turkey*.[124] First, the applicant complained of the disappearance of his two sons, İkram and Servet İpek, as well as the alleged destruction of his family home and property by security forces in the course of an operation conducted in his hamlet of Dahlezeri, outside the village of Türeli, near Lice, on 18 May 1994. The Court found that there was at least a 'low-scale, military operation having been centered on the hamlet within the framework of a larger operation being conducted over the surrounding area'.[125] The Court also accepted that the hamlet had been set alight by the Turkish military and that civilians were prevented from fighting the fires.[126] Importantly, the Court found that this operation was not an isolated one and that during the same period other hamlets and villages suffered the same fate.[127] Although the Court did not go into detail in consideration of whether the villages or hamlets had been an appropriate target, the Court found a violation of Article 1, Protocol 1 in finding a serious violation of the right to peaceful enjoyment of possessions.

Another case of burning of property in the context of disappearances was *Orhan v Turkey*.[128] The applicant alleged that Turkish soldiers burned and evacuated the hamlet where he lived in southeast Turkey and had apprehended and killed his two brothers (Selim and Hasan) and his son (Cezayir).[129] After careful consideration of the testimony of a number of witnesses, the Court found that

the Turkish soldiers had indeed burned the village and that before their disappearance the Orhans had been in Turkish custody. As they had not been seen
for 8 years the Court found that they could be assumed to be dead and found a
violation of Article 2 of the European Convention on Human Rights. Although
the Court found other violations of the Convention, its finding of the violation of
the right to property is most relevant to our discussion. The Court held:

> The Court has found it established that the homes and certain possessions of
> the applicant and of the Orhans were deliberately destroyed by the security
> forces. The applicant's house continued to be Cezayir Orhan's home in
> Deveboyu. In addition, the village had to be evacuated after the harvest.
> There is no doubt that these acts constituted particularly grave and unjusti-
> fied interferences with the applicant's and the Orhans' right to respect
> for their private and family lives and homes. Such acts also amounted to
> serious and unjustified interferences with the peaceful enjoyment by the
> applicant, by Hasan Orhan and by Selim Orhan of their property and
> possessions. ... The Court does not find it necessary to consider whether the
> forced evacuation of the village is sufficient, of itself, to constitute a violation
> of these Articles.
>
> Accordingly, the Court finds a violation of Article 8 and of Article 1 of
> Protocol No. 1 in respect of the applicant, Selim Orhan and Hasan Orhan
> and of Article 8 only in respect of Cezayir Orhan.[130]

It is regrettable that the Court did not consider the forced evacuations in themselves as it is such a feature of this conflict and a clear violation of international
humanitarian law, unless the security situation demands such an action, which
in this case was not established.

3.4.2 Rights to property

The European Court of Human Rights has considered destruction of property in
the context of the ongoing conflict which, as can be seen from Chapter 1, has
resulted in widespread destruction and clearances of Kurdish villages. In the
case of *Altun v Turkey*[131] the applicant made a claim to the Court following the
destruction of his house and property in November 1993. His house along with
five others was burned down by a group of soldiers. The Court considered that
the destruction of the applicant's home and possessions in the above circumstances caused him suffering of sufficient severity for the acts of the security forces
to be categorised as inhuman treatment within the meaning of Article 3.
The Court also found it established that the security forces deliberately
destroyed the applicant's house and property, obliging his family to leave their
village. There was no doubt that these acts, in addition to giving rise to a violation of Article 3, constituted a grave and unjustified interference with the
applicant's rights to respect for his private and family life and home, and to the
peaceful enjoyment of his possessions.[132] The Court therefore concluded that

there has been a violation of Article 8 of the Convention and of Article 1 of Protocol No 1.

There is another critical case considering the right to property in the context of village clearance in *Doğan and others v Turkey*,[133] where 15 applications in cases of displacement from home by Kurdish people were brought together in one case. First, the Court discussed the violent conflict going on in the region of southeast Turkey between the security forces and sections of the Kurdish population in favour of Kurdish autonomy, in particular members of the PKK.[134] This is as close the Court would get to acknowledge an armed conflict and that in this case the applicants were forced by authorities to leave their homes in the conflict zone. The Court considered in depth the village clearances and stated:

> ... armed clashes, generalised violence and human rights violations, specifi-
> cally within the context of the PKK insurgency, compelled the authorities to
> take extraordinary measures to maintain security in the state of emergency
> region. These measures involved, among others, the restriction of access to
> several villages, including Boydaş, as well as evacuation of some villages on
> the ground of the lack of security. However, it observes that in the circum-
> stances of the case the refusal of access to Boydaş had serious and harmful
> effects that have hindered the applicants' right to enjoyment of their posses-
> sions for almost ten years, during which time they have been living in other
> areas of the country in conditions of extreme poverty, with inadequate
> heating, sanitation and infrastructure.[135]

As a result the court did not consider the interference in property to be proportionate to the security interests. Furthermore, the court held:

> The Court is of the opinion that there can be no doubt that the refusal of
> access to the applicants' homes and livelihood, in addition to giving rise to a
> violation of Article 1 of Protocol No. 1, constitutes at the same time a serious
> and unjustified interference with the right to respect for family lives and
> homes.[136]

It is regrettable that the court did not have reference to the applicable humanitarian law guarantees as these measures of village clearances bore all the hallmark
of deportations. The press release concerning this judgement said there were
1500 other cases pending concerning inability of Kurdish people to return to
villages in southeast Turkey.[137]

Although it is clear that the European Court of Human Rights does not have
the jurisdiction to find violations of international humanitarian law, nor does it
have the specific expertise to consider the law of armed conflict, these three cases
confirm that Turkey is arguably violating the customary law of targeting with
respect to the cardinal rules of distinction, necessity and proportionality by
targeting civilians and civilian objects. The general allegation is that the military

operations in southeast Turkey as described in Chapter 1 have involved the destruction and clearing of civilian villages and the killing of civilians within those targeted villages.

3.4.3 Freedom from torture

As with the first case described above, the other part of the security operations have been the detention of civilians who are suspected in involvement in the PKK. There have been many other cases of torture in detention but the most heinous of these is one of the earlier decisions: the case of *Aydin v Turkey* decided in 1997.[138] Although this case dealt specifically with a civilian, it concerned the treatment of women in custody which would apply for suspected PKK members as well. In June 1993, the applicant, aged 17, her father and sister-in-law were detained for suspected connections with the PKK. The applicant alleged that in what she referred to as the 'torture room' she was stripped of her clothes, put into a car tyre and spun round and round. She was beaten and sprayed with cold water from high-pressure jets. At a later stage she was taken clothed but blindfolded to an interrogation room. With the door of the room locked, an individual in military clothing forcibly removed her clothes, laid her on her back and raped her. By the time he had finished she was in severe pain and covered in blood. She was ordered to get dressed and subsequently taken to another room. According to the applicant, she was later brought back to the room where she had been raped. She was beaten for about an hour by several persons who warned her not to report on what they had done to her.[139] The injuries sustained during the rape were confirmed by medical examination.[140] The Court held, first:

1. As it has observed on many occasions, Article 3 of the Convention enshrines one of the fundamental values of democratic societies and as such it prohibits in absolute terms torture or inhuman or degrading treatment or punishment. Article 3 admits of no exceptions to this fundamental value and no derogation from it is permissible under Article 15 even having regard to the imperatives of a public emergency threatening the life of the nation or to any suspicion, however well-founded, that a person may be involved in terrorist or other criminal activities ...

The Court considered the aggravating factor of detention stating:

2. While being held in detention the applicant was raped by a person whose identity has still to be determined. Rape of a detainee by an official of the State must be considered to be an especially grave and abhorrent form of ill-treatment given the ease with which the offender can exploit the vulnerability and weakened resistance of his victim. Furthermore, rape leaves deep psychological scars on the victim which

do not respond to the passage of time as quickly as other forms of physical and mental violence. The applicant also experienced the acute physical pain of forced penetration, which must have left her feeling debased and violated both physically and emotionally.

The Court accepted the facts given by the applicant and ruled:

3.   Against this background the Court is satisfied that the accumulation of acts of physical and mental violence inflicted on the applicant and the especially cruel act of rape to which she was subjected amounted to torture in breach of Article 3 of the Convention. Indeed the Court would have reached this conclusion on either of these grounds taken separately.

4.   In conclusion, there has been a violation of Article 3 of the Convention.

An important aspect of this case was that the applicant was clearly a civilian and not a combatant in this non-international armed conflict. This was a landmark decision as it held that rape in detention was torture. Yet in both sets of cases of suspected fighters and civilians in detention, the same fundamental guarantees applied, which is discussed in Chapter 4.

Conclusion

This chapter demonstrates that it can be argued that a whole range of humanitarian guarantees are offered to both civilians and combatants in a non-international armed conflict. In fact, customary international law, the case law of the international tribunals, the Statute of the International Criminal Court and the various manuals and declarations mean that almost all of the rules of humanitarian law applicable in international armed conflict are applicable in non-international armed conflict.

The particular emphasis in this chapter is on two aspects, the humanitarian guarantees in Common Article 3 and the law of targeting. There are many more rules that could be canvassed but they would merit a separate publication. The choice of these two primary areas are due to the fact that many of the purported violations have either to do with abuse of civilians and combatants or targeting of civilian objects.

It has to be pointed out again that these specific rules apply to both sides in this conflict. Allegations of terrorism on the part of insurgency groups often relate to the use of methods that target civilians. However, in armed conflict civilians might be killed if they are present at a military objective, for example civilians working in an arms factory or military base. The obligations expressed in the established rules of customary international law prohibit any targeting of civilians to spread terror. Notwithstanding the label of 'terrorist', a belligerent can still be a participant in an armed conflict and bound by the customary and treaty rules of international humanitarian law.

There are other guarantees that are also important in the analysis of the conflict in southeast Turkey and northern Iraq and they are the rights of combatants both on the battlefield and in detention. In Chapter 4, however, we turn to the fundamental question of who is a civilian and who is a combatant, known in international humanitarian law as belligerent status. Once again there is a large volume of human rights cases with direct applicability to the conflict.

4 Belligerents

Introduction

One of the most controversial chapters in the history of armed conflict was the opening and maintenance of the detention facilities at Guantanamo Bay, Cuba after 11 September 2001. In this facility is detained suspected terror suspects from around the world and for the first few years of the camp's operation, detainees were unable to challenge the lawfulness of this detention. It brought the rights of detainees in armed conflict to the attention of the international law community and resulted in a number of domestic cases considering both the Geneva Conventions and international human rights law. The application of this new body of law is of direct relevance to the conflict in southeast Turkey.

First, this chapter reviews the definition of belligerents or combatants within the treaties constitutive of international humanitarian law, in both international and non-international armed conflict. It also discusses the various protections afforded to belligerents in the various types of armed conflict. It must be noted that unless a status of belligerency is conferred in a non-international armed conflict, then Common Article 3, as discussed in Chapter 3, only applies to those who are *hors de combat* or are sick and wounded, not those still involved in combat. Furthermore, all of the extensive guarantees available to combatants in Geneva Convention (III) relative to the Treatment of Prisoners of War are not applicable to fighters in non-international armed conflict. Further complicating this issue is the lack of acceptance by many sovereign states including Turkey of the minimum protections contained in Additional Protocol II of 1977 to the Geneva Convention. Once again it is the consideration of customary international law which is pertinent to this situation.

One of the most important and most complex aspects of international humanitarian law is the obligation to distinguish between civilians and combatants. Although it is true that combatants can be targeted and killed, it is also confirmation of that status that leads to extensive obligations to treat those combatants with dignity and, in an international armed conflict, to give them the status of prisoners of war. Nowhere in international humanitarian law is the contrast between international and non-international armed conflict so evident. As is discussed in Chapter 3, the issue of participation in armed conflict has recently been under examination by a committee convened by the International Committee of the Red Cross (ICRC). The issue is of 'direct participation' of those who would normally be classified as civilians which would deprive them of the protection of their right to life but for the purposes of this chapter, the detention of these persons is also an issue particularly with respect to the so called 'war on terror'.

Second, this chapter focuses on the important issue of detention and discusses the issue of prisoner of war status – limited to the situation of international armed conflict. Detention issues in non-international armed conflict are part of domestic law but, notwithstanding the domestic regime, there are important international legal obligations both in international humanitarian law and human rights law that apply to detainees. This part of the chapter discusses the relevant jurisprudence from the European Court of Human Rights specifically with reference to the conflict in southeast Turkey as, although the standards of the court may be slightly different, the discussion of detention issues is equally pertinent to the humanitarian law guarantees.

4.1 Definition of belligerents

Although Additional Protocol I contains the most comprehensive definition of combatants, as Turkey is not a party to that convention we must review the definition of combatants in the Geneva Conventions and customary international law and whether those definitions are applicable to a non-international armed conflict. At each level of armed conflict definitional problems arise as to the distinction between those who are civilians and those who are combatants. However, this is particularly pertinent in situations of civil wars, which often engage large portions of the rebelling population who may not necessarily be members of the rebel group.

4.1.1 Belligerents in international armed conflict

Within the negotiation of the definition of a combatant, according to Draper, there have been two schools of thought which emerged in the 1870s. The first is the military school which prefers an exclusive definition of combatant to regular armed forces, with severe penalties for the excluded if they dare to take part in hostilities. The second school of thought is the patriotic school which proposes a much wider definition of combatant to include irregular forces. Countries which have histories of rising up against colonial domination prefer the patriotic school, which considers it the duty of every citizen to rise up and repel an invasion.[1]

One of the first international humanitarian law instruments was drafted in the midst of the US Civil War by an international lawyer, Francis Lieber, who subscribed to the military school. The Lieber Code of 1869, Article 155 states:

> All enemies in regular war are divided into two general classes – that is to say, into combatants and non-combatants, or unarmed citizens of the hostile government.[2]

The Hague Regulations of 1907 was a notable international instrument to deal with the issue of combatants and these regulations were a compromise between the patriotic and military schools of thought. These regulations were under Section 1 entitled 'On Belligerents' and Chapter 1 'The qualifications of Belligerents', and the definitions were as follows:

> Art. 1. The laws, rights, and duties of war apply not only to armies, but also to militia and Volunteer corps fulfilling the following conditions:
>
> 1.   To be commanded by a person responsible for his subordinates;
> 2.   To have a fixed distinctive emblem recognizable at a distance;
> 3.   To carry arms openly; and
> 4.   To conduct their operations in accordance with the laws and customs of war.
>
> In countries where militia or volunteer corps constitute the army, or form part of it, they are Included under the denomination 'army'.
>
> Art. 2. The inhabitants of a territory which has not been occupied, who, on the approach of the enemy, spontaneously take up arms to resist the invading troops without having had time to organize themselves in accordance with Article 1, shall be regarded as belligerents if they carry arms openly and if they respect the laws and customs of war.
>
> Art. 3. The armed forces of the belligerent parties may consist of combatants and non-combatants. In the case of capture by the enemy, both have a right to be treated as prisoners of war.[3]

Geneva Convention III Relative to the Treatment of Prisoners of War 1949 set out a definition of those who were entitled to prisoner of war status very similar to the wider definition in the Hague Regulations. The provisions provided that:

> Article 4
>
> A. Prisoners of war, in the sense of the present Convention, are persons belonging to one of the following categories, who have fallen into the power of the enemy:
>
> 1.   Members of the armed forces of a Party to the conflict as well as members of militias or volunteer corps forming part of such armed forces.
> 2.   Members of other militias and members of other volunteer corps, including those of organized resistance movements, belonging to a Party to the conflict and operating in or outside their own territory, even if this territory is occupied, provided that such militias or volunteer corps, including such organized resistance movements, fulfil the following conditions:
>
>   (a) That of being commanded by a person responsible for his subordinates;
>   (b) That of having a fixed distinctive sign recognizable at a distance;

(c) That of carrying arms openly;

(d) That of conducting their operations in accordance with the laws and customs of war.

3. Members of regular armed forces who profess allegiance to a government or an authority not recognized by the Detaining Power.

4. Persons who accompany the armed forces without actually being members thereof, such as civilian members of military aircraft crews, war correspondents, supply contractors, members of labour units or of services responsible for the welfare of the armed forces, provided that they have received authorization from the armed forces which they accompany, who shall provide them for that purpose with an identity card similar to the annexed model.

5. Members of crews, including masters, pilots and apprentices, of the merchant marine and the crews of civil aircraft of the Parties to the conflict, who do not benefit by more favourable treatment under any other provisions of international law.

6. Inhabitants of a non-occupied territory, who on the approach of the enemy spontaneously take up arms to resist the invading forces, without having had time to form themselves into regular armed units, provided they carry arms openly and respect the laws and customs of war.[4]

As can be seen this is a comprehensive definition of the combatant and prisoners of war – a broader category than combatant, again evidence of combining both schools of thought. As the Convention also included members of organised resistance movements in the list of those entitled to prisoner of war status, it indicates an acceptance by state parties that combatant status is also due to members of resistance movements provided they fulfil certain conditions (which in many cases might not be possible if the resistance members intend on concealing their identities).[5] Therefore, if the conflict in southeast Turkey was an international armed conflict, members of such groups as the Kurdistan Workers Party (PKK) must distinguish themselves from civilians by wearing uniforms, by carrying their arms openly and by subjecting themselves to military discipline. It seems from most information received that they indeed do so and are subject to military discipline and an organised military structure.[6]

If this conflict is accepted to be an international armed conflict due to the status of a war of national liberation or the spill over into southeast Turkey, it can be asserted on the facts that the PKK fulfils the detailed requirements. The PKK appears to fulfil the first three criteria of prisoner of war status, and that with respect to the fourth, it has filed a declaration to the United Nations (Geneva, 24 January 1995) that announces that it will comply with international humanitarian law, including agreeing to treat captured Turkish security forces as prisoners of war.[7] This fourth criterion of respect for the laws and customs of war, however, remains unfulfilled, as in spite of this extensive declaration the PKK has been resorting to military as well as non-military means such as the taking of hostages, which is clearly prohibited in international humanitarian law.[8] If the members of the PKK are lawful belligerents who have agreed to abide by international law then they too must follow the rules of international humanitarian law and will be subject to criminal penalties if they do not do so.

As opposed to previous treaties on prisoners of war an important new innovation was introduced to prevent suspected non-combatants being shot on sight as spies or mercenaries, and that was Article 5 of the Convention which provided that:

> Should any doubt arise as to whether persons, having committed a belligerent act and having fallen into the hands of the enemy, belong to any of the categories enumerated in Article 4, such persons shall enjoy the protection of the present Convention until such time as their status has been determined by a competent tribunal.[9]

Additional Protocol I to the Geneva Convention of 1977 provides the most comprehensive definition of combatant as it has sections dealing directly with the classification of combatant with several different categories of participants within an armed conflict; armed forces, civilians who participate in the conflict, spies and mercenaries. Only spies and mercenaries are not entitled to the special protection of prisoner of war status.[10] The question is whether these provisions are part of customary international law and thus would be binding on Turkey if an international armed conflict exists.

The ICRC Customary International Humanitarian Law Study (ICRC Customary International Law Study) proposes a series of customary rules on combatant status and the protection of prisoners of war.[11] Rogers, in examining the various rules that are relevant to combatant status (Rules 1, 3, 4, 5, 6, 106, 107 and 108), has put together a composite customary definition of combatant status which would be applicable in international armed conflict, even if the parties did not ratify Additional Protocol I:

> Definitions
>
> All members of the armed forces of a party to the conflict are combatants, except medical and religious personnel. The armed forces of a party to the conflict consist of all organised armed forces, groups and units, which are under a command responsible to that party for the conduct of its subordinates. Civilians are persons who are not members of the armed forces. The civilian population comprises all persons who are civilians. Mercenaries are as defined in Additional Protocol I.
>
> Operative rules on combatant status
>
> The parties to the conflict must at all times distinguish between civilians and combatants. Attacks may only be directed at combatants.[12] Attacks must not be directed against civilians. Civilians are protected against attack unless and for such time as they take a direct part in hostilities. Combatants must distinguish themselves from the civilian population while they are

engaged in an attack or in a military operation preparatory to an attack. If they fail to do so, they do not have the right to prisoner-of-war status. Combatants who are captured while engaged in espionage do not have the right to prisoner-of-war status. They may not be convicted or sentenced without previous trial. Mercenaries do not have the right to combatant or prisoner-of-war status. They may not be convicted or sentenced without previous trial.[13]

By and large this statement confirms the customary status of the detailed definition of combatant contained in Additional Protocol I, so that if the Kurdish conflict is an international armed conflict, the supplemental material expanding the definition of combatant in that treaty is relevant.

4.1.2 Definition of belligerents in non-international armed conflict

It is unfortunately the case that treaties dealing with non-international armed conflicts such as Additional Protocol II and Common Article 3 of the Geneva Conventions contain no provisions on a definition of combatant status. Rogers argues that it can be inferred from this silence that the status of persons who participate in non-international armed conflict is governed by the law of the state where the conflict is taking place.[14] In spite of that fact, the ICRC Customary International Law Study attempts to have the status of combatant rules applicable in non-international armed conflict. Rogers points out that this might be difficult as the use of combatant in a non-international armed conflict will cause confusion as this designation will not mean that there is a right to combatant status or prisoner of war status.[15] However, there is an important recent study that examines the status of a belligerent in non-international armed conflict which does confirm the applicability of a number of customary rules to non-international armed conflict. This source is 'The Manual on Non-International Armed Conflict' ('The Manual') which proposes a new term for the belligerents. This new category is called 'Fighters':

1.1.2 Fighters

a. For the purposes of this Manual, fighters are members of armed forces and dissident armed forces or other organized armed groups, or taking an active (direct) part in hostilities.

b. Medical and religious personnel of armed forces or groups, however, are not regarded as fighters and are subject to special protection unless they take an active (direct) part in hostilities.

   1. The term 'fighters' does not appear in any binding treaty and is used here solely for the purposes of the present Manual. It must be appreciated that fighters include both members of the regular armed forces fighting on behalf of the government and members of armed

groups fighting against the government. The term 'fighters' has been employed in lieu of 'combatants' in order to avoid any confusion with the meaning of the latter term in the context of the international law of armed conflict.

2.   The phrases 'active participation' and 'direct participation' in hostilities are often used interchangeably. For example, Common Article 3 of the Geneva Conventions uses the word 'active', whereas Article 13.3 of Additional Protocol II uses the word 'direct.' There is no substantive distinction between the two terms in this context. What is required is 'a sufficient causal relationship between the active participation and its immediate consequences.'

3.   It is important to distinguish active (direct) participation in hostilities from participation in the war effort. The former term is much more restrictive. Examples of active (direct) participation in hostilities include such activities as attacking the enemy, his materiel or facilities; sabotaging enemy installations; acting as members of a gun crew or artillery spotters; delivering ammunition; or gathering military intelligence in the area of hostilities. It would not include, however, general contributions to the war effort, such as working in a munitions factory.

4.   Under Article 13.3 of Additional Protocol II, the loss of protection exists only 'for such time as [civilians] take a direct part in hostilities.' However, this limitation is not confirmed by customary international law. Such an approach would create an imbalance between the government's armed forces on the one hand and members of armed groups on the other, inasmuch as the former remain legitimate targets (under international law) throughout the conflict. Moreover, the proposition is impractical to implement on the ground. Ordinary soldiers would be required to make complex and immediate assessments as to whether an individual's participation in hostilities is ongoing, at a time when the facts available are incomplete or unclear.

1.1.3 Civilians

Civilians are all those who are not fighters.

For the purposes of this Manual, civilians who actively (directly) participate in hostilities are treated as 'fighters'.[16]

'The Manual' is of great assistance in determining who is a fighter in a non-international armed conflict, but does not specify those traditional treaty conditions as military organisation, carrying arms openly and wearing uniforms. It may be then that a fighter is a broader definition. Therefore, the issue is distinction between civilians and combatants as Common Article 3 provides protection to those that are civilians and *hors de combat* but none of the extensive protections available to combatants are available to fighters.

As can be seen in the discussion in 'The Manual' on the definition of 'fighter', the issue of direct participation in armed conflict as mentioned in the Rogers definition is pertinent to this situation as the issue of civilian participation in armed conflict has come to the forefront with the conflicts in Afghanistan and Iraq and is also an issue in the non-international armed conflict in southeast Turkey.[17] Article 51.3 of Additional Protocol I states that 'Civilians shall enjoy the protection afforded by this section [entitled Protection of the Civilian Population], unless and for such time as they take a direct part in hostilities'.[18] This is also confirmed in Article 13 of Additional Protocol II, which in its part 2 provides that the civilian population shall not be the object of attack, which is limited by the phrase in part 3 'unless and for such time as they take a direct part in hostilities'.[19] Common Article 3 to the four Geneva Conventions of 1949 applies to 'persons taking no active part in hostilities'. Schmitt argues that although Common Article 3 and Protocol II employ different terminology (active and direct respectively), the International Criminal Tribunal for Rwanda judgment held that the terms are so similar they should be treated synonymously.[20] Thus, he argues, civilians lose their immunity from attack while they are taking a direct part in hostilities.[21] There is controversy over what direct participation actually means and the demarcation between combat and the general war effort. Schmitt argues:

> Direct participation, therefore, seemingly requires 'but for' causation (i.e., the consequences would not have occurred but for the act) and causal proximity to the foreseeable consequences of the act. Returning to the ammunition truck driver, one who transports ammunition from the factory to ammunition depots would clearly not be directly participating; an individual who delivered it to the front lines, however, arguably would.[22]

This will have to be assessed on a case-by-case basis but there is no real international agreement on where that dividing line lies. The ICRC has recently released its interpretive guidance on the notion of direct participation in hostilities under international humanitarian law.[23] The key questions considered in the ICRC document are: (1) Who is considered a civilian for the purpose of the principle of distinction? (2) What conduct amounts to direct participation in hostilities? (3) What modalities govern the loss of protection against direct attack?[24] These are crucial questions with respect to Common Article 3 as only those who are not actively participating in hostilities are entitled to protection and it is argued that direct and active participation are synonymous.[25]

Within the guidance, there is a specific section on non-international armed conflict. The proposed guidance states:

> For the purposes of the principle of distinction in *non-international* armed conflict, all persons who are not members of State armed forces or organized armed groups of a party to the conflict are civilians and, therefore, entitled to protection against direct attack unless and for such time as they take a direct

part in hostilities. In non-international armed conflict, organized armed groups constitute the armed forces of a non-State party to the conflict and consist only of individuals whose continuous function it is to take a direct part in hostilities ('*continuous combat function*').

The commentary to this provision acknowledges that, with respect to Common Article 3, it does not govern the conduct of hostilities. Nevertheless, its wording allows conclusions to be drawn with regard to the distinction between armed forces and the civilian population in non-international armed conflict. As the article provides that 'each party to the conflict' must afford protection to those who take no active part in the hostilities, it implies that both state and non-state parties have armed forces distinct from the civilian population. The article also makes clear that members of such forces are considered to take no active part in hostilities once they have 'disengaged from fighting' or are *hors de combat*.[26] This is criticised by Schmitt as the approach based on continuous direct participation blurs the distinction made by international humanitarian law between loss of protection based on conduct (for civilians) and on status or function (members of armed forces or organized armed groups).[27]

The Guidance goes on to define what constitutes direct participation in hostilities by three cumulative requirements:

> The act must be likely to adversely affect the military operations or military capacity of a party to an armed conflict or, alternatively, to inflict death, injury, or destruction on persons or object protected against direct attack (*threshold of harm*), and there must be a direct causal link between the act and the harm likely to result either from that act, or from a coordinated military operation of which that act constitutes an integral part (*direct causation*), and the act must be specifically designed to directly cause the required threshold of harm in support of a party to the conflict and to the detriment of another (*belligerent nexus*).[28]

The Guidance also proposes that direct participation includes 'measure preparatory to the execution of such an act, as well as the deployment to and return from the location of its execution when they constitute an integral part of such a specific act or operation'.[29] There is also a temporal scope of these activities which involve a distinction between civilians and non-state armed groups:

> Civilians lose protection against direct attack for the duration of each specific act amounting to direct participation in hostilities, whereas members of organized armed groups belonging to a non-State party to an armed conflict cease to be civilians ... , and lose protection against direct attack, for as long as they assume their continuous combat function.[30]

In this case however, the PKK does not assert that it is a group of civilians but that it is an organised armed force entitled to combatant status. However, there are clearly civilians involved in this civil war and the ICRC Guidance, in spite of the controversy, offers assistance in the rules on targeting.

Yet although it is clear that participants or 'fighters' are liable to be killed, wounded or captured, there are some basic guarantees offered to this wider category of fighter contained in 'The Manual', which describes basic protections that are also to be found in the Customary International Humanitarian Law Study. These are a series of rules that reflect long-standing customary law since the inclusions of the Martens Clause in the Hague Conventions which specified that the laws of war were to be subject to the laws of humanity and the requirements of public conscience.[31] 'The Manual' sets out:

1.2.3 Unnecessary Suffering
Using means or methods of combat that are of a nature to cause superfluous injury or unnecessary suffering to fighters is forbidden.[32]

2.2.1 General principles
Weapons and the use thereof must comply with the principles of distinction and unnecessary suffering.

2.2.1.1 Indiscriminate weapons
Weapons that are indiscriminate by nature are forbidden. An indiscriminate weapon is one incapable of being specifically directed against fighters or military objectives or which has effects on civilians and civilian objects that are uncontrollable.

2.2.1.2 Indiscriminate use of weapons
Using weapons indiscriminately is forbidden.

2.2.1.3 Unnecessary suffering
Using weapons of a nature to cause unnecessary suffering or superfluous injury to fighters is forbidden.

The customary nature of these rules was confirmed in the *Tadić* case where the International Criminal Tribunal for the Former Yugoslavia Appellate Chamber stated:

Elementary considerations of humanity and common sense make it preposterous that the use by States of weapons prohibited in armed conflict between themselves be allowed when States try to put down rebellion by their own nationals on their own territory. What is inhumane and consequently proscribed in international wars, cannot be inhumane and inadmissible in civil strife.[33]

'The Manual' goes on to outline these prohibited weapons including: poison and poisoned weapons; biological and bacteriological weapons; gas, and other chemical weapons, including riot control agents when such agents are used as a method of warfare; exploding anti-personnel bullets; weapons that mainly injure by fragments which escape detection by X-rays; and laser weapons designed to cause permanent blindness:[34] all of which are argued to have customary status when it comes to non-international armed conflict. This is confirmed in the Customary International Humanitarian Law Study.[35]

There are also specific protections given, and duties specified, for means and methods of combat including:

2.3 Methods of combat

2.3.1 No quarter
It is forbidden to order that there shall be no survivors, to threaten an adversary therewith, or to conduct hostilities on this basis.

2.3.2 Surrender
Killing or wounding fighters who have effectively indicated their wish to surrender or are defenceless is forbidden. Fighters lose this protection if they subsequently engage in any hostile action.

2.3.3 Flag of truce
Attacking fighters who are displaying a white flag is forbidden, provided those displaying it have ceased all hostile action.

2.3.4 Improper use of protected distinctive emblems or neutral military emblems, insignia, flags or uniforms
It is prohibited to make improper use of protected distinctive emblems or neutral military emblems, insignia, flags, or uniforms, including those of the United Nations.

2.3.5 Improper use of enemy military emblems, insignia, flags or uniforms
It is prohibited to make use of enemy military emblems, insignia, flags, or uniforms during combat.

2.3.6 Perfidy
Displaying the white flag falsely, or pretending to surrender, be wounded, or otherwise have a protected status is forbidden if the intent in doing so is to kill or wound an adversary.

2.3.7 Location of military objectives
Whenever feasible, military objectives must not be located within or near densely populated areas.

2.3.8 Human shields
The use of civilians (as well as captured enemy personnel) to shield a military objective or operation is forbidden. It is also forbidden to use them to obstruct an adversary's operations.

2.3.9 Terrorising civilians

Acts or threats of violence intended primarily to spread terror among civilians are forbidden, even if this is done for military purposes.

2.3.10 Starvation of civilians

Deliberate starvation of civilians as a method of warfare is forbidden.[36]

As a result of the customary status of many of the protections and obligations applicable to combatants in international armed conflict, they are also applicable to fighters in non-international armed conflict.[37] However, in spite of all of the developments in customary international law rules that specifically apply in non-international armed conflict, there is one area where there is a clear distinction of status and that is when a combatant or fighter is captured by the enemy. Regrettably, there are two entirely separate regimes, one international and one largely domestic. It is to this complex issue we now turn.

4.2 Detention issues

The issue of the rights of fighters or combatants deprived of their liberties is very relevant to the status of the PKK in Turkish custody and the Turkish army soldiers in custody of the PKK. It is within detention that it is alleged that many of the violations of humanitarian law and human rights occur on the part of both sides of this conflict. Although within non-international armed conflict this engages the previous discussion on Common Article 3, there is also an important overlap with the law concerning the international protection of human rights. It is important first to examine the extensive treaty protections offered to detainees in international armed conflict before turning to the thorny issue of internal armed conflict.

4.2.1 Detainees in international armed conflict

Unless the conflict is classified as an international armed conflict, prisoner of war status is not available to combatants. In our previous discussion we saw that there could be an argument for an international armed conflict either based on a war of national liberation or belligerency. In those cases the PKK fighters and the Turkish army are entitled to prisoner of war status. This makes the assumption that they meet the criteria established within the Prisoner of War Convention on combatants as: being commanded by a person responsible for his subordinates; having a fixed distinctive sign recognisable at a distance; carrying arms openly; and conducting their operations in accordance with the laws and customs of war. Once this is established, detailed provisions of the Geneva Prisoner of War Convention are applicable. Prisoners of war are entitled to many protections including appropriate health care, nutrition and payment for work performed. They also have important guarantees of fair trial, including due process for hearings to determine their combatant status and for disciplinary offences.[38]

Prisoners of war also have the important services of the ICRC, which makes sure families are notified as to the whereabouts of their loved ones, correspondence is respected, aid parcels are delivered and prisoner of war camps are inspected so that conditions of detention are monitored. It also maintains an international database of those persons who are in prisoner of war camps so that there is no issue of accounting for persons captured by the enemy. These types of arrangements are obligatory in international armed conflict.

Although Article 118 of Geneva Convention III indicates that Prisoners of War shall be released and repatriated without delay after the cessation of active hostilities,[39] an important limitation exists as prisoner of war status can be of unlimited duration as release depends on cessation of hostilities. There have historically been prisoner exchanges before the end of hostilities but this is not legally obligatory. Therefore, in practice, prisoners of war can be incarcerated without any type of parole for long periods of time. Civil wars can be of long-standing duration. However, this distinction might not be that significant as the fact of participating in rebellion in domestic law can often lead to charges of sedition, treason, murder or kidnapping with imposition of life sentences and in certain circumstances death.[40]

None of these arrangements is currently in place in the southeast Turkey/ northern Iraq conflict. There is a voluntary presence of the ICRC, but there are no prisoner of war camps set up on either side. The difficulty is that if this conflict is a non-international armed conflict, compliance with any of these obligations is strictly voluntary. The PKK has indicated in a critical statement to the Swiss government that it intends to accord prisoner of war status to Turkish security forces, although there is no indication of separate prisoner of war facilities.[41]

4.2.2 Detainees in non-international armed conflict

Rogers argues that in a non-international armed conflict in the absence of recognition or agreement, members of armed opposition groups are simply subject to the domestic law of the state concerned and answerable for any violations of the law that they may have committed.[42] Any claim that they are combatants legitimately engaged in an armed conflict provides no defence to a domestic law unless an amnesty is granted. This also applied to members of the armed forces of the state who also have no claim to prisoner-of-war status unless there is an agreement or the status of belligerency is recognised.[43] However, in spite of the fact that Geneva Convention III Relative to the Treatment of Prisoners of War is not applicable to non-international armed conflict, there are humanitarian law and human rights guarantees for detainees. Chapter 6 analyses whether the label of 'terrorist' might alter in any way legal guarantees for detainees. Despite the label of 'fighter' or 'terrorist', detainees in a civil war, although subject to their state's domestic legal system, are also entitled to the minimum humanitarian guarantees in Common Article 3 of the Geneva Conventions. There is also strong opinion that Article 75 of Additional Protocol I, with its more extensive guarantees, has customary status in non-international armed conflict.[44] We have discussed these guarantees with respect to Common Article 3 but there are more extensive due process guarantees included in this article. The part of Article 75 on rights in detention is so fundamental that it is set out in full:

3. Any person arrested, detained or interned for actions related to the armed conflict shall be informed promptly, in a language he understands, of the reasons why these measures have been taken. Except in cases of arrest or detention for penal offences, such persons shall be released with the minimum delay possible and in any event as soon as the circumstances justifying the arrest, detention or internment have ceased to exist.

4. No sentence may be passed and no penalty may be executed on a person found guilty of a penal offence related to the armed conflict except pursuant to a conviction pronounced by an impartial and regularly constituted court respecting the generally recognized principles of regular judicial procedure, which include the following:

    (a) The procedure shall provide for an accused to be informed without delay of the particulars of the offence alleged against him and shall afford the accused before and during his trial all necessary rights and means of defence;

    (b) No one shall be convicted of an offence except on the basis of individual penal responsibility;

    (c) No one shall be accused or convicted of a criminal offence on account of any act or omission which did not constitute a criminal offence under the national or international law to which he was subject at the time when it was committed; nor shall a heavier penalty be imposed than that which was applicable at the time when the criminal offence was committed; if, after the commission of the offence, provision is made by law for the imposition of a lighter penalty, the offender shall benefit thereby;

    (d) Anyone charged with an offence is presumed innocent until proved guilt according to law;

    (e) Anyone charged with an offence shall have the right to be tried in his presence;

    (f) No one shall be compelled to testify against himself or to confess guilt;

    (g) Anyone charged with an offence shall have the right to examine, or have examined, the witnesses against him and to obtain the attendance and examination of witnesses on his behalf under the same conditions as witnesses against him;

    (h) No one shall be prosecuted or punished by the same Party for an offence in respect of which a final judgement acquitting or convicting that person has been previously pronounced under the same law and judicial procedure;

(i)   Anyone prosecuted for an offence shall have the right to have the judgement pronounced publicly; and

(ii) A convicted person shall be advised on conviction of his judicial and other remedies and of the time-limits within which they may be exercised.

5.   Women whose liberty has been restricted for reasons related to the armed conflict shall be held in quarters separated from men's quarters. They shall be under the immediate supervision of women. Nevertheless, in cases where families are detained or interned, they shall, whenever possible, be held in the same place and accommodated as family units.

6.   Persons who are arrested, detained or interned for reasons related to the armed conflict shall enjoy the protection provided by this Article until their final release, repatriation or re-establishment, even after the end of the armed conflict.

7.   In order to avoid any doubt concerning the prosecution and trial of persons accused of war crimes or crimes against humanity, the following principles shall apply:

(a) Persons who are accused of such crimes should be submitted for the purpose of prosecution and trial in accordance with the applicable rules of international law; and

(b) Any such persons who do not benefit from more favourable treatment under the Conventions or this Protocol shall be accorded the treatment provided by this Article, whether or not the crimes of which they are accused constitute grave breaches of the Conventions or of this Protocol.[45]

It is evident that these provisions bear a strong resemblance to human rights due process, detention and fair trial guarantees, which are discussed in Chapter 2.

The Customary International Humanitarian Law Study contains Part V on the Treatment of Civilians and Persons Hors de Combat. In Chapter 32, it adduces strong evidence that Article 75 of Additional Protocol I is of customary status in non-international armed conflict. Indeed, the study states that the 'fundamental guarantees listed in this chapter all have firm basis in international humanitarian law applicable in both international and non-international armed conflict'.[46] There is no question that the fundamental guarantees are based both in international humanitarian law and international human rights law, particularly the Universal Declaration of Human Rights and the International Covenant of Civil and Political Rights. As the study states, 'international humanitarian law and human rights law reinforce each other, not only to reaffirm rules applicable in times of armed conflict, but in all situations'.[47]

The specific rules of customary international humanitarian law concerning apprehension, investigation and detention regarding of the status of the individual[48] are as follows:

Rule 89
Murder is prohibited.

Rule 90
Torture, cruel or inhuman treatment and outrages upon personal dignity, in particular humiliating and degrading treatment, are prohibited.

Rule 91
Corporal punishment is prohibited.

Rule 92
Mutilation, medical or scientific experiments or any other medical procedure not indicated by the state of health of the person concerned and not consistent with generally accepted medical standards are prohibited.

Rule 93
Rape and other forms of sexual violence are prohibited.

Rule 94
Slavery and the slave trade in all their forms are prohibited.

Rule 95
Uncompensated or abusive forced labour is prohibited.

Rule 96
The taking of hostages is prohibited.

Rule 97
The use of human shields is prohibited.

Rule 98
Enforced disappearance is prohibited.

Rule 99
Arbitrary deprivation of liberty is prohibited.

Rule 100
No one may be convicted or sentenced, except pursuant to a fair trial affording all essential judicial guarantees.

Rule 101
No one may be accused or convicted of a criminal offence on account of any act or omission which did not constitute a criminal offence under

national or international law at the time it was committed; nor may a heavier penalty be imposed than that which was applicable at the time the criminal offence was committed.

Rule 102
No one may be convicted of an offence except on the basis of individual criminal responsibility.

Rule 103
Collective punishments are prohibited.

Rule 104
The convictions and religious practices of civilians and persons *hors de combat* must be respected.

Rule 105
Family life must be respected as far as possible.[49]

These rules are much more extensive than the one paragraph on detention included in Common Article 3 which states:

(d) the passing of sentences and the carrying out of executions without previous judgment pronounced by a regularly constituted court affording all the judicial guarantees which are recognized as indispensable by civilized peoples.

These rules also include the due process guarantees contained in Article 75 of Additional Protocol I.

Francoise Hampson, in her chapter in *Perspectives on the ICRC Study on Customary International Humanitarian Law* (*Perspectives*), discusses the significance of these rules applicable to the treatment of detainees.[50] Arguing that international humanitarian law is virtually silent as to the grounds of detention in non-international armed conflict, she proposes that the evidence cited with regard to state practice in regard to non-international armed conflicts may establish that unlawful/illegal detention is prohibited in non-international armed conflict, but cautions that the practice does indicate what constitutes unlawful detention. It is left to states to determine what constitutes arbitrary detention in non-international armed conflict.[51] However, human rights bodies have developed a body of case law on what constitutes arbitrary detention and the Human Rights Committee issued an influential General Comment on derogations from human rights obligations in states of emergency which indicate that although some of the guarantees are derogable, the prohibition against arbitrary detention has a non-derogable core, notably with regard to *habeas corpus*.[52]

In addition to the guarantee against arbitrary detention, there are important procedural guarantees in the rules confirming the customary status of those guarantees in Article 75. Hampson accepts that these rules including 'the right to be told why one is being detained and, most importantly, the right promptly to challenge the lawfulness of detention' also exist in non-international armed conflict, even if the state practice is limited in non-international armed conflict.[53]

In addition, there are the due process guarantees which were also included in Common Article 3. Although, once again, these can be argued to be customary in non-international armed conflict, Hampson cannot resist commenting that few states afford such guarantees even in peacetime. Another difficulty is that non-state armed groups must also comply with these guarantees and it would be difficult to have a lawfully constituted court unless there is a type of break-away republic.[54] The specificity of the fair trial provisions mean that a person must be tried for existing offences with full due process guarantees.

The fundamental guarantees with their customary status impose on Turkey and the PKK extensive obligations on the treatment of detainees. In addition to these fundamental guarantees there are also arguably customary rules applicable in non-international armed conflict concerning the actual practical arrangements for persons deprived of their liberty. Once again these are set out in the ICRC Customary International Law Study:

> Rule 118
> Persons deprived of their liberty must be provided with adequate food, water, clothing, shelter and medical attention.

> Rule 119
> Women who are deprived of their liberty must be held in quarters separate from those of men except where families are accommodated as family units, and must be under the immediate supervision of women.

> Rule 120
> Children who are deprived of their liberty must be held in quarters separate from those of adults, except where families are accommodated as family units.

> Rule 121
> Persons deprived of their liberty must be held in premises which are removed from the combat zone and which safeguard their health and hygiene.

> Rule 122
> Pillage of the personal belongings of persons deprived of their liberty is prohibited.

> Rule 123
> The personal details of persons deprived of their liberty must be recorded.

Rule 124

In international armed conflicts, the ICRC must be granted regular access to all persons deprived of their liberty in order to verify the conditions of their detention and to restore contacts between those persons and their families.

In non-international armed conflicts, the ICRC may offer its services to the parties to the conflict with a view to visiting all persons deprived of their liberty for reasons related to the conflict in order to verify the conditions of their detention and to restore contacts between those persons and their families.

Rule 125

Persons deprived of their liberty must be allowed to correspond with their families, subject to reasonable conditions relating to the frequency and the need for censorship by the authorities.

Rule 126

Civilian internees and persons deprived of their liberty in connection with a non-international armed conflict must be allowed to receive visitors, especially near relatives, to the degree practicable.

Rule 127

The personal convictions and religious practices of persons deprived of their liberty must be respected.

Rule 128

Prisoners of war must be released and repatriated without delay after the cessation of active hostilities.

Civilian internees must be released as soon as the reasons which necessitated internment no longer exist, but at the latest as soon as possible after the close of active hostilities.

Persons deprived of their liberty in relation to a non-international armed conflict must be released as soon as the reasons for the deprivation of their liberty cease to exist.

The persons referred to may continue to be deprived of their liberty if penal proceedings are pending against them or if they are serving a sentence lawfully imposed.

Agnieszka Jachec-Neale, in her chapter, Status and Treatment of Prisoners of War in *Perspectives*, only partly agrees with the study in confirming the customary status of some these rules in non-international armed conflict as she is generally critical of the lack of evidence of widespread state practice to support the applicability of these rules in a civil war.[55] In spite of the lack of evidence of state practice, these rules provide important evidence in themselves of what should be the standards in non-international armed conflict. These rules could then provide the yardstick by which the detention of Öcalan and other PKK detainees should be measured and it seems clear that in many cases the conditions will not conform to these international customary obligations. As there is no process of humanitarian law determination of the conditions of detention within this conflict, the human rights cases considering this issue are extremely important.

4.2.3 Human rights of detainees suspected of being PKK members

As mentioned by Hampson, there is a body of human rights law that considered detention of participants in internal armed conflict, and indeed there are a number of European Court of Human Rights cases considering detention issues in the context of the conflict in southeast Turkey. These cases consider loss of life in detention, torture in detention and lack of due process guarantees including access to counsel to challenge detention.

The key case in the context of the conflict in southeast Turkey on rights of detainees who are suspected of being fighters is the case of *Öcalan*.[56] The applicant was accused of founding an armed gang (the PKK) in order to destroy the territorial integrity of the Turkish state and of instigating various terrorist acts that had resulted in loss of life.[57] He admitted being the leader of the PKK. Öcalan was arrested in Kenya in February 1999 and taken back to Turkey and detained on the island of İmralı. The Grand Chamber of the European Court of Human Rights determined that there were a number of violations of the European Convention on Human Rights by Turkey. The court held that there was a violation of Article 5(4) in that there was a lack of remedy by which the applicant could have the lawfulness of his detention in police custody decided[58] and also a violation of Article 5(3), given the failure to bring Öcalan before a judge promptly after his arrest as he was held for 7 days before being brought before a judge.[59] The Court agreed with the statement of the previous Court consideration that in spite of the contention that Öcalan was a terrorist the court could not 'accept that it was necessary for the applicant to be detained for seven days without being brought before a judge'.[60]

Turkey was also held to be in violation of fair trial rights as set out in Article 6(1) as Mr Öcalan had not been tried by an independent and impartial tribunal and was not afforded the right to adequate time and facilities for preparation of his defence or the right to legal assistance.[61] However, there is one ruling by the Court that may well be controversial for the purposes of this book. The Court assessed the fairness of the proceedings based on the fact that Öcalan was a civilian. The court stated:

> In its previous judgments, the Court attached importance to the fact that a civilian had to appear before a court composed, even if only in part, of members of the armed forces (see, among other authorities, *Incal*, cited above, p. 1573, § 72). Such a situation seriously affects the confidence the courts must inspire in a democratic society ... [62]

The European Court of Human Rights, in spite of the fact that it had extensive admitted evidence before it that there had been a military conflict since 1984, never considered the status of Öcalan as a combatant. Although these determinations were under human rights law, the specific findings of lack of due process and arbitrary detention were also violations of customary international humanitarian law as Öcalan as head of the PKK was a fighter in a non-international armed conflict. The fundamental guarantees in Common Article 3 and in customary international law (Rule 99) all provide that arbitrary deprivation of liberty is prohibited, Customary Rule 100 provides that no one may be convicted or sentenced, except pursuant to a fair trial affording all essential judicial guarantees. However, the status of fighter in non-international armed conflict provides no separate prisoner of war status, so that one must assume that the standards of treatment of civilians must apply. The consideration of conditions of detention was interesting. The Grand Chamber stated:

> Further, the Court considers that the applicant cannot be regarded as being kept in sensory isolation or cellular confinement. It is true that, as the sole inmate, his only contact is with prison staff. He has books, newspapers and a radio at his disposal. He does not have access to television programmes or a telephone. He does, however, communicate with the outside world by letter. He sees a doctor every day and his lawyers and members of his family once a week (his lawyers were allowed to see him twice a week during the trial). The difficulties in gaining access to İmralı Prison in adverse weather conditions appear to have been resolved, as the prison authorities were provided with a suitable craft at the end of 2004.[63]

These considerations of conditions of detention also comply with consideration of the customary guarantees as discussed in Rules 118 to 128.

Following on from these findings on the unfairness of the pre-trial and trial process, the Grand Chamber held that the imposition of the death penalty was a violation of Article 3 due to its imposition following these proceedings. The Court only considered the imposition as inhuman treatment (particularly as the applicant faced the possibility for 3 years) because the actual imposition of the sentence was not going to take place since Turkey abolished the death penalty before these final proceedings.[64] However, the Court, in spite of the pleas of Öcalan's counsel, did not consider that the detention on an island at İmralı Prison as constitutive of inhuman or degrading treatment within the meaning of Article 3.[65]

Many of the cases before the European Court of Human Rights dealing with the conflict in southeast Turkey concern the disappearance of persons while in Turkish custody. An early case was *Çiçek v Turkey* where a mother of Kurdish extraction brought a case against Turkey as a result of the disappearance of her two sons, and where the Court found a violation of the right to life set out in Article 2 of the European Convention on Human Rights as the two men had been taken into custody by Turkish security forces and never seen again.[66]

Another example of a case of loss of life in detention is *Yasin Ateş v Turkey*, decided in 2005, 10 years after the death of the applicant's son.[67] The applicant alleged that his son had been arrested in the morning of 13 June 1995 at the Lice-Kulp fork, and that he had subsequently been transferred to the Diyarbakır Security Directorate where he was handed over to the special teams who thereafter tortured and then executed him either in Diyarbakır or in the district of Lice. The government countered and stated that on 13 June 1995 the Diyarbakır Security Directorate received information to the effect that a small lorry would be carrying logistical equipment to PKK terrorists, and that the terrorists would meet with Kadri Ateş and others travelling in the lorry. Turkey argued that necessary security measures were taken and at about 7.35 pm the lorry was stopped at the Lice-Kulp fork and Kadri Ateş was questioned. He stated that he was going to deliver the equipment to the PKK terrorists at a location close to the Aksu petrol station near the Lice-Kulp fork at approximately 9 pm. Thereafter he was arrested in order to be taken to the meeting point. The others were taken to the Diyarbakır Security Directorate for questioning.

Upon reaching the meeting point, the government alleged that the necessary security measures were taken and at approximately 11.45 pm five PKK terrorists arrived to collect the equipment from Kadri Ateş. At that point the police asked the terrorists to surrender. However, instead of surrendering, the terrorists opened fire at the security forces and the firing continued for approximately half an hour. Kadri Ateş made an attempt to escape from the security forces but was shot and killed in the crossfire. Two terrorists were also shot and killed but the others managed to escape.

The Court held that the respondent state was liable for the death of the applicant's son in violation of Article 2 of the Convention. In the operative part of the ruling the Court stated:

5. This does not, however, mean that the respondent Government are absolved from their responsibility to account for Kadri Ateş' death, which occurred while he was under arrest. In this connection the Court reiterates that persons in custody are in a vulnerable position and that the authorities are under a duty to protect them. The Court has previously held that, where an individual is taken into police custody in good health and is found to be injured on release, it is incumbent on the State to provide a plausible explanation of how those injuries were caused (see, among other authorities, *Selmouni v. France* [GC], no. 25803/94, § 87, ECHR 1999-V). The obligation on the authorities to account for the treatment of an individual in custody is particularly stringent where that individual dies (see *Salman*, cited above, § 99) ...

6. Article 2, which safeguards the right to life and sets out the circumstances when deprivation of life may be justified, ranks as one of the most fundamental provisions in the Convention, of which no derogation is permitted. Together with Article 3, it also enshrines one of the basic values of the democratic societies making up the Council of Europe. The

circumstances in which deprivation of life may be justified must therefore be strictly construed. The object and purpose of the Convention as an instrument for the protection of individual human beings also requires that Article 2 be interpreted and applied so as to make its safeguards practical and effective (see *McCann and Others v. the United Kingdom*, judgment of 27 September 1995, Series A no. 324, pp. 45–46, paras. 146–47).

7. The text of Article 2, read as a whole, demonstrates that it covers not only intentional killing but also situations where it is permitted to 'use force' which may result, as an unintended outcome, in the deprivation of life. The deliberate or intended use of lethal force is only one factor, however, to be taken into account in assessing its necessity. Any use of force must be no more than 'absolutely necessary' for the achievement of one or more of the purposes set out in sub-paragraphs (a) to (c). This term indicates that a stricter and more compelling test of necessity must be employed from that normally applicable when determining whether State action is 'necessary in a democratic society' under paragraphs 2 of Articles 8 to 11 of the Convention. Consequently, the force used must be strictly proportionate to the achievement of the permitted aims (*ibid.*, p. 46, paras. 148–149).

8. In the light of the importance of the protection afforded by Article 2, the Court must subject deprivations of life to the most careful scrutiny, taking into consideration not only the actions of State agents but also all the surrounding circumstances. The use of force by State agents in pursuit of one of the aims delineated in paragraph 2 of Article 2 may be justified where it is based on an honest belief which is perceived, for good reasons, to be valid at the time but which subsequently turns out to be mistaken (*ibid.*, pp. 58–59, para. 200).

9. In the present case, the Court has already established that the Government have failed to account for the killing of Kadri Ateş (see paragraph 115 above). It follows that there has been a violation of Article 2 of the Convention in respect of his death.

The Court further held that there had been a violation of Article 5 (1) (the arbitrary detention provision) of the Convention. It determined that none of the necessary safeguards were observed during and after the arrest of the applicant's son, such a failure meaning that the act of deprivation of liberty was not amenable to independent judicial scrutiny to secure the accountability of the authorities. In the light of the failures and contradictions concerning the arrest of the applicant's son – which have already contributed to discrediting the government's attempt to account for the death of the applicant's son – the Court concluded that the applicant's son was deprived of his liberty in an arbitrary manner contrary to the aim and purpose of Article 5 of the Convention and it followed that there had been a violation of Article 5 (1) of the Convention.

A similar case of loss of life is the case of *Tanli v Turkey* decided in 2001.[68] Mahmut Tanli, the applicant's son and a suspected armed militia man in the

PKK, was arrested and in detention in police custody from 27 to 28 June 1994. The applicant had been informed on 29 June 1994 that his son had died of a heart attack while in custody but he suspected that his son had been tortured to death. The Court held that the government of Turkey was liable for the death of Mahmut Tanli in violation of Article 2 of the Convention. The Court in considering its ruling was influenced by the reports of eight visits of the European Committee for the Prevention of Torture reporting that 'resort to torture and other forms of severe ill-treatment remained a common occurrence in police establishments in Turkey'.[69] Once again the court asserted that '[t]he obligation on the authorities to account for the treatment of an individual in custody is particularly stringent when that individual dies'.[70] Therefore, the Court found that the government had not accounted for the death of Mahmut Tanli during his detention at a Turkish police station and that its responsibility for his death was engaged.[71]

The second group of cases are those where death does not result but there are serious allegations of torture of suspect PKK fighters. An example is the case of *Abdülsamet Yaman v Turkey* decided in 2004.[72] Yaman was detained in prison and he was the provincial leader of HADEP (People's Democracy Party) in Adana. When he was arrested on 3 July 1995 on suspicion of being connected with the PKK he was taken to the Adana Security Directorate. He alleged that he was blindfolded, stripped naked and immersed in cold water in the Security Directorate. He was attached by the arms to the ceiling pipes and made to stand on a chair. Electric cables were attached to his body, in particular to his sexual organs. The chair was then pulled away and he was left suspended while electric shocks were administered. From time to time the shocks were stopped and his testicles were squeezed. The Court largely agreed with his recounting of events and held that had been a violation of Article 3 of the Convention in regards to the nature and degree of the ill-treatment and to the strong inferences that can be drawn from the evidence that it was inflicted in order to obtain information from Abdülsamet Yaman about his suspected connection with the PKK, the Court finds that the ill-treatment involved very serious and cruel suffering that only be characterised as torture.

The Court also held that there had been a violation of Article 5 (3) of the Convention as the applicant's detention had lasted 9 days and reiterated that in the *Brogan and Others*[73] case it held that detention in police custody which had lasted 4 days and 6 hours without judicial control fell outside the strict constraints as to the time laid down by Article 5 (3) of the Convention, even though its purpose was to protect the community as a whole against terrorism. Even supposing that the activities of which the applicant stood accused were linked to a terrorist threat, the Court could not accept that it was necessary to detain him for 9 days without judicial intervention. This also led to a violation of Article 5 (4) as the Court considered that the period in question (9 days) sits ill with the notion of 'speedily' under Article 5 (4) of the Convention.

A similar case is the case of *Çelik and Imret v Turkey*, decided in October 2004.[74] The two applicants were accused in 1998 of acting as couriers for the PKK, and were arrested by police officers from the Batman Security Directorate. The applicants alleged that they were subjected to various types of torture and inhumane treatment during their detention in police custody. They claim they were blindfolded and immersed in high pressure cold water. They had to stand naked and electric shocks were administered to various parts of their bodies including their sexual organs. They state that their testicles were squeezed and that their hands and legs were tied. They were severely beaten and deprived of food and water and prevented from using toilet facilities. They were also kept in isolation, subjected to unbearable noises, insulted and threatened with death. From time to time, police officers applied medication to their injuries. The Court found with respect to Abdurrahman Çelik that there had been a violation of Article 3 of the Convention. The Court found that the respondent state was responsible under Article 3 of the Convention. As regards the other applicant, Kasım İmret, there has been no violation of Article 3 of the Convention. The Court found that Kasım İmret did not establish that there had been a violation of Article 3 of the Convention in respect of his allegation that he was subjected to ill treatment in police custody.

In one of the decisions the court was explicit about the responsibility on the detaining authorities. In the case of *Çolak and Filizer v Turkey*[75] the court considered two applicants who were arrested by the anti-terrorist branch of the Istanbul Security Directorate on suspicion of membership of an illegal organisation, the PKK, and placed in custody on 28 and 29 April 1995 respectively.

Both applicants alleged that they had been beaten and insulted by policemen on the way to the Security Directorate Building. The applicants alleged that during their interrogation by the police, they had been kept blindfolded and forced to give information about persons they did not know. They were allegedly subjected to various forms of ill treatment by police officers. They claimed they were beaten, strung up by the arms, threatened with death and given electric shocks. The Court held that there had been a violation of Article 3 of the Convention. The Court reiterated that a state is responsible for any person in detention who is in a vulnerable situation while in its charge, and that the authorities have a duty to protect such a person. Bearing in mind the state authorities' obligation to account for injuries caused to persons within their control in custody, the Court considered that the acquittal of the police officers suspected of inflicting ill treatment cannot absolve the state of its responsibility under the Convention.[76]

These cases stood for the proposition that there was a positive obligation on the state to protect detainees, even those suspected of being PKK fighters, from injury and that the state would have to explain any injuries that occurred. Both the cases of death in detention and torture have applicable customary humanitarian law guarantees (Rules 89, 90, 93 and 98). The similarity in the human rights provisions and customary humanitarian law means that these cases are very influential in determining violations of international humanitarian law which are classified as war crimes.

Conclusion

This chapter illustrates that for both fighters in a non-international armed conflict and combatants in international armed conflict, a full range of humanitarian protections apply due to their customary status. The rules for the conduct of hostilities are very similar with basic rules of humanity applying both types of conflict. It is these rules that the conduct of the conflict in southeast Turkey must be measured against and once again the conduct may be found wanting. Any international assessment must base its analysis on these customary rules in addition to the concurrently applicable human rights provisions.

Regrettably, when a fighter is captured the status of the conflict again becomes material. Although there are a full range of treaty protections for prisoners of war, the status of captured fighters is not so definitive. There are, however, extensive guarantees for detainees based on Article 75 of Additional Protocol I and human rights law. This chapter establishes that there are specific procedural guarantees to challenge the lawfulness of detention and then once detention has been lawfully constituted a number of rules of treatment of detainees. Detainees and prisoners of war in all non-international and international armed conflicts are entitled to these basic standards.

It is clear again from the history set out in Chapter 1 that neither Turkey nor the PKK has respected these customary rules towards each other's fighters that find themselves *hors de combat*. It is necessary for both parties to be aware of the customary and treaty rules in both international humanitarian and human rights law and to apply them to their conduct in this conflict. The body of case law from the European Court of Human Rights, the investigations of the European Committee on the Prevention of Torture, and human rights reports reveal that these basic and fundamental guarantees towards both civilians and combatants are not being respected.

5 The international law of armed conflict – *jus ad bellum*

Introduction

In considering the armed conflict in southeast Turkey between Kurdish armed groups and Turkish armed and security forces one cannot ignore issues surrounding the legality of the conflict itself, which in international law is known as the *jus ad bellum*. Two major armed conflict issues are canvassed in this chapter: the first is whether international law prohibits wars of secession – are non-state actors prohibited in international law from resorting to force to compel rights of self-determination or to defend themselves against major abuses of human rights? Furthermore, there is the related question of whether other states can assist these non-state actors in their efforts to secure a new political arrangement. The second issue is to assess the legality of the several Turkish incursions into northern Iraq, the most recent one in February 2008, to pursue those same fighters. This involves considering whether other states in this case Iraq and the United States can assist a sovereign state in its struggle against an insurgency.

Both of these important questions involve the same basic difficulty, the lack of development of *jus ad bellum* within internal armed conflict. The collective security system in the United Nations Charter was developed in order to prevent those international armed conflicts that had threatened peace and security in the 20th century. However, the reality is that in the decades since the end of the Second World War, by far the greater number of conflicts (often called insurgencies) have been those waged within a state, between the governmental authorities and a group that seeks to secure its own political arrangement. There are many examples including Ethiopia/Eritrea, Pakistan/Bangladesh, Yugoslavia/Kosovo, United Kingdom/Irish independence movement represented by the IRA, Nigeria/Biafra, Spain/Basque independence movement represented by ETA and Canada/Quebec independence movement represented by the FLQ. In later chapters we discuss issues of self-determination and terrorism in reference to internal secessionist movements but in this chapter we examine the narrower issues of lawfulness of resort to armed force by the independence movement and the use of force to be used against the independence movement. Finally, we introduce ideas of aggravated state responsibility to argue that regardless of the lawfulness of the use of force, such sustained and severe violence triggers the international responsibility of all states within the international community to respond to situations of non-international armed conflict, which involve violations of peremptory norms of public international law known as norms of *jus cogens*.

5.1 The right to use force in self-determination

On the one side of the conflict in southeast Turkey has been a long-standing armed rebellion by the Kurdish peoples against Turkish authorities, particularly embodied in the activities of the Kurdistan Workers Party (PKK). Saul in his influential work on terrorism argues that the existence of an international legal right to resist or rebel against tyranny or oppression is doubtful.[1] Gray argues that this issue is 'of reduced practical importance' and that 'there is no support for the right to use force to attain self-determination outside the context of decolonization or illegal occupation'.[2] Yet provocatively, she argues that when claims to secession, or even more limited autonomy, are met with forcible repression, as in the cases of Kosovo, the Chechens and the Kurds, the use of force against a people may strengthen its case for self-determination.[3] Yet in spite of these opinions, many groups seeking self-determination resort to armed conflict. Honoré disagrees with Gray and Saul's conclusions and defines a proposed right to rebel which would be:

> The right of an individual or group to resort to violence, if necessary on a large scale, in order either:
>
> (a) to secure on behalf of individuals or groups conceived as exploited or oppressed a change in the government, structure or policies of the society to which they belong (radical rebellion) or
> (b) to resist on behalf of individuals or groups who are attached to their way of life a change in the government, structure or policies of their society which the rulers of the society intend to bring about (conservative rebellion), or
> (c) to secure on behalf of a group conceived as distinct the right to independence from the society to which it at present belongs (rebellion in aid of self-determination).[4]

It is the third category, rebellion in self-determination which is the focus of analysis of this book. Even though many modern states such as the United States and the Republic of France were founded as a result of revolutions, in the modern era there are no treaty provisions that contain the right to rebel against oppressive regimes.[5]

The major international treaty concerning *jus ad bellum* is the United Nations Charter drafted to save succeeding generations from the scourge of war. The prohibition on the use of force is contained in Article 2(4) which states:

> All Members shall refrain in their international relations from the threat or use of force against the territorial integrity or political independence

of any state, or in any other manner inconsistent with the Purposes of the
United Nations.

As Gray argues, Article 2(4) was drafted in response to the Second World War
and was directed towards prohibiting inter-state conflicts. Internal armed conflicts
were seen initially as domestic matters unless they posed a threat to international
peace and security as delineated under Chapter VII of the United Nations
Charter.[6] Therefore, the legal rules with respect to forcible intervention in
civil conflicts have been developed through widespread acceptance of a series of
UN General Assembly Resolutions drafted in response to the reality of internal
armed conflict since the Second World War.[7]

The question for further discussion is: Given the absence of international
instruments is there is an arguable customary right to rebel? Grotius often named
as the 'father of public international law', argued that the people have a right to
make war against rulers who derive their sovereign authority from the people and
then transgress against the law and the state.[8] He also maintained that people
have a right of self-defence if a ruler used 'atrocious cruelty'.[9] Later the famous
philosopher John Locke also formulated a right to rebel. He perceived an
individual has having rights in a state of nature which were to be retained in the
formation of a state based on a social contract. However, when these rights
are infringed such as the denial of property, a right to rebel existed.[10] Vattel
writing a century later also argued a right to rebel within international law and
discussed the involvement of other states. He stated:

> If a prince, by violating the fundamental laws, gives his subjects a lawful
> cause for resisting him; if by his insupportable tyranny, he brings on a
> national revolt against him, any foreign power may rightfully give assistance
> to an oppressed people who ask for its aid ... when such dissension reaches
> the state of civil war, foreign Nations may assist one of the two parties
> which seems to have justice on its side. But to assist a detestable tyrant, or to
> come out in favour of an unjust and rebellious people, would certainly be a
> violation of duty.[11]

This assertion of a right to rebel against a tyrannical regime inspired the
American Declaration of Independence (1776), the French Declaration of the
Rights of Man and Citizen (1789 and 1793), and the revolutions that followed
in those countries. In recent literature, Cutler argues that the principle of the
right of any people to rebel by force against a tyrannical regime has achieved
'world-wide acceptance'.[12] In the modern era this view is certainly not the view
of the majority of states as rebellion is often criminalised as treasonous or as
terrorism. Within international law the view of a right to rebel against tyranny
seems to be out of fashion as it harkens back to an era of just wars within
a natural law framework, first developed by Grotius.[13] Nevertheless, this
debate has continued into the modern era, particularly in light of the post-war
de-colonisation movement.

An avenue of exploration to assess the views of states in this debate is to view the numerous declarations in the UN General Assembly concerning self-determination and the use of force, some of which may have developed into statements of customary international law.[14] First, the Universal Declaration of Human Rights of 1948 contains a preamble that alludes to the possibility of the use of force as a last resort for an oppressed people. The preamble states:

> Whereas it is essential, if man is not to be compelled to have recourse, as a last resort, to rebellion against tyranny and oppression, that human rights should be protected by the rule of law.

Most of the rights in the Universal Declaration of Human Rights have been declared to be customary but this would not extend to this preamble.[15] Yet the wording of the preamble implies that if human rights are not protected by the rule of law, the possibility of a rebellion exists. This does not mean that this statement supports the lawfulness within an international law framework.

An early declaration directed towards prohibiting other states from assisting in rebellion was UN General Assembly Resolution 375 (IV) (1949) on the Rights and Duties of States. Article 3 specified that every state has the duties to refrain from intervention in the internal or external affairs of any other state. Article 4 stated that every state had the duty to refrain from fomenting civil strife in the territory of another state and to prevent the organisation within its territory of activities calculated to foment civil strife.[16] These provisions seem to be directed at other states and seems to accord with Resolution 2131 (1965) on the Declaration on the Inadmissibility of Intervention in the Domestic Affairs of States and the Protection of Their Independence and Sovereignty, which states in Article 1:

> No State has the right to intervene, directly or indirectly, for any reason whatever, in the internal or external affairs of any other State. Consequently, armed intervention and all other forms of interference or attempted threats against the personality of the State or against its political, economic and cultural elements, are condemned.[17]

It was the third and one of the most important of these resolutions, the Declaration of Principles of International Law, Friendly Relations and Co-operation among States in Accordance with the Charter of the United Nations, passed in the UN General Assembly in 1970, that directly addressed the issue of rebellion.[18] The preamble of the declaration asserted that the subjection of peoples to alien subjugation, domination and exploitation constituted a major obstacle to the promotion of international peace and security. It also argued that the principle of equal rights and self-determination of peoples constituted a significant contribution to contemporary international law, and that its effective application was of paramount importance for the promotion of friendly relations among states, based on respect for the principle of sovereign equality.

The operative sections of the declaration dealt with the issue of resort to force and self-determination and stated:

> Every State has the duty to refrain from any forcible action which deprives peoples referred to above in the elaboration of the present principle of their right to self-determination and freedom and independence. In their actions against, and resistance to, such forcible action in pursuit of the exercise of their right to self-determination, such peoples are entitled to seek and to receive support in accordance with the purposes and principles of the Charter.[19]

At first glance this part of the resolution seems to authorise groups seeking self-determination to resort to force and indeed to receive assistance very much in accordance with the view of Vattel. Yet a careful review of the statement reveals that the force is only permitted 'against, and resistance to' forcible action. This would seem to be a right of self-defence which could arguably exist within the domestic system. Furthermore, within the declaration is an important limitation which protects states that are providing within their territory the right of self-determination:

> Nothing in the foregoing paragraphs shall be construed as authorizing or encouraging any action which would dismember or impair, totally or in part, the territorial integrity or political unity of sovereign and independent States conducting themselves in compliance with the principle of equal rights and self-determination of peoples as described above and thus possessed of a government representing the whole people belonging to the territory without distinction as to race, creed or colour. Every State shall refrain from any action aimed at the partial or total disruption of the national unity and territorial integrity of any other State or country.[20]

This statement may leave open movements in self-determination against a state that is not fulfilling the basic obligations and attempting to exercise force against the movements. It seems from the Declaration that only those states that fulfil their obligations to provide equal rights and self-determination are spared from dismemberment of their territorial integrity or political independence. Although the International Court of Justice has confirmed on two occasions that the prohibition in the Declaration on every state from refraining from organising, instigating, assisting or participating in acts of civil strife or terrorist acts in another state is declaratory of customary international law, the Declaration as a whole has not been confirmed to be customary.[21] It should also be noted that nowhere within the extensive provisions on self-determination is there a provision that these rights are limited to peoples under colonial domination, yet the context of the drafting of the Declaration was still within the decolonisation period.

  Both of the International Covenants on Human Rights (the ICCPR and the ICESCR) have a provision on self-determination, their common article 1 states that 'all peoples have the right of self-determination. By virtue of that right they freely determine their political status and freely pursue their economic, social and cultural development'.[22] Once again this right is not limited to those under colonial domination but there is also no definition of what constitutes a people. In this context self-determination is a human right, as is discussed in Chapter 8, and consequences for violation of this right are left to the methods of enforcement for human rights violations as set out in Optional Protocol I to the ICCPR, not as an authorisation for the use of force.

Generally, this debate within international law concentrates on the issue of whether another nation has the right to intervene in this type of rebellion and not on the legality of the rebellion itself as that is seen generally as a domestic matter. However, one might extrapolate some academic support for such a right in an article by Reisman when he proposes a framework of a minimum order in a precarious international system where the collective security system is not functioning as it should. He argues that one of the fundamental principles of political legitimacy in contemporary international politics is the ongoing right of peoples to determine their own political destinies.[23] Reisman's view can be supported as two of the purposes of the United Nations are 'equal rights and self-determination of peoples' and 'respect for human rights and for fundamental freedoms' and thus a war in rebellion could be to ensure those purposes.[24] An important precedent that can serve as an example of the emergence of customary international law is the widespread support for the Palestinian people resisting Israeli domination.[25] Quigley contends that the West Bank and the Gaza Strip were part of historic Palestine, which was colonised by the Ottoman Empire in the 16th century and ruled by Great Britain under a League of Nations mandate after the First World War. After the British withdrawal in 1948 the people of Palestine had a right to self-determination. The occupation of Israel did not eradicate the Palestinian right to self-determination.[26] Quigley asserts provocatively that as the Israelis refuse to withdraw voluntarily from these areas, the Palestinians 'are entitled to use force against Israel to secure its withdrawal'.[27] This argument is supported by a resolution of the UN Human Rights Commission, which declared that the force used by the Palestinians in the 1988 uprising was lawful force and that there was a 'right of the Palestinian people to regain their rights by all means in accordance with the purposes and principles of the Charter of the United Nations' and that 'the uprising of the Palestinian people against the Israeli occupation since 8 December 1987 is a form of legitimate resistance, an expression of their rejection of occupation'.[28] The type of force used would still be regulated by international humanitarian law (see earlier chapters), which constrains the ways in which the Palestinians can resist their occupiers (which does not include the use of suicide bombers nor systematic attacks against civilian population).[29]

The right to resist with violence is not universally accepted. Lippman asserts that the means of resistance must be proportionate to the gravity of the human rights that are being violated and that violent resistance must only be used as a last resort in response to situations such as colonialism, genocide and apartheid.[30] Hannum outlines the grievances of the Kurdish people that may well rise to this situation of desperation. He states that '[t]he consistent policy of the state of Turkey from its inception has been the destruction of the Kurdish culture and the forced assimilation of Kurds into a purely Turkish society'.[31]

The vigorous debate concerning the contested concept of humanitarian intervention uses just such a framework of analysis, the most serious violations of human rights within a sovereign state being grounds for armed force being used by other nations in order to preserve and protect human life. The debate however, is whether this is a ground of intervention for any state to act unilaterally or whether it must wait for a UN Security Council authorised collective security action such as Somalia. However, a comprehensive study of the phenomenon reveals that humanitarian intervention as a unilateral use of force is not accepted in customary international law but on the other hand sovereignty is not a defence against a United Nations robust peacekeeping operation such as those currently underway in Darfur and the Democratic Republic of Congo.[32] Such a detailed study should be carried out with respect to the lawfulness of the rebellion itself. It may well be argued that in a situation of colonialism the resort to force is lawful based on the Declaration of Friendly Relations but this may not extend to non-colonial rebellions. The Kurds may well have been colonised in the distant past but they were left out of the decolonisation process and now seek to separate from a sovereign state – Turkey – that is no longer a colonial power as the Ottoman Empire is long gone. Therefore, other venues of legality must be examined.

There is another analysis that argues that wars of national liberation, even though they occur within the sovereign territory of a state, are international armed conflicts. This would mean they are a concern to the international community as a whole and would trigger the operation of the collective security system as being a threat to international peace and security pursuant to Article 39.[33] This is a very controversial opinion and not accepted by academic opinion generally. Yet it is supported in Article 1(4) of the first Additional Protocol to the 1949 Geneva Conventions clearly states that wars of national liberation are international armed conflicts. The provision states:

> 4. The situations referred to in the preceding paragraph include armed conflicts in which peoples are fighting against colonial domination and alien occupation and against racist regimes in the exercise of their right of self-determination, as enshrined in the Charter of the United Nations and the Declaration on Principles of International Law concerning Friendly Relations and Co-operation among States in accordance with the Charter of the United Nations.[34]

However, this treaty has not received universal ratification and it is not directed towards the lawfulness of any such conflict rather to the *jus in bello* that applies to the conflict itself as discussed in Chapters 2, 3 and 4.

Nevertheless, if wars of national liberation are indeed international armed conflicts the national liberation group would be bound by the prohibition on the use of force in Article 2(4) and the only accepted exception to the prohibition would be the right of self-defence as set out in Article 51 of the Charter According to Gorelick the groups seeking national liberation against colonialism used self-defence as justification for their actions.[35] As the threshold for applicability of self-defence was an armed attack, there were lengthy debates as to whether colonialism in itself was some sort of armed attack justifying national liberations groups using violence to secure their freedom but that debate was never resolved and opposed in principal by many Western states particularly in the debates surrounding the Indian intervention in Goa in 1962.[36] Notwithstanding this lack of consensus on self-defence, there the Declaration on Aggression in its Article 7 confirmed the right to self-defence, if and only if force is used against colonial peoples. It states:

> Nothing in this Definition, and in particular article 3, could in any way prejudice the right to self-determination, freedom and independence, as derived from the Charter, of peoples forcibly deprived of that right and referred to in the Declaration on Principles of International Law concerning Friendly Relations and Cooperation among States in accordance with the Charter of the United Nations, particularly peoples under colonial and racist regimes or other forms of alien domination: nor the right of these peoples to struggle to that end and to seek and receive support, in accordance with the principles of the Charter and in conformity with the above-mentioned Declaration.[37]

That does not completely answer the question as consideration must be given to the right to rebel even if force is not used against a group. Controversially, Honoré argues that in certain circumstances there is a right to rebellion based on peremptory notions of human dignity, autonomy and co-operative morality.[38] If so, then it has to be a customary right as Saul is correct about the absence of an international instrument. Honoré provocatively asserts that when there is a fundamental and sustained breach by a state of its obligations, the subject has the right to treat the bond between himself and the state dissolved and therefore may lawfully resort to force to defend himself against the state and its officials.[39] Although philosophically this might indeed be a compelling argument there seems to be no international law justification, for such plea might be a political position not a legal right.[40]

Although written in 1979, Gorelick perceptively concluded that the state of the law with respect to wars of national liberation was unclear. He stated:

> It might be concluded that while all States have acknowledged the existence of self-determination, the question of the means to that end is still a bone of contention. While the Afro-Asian and Socialist States have argued in favor of an unrestricted right to revolt in the case of wars of national liberation, this idea has found little support among the Western States.[41]

There is no question that violent acts have been perpetrated against Kurdish peoples, and they have responded in return with violence and rebellion, but the question remains as to whether they are a colonial people as only colonial peoples may have an unrestricted right of self-defence against their colonisers who are trying to repel their movements by force. The Ottoman Empire did not strictly speaking colonise the area and even though the new Turkish state was supposed to grant independence to the Kurdish people according to the Treaty of Sèvres, after the rise of the Turkish state as is outlined in Chapter 1, the Treaty of Lausanne specified that the Turkish government has the right to control the territory in which the Kurds reside. The Kurds have not recently had their right to self-determination confirmed in the same fashion as the Palestinians. Nevertheless, an analysis of the way in which the Turkish regime has denied self-determination and perpetuated violence against the Turkish people might provide justification for self-defence. But that does not confirm a lawful right of rebellion in international law for non-colonial peoples and the lawfulness of the violence of the PKK in response is very much an open question. If one takes a traditional view of international law as primarily regulating the conduct of states, the question of whether a people have a right to rebel might well be a domestic legal issue, only resolved after a successful rebellion or an internal amnesty process following a peace process, such as the situation in Northern Ireland. The international law question as reflected in the various UN General Assembly Resolutions is whether other sovereign states may become involved in the insurgency rather than the lawfulness of the insurgency itself. In Chapter 8 this discussion continues in an examination of whether there is a right to external self-determination meaning secession from an existing state. The only element of certainty in this discussion is that it seems that is not in accordance with international law for other nations to assist non-state actors in rebellion, this is settled within international jurisprudence and UN General Assembly Resolutions.

However, in the history of liberation movements, particularly during the Cold War, there was assistance given in arms, training and strategy by other powers, particularly the Cold War superpowers, the United States and Russia, in a series of civil wars around the world. Gray used Angola as an example of a civil war that was 'fuelled by outside intervention; states divided on Cold War lines'.[42] Consideration of this issue was the basis of the *Nicaragua* decision. The International Court of Justice supported the Declaration on Friendly Relations on the duty 'not to organise civil strife in another state in support of an opposition party'.[43] The international system is based on respect for sovereign states and to interfere in a civil war is the ultimate violation of that sovereignty. The only possible exception is a declaration of the UN Security Council that such rebellions are threats to international peace and security which has been done only within the context of grievous violations of human rights in cases such as Somalia, Iraq, Darfur and the former Yugoslavia. However, in these situations there are often allegations of genocide, crimes against humanity, grievous war crimes or ethnic cleansing which would justify a UN Security Council resolution and indeed there are often mass refugee movements into other states. In those circumstances, assistance from other states would be lawful with the umbrella of UN Security Council authority.[44] The other side of the coin within this discussion is whether a state might assist another state in quelling such a rebellion and in this case the law is not as clear and this issue is engaged when one considers the various Turkish incursions into northern Iraq.

5.2 The *jus ad bellum* – Turkey in northern Iraq[45]

The second issue is the response by the Turkish forces to this rebellion. There is no question that within a sovereign territory armed and security forces can attempt to quell a rebellion and unless there are sustained violations of human rights law and international humanitarian law (see Chapters 2, 3 and 4) it seems settled that international law has no role in the conflict. However, when a conflict spills over into another sovereign state either by refugee crises or armed conflict, the international community and international law takes precedence. This section applies the facts of the continuing incursions by the Turkish armed and security forces into northern Iraq to the prohibition on the use of force in international law.

5.2.1 The United Nations Charter

There is no doubt that PKK fighters have sought shelter and mounted military operations from the mountains in northern Iraq. On several occasions Turkish armed and security forces have entered into northern Iraqi territory in order to engage in combat with the PKK, as is discussed in detail in Chapter 1. What is rather astonishing is that the several raids by a large group of Turkish armed forces into northern Iraq have attracted very little attention from the experts in armed conflict. As discussed earlier, in 1995, 35,000 Turkish troops were sent into the Kurdistan province of Iraq. Another major incursion occurred in May 1997 when Turkish troops backed by tanks and artillery crossed the border into Iraq with forces numbering some 50,000 soldiers and 250 tanks. The most recent cross-border activity took place on 21 February 2008 with a large number of troops (estimates of between 3,000 to 10,000 troops) supported by aircraft and artillery entered Iraqi territory, this activity following shelling and air strikes across the border, as is outlined in Chapter 1.[46]

In this most recent incursion there was a definitive Iraqi reaction. Reuters reported on 22 February 2008 that Iraq's government protested the invasion and urged Turkey to respect its sovereignty and to avoid any military action which would threaten security and stability. Iraqi Foreign Minister Hoshiyar Zebari summoned the *chargé d'affaires* from the Turkish embassy in Baghdad to protest the incursion.[47] The Turkish ground troops came face to face with Kurdish security forces on the border and these forces blocked the advance of some Turkish troops without any confrontation. However, tensions between the two forces escalated when Turkish tanks in a base just inside northern Iraq tried to leave the compound. They were stopped by Kurdish soldiers. Therefore, there is clearly a use of armed force within another sovereign state by the Turkish government. As with the legality of the uprising of the Kurdish forces discussed in the previous section, the Turkish invasion of another territory results in a number of debates concerning the applicable rules of *jus ad bellum*.

As a peremptory norm of international law, Article 2(4) of the United Nations Charter mandates that all members of the United Nations refrain in their international relations from the threat or use of force against the territorial integrity or political independence of any other state. Any such use of such force can rise to the level of an international armed conflict but it is arguable that even if this is not a full scale international armed conflict, it should engage the responsibility of the international community as represented by the UN Security Council. It is this type of conflict the collective security provisions in Chapter VII of the United Nations Charter were designed 'to save succeeding generations from the scourge of war'.[48] Therefore, a major task for the international lawyer is to assess whether any incident involving the use of force in international relations can be excused by one of the permissible exceptions to the prohibition, the main ones being self-defence or a UN Security Council authorised collective security operation. There is also another possible ground for consideration that is particularly relevant in this case and that is intervention on invitation. A sovereign state can invite troops from another country to enter its territory to give aid and assistance to the legitimate government.[49] Finally, there is a new type of justification coined by Dinstein as extra-territorial law enforcement, also known in other quarters as 'hot pursuit'.[50] This third ground is very controversial and is, ultimately, dismissed in this chapter. If one of the other justifications is not valid then the use of force is illegal and should be labelled as either aggressive or an unlawful use of force.[51] Therefore, the issue of the lawfulness of the use of armed force (the *jus ad bellum*) only arises when the conflict has spilled over international frontiers but in the case of the Kurdish/Turkish conflict this is precisely what has taken place.

It should be noted that Turkey has not felt it necessary to provide an international legal explanation for its invasion of Iraq. President Gül argued his country's 'readiness and right' to intervene in northern Iraq.[52] The country did not inform the UN Security Council about the operation. There was one statement made at the conclusion of 'Operation Sun' when Turkey submitted a *note verbale* to the Human Rights Council, declaring that:

> The counter-terrorism operation carried out … in northern Iraq was limited in scope, geography and duration. It targeted solely the PKK … terrorist presence in the region. Turkish military authorities took all possible measures to ensure the security of civilians and to avoid collateral damage. As a result, there has been no civilian casualty. Turkey remains a staunch advocate of the territorial integrity and sovereignty of Iraq.[53]

This statement made no effort to categorise the incursion within any of the traditional frameworks of exceptions to the prohibition on the use of force as it was an effort to minimise the activity to be under the radar of *jus ad bellum*. Notwithstanding this explanation, thousands of troops have been involved and this issue merits close examination. One use of force can be dismissed without further analysis because there was not a UN Security Council authorisation for this action as the matter was not even reported to the Security Council.

5.2.2 Self-defence

The law of self-defence is set out in both treaty and customary international law. Article 51 of the United Nations Charter provides:

> Nothing in the present Charter shall impair the inherent right of individual or collective self-defence if an armed attack occurs against a Member of the United Nations, until the Security Council has taken measures necessary to maintain international peace and security. Measures taken by Members in the exercise of this right of self-defence shall be immediately reported to the Security Council.

The first condition to be addressed is the issue of an armed attack. One can extrapolate from the statement of the Turkish authorities that they would deny an armed attack has taken place. It is certainly evident that Iraq has not mounted an attack on Turkish territory and any threat to Turkey comes from non-state groups, but has this threat from non-state actors risen to the level of an armed attack justifying a response in self-defence? The analysis of this question is assisted by international jurisprudence. The International Court of Justice has considered the question of what constitutes an armed attack in a series of its cases. The first of these is the *Nicaragua* case. The Court in its judgment on the merits considered whether an armed attack has to be by a regular army. It held relying on the Definition of Aggression that an armed attack must be understood as including not merely action by regular armed forces across an international border, but also 'the sending by or on behalf of a State of armed bands, groups, irregulars or mercenaries, which carry out acts of armed force against another State of such gravity as to amount to' (*inter alia*) an actual armed attack conducted by regular forces, 'or its substantial involvement therein'.[54] The Court goes on to state:

> The Court sees no reason to deny that, in customary law, the prohibition of armed attacks may apply to the sending by a State of armed bands to the territory of another State, if such an operation, because of its scale and effects, would have been classified as an armed attack rather than as a mere frontier incident had it been carried out by regular armed forces.[55]

The first task is to consider what if any argument of legality might be made with respect to this incursion into another sovereign territory. This situation is arguably very similar to the fact situation in the *Nicaragua* decision in that the Court considered cross-border incursions by the Nicaraguan armed forces into Honduras and Costa Rica. The court held that these 35 incursions did not amount to an armed attack justifying collective self-defence.[56] This is supported by the decision in the *Oil Platforms* case where the Court held that the United States response to the bombing of Iranian oil platforms was not justified as this had not risen to the level of an armed attack.[57] As Ruys argues the content of 'minimal gravity' is the subject of disagreement between scholars and judges.[58] However, in the recent *Oil Platforms* case the judgment stated that: 'The Court does not exclude the possibility that the mining of a single military vessel might be sufficient to bring into play the "inherent right of self-defence"' so that a large scale attack may not be needed.[59] Ruys points to an example of recent state practice as when in July 2006 Israel engaged in military operations in Lebanon in response to a Hezbollah attack on an Israeli border patrol, the majority of the international community appeared to agree that Israel had been the victim of an armed attack and could resort to self-defence although there was widespread condemnation of the disproportionate way in which the force was used.[60]

Therefore, there is an indeterminate level of cross-border activity that is required in order for a classification of armed attack which would violate the prohibition on the use of force. However, this Kurdish/Turkish activity has been going on for several years and the level of violence is intense with far more troops involved than the rebel groups in Nicaragua and the attacks on US naval ships in Iran. Therefore, one could assume that there may have been a right of self-defence on the part of Turkish security and armed forces. With respect to northern Iraq, it is the position of this author that the forces of the Turkish armed forces in their interventions have mounted an armed attack on the sovereign territory of northern Iraq. This conflict indeed engages the Article 2(4) prohibition[61] as there are thousands of Turkish military involved in these operations and they exercise control over the territory they enter by setting up military bases and thus they are violating the territorial integrity and political independence of another sovereign state and thus triggering the right of self-defence for Iraq, a right that has not been acted upon, other than by verbal protests.

Gray in her seminal work on the use of force actually examined the issue of Turkey, Iraq and the Kurds. She argued that Turkey had not even attempted to use traditional self-defence as a justification.[62] Instead in a particular statement in 1995 after the major incursion discussed above, Turkey argued that as Iraq had not been able to exercise its authority over Kurdistan, Iraq since 1991, Turkey had to intervene to stop the cross-border attacks of a terrorist organisation because Iraq had not been able to put an end to the attack. Turkey also argued that the operations were of limited time and scope.[63] However, again this situation has changed since the invasion of Iraq and still the Iraqi government has not been given the opportunity to police its own areas. Gray did point out the acquiescence of the United States in the operations by Turkey in the 1990s but that the United States argued self-defence.[64] In the recent invasion of 2008, once again Turkey did not raise self-defence against non-state actors, as was done by the United States with respect to the war in Afghanistan following 11 September 2001. Even if there was a self-defence argument Turkey clearly did not follow the procedural requirements of Article 51 of the Charter as it made no effort to notify the UN Security Council. This in itself would not defeat a claim of self-defence.[65]

The *Nicaragua* judgment stated that 'the absence of a report may be one of the factors indicating whether the state in question was itself convinced it was acting in self-defence'.[66] Gray reports that, since that pronouncement, states on the whole comply with this requirement.[67]

Closely related to the issue of what constitutes an armed attack is the issue of the availability of self-defence against non-state actors, justifying an armed attack against another state. Earlier we discussed the issue of whether non-state actors could act in self-defence. Here we consider the issue of a sovereign state entering another sovereign state to exercise a right of self-defence against non-state actors when the state being entered did not participate in the attack.[68] Any analysis of this issue would view that there is a dividing line, pre-11 September 2001 and then post-11 September 2001. Prior to the Al-Qaeda attacks it might have been safely argued that there was not a right of self-defence against non-state actors unless those actions could be directly attributed to the state. However, after 11 September there is a vigorous debate on this issue particularly in the light of the invasion of Afghanistan in October 2001. However, *jus ad bellum* in its traditional form as embodied in both the United Nations Charter and the Kellogg/Briand Pact clearly regulates the resort to armed force by states, even though Article 51, does not indicate that an armed attack must come from a state, given the context of the prohibition of the use of force, it seems clear that was the implication.[69] Even though there had been many other examples of non-state actor violence the massive loss of life caused by the attack on the World Trade Center and the Pentagon by Al-Qaeda triggered this debate. In fact, prior to 2001 Germany had argued that the attacks on Turkey by the PKK operating from northern Iraq did not qualify as an armed attack with the result that Turkey's military invasion was regarded as self-help and not self-defence.[70] As seen earlier from the discussion of an armed attack which included activities by non-state actors, the Definition of Aggression defined aggression as the sending by or on behalf of a state of armed bands, groups, irregulars or mercenaries, which carry out acts of armed force against another state. Any self-defence is therefore, against the state which sends these armed bands. Yet it is evident that although the Taliban regime may have allowed Al-Qaeda to operate training camps there was no evidence of actual support of the group in the way of training or financial support as was considered in the *Nicaragua* decision. Furthermore, as Ruys argues that it is clear that PKK attacks cannot be imputed to Iraq's federal or regional authorities as there is no evidence of any active support, on the contrary, the Iraqi regime condemned PKK attacks.[71]

Therefore, we are left considering whether 11 September altered what seemed to be settled international law even though there had been previous incidents such as the Turkish incursions and the US bombings in Sudan and Afghanistan after the embassy attacks in Nairobi and Dar es Salaam. Although some international law scholars characterised the Al-Qaeda attacks as a crime against humanity, some experts in armed conflict indicated that this attack could result in self-defence against non-state actors. The German view and indeed most of the international community's view changed on 12 September 2001 with the passage of UN Security Council Resolution 1368 which condemned the attacks on the World Trade Center and the Pentagon and classified these acts as international terrorism constituting a threat to international peace and security and recognised the inherent right to individual or collective self-defence in accordance with the United Nations Charter.[72] The NATO Council expressed its support for the United States on the basis of Article 5 of the NATO Treaty and 'reinterpreted what an armed attack on a Party to the North Atlantic party means' so that a terrorist attack was regarded as an attack on all NATO partners justifying self-defence.[73] Greenwood argues that the international reaction to the events on 11 September 2001 confirms 'the commonsense view that the concept of armed attack is not limited to State acts'.[74] The United States launched Operation Enduring Freedom in October 2001 and in its letter dated 7 October 2001 to the UN Security Council set out its legal grounds for action:

> ... the United States of America, together with other States, has initiated actions in the exercise of its inherent right of individual and collective self-defence following the armed attacks that were carried out against the United States on 11 September 2001 ... my Government has obtained clear and compelling information that the Al-Qaeda organization, which is supported by the Taliban regime in Afghanistan, had a central role in the attacks ... The attacks on 11 September 2001 and the ongoing threat to the United States and its nationals posed by the Al-Qaeda organization have been made possible by the decision of the Taliban regime to allow the parts of Afghanistan that it controls to be used by this organization as a base of operation. Despite every effort by the United States and the international community, the Taliban regime has refused to change its policy ... In response to these attacks, and in accordance with the inherent right of individual and collective self-defence, United States armed forces have initiated actions designed to prevent and deter further attacks on the United States. These actions include measures against Al-Qaeda terrorist training camps and military installations of the Taliban regime in Afghanistan.[75]

This letter is interesting because it does not claim a right to defend solely against a non-state actor and indicates the role of the Taliban regime in supporting Al-Qaeda. The operation was supported by a majority of United Nations members.

Gray is not as sure this operation as resulted in a change in the *jus ad bellum* as she indicates that those who argue that self-defence may be invoked against non-state actors have not been able to adduce state practice to support their argument other than Operation Enduring Freedom in Afghanistan.[76] Her view is supported by recent case law in the International Court of Justice. In the *Legal Consequences of the Construction of a Wall in the Occupied Palestinian Territory* Advisory Opinion the Court referred to a statement made by Israel's Permanent Representative in the UN General Assembly that the resolutions by the UN Security Council on terrorism (1363 and 1373) 'clearly recognized the right of States to use force in self-defence against terrorist attacks'.[77] Interestingly, the Court responded that Article 51 of the Charter recognises the existence of 'an inherent right of self-defence in the case of armed attack by one State against another state' and that 'Israel does not claim that the attacks against it are imputable to a foreign State'.[78] The next case to consider the issue of self-defence against non-state actors was the *Armed Activities on the Territory of the Congo (Democratic Republic of the Congo v Uganda)*.[79] The Court considered Uganda's argument of self-defence based on attacks from a rebel group based in the Congo, the ADF. The court did not accept the claim:

> The Court has found ... that there is no satisfactory proof of the involvement in these attacks, direct or indirect, of the Government of the DRC. The attacks did not emanate from armed bands or irregulars sent by the DRC or on behalf of the DRC, within the sense of Article 3 *(g)* of General Assembly resolution 3314 (XXIX) on the definition of aggression, adopted on 14 December 1974. The Court is of the view that, on the evidence before it, even if this series of deplorable attacks could be regarded as cumulative in character, they still remained non-attributable to the DRC ... For all these reasons, the Court finds that the legal and factual circumstances for the exercise of a right of self-defence by Uganda against the DRC were not present.[80]

The Court indicated that it had no need to respond to the contentions of the Parties as to whether and under what conditions international law provided for a right of self-defence against large-scale attacks by irregular forces.[81] The Court seems unwilling to depart from the ruling in the *Nicaragua* case that regards imputability to a state as a precondition for self-defence.[82] The case law seems to support Gray's concern that operations solely against non-state actors is not confirmed as lawful in the customary development of the law of self-defence.

There are two further conditions within the customary law of self-defence that merit examination in the Turkish operation in northern Iraq. These are necessity and proportionality.[83] With respect to necessity, there is no evidence of allowing the Iraqi government police its own territory. Comparisons can also be drawn to the tribal areas of Pakistan where it can be argued that the government does not have control over that portion of the territory where the rebels have their bases of operations. However, in this case Kurdistan, Iraq is one of the few areas in the country that is relatively stable and control does exist over the territory by the Kurdish administration. However, there is no question that the border area is porous as Kurdish people consider both sides of the border to be their territory and therefore, PKK bases in northern Iraq are a long-standing feature of the landscape. This would indeed constitute a problem for the Turkish government and security forces but notwithstanding this fact, the test of necessity as established in the various cases is stringent. Furthermore, in respect of proportionality, mounting a major invasion with thousands of troops in response to the cross border activity by small groups of rebels may well be seen as disproportionate and unnecessary.

5.2.3 Intervention by consent

Another possible justification within *jus ad bellum* is intervention by consent. This would mean that the troops who entered northern Iraq were there with the actual or tacit consent of the Iraqi regime. As the rules under the Charter deal with international armed conflicts, assistance to another nation in a situation of civil war is an area of controversy. The basic principle of the right of a government to invite another state to use force on its territory in contrast with the prohibition of aiding an opposition movement has been accepted, but as Gray asserts, its application has not been simple.[84] It is particularly controversial in civil war due to the duty of non-intervention and the right of every state to choose its political, economic and social systems.[85] The United Kingdom issued a Foreign Policy document in 1984 in which it was argued that any form of interference or assistance was prohibited when a civil war was taking place and control of that state's territory was divided between warring parties.[86] The right of a third state to use force at the invitation of a government in order to keep that government in power or in order to maintain to domestic order, 'has apparently been taken for granted by states since 1945 if the domestic unrest falls below the threshold of a civil war'.[87] However, in this case the threshold has been reached of a civil war and it is not Turkey going in to aid Iraq with its rebels but rather pursuing their rebels into another country and the issue is the consent of the Iraqi regime for that incursion.

This is a very difficult area as one does not know for certain what level of discussion has taken place between the new Iraqi government, the US authorities and the Turkish government. If there was at least a tacit consent by the Iraqi government to the incursions which would mean that the prohibition on the use of such force would not be engaged if the state involved gives its consent. Another complicating factor is that United States has assisted with intelligence to identify the targets.[88]

It is indeed very significant that the issue of the invasion of northern Iraq has not been brought to the UN Security Council by the government of Iraq. Nevertheless, there is the clear reported evidence of protests by the Iraqi government against the incursion and no public evidence of tacit consent. As Gray reports since 1991, Iraq has repeatedly protested at Turkey's incursions and that it did not accept the pretext that they were in pursuit of separatist terrorists and stated that the incursion was a violation of the United Nations Charter and of international law.[89] Therefore, as with the argument of self-defence, there may be no clear legal justification on the basis of invitation for the use of force in northern Iraq as there is no evidence of an actual and clear invitation for assistance in ridding northern Iraq of PKK camps.[90]

5.2.4 'Hot pursuit'

Dinstein calls this phenomenon 'extra-territorial law enforcement'. He poses the question of what is the lawful action when hostile paramilitary groups operate against a state from another territory. If indeed the state is unable or unwilling to act Dinstein asserts that the victim state can dispatch military units into the other territory in order to destroy the bases of the armed bands or terrorists (provided that the destruction is the sole object of the operation).[91] Dinstein labels this type of action as self-defence but that the situation is short of an international armed conflict. He does not accept the appellation 'hot pursuit' but rather argues that this does not need to be a 'hot pursuit' as it can be begun after the insurgents are in the other territory. He calls this action 'extra-territorial law enforcement' as a form of self-defence to operate if and only if the other state is unwilling or unable to stop further armed attacks launched from within its territory.[92] Dinstein uses the example of the repeated crossings by the Turkish troops into northern Iraq to attempt to deny Kurdish armed bands a sanctuary as an example of state practice of this type of activity. He also uses the examples of the Israeli incursion into Lebanon in 1982, the American military expedition of 1916 into Mexico and the famous Caroline incident.[93] It remains an issue however, if these cross-border incursions are part of customary international law particularly when one views the pronouncements in the *Nicaragua*, the *Wall* and the *Armed Activities in the Congo* cases.

This justification for the use of force seems to this author to be an attempt to resolve the confusion in the law of self-defence over non-state actors. This type of hot pursuit surely cannot be extra-territorial law enforcement and should be viewed within the lens of self-defence. However, Dinstein is attempting to expand the law of self-defence into law enforcement operations, surely a troubling development within the law of armed conflict. However, this type of action might be the closest to the fact situation of the Turkish actions. Turkey, unlike the United States and its coalition partners and Afghanistan nor Israel and Lebanon, confined its operations within the mountainous areas where the PKK might be located and did not initiate action against Iraqi government facilities or troops.

The issue of whether the United States assistance to Turkey in identifying targets is not as controversial in international law. In spite of the declarations of non-assistance to either side in a self-determination struggle, as discussed above, the law of self-defence provides that a country can come to the aid of another country in its struggle with rebellion.

The analysis of the operation in northern Iraq reveals no clearly lawful justification for entry of thousands of troops into the sovereign territory of Iraq. The law of self-defence has not clearly evolved towards operations against non-state actors without some connection to the state where the rebels are located. Ruys argues that the Iraqi authorities have been unwilling to expel the PKK nor arrest them and that in itself may be enough to establish a connection with a state, that is certainly far beyond the *Nicaragua* standard.[94] It also has the potential to destabilise a critical area and this is evident by the concurrent involvement by the Republic of Iran in operations in northern Iraq.

5.3 The law of state responsibility

There is an important political and legal consequence of long-standing non-international armed conflict aggravated by the incursion into northern Iraq.

This is the responsibility set out in international law of the international community to address situations of armed conflict. The astonishing fact about this intervention is that the international community has barely reacted to the situation. Ruys in his article gives a complete account of the lack of reaction but the highlights can be summarised as follows:

1. Iraq

   The operation was denounced by the Iraqi government as a violation of Iraqi sovereignty and the government demanded an immediate withdrawal from the region. Foreign Minister Zebari argued that even though the operation was a 'limited military incursion into a remote, isolated and uninhabited region' it could destabilise the region and the operation should end as soon as possible. It was also condemned by the Kurdish regional government as Kurdish region leader Masoud Barzani said that the regional government would not be part of the conflict between the Turkish government and the PKK fighters '[b]ut at the same time, we stress that if the Turkish military targets any Kurdish civilian citizens or any civilian structures, then we will order a large-scale resistance;' but the matter was not reported by the Iraqi government to the United Nations Security Council.[95] Notwithstanding these statements Iraq did not report the matter to the United Nations Security Council.

2. The United States

   As Ruys states 'The United States never explicitly endorsed the intervention, yet it certainly never condemned it'.[96] It is asserted in media reports that the United States assisted the Turkish invasion by providing 'actionable military intelligence' about where the PKK might be located in Northern Iraq and cleared northern Iraqi airspace to enable the Turkish air strikes.[97] The Turkish government notified the US and the Kurdish government about the invasion and on his first official visit to the United States on 8 January, prior to the operation, President Gül thanked the US for its support for the Turkish campaign. On 28 February President Bush gave a news conference and told the reporters assembly that the Turks needed to 'move quickly, achieve their objective and get out! On the same day US Defence Secretary Gates declared that Turkey's operation 'should be as short and precisely targeted as possible.'[98]

3. The European Union

   The European Union has been heavily involved in this conflict due to the Turkish accession process.[99] However, in this case they also seemed to support the Turkish action. When the air raids increased in December 2007, the EU presidency expressed 'concern' over the action and called upon Turkey 'to exercise restraint, to respect the territorial integrity of Iraq and refrain from taking any military action that could undermine regional peace and stability.'[100] Notwithstanding this warning, when 'Operation Sun' commenced the Presidency statement recognised 'Turkey's need to protect its population from terrorism' and called on Turkey 'to refrain from taking any disproportionate military action and to respect Iraq's territorial integrity.'[101] These statements are hardly a sound condemnation of an invasion of another territory.

4. The United Nations
    There was no action by the United Nations. As a Member State did not report a potential or actual threat to international peace and security pursuant to Article 39 of the UN Charter, the Security Council did not meet concerning the invasion and there is also no evidence of action by the General Assembly. The Secretary-General of the United Nations Ban Ki-Moon expressed his concern on more than one occasion urging restraint and respect for the border between the two countries and stressed the need to protect civilian life.[102] Nevertheless he did not report the matter to the Security Council.

Given the analysis completed above and the conclusion that there may have been a breach of the international law of *jus ad bellum*, particularly a violation of the United Nations Charter prohibition on the use of force and a peremptory norm of customary international law, there surely should have been a referral to the United Nations.

A branch of international law that is particularly relevant is the law of state responsibility and the new concept of aggravated state responsibility set out in the Articles of State Responsibility which have been recommended to the international community by a UN General Assembly Resolution.[103] The third chapter of the Articles is entitled 'Serious Breaches of Obligations under Peremptory Norms of General International Law', contains two significant articles.

Article 40 states:

1. This chapter applies to the international responsibility which is entailed by a serious breach by a State of an obligation arising under a peremptory norm of general international law.
2. A breach of such an obligation is serious if it involves a gross or systematic failure by the responsible State to fulfil its obligation.

To begin with, Article 40 defines serious breaches as those involving gross or systematic failure by the responsible state to fulfil its obligation arising under a peremptory norm of general international law. The community obligation is owed to all other members of the international community and, therefore, there is a community right belonging to any other state. As a result, this community right can be exercised by any other state, whether or not damaged by the breach. However, this right is exercised on behalf of the international community, not on the part of the claimant state.[104] Article 40 (?) specifies that the breach must be gross or systematic, serious or large scale, and examples given are aggression, genocide, or grave atrocities against one's own nationals or all persons

belonging to an ethnic group.[105] However, another important example is violation on the prohibition against the illegal use of force which is a norm of jus
cogens and therefore triggers this argument of aggravated state responsibility. It is
therefore clear that all members of the international legal community become
victims of the breach of their community rights or dare we say, constitutional
values.[106]

Cassese argues that this new form of responsibility has come into being as a
result of a number of factors. First of all, there is the United Nations Charter
provisions on the ban of force and the methods within the Charter of responses
to acts of aggression which support the fact that there can be serious responses
on the part of the whole international community. Second, he argues the
emergence in the world community of values such as peace, human rights, and
self-determination which are deemed of universal significance not subject to
derogation. This has led many states to believe that gross infringements of
such values must require a stronger reaction than those normally taken in
response to violation of bilateral legal relations. The reaction should be public
and reactive.[107] Clear examples of collective action by states are of course the
actions of the UN Security Council in situations of a breach of the United
Nations Charter which is a multilateral treaty. Examples given are the economic
measures against Southern Rhodesia, South Africa, the Federal Republic of
Yugoslavia, Libya, Liberia and Haiti.[108]

At the core of the Article 40 category of aggravated state responsibility is the
notion of *obligations erga omnes* as set out in the *Barcelona Traction* case, the *Namibia
Advisory Opinion*, the *Case concerning East Timor* and the *Application of the Convention
on the Prevention and Punishment of the Crime of Genocide, Bosnia and Herzegovina v
Yugoslavia* case.[109] The types of serious breaches as set out in those cases were
genocide, aggression, apartheid and forcible denial of self-determination. These
breaches 'shock the conscience of mankind' and as such should attract serious
consequences and thus merit a separate Chapter in the Draft Articles.[110] As
Crawford states, the *Barcelona Traction* case was the first to make a distinction
between 'the position of an injured State in the context of diplomatic protection
with the position of all States in respect of the breach of an obligation towards the
diplomatic community as a whole'.[111] In the *East Timor* case the Court held that
'Portugal's assertion that the right of peoples to self-determination, as it evolved
from the Charter and from United Nations practice, has an *erga omnes* character is
irreproachable'.[112] In a critical Statement the Court in the Application of the
Convention on the Prevention and Punishment of the Crime of Genocide case
states that 'the rights and obligations enshrined by the [Genocide] Convention
are rights and obligations *erga omnes*'.[113]

Articles 53 and 64 of the Vienna Convention on the Law of Treaties are cited
by the drafters of these articles as the Convention recognises the existence of
substantive norms of a fundamental character from which no derogation is
permitted.[114] In the same way, this chapter of the articles recognises that there
could be 'egregious breaches of obligations owed to the community as a whole,
breaches which warrant some response by the community and its members'.[115]

The second article in Chapter 3 outlines the consequences of such a breach.

Article 41 states:

1. States shall cooperate to bring to an end through lawful means any serious breach within the meaning of article 40.
2. No State shall recognize as lawful a situation created by a serious breach within the meaning of article 40, nor render aid or assistance in maintaining the situation.
3. This article is without prejudice to the other consequences referred to in this part and to such further consequences that a breach to which this chapter applies may entail under international law.

It was the consequences of serious breach of obligations under peremptory norms that are a dramatic departure from ordinary state responsibility. The first important factor is that *all* other states can take action. All other states are entitled to: (a) invoke the aggravated responsibility by bringing their claim to the notice of the state; (b) demand cessation of the wrong; (c) claim reparation on behalf of the victims; (d) bring the matter to competent international bodies such as the United Nations or regional organisation; (e) if that international organisation took no action then states could take peaceful countermeasures on an individual basis; and finally (f) to resort to collective self-defence in the case of aggression subject to their consent.[116] States are placed under a positive obligation by the term 'shall' to cooperate in order to bring an end to serious breaches of obligations owed under a peremptory norm of international law. Article 41 regrettably does not specify the form this cooperation should take although it could be organised under the auspices of the United Nations but it also could be undertaken by such regional organisations as the European Union which has been dealing with Turkey in discussions on membership of the European Union.

Article 41(2) obliges other states not to recognise as lawful a situation created by a serious breach nor render aid or assistance to that state. Later in the book we discuss the possible reactions that should be taken in response to the illegal use of force by Turkey as due to the existence of these obligations, it seems that there is a duty on the international community to seek a solution to the armed conflict, even if Iraq fails to act. It has to be acknowledged that Professor Crawford has acknowledged that, as of yet, these provisions are not part of customary international law. Nevertheless, they set out an important mechanism for international action when peremptory norms are violated.

In Chapter 9 we see that the international community is, indeed, responding and proposing solutions to this long-standing internal armed conflict which has spilled over into Iraq.

Conclusion

This chapter considers problems with considering the lawfulness of resorting to force within the paradigm of a non-international armed conflict. In the same way that the existence of an armed conflict is such a difficult task within the *jus in bello*, assessing legality within *jus ad bellum* is an equally difficult task. The first question about whether, in a post-colonial era, there is a right to rebel is an extremely controversial topic. It threatens the stability of the international system. A review of existing academic opinion reveals a lack of consensus on this issue. Certainly no group should be encouraged to wage a war of independence unless the most extreme circumstances exist of widespread and systematic violation of human rights.

The second question of whether the Turkish invasion of northern Iraq was lawful may be an easier question as it seems that Turkey does not have a clear justification for its incursions into the sovereign territory of Iraq. It seems clear that in spite of a lack of international reaction, the incursions are not justified by any of the legal exceptions to the prohibition on the use of force and this action could be characterised as at least a breach of the peace, if not aggression.

Finally, both the rebellion within southeast Turkey and the spill over of the response to the rebellion into northern Iraq compels within the law of aggravated state responsibility a response from the international community. Chapter 6 provides even more complexity to this situation as the rebels in this situation (the PKK) have been classified as terrorists. This provides a further impetus to the international community to respond because, since the 11 September attacks, terrorism is viewed as a threat to international peace and security and is a major priority for the UN Security Council. The long-standing conflict in Turkey, however, failed to attract the attention of the UN Security Council in the past which seems to have been a major oversight given the number of casualties and the involvement of other sovereign states. Perhaps the terrorism paradigm will provide the needed pressure for a resolution to this conflict.

6 Terrorism, the law of armed conflict and the PKK

Introduction

The inclusion of the Kurdish conflict within the definition and legal regime of a non-international armed conflict can be contrasted with the current characterisation of the situation as a series of terrorist attacks conducted by a proscribed terrorist group, the Kurdistan Workers Party (PKK).[1] Terrorism has been a very controversial area of international law with a lack of consensus on the definition of terrorism, or what constitutes a terrorist.[2] Although terrorist attacks have long been a feature of international relations, the situation materially changed with the Al-Qaeda attacks on the World Trade Center and the Pentagon on 11 September 2001. The global community began to focus on the phenomenon of terrorism as a high priority political issue and the term 'global war on terror' joined the lexicon of armed conflict. This resulted in a series of legal measures including the establishment of a UN Security Council mandated counter-terrorism committee with mandatory legal obligations on sovereign states to report on the measures they are taking to combat terrorist attacks.[3]

The various legal methods to combat terrorism has resulted in significant impact on already existing internal armed conflicts as groups that are involved in long-standing independence struggles are looked upon as terrorist groups, not only within their own countries but into the international community at large. This includes the PKK in southeast Turkey, included on the European Union, NATO and the US State Department list of terrorist groups.[4] It is, however, not on the United Nations list, so far limited to Al-Qaeda and Taliban suspects.[5] Being on such lists means that within an international criminal law framework, terrorists are to be apprehended and prosecuted or extradited to their home countries to stand trial. Within an armed conflict framework, their domestic activities constitute a threat to international peace and security rather than just internal threats. Within the context of the armed conflict in southeast Turkey, the PKK has challenged the EU designation in the European Court of Justice, and a significant decision has been delivered by the European Court of Justice that throws into question the whole issue of designation.[6]

This chapter examines the international legal framework of terrorism and Chapter 7 places terrorism in the political context of negotiations for a peaceful settlement of this dispute. The first part of the chapter discloses the lack of an agreed definition of terrorism. In spite of that fact, international, regional and national organisations have taken concerted action against terrorist activities, resulting in a significant impact on this conflict which is discussed in Chapter 7. The second part of this chapter discusses the lack of an agreed definition of who is a terrorist in the context of the traditional disagreement between viewing these persons as freedom fighters and terrorists. The third part of the chapter reviews the encouraging jurisprudence on terrorism from several countries which confirm the continued co-applicability of international humanitarian law and international human rights law even if an allegation is made of terrorist activity. The European Court of Justice and courts in the United Kingdom and the United States lead the way in confirming that the label of 'terrorist' does not eliminate the necessity of all of the international law guarantees discussed in previous chapters. Finally, we examine the legal implications for the PKK and the Kurdish struggle by imposing the label of 'terrorist' on the PKK. This part of the chapter analyses the important decision rendered by the European Court of Justice which calls into question the notion of the designation of this group as a terrorist organisation.

Due to the important jurisprudence subsequent to the measures imposed post-11 September 2001, the controversy over definitions and applicability of terrorist measures does little to change the legal regimes applicable to the non-international armed conflict in southeast Turkey. If anything, the cases on terrorism have clarified and confirmed the importance of international human rights law and international humanitarian law in internal armed conflict.

6.1 Definition of terrorism

The international community has long been unable to agree on a definition of terrorism even though terrorist attacks have been a phenomenon for centuries. Higgins asserts that:

> 'Terrorism' is a term without legal significance. It is merely a convenient way of alluding to activities, whether of States or of individuals, widely disapproved of and in which either the methods used are unlawful, or the targets protected, or both.[7]

Notwithstanding this reservation the international community has sought a legal definition for generations. One very famous example of a terrorist attack was the assassination of Grand Duke Franz Ferdinand and his wife in Sarajevo, an event that triggered the First World War.[8] Gasser characterises these types of attacks on bystanders or government officials as 'unchecked and indiscriminate violence'.[9] In 1937 the League of Nations drafted the Convention for the Prevention and Punishment of Terrorism which unsurprisingly never entered into force.[10] The Convention was signed by 24 states but only ratified by one.[11] Acts of terrorism were defined in Article 1 as 'criminal acts directed against a State and intended or calculated to create a state of terror in the minds of particular person, or a group of persons or the general public'. Article 1(1) reaffirmed the principle in international law that it was the duty of every state to refrain from any act designed to encourage terrorist activities directed against another state. Article 2 obliged a contracting state to make the following acts committed on its own territory criminal offences. Those acts were:

(1) Any willful act causing death or grievous bodily harm or loss of liberty to heads of state, their spouses, or persons holding a public position 'when the act is directed against them in their public capacity';
(2) Willful damage to public property belonging to another contracting party;
(3) Any willful act calculated to endanger the lives of members of the public;
(4) Any attempt to commit the above offences;
(5) The dealing with arms and ammunitions with a view to the commission of one of the above offences in any country whatsoever.[12]

The Convention was the first and last international treaty to comprehensively define the concept and contains many of the elements still discussed by the international community today. A major criticism of this effort was the focus on protection of head of state and other public figures occasioned by the assassination of King Alexander I of Yugoslavia and the President of the Council of the French Republic.[13] This first failure of this definition process continues into the 20th and 21st centuries and it may well be that this Convention was as close as the international community ever got.

There have been repeated concerted efforts to define terrorism since the founding of the United Nations. A major initiative occurred in 1972 a year in which, as Dugard described, resulted in the proliferation of new forms of terrorism, the Lod Airport Massacre in Tel Aviv, the Munich Olympic Games disaster and a wave of letter bombs directed at Israeli diplomats.[14] In response, the Secretary-General of the United Nations requested the UN General Assembly to consider measures to prevent terrorism. The item was referred to the UN General Assembly 6th Committee which had before it a 'Draft Convention for the Prevention and Punishment of Certain Acts of International Terrorism' that had been submitted by the United States.[15] The Committee did not recommend the Convention to the UN General Assembly and the United States proposed in early 1973 a UN General Assembly Resolution calling for an international convention to adopt the Convention. This was rejected by the UN General Assembly, which instead passed a resolution inviting states to make proposals to be considered in the next session in a committee of 35 states. This committee of 35 states met in July and August 1973 and it was unable to agree on a definition of 'terrorism' let alone a Convention. In both the UN General Assembly and the 6th Committee the focus was on the legitimacy of wars of national liberation, and many states especially the Afro-Arab and eastern European states refused to support 'any measures which might interfere with the activities of liberation movements'.[16] This would become the theme for the objection to a global definition of terrorism that has occupied the international community ever since.

The next major push to adopt an international instrument was the effort to adopt a Comprehensive Convention on International Terrorism (CCIT). The UN General Assembly in 1994 adopted a Declaration on Measures to Eliminate International Terrorism which included in paragraph 1:

> The States Members of the United Nations solemnly reaffirm their unequivocal condemnation of all acts, methods and practices of terrorism, as criminal and unjustifiable, wherever and by whomever committed, including those which jeopardize the friendly relations among States and peoples and threaten the territorial integrity and security of States.[17]

Two years later in 1996 the UN General Assembly created an Ad Hoc Committee 'to address means of further developing a comprehensive legal framework of conventions dealing with international terrorism'.[18] In the same year India presented a draft CCIT. The Ad Hoc Committee and a Working Group of the Sixth Committee worked on separate but related aspects of the treaty negotiations. The draft CCIT has been the subject of discussion, debate and modification since its proposal but its features are:

i) all States have a responsibility not to support terrorist acts and/or to provide any assistance, training, safe haven etc.;
ii) all States should adopt measures to ensure that terrorist acts within the scope of the Convention are, under no circumstances, justified by considerations of political, philosophical, ideological, racial, religious or other similar nature;
iii) all States should take all practicable measures to prohibit the establishment and operation of terrorist installations and training camps;
iv) terrorists should either be prosecuted or extradited.

As Clapham indicates, the historical obstacle confronting the achievement of an agreed definition of terrorism has been the support of some governments for 'the legitimacy of the use of force by peoples subjected to oppressive regimes'.[19] This is particularly the case for those countries that won their independence through struggle against colonialism or alien domination.[20] In fact, some regional conventions have specific exclusions including the Convention of the Organisation of Islamic Conference on Combating International Terrorism of 1999 which in Article 2(a) states:

> Peoples' struggle including armed struggle against foreign occupation, aggression, colonialism, and hegemony, aimed at liberation and self-determination in accordance with the principles of international law shall not be considered a terrorist crime.[21]

The Organisation of African Unity Convention on the Prevention and Combating of Terrorism 1999 in Article 3 (1) similarly specifies:

> Notwithstanding the provisions of Article 1, the struggle waged by peoples in accordance with the principles of international law for their liberation or self-determination, including armed struggle against colonialism, occupation, aggression and domination by foreign forces shall not be considered as terrorist acts.[22]

In 1997, a United Nations Convention, the International Convention for the Suppression of Terrorist Bombings, did not include any such exception and neither did the 1999 Convention for the Suppression of the Financing of Terrorism, but these Conventions criminalised certain activities, not terrorism in itself.[23] Within the 1999 Convention is an important part of the contested definition of terrorism:

> (b) Any other act intended to cause death or serious bodily injury to a civilian, or to any other person not taking an active part in the hostilities in a situation of armed conflict, when the purpose of such act, by its nature or context, is to intimidate a population, or to compel a government or an international organization to do or to abstain from doing any act.[24]

The turning point which added urgency to the efforts to define terrorism was the Al-Qaeda attacks on the World Trade Center and the Pentagon on 11 September 2001. After these horrific attacks UN Security Council Resolution 1373 of 28 December 2001 in its preamble stated ' … that such acts, like any act of international terrorism, constitute a threat to international peace and security'. Thus there has been a new element introduced in the debate, not only are terrorist acts crimes, they may constitute armed attacks and as a result there has been a new element introduced of the 'global war on terror'. Nowhere does this pivotal resolution define terrorist acts. In spite of the impetus provided by the Al-Qaeda attacks, the general roadblocks remained within the decades-old process of attempting to conclude a CCIT.

Therefore, in spite of over a decade of negotiations in the Ad Hoc Committee, the final CCIT has not yet been concluded. The purpose of the draft CCIT was for an instrument that would serve as a binding and enforceable instrument of international criminal law. In an initial attempt to define terrorism, the draft CCIT states that it is an offence to:

- Unlawfully and intentionally cause death or serious bodily injury;
- Unlawfully and intentionally cause serious damage to public or private property or damage such property as to result, or likely to result, in major economic loss; and
- Purposefully intimidate or population or compel a government or an international organization to act, or abstain from acting.[25]

In the deadlock to obtain a CCIT, the most problematic issues are summarised as:

1. Whether the definition of terrorism should include State-sponsored terrorism and acts of State terrorism. Some delegations (including Cuba, Iraq, Iran, Lebanon, Libya, Pakistan, Syria and Sudan) previously have expressed the view that State, and State-sponsored, terrorism should be included in the definition. Other delegations have countered that State and State-sponsored terrorism already are subject to international conventions (including the Prohibition of the Use of Force under Article 2(4) of the United Nations Charter);

2. Whether the activities of armed forces should fall under the scope of the Convention. Some delegations (including the EU states, Canada, China and Japan) wish to exclude military activities from the Convention, arguing that military activity is already subject to international conventions and treaties;

3. How to resolve use of the term 'terrorism' to ensure that it is not left open to unchecked politicization. Currently, the draft refers to terrorist 'offences,' but some Member States are concerned that 'terrorism' also should be included in the draft, so as to differentiate it from terrorist 'offences' and to endow it with a legal definition.

4. The legitimacy of armed struggle against foreign occupation, aggression or colonialism. Some delegations consider such armed struggle to be aimed self-determination and believe that the Convention should in no way hinder any people's legitimate right to self-determination, whilst others argue that the Convention should identify any act that falls beyond the defined parameters of armed conflict as terrorism.

5. How to situate a 'comprehensive convention' in an international system that already includes multiple conventions, while ensuring that no terrorist activity escapes through legal loopholes. No state wishes to be subject to a 'double regime' of anti-terrorism legislation. This is especially problematic because not all States are subject to all conventions, but no State wishes to have to duplicate their counterterrorism efforts.[26]

The Ad Hoc Committee has now proposed that there be an international conference to discuss the CCIT but that has not yet been convened.[27]

A report on the activities of the Ad Hoc Committee summarised the position of several delegations that would be relevant to the activities of the PKK. The report stated that:

> Several delegations expressed the view that the draft convention should contain a universally accepted definition of terrorism, which would, in principle, differentiate it from the legitimate struggle of peoples in the exercise of their right for self-determination from foreign occupation or colonial domination.[28]

There has been one success in this herculean effort to agree on a definition. The international community acting on the recommendation in the 2005 World Summit Outcome document[29] has adopted a UN global counter-terrorism strategy:

- Improving the coherence and efficiency of counter-terrorism technical assistance delivery so that all States can play their part effectively;
- Voluntarily putting in place systems of assistance that would address the needs of victims of terrorism and their families;
- Addressing the threat of bioterrorism by establishing a single comprehensive database on biological incidents, focusing on improving States' public health systems, and acknowledging the need to bring together major stakeholders to ensure that biotechnology's advances are not used for terrorist or other criminal purposes but for the public good;
- Involving civil society, regional and sub regional organizations in the fight against terrorism and developing partnerships with the private sector to prevent terrorist attacks on particularly vulnerable targets;
- Exploring innovative means to address the growing threat of terrorist use of the Internet;
- Modernizing border and customs controls systems, and improving the security of travel documents, to prevent terrorist travel and the movement of illicit materials;
- Enhancing cooperation to combat money laundering and the financing of terrorism; and
- Intensification of its counter-terrorism work since 2001 9/11.[30]

Furthermore, there are now 16 international instruments dealing with the phenomenon of terrorism, 12 dating before 11 September but none of these contains an agreed definition of 'terrorism', rather they criminalise activities such as hijacking and the taking of hostages.[31] These Conventions are summarised in Appendix 2 along with their major provisions.[32]

Regional organisations such as the European Union and the Council of Europe have also embarked on a search for a comprehensive definition of terrorism and it is to their efforts that this analysis now turns, as their activities have a direct bearing on the Kurdish conflict.[33]

6.1.1 Council of Europe and European Union action

The Council of Europe also had a long-standing experience with terrorism. As early as 1977, it adopted a Convention entitled, European Convention on the Suppression of Terrorism:[34]

Article 1
For the purposes of extradition between Contracting States, none of the following offences shall be regarded as a political offence or as an offence

connected with a political offence or as an offence inspired by political motives:

a.   an offence within the scope of the Convention for the Suppression of Unlawful Seizure of Aircraft, signed at The Hague on 16 December 1970;

b.   an offence within the scope of the Convention for the Suppression of Unlawful Acts against the Safety of Civil Aviation, signed at Montreal on 23 September 1971;

c.   a serious offence involving an attack against the life, physical integrity or liberty of internationally protected persons, including diplomatic agents;

d.   an offence involving kidnapping, the taking of a hostage or serious unlawful detention;

e.   an offence involving the use of a bomb, grenade, rocket, automatic firearm or letter or parcel bomb if this use endangers persons;

f.   an attempt to commit any of the foregoing offences or participation as an accomplice of a person who commits or attempts to commit such an offence.

After 11 September 2001, the Council of Europe revisited this Convention and in 2003 an amending protocol was negotiated that updated the treaties mentioned in Article 1, strengthened measures for implementation, and importantly barred extradition to countries that practice torture or use the death penalty.[35] In 2005 the Council of Europe Convention on the Prevention of Terrorism was adopted in Warsaw.[36] This treaty entered into force on 1 June 2007 and now has 20 ratifications. As Saul points out, the Convention does not attempt to generically or comprehensively define terrorism rather it is defined as any offence listed in listed 10 sectoral treaties (10 of those 16 listed in Appendix 2).[37] However, the preamble is informative stating:

> Recalling that acts of terrorism have the purpose by their nature or context to seriously intimidate a population or unduly compel a government or an international organisation to perform or abstain from performing any act or seriously destabilise or destroy the fundamental political, constitutional, economic or social structures of a country or an international organization.[38]

The focus of this important Convention is once again on acts of terrorism rather than attempting a controversial and problematic definition.

The European Union has also long been concerned with the phenomenon of terrorism. The Amsterdam Treaty of the European Union states that one of the tasks of the European Union is 'preventing and combating crime, organized or otherwise, in particular terrorism' and that will 'provide citizens with a high level of safety within an area of freedom, security and justice'.[39] There was long-standing cooperation on terrorism, dating back to the 1975 TREVI group

(French acronym for *Terrorisme, Radicalisme, Extremisme et Violence Internationale*), where Interior Ministers met in order to enhance police cooperation to combat terrorism.[40] In 1996, the Council decided by Joint Action to create and maintain a directory of counter-terrorism competencies to facilitate cooperation between the member states of the European Union.[41] After the 11 September attacks on the World Trade Center, the EU activities in terrorism increased exponentially, resulting in action by the European Union.

The European Union indeed adopted a Council Framework Decision on Combating Terrorism[42] and a Framework Decision on the European Arrest Warrant.[43] The Framework Decisions included a list of terrorist offences which, by their nature or context, may seriously damage a country or an international organisation where committed with the aim of:

— seriously intimidating a population, or
— unduly compelling a Government or international organization to perform or abstain from performing any act, or
— seriously destabilising or destroying the fundamental political, constitutional, economic or social structures of a country or an international organisation, shall be deemed to be terrorist offences.

These offences would include with the above intention:

(a) attacks upon a person's life which may cause death;
(b) attacks upon the physical integrity of a person;
(c) kidnapping or hostage taking;
(d) causing extensive destruction to a Government or public facility, a transport system, an infrastructure facility, including an information system, a fixed platform located on the continental shelf, a public place or private property likely to endanger human life or result in major economic loss;
(e) seizure of aircraft, ships or other means of public or goods transport;
(f) manufacture, possession, acquisition, transport, supply or use of weapons, explosives or of nuclear, biological or chemical weapons, as well as research into, and development of, biological and chemical weapons;
(g) release of dangerous substances, or causing fires, floods or explosions the effect of which is to endanger human life;
(h) interfering with or disrupting the supply of water, power or any other fundamental natural resource the effect of which is to endanger human life;
(i) threatening to commit any of the acts listed in (a) to (h).

The aim of this decision was to enable a common European arrest warrant and the mutual recognition of legal decisions and verdicts among EU member states.[44] On the same day, 13 June 2002, the European Union adopted another Framework Decision on the European Arrest Warrant which would eliminate the necessity for extradition and streamline procedures for arresting terror suspects.[45] Given that the PKK is included on the terrorist designation list, this would have a significant impact on any members of the organisation. In December 2005 the Justice and Home Affairs Council adopted the European Union Counter-Terrorism Strategy. The four pillars of the strategy were to prevent, protect, pursue and respond, the ultimate goal being to combat terrorism globally while respecting human rights.

With the Council Framework Decision and the Council of Europe Convention, the European States have been able, therefore, to make more progress than the international community. However, as we discuss later in the chapter, the proscription of terrorist groups in the European Union has led to a direct legal challenge by the PKK to its designation as such.

6.2 Definition of terrorist

The international community is also divided over the definition of what would constitute a terrorist, and the long-standing schism between the freedom fighter and the terrorist is the main difficulty in arriving at such a definition. A proposal could be that a definition should relate to the actions taken by the fighters not the political cause they represent. Reinisch argues that the most difficult legal and political issue in the Framework Convention discussed above was the definition of terrorist acts. He argues that the difficulty internationally was, first, about the role of 'state terrorism' and the other a possible exception for 'freedom fighters'.[46] The argument with respect to the definition of a terrorist relates to the oft-quoted phrase that one man's terrorist is another man's freedom fighter.[47]

There are two approaches to this thorny issue: to apply a general statement that those who belong to a proscribed group can be labelled as terrorists, or to call those who commit terrorist offences terrorists even though they might not be a member of such a group. The international community generally seems to follow the second approach by means of the avenue of criminalisation. Many of the International Conventions that deal with terrorism designate individual criminal responsibility for terrorist acts.[48]

When the Preparatory Committee for the Statute of the International Criminal Court met to discuss international crimes, the representative of India stated that international terrorism posed a challenge to the international community that had been recognised by world public opinion, as well as by world leaders. The argument went on to point out that the vast destruction of lives and property caused by international terrorism qualified that crime to be included among the 'core crimes' over which the proposed international criminal court should have jurisdiction. The representative of the Russian Federation supported the inclusion of terrorism among the core crimes, but said that only the most serious cases should be prosecuted. The court should not move against isolated cases of kidnapping, hijacking and other incidents.[49] The vast majority of nations argued that terrorism should not be included among the core crimes as it would result in could result in 'protracted discussions, which could lead to further delay in the establishment of an international criminal court'.[50]

The UN Counter-Terrorism Strategy takes the same criminal law approach stating in its action plan that states should agree to:

> ... ensure the apprehension and prosecution or extradition of perpetrators of terrorist acts, in accordance with the relevant provisions of national and international law, in particular human rights law, refugee law and international humanitarian law. We will endeavour to conclude and implement to that effect mutual judicial assistance and extradition agreements and to strengthen cooperation between law enforcement agencies.[51]

This strategy only defines perpetrators not terrorists. This is in keeping with previous UN Security Council Resolutions such as the famous 1373, which stated that nations should deny safe haven to those who finance, plan, support, or commit terrorist acts, or provide safe havens.[52]

In spite of the fact that there is a debate on individual international criminal responsibility, nowhere is there a definition of who might be considered a terrorist. This is a critical issue as most countries exclude from admission those who might be considered terrorists and will detain those asylum seekers who are suspected of being terrorists. In the United States, for instance, persons associated with groups such as the PKK listed on the 'Terrorist Exclusion List' may be found 'inadmissable' to the United States, and thus be prevented from entering the United States or may be liable for deportation if already in US territory. Therefore, it seems that the first approach is also being followed particularly in the activity of the European Union which is to list terrorist groups, and thus membership in such a group will result in a designation of terrorist. Unlike the United Nations lists being limited to those resulting from Al-Qaeda and Taliban activity, the European list is extensive and includes many groups seeking statehood for their ethnic group. The first action by the European Union took place shortly after 11 September 2001, in the form of Council Regulation 2580/2001 dated 27 December 2001 that listed a number of measures against terrorists including the freezing of all funds, financial assets and economic resources belonging to a group listed under this Regulation.[53] Article 2(3) established the procedure for including a group on a list of terrorist organisations as follows:

> 3. The Council, acting by unanimity, shall establish, review and amend the list of persons, groups and entities to which this Regulation applies, in accordance with the provisions laid down in Article 1(4), (5) and (6) of Common Position 2001/ 931/CFSP; such list shall consist of:
>
> (i)   natural persons committing, or attempting to commit, participating in or facilitating the commission of any act of terrorism;
> (ii) legal persons, groups or entities committing, or attempting to commit, participating in or facilitating the commission of any act of terrorism;

(iii) legal persons, groups or entities owned or controlled by one or more natural or legal persons, groups or entities referred to in points (i) and (ii); or

(iv) natural legal persons, groups or entities acting on behalf of or at the direction of one or more natural or legal persons, groups or entities referred to in points (i) and (ii).[54]

In the subsequent Framework Decision a terrorist group is defined in Article 2(1) as a 'structured group of more than two persons, established over a period of time and acting in concert to commit terrorist offences'. The structured group is defined as 'a group that is not random formed for the immediate commission of an offence and that does no need to have formally defined roles for its members, continuity of membership or a developed structure'.[55] Article 2 (2) requires member states to punish those accused of: (a) directing a terrorist group; and (b) participating in the activities of a terrorist group. This would include providing information, material resources or funding but mere membership, according to Saul, may not attract criminal liability.[56]

Clapham discusses the distinction between a terrorist and rebel. He argues that 'governments are more interested in painting their opponents as criminal elements or terrorists rather than insurgents or rebels … '.[57] Therefore, the conundrum between the two remains unresolved and seems that it may be a political rather than legal decision. It makes far more sense to view the acts as criminal and that those acts may be proscribed, rather than attempt to determine the distinction between freedom fighter and terrorist. The bulk of the terrorist conventions and actions discussed here do just that but the EU action on proscribed groups necessitates consideration of who might be a terrorist in spite of the disagreement over the definition. With respect to the PKK in Europe and the United States even though mere membership may not be sufficient, 'participating in the activities of a terrorist group' is a wide ambit indeed. However, within one Convention at least there is an exclusion from its ambit for armed conflict. Within the 1997 Terrorist Bombing Convention there is an exception for armed conflict which states:

Article 19

Nothing in this Convention shall affect other rights, obligations and responsibilities of States and individuals under international law, in particular the purposes and principles of the Charter of the United Nations and international humanitarian law.

The activities of armed forces during an armed conflict, as those terms are understood under international humanitarian law, which are governed by that law, are not governed by this Convention, and the activities undertaken by military forces of a State in the exercise of their official duties, inasmuch as they are governed by other rules of international law, are not governed by this Convention.[58]

Within this Convention, if the secessionist struggle rises to the level of an armed conflict the activities of that group are not terrorist but rather are governed by international humanitarian law.[59]

It is evident that the definitional issue of what constitutes terrorism or a terrorist group remains unresolved. In the following section we review the burgeoning jurisprudence of terrorism much of which concentrates on the human rights obligations of the state that apprehends terrorists. Once again, the lack of a definition of who is a terrorist has serious implications for the jurisprudence but there have been significant cases on the designation issue as well.

6.3 Jurisprudence of terrorism

Notwithstanding the lack of an agreed definition of 'terrorism' or 'terrorist', there have been numerous cases dealing with those suspected of terrorist activities who have challenged their treatment before domestic and regional courts. In some respects many of the cases we have already discussed concerning the treatment of civilians and alleged PKK members provide a framework for human rights guarantees within terrorism, but since 11 September 2001 there have also been highly influential domestic decisions. These are essential as Gasser summarises the activities of states post-11 September, which curtail the rights of individuals. He outlines these activities as:

- tightening police surveillance, particularly of foreign residents;
- adopting more 'vigorous' interrogation procedures, which may amount to inhumane treatment or even to torture;
- curtailing the right of alleged terrorists to a fair trial by, eg establishing limits to access to witnesses and to the exercise of other rights of the defendant, measures which may sometimes be equivalent to abolishing the presumption of the defendant's innocence;
- toughening attitudes vis-à-vis asylum-seekers, refugees and migrants, eg by ignoring the prohibition on returning such persons against their will to a country where they have to fear for their lives (principle of *non-refoulement*).[60]

The case law of the European Court of Human Rights, European Court of Justice, United States Supreme Court, the United Kingdom House of Lords, the Inter-American Court of Human Rights and an important case from the Italian Court of Cassation, have all affirmed the position that even those persons labelled as potential terrorists are entitled to human rights and international humanitarian law protections, the very protections applicable in armed conflict that are discussed in previous chapters.[61] A significant body of jurisprudence particularly in the United States and the United Kingdom has significantly moderated the effects of the legislative and administrative acts being employed against terrorists and held these measures up to the standards of international legality. These courts are refusing to allow legislation or administrative measures to stand that allows people to be detained without trial or permit evidence to be adduced that was obtained by torture. These courts have now been joined by significant jurisprudence from the European Court of Justice dealing with the proscription of terrorists or terrorist groups. All of these cases describe standards of conduct that are relevant to the way in which Turkish officials deal with suspected PKK members, as the standards used by these courts are international law norms. These cases should be viewed alongside the extensive jurisprudence of the European Court of Human Rights, which is discussed in earlier chapters.

6.3.1 Detention provisions in the United Kingdom[62]

A major issue under the United Kingdom Anti-Terrorism Crime and Security Act 2001 was the unlimited detention of terror suspects within the United Kingdom pursuant to Article 23 in Part IV of this Act.[63] In the derogation from the Article 5 liberty and security of the person provisions in the European Convention on Human Rights which was filed in the Council of Europe following the 11 September attacks, the government outlined the scope of this provision:

> ... an extended power to arrest and detain a foreign national which will apply where it is intended to remove or deport the person from the United Kingdom but where removal or deportation is not for the time being possible, with the consequence that the detention would be unlawful under existing domestic law powers. The extended power to arrest and detain will apply where the Secretary of State issues a certificate indicating his belief that the person's presence in the United Kingdom is a risk to national security and that he suspects the person of being an international terrorist. That certificate will be subject to an appeal to the Special Immigration Appeals Commission ('SIAC'), established under the Special Immigration Appeals Commission Act 1997, which will have power to cancel it if it considers that the certificate should not have been issued. There will be an appeal on a point of law from a ruling by SIAC. In addition, the certificate will be reviewed by SIAC at regular intervals.[64]

Under Article 15 (1) of the European Convention on Human Rights, where a public emergency threatening the life of the nation is shown to exist, a member state may lawfully derogate from some human rights protections, provided that the measures taken are strictly required by the situation. No other European country has taken such a step in the wake of the 11 September attacks. This derogation from the European Convention on Human Rights has been the focus of sustained legal challenge in the United Kingdom.

The House of Lords considered unlimited detention in *A (FC) and others (FC) (Appellants) v Secretary of State for the Home Department (Respondent)* decided on 16 December 2004.[65] The case concerned the nine appellants, all of whom were detained under section 23 of the Anti-Terrorism, Crime and Security Act 2001. The legal issue was that the detention provision was inconsistent with the obligations binding on the United Kingdom by the European Convention on Human

Rights and given domestic effect by the Human Rights Act 1998. Lord Bingham, speaking for the majority, referred to a previous influential decision on detention, *Chahal v United Kingdom*, in which the European Commission on Human Rights unanimously rejected qualification of the Article 3 prohibition against torture for security reasons.[66] The Commission held that if a person could not be deported due to risk of torture and there were no criminal charges pending, then he or she should not be detained.[67]

Lord Bingham agreed that the emergency triggered by the 11 September attacks caused a public emergency threatened the 'life of the nation' and therefore, derogation from the detention provisions in the European Convention on Human Rights might be justified. However, even though the derogation might be permissible the actual measure of unlimited detention was not. Part of the material relied upon in making this decision was the Privy Counsellor Review Committee known as the Newton Committee's recommendation that the detention provisions be replaced. Lord Bingham held that even if there was a public emergency threatening the life of the nation, measures that derogate from Article 5 of the European Convention on Human Rights were permissible only to the extent strictly required by the exigencies of the situation. Amongst his reasons were that the state had not proved that the measures were proportional as it had not explained why the measures were directed only to foreign nationals and why a terrorist, if a serious threat to the United Kingdom, ceases to be so elsewhere. He held later that these measures also violated Article 14, the discrimination provision of the European Convention on Human Rights. Lord Bingham ruled that there would be a declaration under section 4 of the Human Rights Act 1998 that section 23 of the Anti-Terrorism, Crime and Security Act 2001 is incompatible with Articles 5 and 14 of the European Convention on Human Rights insofar as it was disproportionate and permitted detention of suspected international terrorists in a way that discriminated on the ground of nationality or immigration status. Most of the other members of the House of Lords Appellate Committee supported the opinion of Lord Bingham.

Part of the basis of the decision was the Newton Committee report reviewing the Anti-Terrorism, Crime and Security Act 2001 released in December 2003. Lord Rooker, then a Minister in the Home Office, explained to the Lords that '[t]he committee will complete a review of the operation of the Act with full access to all the information including that from the security services and so forth'.[68] The Newton Committee report stated that 'we have taken evidence from the police, the security and intelligence agencies and other counter terrorist officials'.[69] The report contained significant findings. First of all, the Privy Counsellors agreed that counter-terrorism legislation may be justified because of the way terrorists operate but any such legislation had to contain proper protection for the privacy and liberty of the individual.[70] Their major recommendation was that the powers allowing foreign nationals to be detained potentially indefinitely as set out in Part IV of the Act should be replaced as a matter of urgency.[71] The committee would not, and indeed could not, have made such a recommendation had it believed that the derogation was warranted.[72] The Newton

Committee strongly recommended that 'Part 4 powers which allow foreign nationals to be detained potentially indefinitely should be replaced as a matter of urgency. New legislation should ... not require derogation from the European Convention on Human Rights'.[73]

The Parliamentary Joint Human Rights Committee had also expressed doubts about the necessity of derogation from the right to liberty under the European Convention on Human Rights. In its first report on the Anti-Terrorism Crime and Security Act 2001, published in November 2001, the committee stated that there were not enough safeguards 'to ensure that the measures in the Bill could be said to be strictly required by the exigencies of the situation' and concluded that 'we are not persuaded that the circumstances of the present emergency or the exigencies of the current situation meet the tests set out in Article 15 of the ECHR'.[74] The report of the Committee in February 2004 report stated: 'we continue to doubt whether the very wide powers conferred by Part 4 are, in Convention terms, strictly required by the exigencies of the situation'.[75]

As a result of this case and the critical committee reports, the government introduced new legislation and the Prevention of Terrorism Act 2005 came into force on 11 March 2005.[76] The Act replaced section 4 – the unlimited detention provision – of the Anti-Terrorism, Crime and Security Act 2001. This Act gave the Home Secretary the power to make Control Orders in respect of suspected terrorists, whether British or foreign nationals.

These Control Orders include a range of possible conditions such as a ban on mobile phone or internet use, restrictions on movement and travel, restrictions on associations with named individuals, and the use of tagging for the purposes of monitoring curfews. This is not an ideal situation again and was the subject of further court challenges. On 31 October 2007 the House of Lords issued three opinions on Control Orders and although they stopped short of striking down the provisions, the Lords held that the most restrictive part of the Control Orders, the 18-hour home curfew, were so restrictive of liberty as to amount to a deprivation of liberty for the purposes of Article 5(1) of the European Convention on Human Rights. However, the Lords did agree that shorter curfews were acceptable.[77] In another critical aspect of these decisions the Lords held intelligence-based evidence that might constitute the evidence for the Control Orders could not be withheld from suspects and their lawyers.[78] To do so was incompatible with the fair trial guarantees of Article 6 of the European Convention on Human Rights.

Furthermore, after the 7 July 2005 bombings, the government attempted to introduce longer detention provisions from the current 14 days without a hearing up to 3 months.[79] This effort was not successful but a compromise was adopted of 28 days detention without review. This is far outside the allowable limit in the European Convention on Human Rights jurisprudence and it will likely face further challenge.[80] There has not yet been a hearing on this particular issue but it is clear that UK courts at least will not accept unreasonable limitations on the liberty of the individual. Given the human rights case of unlimited detentions in Turkey, while not binding, the House of Lords has given proper and

reasonable consideration of detention of terror suspects preserving the fundamental guarantees of detainees.

6.3.2 Detention of terror suspects abroad

The second major issue in counter-terrorism has been the detention of terror
suspects abroad in either secret detention facilities or in Guantanamo Bay. The
courts in the United Kingdom have also faced litigation dealing with this
issue with respect to citizens of the United Kingdom. This litigation on first
glance has not yielded the same positive results but has resulted in significant
pressure on politicians to deal with the issue. In the case of *Abbasi and Another v
Secretary of State for Foreign and Commonwealth Affairs*,[81] the Court of Appeal rejected
the request of Mr Abbasi, a UK national held in Guantanamo Bay, to compel the
Foreign and Commonwealth Office to 'make representations on his behalf to
the United States government or to take other appropriate action or at least to
give an explanation as to why this has not been done'.[82] The court agreed with
the submissions for Mr Abbasi that at present he was being arbitrarily detained
'in present contravention of fundamental principles recognised by both jurisdictions and by international law'. The court memorably described this phenomenon
as a 'legal black-hole'.[83] The court went on to say:

> What appears to us to be objectionable is that Mr. Abbasi should be subject
> to indefinite detention in territory over which the United States has exclusive
> control with no opportunity to challenge the legitimacy of his detention
> before any court or tribunal.[84]

Regrettably, the court held that it could do nothing about the situation stating
that international law had not recognised that a state was under to duty to
intervene by diplomatic or other means to protect a citizen who if suffering or
threatened with injury in a foreign state.[85] The court also analysed the decisions
of the European Court of Human Rights in *Al-Adsani*[86] and *Bankovic*[87] and held
that they stood for the principles: that the jurisdiction referred to in Article 1 of
the European Convention on Human Rights would normally be territorial; where
a state enjoyed effective control of a foreign territory that territory would fall into
the jurisdiction for the purposes of Article 1; and where, under the principles of
international law, a state enjoyed extra-territorial jurisdiction over an individual
and acted in the exercise of that jurisdiction, that individual could be deemed
to be within the jurisdiction of the state. None of these criteria applied to
Mr Abbasi. The court held that the European Convention on Human Rights and
the Human Rights Act 1998 did not afford any support to the contention that the
Foreign Secretary owed Mr Abbasi a duty to exercise diplomacy on his behalf.[88]
    Another significant part of the judgment discussed the discretion of the Foreign
Office in protecting British citizens. This was a very wide discretion both to
exercise the right to protect citizens in the first place and what measures to take if
it decided to intervene. Decisions to make representations on a diplomatic level

were 'intimately connected with decisions relating to this country's foreign policy'.[89]

This decision was made in spite of evidence in the *First Report on Diplomatic Protection*, from the UN Special Rapporteur on diplomatic protection, Professor Dugard. The Dugard Report proposed that a state should have a legal duty 'to exercise diplomatic protection on behalf of an injured [national] upon request, if the injury results from a grave breach of a jus cogens norm attributable to another State'.[90]

Although this decision was clearly disappointing for the advocates for Guantanamo Bay prisoners, the phrase 'the legal black-hole' has been adopted in a subsequent influential address by Lord Steyn 'Guantanamo Bay: The Legal Black Hole'. In a speech made at the British Institute of International and Comparative Law, Lord Steyn engaged in a blistering attack on the lawfulness of detention and urged the US court system to take into account the statement of Master of the Rolls, Lord Phillips of Worth Matravers, who called the lack of challenge to the legitimacy of detention 'objectionable'.[91] Lord Steyn stated:

> By denying the prisoners the right to raise challenges in court about their alleged status and treatment, the United States government is in breach of the minimum standards of customary international law.[92]

Addressing the issue of military commissions he stated that they were not independent courts or tribunals and that the term 'kangaroo court' sprang to mind and conveyed the idea 'of a pre-ordained arbitrary rush to judgment by an irregular tribunal which makes a mockery of justice'.[93] These are eloquent words from a member of the Law Lords.

It has to be noted that the British government was able to secure the release of all the UK detainees from Guantanamo Bay by diplomatic negotiations, and the pressure of the dicta in *Abbasi* and from various parliamentarians and Law Lords had to be influential. Furthermore, in the United States there was a concerted effort on the part of legal experts to challenge the legality of detention in Guantanamo Bay, ultimately resulting in President Obama's decision to close the facility which is underway at the time of the writing of this chapter. This again is an important discussion with relation to PKK suspects, as the importance of access to counsel, and the right to challenge detention is also relevant to the conflict in southeast Turkey as established in the case law of the European Court of Human Rights; these rights extend even to those suspected of being involved in the most heinous crimes.

The US Supreme Court, in a series of influential decisions, has also considered the issue of detention in Guantanamo Bay and other locations, and reviewed the arrangement for proposed military commissions set up to try the suspects. In two critical decisions by the Court on 28 June 2004, the Court considered the applications of *Hamdi* and *Rasul*.[94] In *Hamdi* an American citizen was arrested by the US military in Afghanistan. He was declared to be an 'enemy combatant' for fighting for the Taliban. The question before the Court was whether the government had violated Hamdi's Fifth Amendment right to due process by holding him indefinitely without access to a lawyer due to his designation as an enemy combatant. A further question was whether the separation of powers doctrine required federal courts to defer to the Executive's determination that an American citizen was an enemy combatant. Justice O'Connor for the majority ruled that although the US Congress had authorised Hamdi's detention, Fifth Amendments rights of due process guarantees a US citizen the ability to challenge the detention before a neutral decision maker.[95] In *Rasul v Bush*, an even more significant decision, four British and Australian citizens were captured by the US military in Pakistan or Afghanistan and transported to Guantanamo Bay. The question before the US Supreme Court was whether the US courts had jurisdiction to consider legal appeals filed on behalf of foreign citizens held by the United States on Guantanamo Bay. Justice Stevens for the majority held that the degree of control exercised by the United States over Guantanamo Bay, Cuba was sufficient to allow for the application of *habeas corpus* rights to challenge the constitutionality of their detention, once again under the Fifth Amendment due process rights.[96]

Two other cases also provided significant guarantees for detained persons. *Hamdan v Rumsfeld* was decided on 29 June 2006.[97] Osama bin Laden's former chauffeur, Hamdan was captured by the Afghan forces and held in Guantanamo Bay. The main question considered in the opinion were whether the rights for prisoners of war protected by the Geneva Conventions can be enforced in federal courts through *habeas corpus*. The second question was concerning the legality of the establishment of military commissions to try Hamdan and others. Justice Stevens for the majority held that neither an Act of Congress nor the inherent powers of the Executive laid out in the Constitution expressly authorised the sort of military commission set up in this case. Military commissions had to comply with the ordinary laws of the United States and the laws of war. The Geneva Conventions along with the Statutory Uniform Code of Military Justice could be enforced by the Supreme Court. The exclusion of Hamdan from certain parts of his trial deemed classified violated both of these laws and therefore, his trial was illegal.[98]

The *Boumediene v Bush* decision was rendered by the court on 12 June 2008.[99] In a now familiar story, Boumediene and five other Algerians were seized by Bosnian police under suspicion of a plot to attack the US Embassy in Sarajevo. They were classified as enemy combatants, sent to Guantanamo Bay and subsequently faced trial by military commission. The court considered four questions: (a) Should the Military Commissions Act of 2006 be interpreted to deny federal courts jurisdiction over *habeas corpus* petitions filed by foreigners detained at Guantanamo Bay?; (b) If so, was the Military Commissions Act of 2006 a violation of the suspension Clause of the Constitution?; (c) Are the detainees at Guantanamo Bay entitled to the protection of the Fifth Amendment right not to be deprived of liberty without due process of law and of the Geneva Conventions?; and (d) Can the detainees challenge the adequacy of the judicial review provisions of the Military Commissions Act of 2006 before they have sought to invoke that review? In the opinion, delivered by Justice Kennedy, it stated that the Military Commissions Act of 2006 operated as an unconstitutional suspension of the writ of *habeas corpus*. The detainees were not barred from seeking *habeas corpus* or invoking the Suspension Clause merely because they were declared to be enemy combatants or held at Guantanamo Bay.[100]

6.3.3 Torture of terrorism suspects

Another important human rights concern is the issue of torture of terrorist suspects, which is considered in previous chapters. This has a significant extra-territorial aspect. It is clear that the European Convention on Human Rights prohibits torture and inhuman or degrading treatment or punishment. In the landmark case of *Ireland v United Kingdom*,[101] the United Kingdom was found to have committed acts of inhuman and degrading treatment (not torture) in dealing with terrorist suspects in the Irish troubles but the practices described had already been discontinued by the United Kingdom. These practices included hooding, wall standing and sleep deprivation. Since that case there had been a clear commitment on the part of the UK government not to tolerate torture of any kind on its territory. However, an influential House of Lords case considered whether a court in the United Kingdom can use evidence in hearings that might have been obtained by torture elsewhere.

The House of Lords considered this issue in a case with the same name as a case on detention: *A (FC) and others (FC) (Appellants) v Secretary of State for the Home Department (Respondent)*.[102] This decision was released on 8 December 2005. The question before the Lords was:

> May the Special Immigration Appeals Commission (SIAC), a superior court of record established by statute, when hearing an appeal under section 25 of the Anti-terrorism, Crime and Security Act by a person certified and detained under sections 21 and 23 of that Act, receive evidence which has or may have been procured by torture inflicted, in order to obtain evidence, by officials of a foreign state without the complicity of the British authorities?

Lord Bingham (in the minority in this case) analysed this question from three perspectives: English common law; the European Convention on Human Rights; and international law. He first summarised the common law position stating 'It is, I think, clear that from its very earliest days the common law of England set its face firmly against the use of torture'.[103] He also relied upon section 78 of the Police and Criminal Evidence Act 1984 which gave effect to the intent of Article 15 of the International Convention against Torture and other Cruel, Inhuman or Degrading Treatment or Punishment 1984 (CAT).

In considering the European Convention on Human Rights, Lord Bingham indicated that as SIAC was a public authority within the meaning of section 6 of the Human Rights Act 1998 it, therefore, was forbidden to act incompatibly with Convention rights. The two primary rights affected were the Article 3 – absolute prohibition against torture and the Article 6 – fair trial guarantee. Although Lord Bingham acknowledged that the European Court of Human Rights had consistently declined to articulate evidential rules to be applied, the Court did mandate that proceedings be fair which it would not be if evidence was obtained by torture.

The third consideration was public international law and the proposition that the prohibition of torture enjoyed the highest normative force recognised by international law. Lord Bingham held that the prohibition against torture imposed on states obligations towards all other members of the international community and, therefore, there would be a claim to compliance on the part of all states (even if the torture took place elsewhere). Furthermore, torture had acquired the status of a peremptory norm of customary international law and thus one of the most fundamental standards of the international community. Lord Bingham held there was a duty on states to reject the fruits of torture inflicted in breach of international law. This discussion of the binding force of international legal obligations will be an important precedent in subsequent decisions.

Although the sentiments expressed by Lord Bingham on evidence obtained by torture abroad was shared by all the Law Lords, they disagreed on the burden of proof needed to establish that this torture had occurred. Lord Bingham who was joined by Lord Nicholls and Lord Hoffmann, did not agree with the Secretary of State that it was for the party seeking to challenge the admissibility of evidence based on it being obtained by torture to prove the factual grounds on to base the challenge. Lord Bingham proposed that all the appellant should have to do is advance some plausible reason why the evidence may have been procured by torture and then the SIAC would have to make inquiries to conclude that there is not a real risk that the evidence was obtained by torture. Lord Hope, who was joined by Lord Rodger, Lord Carswell and Lord Brown for the majority, on the other hand proposed the following test: Is it established by means of such diligent enquiries into the sources that it is practicable to carry out and on a balance of probabilities, that the information relied on by the Secretary of States was obtained under torture? This would mean that the onus remains with the person seeking to exclude the evidence as Lord Nicholls stated to 'place on the detainee a burden of proof which, for reasons beyond his control, he can seldom discharge'.[104] This is a most disappointing aspect of the judgment as it will be very difficult to establish torture and thus to exclude evidence.

In spite of the disagreement on the test for proving torture it is clear that British courts will not accept evidence obtained by torture from third countries. The aspect of the judgment relevant for the purposes of this chapter was the extensive reference to international standards for fair trial and on the prohibition against torture which included even those suspected of planning serious terrorist offences.

6.3.4 Deaths of suspected terrorists while in detention

In *The Queen (on the application of Mazin Mumaa Galteh Al-Skeini and Others) v The Secretary of State for Defence*[105] decided by the Court of Appeal on 21 December 2005 and the House of Lords in June 2007, the issue before the court was the extra-territorial application of the European Convention on Human Rights. However, one of the applicants, Iraqi Police Colonel Daoud Mousa, was bringing a claim on behalf of his son, Baha Mousa, aged 26 who had died while in the custody of the British army.[106] The Secretary of State for Defence conceded that the United Kingdom was exercising extra-territorial jurisdiction for European Convention on Human Rights purposes. The Court of Appeal upheld the High Court's finding that the Human Rights Act 1998 and the European Convention on Human Rights apply to Mr Mousa's case on the basis that he came within the authority and control of British forces in Iraq. The Court of Appeal went further and held that not only those in British prisons were protected by the Human Rights Act 1998 and the European Convention on Human Rights, but individuals whose liberty had been restricted by British forces were also covered, regardless of whether they were detained in a prison, as they came under British authority and control. The Court of Appeal further highlighted the defects in military investigations, in particular, the role of the Commanding Officer and the inherent problems resulting from investigations lacking independence from the military chain of command. The Court recognised the important and unique protection provided by the European Convention on Human Rights, through the positive obligation under Articles 2 and 3, to conduct an independent investigation and that such protection could extend to territory outside Europe where a state party was found to have effective control over such territory.

On 13 June 2007 in the House of Lords, the Law Lords upheld the lower court ruling that UK human rights laws did apply to Mousa because he was in British custody in Iraq. Therefore, according to Baroness Hale, the United Kingdom 'would be answerable in Strasbourg for the conduct of the British army while Mr. Mousa was detained'.[107] This crucial case confirms the continued applicability of human rights law in armed conflict. Furthermore, for the purposes of the duties of the detaining powers, as is discussed in Chapter 4, there must be a proper and thorough investigation of suspicious deaths while in custody.

6.3.5 Designation of a group as a terrorist organisation or designation of an individual as a terrorist

Finally, within this survey of the jurisprudence of terrorism is consideration of the designation of groups as terrorist and the issue of membership in that group, an issue that is so significant for the PKK. First, in 2007, the Italian Court of Cassation considered three Moroccan and Tunisian nationals, Abdelaziz, Sassi and Mohammed, accused in 2003 of 'association with the aim of committing international terrorism' in Italy and abroad, a crime which was proscribed at that time by Article 270 *bis*(3) of the Italian Criminal Code.[108] They were charged with taking part in the recruitment and dispatching to Iraq and other war zones of volunteers to be trained as Islamic fighters, mainly within the framework of the Islamic organisation Ansar-al-Islam. Abdelaziz, Sassi and Mohammed were also accused of several other crimes, such as aiding and abetting illegal emigration and immigration from and into Italy, and providing false identity documents. The Court of Cassation considered the international Conventions with respect to terrorism, and more particularly the 1999 Convention on the Suppression of Terrorism Financing and the European Framework Decision on Terrorism. However, the Court indicated that the absence of a global convention on international terrorism was due to a disagreement among states over whether acts of freedom fighters engaged in wars of liberation, or in the course of an armed struggle for the right of self-determination, should be exempted from the category of terrorist conduct. The Court stated:

> Lacking such an instrument, one has to understand Article 2(1)(b) of the 1999 Convention as providing a general definition of international terrorism, applicable both in times of peace and during armed conflict. According to a customary international rule whose existence is confirmed in various resolutions of the UN General Assembly and UN Security Council, as well as in the International Convention for the Suppression of Terrorist Bombings (15 December 1997) UNGA Res 52/164 UN Doc A/RES/52/164, entered into force 23 May 2001, the notion of international terrorism also requires a psychological element: the criminal conduct must be based on political, ideological, or religious motivations, and must not be undertaken for a personal end.[109]

Italy had expressly introduced a new Article 270 into the Criminal Code in 2005 in order to implement the European Union Framework Decision. Unlike the 1999 Convention, the Framework Decision was based on a list of offences under national law. The Italian provision also affirmed that international terrorist acts are also those set out in the international Conventions. On the basis of both the international and European standard the court concluded that terrorist conduct depended on the identity of the perpetrators and of the victims, and could also constitute war crimes and crimes against humanity. With respect to the group the defendants supported, the court held that the inclusion of Ansar-al-Islam among the organisations listed in UN Security Council Resolution 1267 of 15 October 1999 was not conclusive evidence of its terrorist nature. The list, according to the Italian Court, was to identify groups and individuals targeted by UN sanctions and, accordingly, it only had an administrative character. Inclusion on the list could not override the principle of the free assessment of evidence by an independent judge. Therefore, the Court of Appeal (which upheld the charges against these persons) ought to have investigated more thoroughly what kind of relationship existed between the accused and this organisation and other transnational Islamic organisations actively engaged in terrorist activities abroad. The Court should have ascertained whether the accused were aware of terrorist methods being used by their organisation. The decision of the Court of Appeal was quashed and the case remanded to a different section of the Court where, in the new proceeding, the Court would have to reassess the collected evidence in order to reassess whether the accused were guilty of 'association for the purposes of international terrorism'.[110] This is indeed significant as the Court considered that it had the legal jurisdiction to consider terrorist designation and acts of terrorism independently of any listing of persons or individuals. This case supports the contention in this chapter that it is the activity that needs to be assessed not the label.

The European Court of Justice has also considered the issue of designation of individuals and groups as terrorists in several cases. However, the landmark case has been the case of *Ahmed Ali Yusuf & Al Barakaat International Foundation v Council and Commission* and *Yassin Abdullah Kadi v Council of the European Union and Commission of the European Communities*, known in academic literature as the *Kadi* case.[111] The case dealt with the European Community (EC) Regulation that implements the UN Security Council's orders to freeze the assets of alleged terrorists or terrorist supporters. The Court of First Instance had refused to review the Regulation fully, on the ground that its basis lay in UN Security Council Resolutions which were binding on all member states. However, on appeal, the European Court of Justice stressed that all legislative acts issued by Community organs had to comply with the fundamental rights guaranteed under European Community law, even when those acts were designed to implement resolutions of the UN Security Council, which are binding on UN member states under international law. The Court held that the regulation violated the appellants' rights to be heard, to effective judicial review, and to have their property respected, and the European Court of Justice set aside the judgments of the Court of First Instance and annulled the contested regulation insofar as it applied to the appellants.[112] Once again, this jurisprudence confirmed the continued applicability of human rights guarantees even where terrorism is suspected.

6.4 Consequences of the definition of the PKK as terrorists

Although the PKK was not included on the original list of terrorism groups on 27 December 2001,[113] it was included on a later list promulgated on 2 May 2002.[114,115] The PKK has not accepted this designation and has embarked on long protracted litigation in the European Court of Justice to appeal this designation and seek to have the PKK taken off the list of terrorist groups. On 18 January, the European Court of Justice released its decision in the case *The Kurdistan Workers Party (PKK) and the Kurdistan National Congress (KNK) v Council*.[116] The PKK and the KNK appealed a 2005 order of the Court of First Instance which dismissed the action on inadmissibility grounds. The parties sought annulment of a Council anti-terrorist measure. The European Court of Justice held that the action was in fact partly admissible with reference to the PKK and referred the case back to the Court of First Instance for judgment on substance. As at the time of the writing of this book this important legal issue has not concluded and it is difficult to predict what the ultimate result might be, but one of the problems with the process is some of the tactics that have been used by the PKK in its struggle, which might constitute terrorist acts. It is to this we now turn.

6.4.1 Alleged acts of terrorism and the PKK

As discussed in Chapters 2 and 3, the non-international armed conflict in southeast Turkey is subject to the rules of international humanitarian law both customary and treaty-based. There is a primary rule of customary international humanitarian law that is applicable to this discussion. Rule 2 as proposed by the ICRC Customary International Humanitarian Law Study applicable in both international and non-international armed conflict states that:

> Acts or threats of violence the primary purpose of which is to spread terror among the civilian population are prohibited.

Article 33 of the Fourth Geneva Convention states that 'Collective penalties and likewise all measures of intimidation or of terrorism are prohibited', while Article 4 of Additional Protocol II prohibits 'acts of terrorism' against persons not or no longer taking part in hostilities. The purpose of these provisions was to emphasise that neither individuals, nor the civilian population may be subject to collective punishments, which, among other things, obviously induce a state of terror.[117]

Both Additional Protocols to the Geneva Conventions contain provisions that prohibit acts aimed at spreading terror among the civilian population. 'The civilian population as such, as well as individual civilians, shall not be the object of attack. Acts or threats of violence the primary purpose of which is to spread terror among the civilian population are prohibited'.[118] Yet as mentioned previously, Turkey is not a party to these provisions, which is why the customary rule is so important.

Although it is highly unlikely that the PKK is a terrorist organisation in the face of the controversy over national liberation groups, allegations that the PKK engages in acts of violence the purpose of which is to spread terror among the civilian population must be addressed. As the PKK signed the document agreeing to comply with international humanitarian law, activities such as this would constitute a war crime.

On an annual basis the US Department of State, Office of the Coordinator for Counterterrorism, releases its *Patterns of Global Terrorism* report, which contains country reports, including an annual report on Turkey.[119] A review of these reports contains few attacks that could constitute a violation of customary and treaty law prohibitions against acts of terror. In 1996, the report stated that on 30 June 1996 there was a suicide bombing against a Turkish military parade in Tunceli which killed nine security forces personnel and wounded another 35. In October, four schoolteachers were murdered outside Diyarbarkir and in October three tourists were kidnapped outside Bingol. There were also two more suicide bombings in late October that killed two civilians in addition to eight security forces personnel in Adana and Sivas.

There were no reports of terrorist activity in 1997 but some disturbing incidents in 1998. On 10 April it was alleged in the report that PKK terrorists on a motorcycle threw a bomb into a park near the Blue Mosque in Istanbul. The explosion injured two Indians, a New Zealander and four Turkish citizens. In southeast Turkey in early June 1998 it was reported that the PKK kidnapped a German tourist and a Turkish truck driver with the truck driver remaining missing. After their leader Öcalan was arrested in Italy, the PKK conducted three suicide bombings in southeastern Turkey killing three persons and injuring dozens.

Öcalan was tried and sentenced to death in 1999, and the PKK did not conduct operations answering a call from him for a ceasefire. This pattern of pursuing a peace initiative continued in 2000 and 2001. In April 2002 the PKK changed its name to the Kurdistan Freedom and Democracy Congress (KADEK) and declared its commitment to political versus armed tactics to advance Kurdish rights in Turkey, during this same year Öcalan's death sentence was commuted. In October 2003 KADEK made yet another name change to the Kurdistan People's Congress (KHK or Kongra-Gel). The State Department alleged that the KHK had launched several attacks in retaliation for losses the group suffered from Turkish counter-insurgency operations, but there was no allegation of civilian targets or terrorist tactics. In the summer of 2004, PKK/KADEK/Kongra-Gel renounced its cease fire and the Turkish press reported multiple incidents in the southeast of PKK/KADEK/Kongra-Gel terrorist actions or clashes between Turkish security forces and PKK/KADEK/Kongra-Gel militants. The State Department reported an escalation in 2005. The report stated that there were a number of bombings and attempted bombings in resort areas in western Turkey and Istanbul, some of which resulted in civilian casualties. However, as is discussed in earlier chapters, the report acknowledged that it was another Kurdish separatist group calling itself the Kurdish Freedom Falcons (TAK), which claimed responsibility for many of these attacks.

In 2006 the report indicated that the KHK/PKK attacks against Turkey increased significantly and claimed as many as 600 lives in 2006. However, in October, the KHK/PKK declared a unilateral cease-fire that slowed the intensity and pace of its attacks, but attacks continued in response to Turkish security forces significant counter-insurgency and counter-terrorism operations, especially in the southeast. However, the report did not indicate that there had been attacks on civilian targets or persons. This activity continued in 2007, but once again the report alleged that it was the TAK that claimed responsibility for a series of deadly attacks on Turkish and foreign citizens in Turkish cities. On 25 May 2007, the KHK/PKK claimed responsibility for the bombing of a cargo train in Bingol Province, which could be a civilian target but not necessarily a terrorist attack. During this time of sustained violence, the Turkish Parliament on 17 October 2007 overwhelmingly passed a motion authorising cross-border military operations against KHK/PKK targets in northern Iraq. Turkish forces carried out extensive operations along the Turkey-Iraq border in the latter part of the year. On 5 November 2007 President Bush committed to provide Turkey 'real-time, actionable intelligence' to counter the KHK/PKK in northern Iraq.

The TAK, a group designated as terrorists, has claimed responsibility for a series of deadly attacks in Turkish cities in recent years. On 19 February 2007, the TAK announced it would engage in a renewed campaign of violence in Turkey. On 27 July 2007, two bombs exploded in the Istanbul working-class neighbourhood Güngören, killing 17 and injuring more than 150. No group claimed responsibility, but Turkish authorities blamed the PKK. On 19 August 2007, both the TAK and the PKK claimed responsibility for a 19 August 2007 car bomb at a Mersin police checkpoint and for a 23 August 2007 car bomb in a residential area of Izmir. The PKK also claimed responsibility for a car bomb in Diyarbakir on 3 January 2007, which killed six civilians and wounded 70; it apologised for this attack, claiming that the attackers were PKK members acting independently of orders.

The Turkish military and the PKK engaged in constant skirmishes in the southeast throughout the year, the largest of which was a 4 October 2007 attack against a military outpost at Aktutun, in which 15 soldiers were reported killed. On 17 October 2007, in the midst of weeks of violence, during which PKK attacks claimed scores of killed or wounded Turkish soldiers and citizens, the Turkish Parliament overwhelmingly passed a motion authorising cross-border military operations against PKK targets in northern Iraq, which it renewed in October 2008. US information-sharing, begun in November 2007, helps ensure these Turkish actions hit terrorist rather than civilian targets. Turkish forces carried out extensive operations along the Turkey-Iraq border in the latter part of the year and continued to carry out strikes along the Turkey-Iraq border throughout 2008. In February, the Turks launched ground operations into northern Iraq, targeting PKK locations, and then disengaged by the end of the month. The Turkish government claimed that 657 PKK members were killed, 161 were captured, and 161 had surrendered in skirmishes throughout the year. In addition, 120 PKK members turned themselves over to Turkish authorities under the terms of a repentance law passed in 2005.

A careful review of these reports indicate that by and large the attacks that could clearly be labelled as terrorist have been conducted since the arrest of Öcalan by those who are not members of the PKK but rather by the TAK. The US State Department alleges that these two groups are connected but this is strenuously denied by the PKK which condemns attacks on civilians. It will be this type of evidence that will be assessed by the European Court of First Instance when the matter of terrorist designation returns to the Court.

Conclusion

The complication of the legal designation of terrorism or terrorist adds little to the analysis of the Kurdish conflict and that it is within the traditional *jus in bello* or *jus ad bellum* rules that this situation should be addressed. However, it is clear that within international humanitarian law, acts of terror constitute war crimes and are prohibited. The PKK has an obligation to comply with the rules of armed conflict and by and large it has done so. Yet the acts of terror outlined above, even though largely historical, put the organisation at risk of being labelled as a terrorist organisation because of the criminal acts it might perpetrate under terrorism conventions (particularly prohibitions against the taking of hostages) and under international humanitarian law. It is vital that the PKK as the armed group involved in the insurgency refrains from any acts that might conceivably be labelled as terrorist.

Nevertheless, due to the existence of the armed conflict there is a political obligation to address the issues surrounding the conflict and that the international community should not hide behind the designation of terrorism. Pursuing terrorist groups and the terrorists does little to resolve the underlying conflict discussed in earlier chapters. Chapter 7, the beginning of the section on political solutions to this crisis, addresses the issue of terrorism and the solution to armed conflict by political negotiation.

Part 2

7 Terrorism

Historical engagement and the global war on terror

Introduction

This chapter examines the current predominant approach, both regionally and in the wider international community, to the conflict in southeast Turkey and, to some extent the cross-border operations into Kurdistan, Iraq as one of 'combating terrorism'. Following from the conclusions of Chapter 6, which resolve that terrorism is not a useful legal designation, this chapter examines politicised applications of terrorism to the Kurdish conflict, and analyses the implications for resolution of the conflict and post-conflict mechanisms. First, the impact of the so-called 'global war on terror' on the political dynamics of the Kurdish conflict are considered, before an in-depth analysis of international responses to the conflict. Then, the chapter examines the role of the international community and regional actors in comparative scenarios of 'terrorism', looking at when they have and have not been successful in reducing conflict and establishing sustainable post-conflict mechanisms.

7.1 The global 'war on terror'

The attacks of 11 September 2001 on the World Trade Center and the Pentagon sparked a renewed zeal in the international community to prevent and counter similar occurrences.[1] At the same time, the US administration, in both its rhetoric and policy, treated this as an armed attack rather than a criminal act.[2] The United States emphasised the military dimension of its response, referring to Al-Qaeda[3] as 'the enemy' and its 'defeat' the objective of the 'war' the United States pledged to wage. Yet while Al-Qaeda was the primary target, the scope of the war was to defeat all 'terror', directed at a type of activity (akin to the 'war on drugs') rather than specific places or persons.[4] Many scholars have questioned the feasibility of such a construction.

In light of the issues, as outlined in Chapter 6, of using terrorism as a consistent legal framework, approaches to terrorism have tended to reflect political considerations. The US approach to terrorism, for example, has been 'extra-ordinarily politicized'.[5] Strident military framing of a battle with terrorism shifted when it became clear than neither the war in Iraq nor Afghanistan was going to be a quick victory. The tone of US counter-terror strategy gradually began to reflect this in the latter half of the decade.[6]

The politicisation of the 'war on terror' has had international reverberations. The US approach was replicated by states across the world to counter their own threats. Further, the continued failure to agree on an international definition of terrorism[7] enabled domestic problems to take the tenor of an international war, and specific policies of the United States were imitated and justified on these terms. As the Supreme Court of Canada warned 'the absence of an authoritative definition means that, at least at the margins, "the term is open to politicised manipulation, conjecture and polemical interpretation".[8]

The US war on terror classified states as either allies or foes, leaving no room for debate or ambiguity. As then President George W Bush famously stated during an address to a joint session of Congress on 20 September 2001, 'Either you are with us, or you are with the terrorists'.[9] Other states took advantage of this simplification and used it to cast domestic problems as part of their participation in the US war on terror. Many states introduced legislation designed specifically to counter terrorism, which while extraordinary measures were allowed perpetual application. The blurring of the criminal and military approaches led to a host of legal problems including the struggle over the definition of detainees,[10] proportionality of response, justification of foreign military intervention, tactics – such as targeted killings.[11]

The next part of the chapter examines the link between the language and policy of the US and European 'war on terror' and consequences they have had on the conflict in the Kurdish regions of Turkey.

7.1.1 The United States and Europe

The attack on the World Trade Center in 1993 and the Oklahoma bombing in 1995 initiated the creation of anti-terrorism measures in the United States. However, it was not until the events of 11 September 2001 that the US Congress passed a new, more stringent, set of measures. For example, the US Patriot Act introduced in October 2001,[12] which expanded the ability of law enforcement to conduct secret searches, gives them wide powers of phone and internet surveillance, and access to highly personal medical, financial, mental health and student records with minimal judicial oversight.[13]

The US Office of the Coordinator for Counterterrorism, whose aim it is to engage with non-state actors, multilateral organisations and foreign governments to promote the country's counter-terrorism objectives was first created in 1972 in response to the attack on the Munich Olympics.[14] This office annually publishes a report on the *Patterns of Global Terrorism* within certain groups and states.[15] In an attempt to enhance strategic and operational coherence, an inter-agency body, the National Counterterrorism Center (NCTC), reporting to the Office of the Director of National Intelligence (ODNI),[16] was established in 2004 to head intelligence analysis and strategic planning for both domestic and international terrorism.

As is discussed in Chapter 6, the inability of the international community to agree on a definition of what constitutes terrorism has proved problematic. Often there is confusion and disagreement over defining what terrorism is within states themselves. In the United States alone the US Law Code, Department of Defense, the USA Patriot Act, the NCTC and the Federal Bureau of Investigation (FBI) all have different definitions of terrorism.[17] Human rights scholars have pointed out the difficulty this poses in aligning anti-terror laws with international human rights law. For example, Article 7 of the European Convention on Human Rights requires that any law creating a criminal offence must be clear and precise enough for people to understand what conduct is prohibited and to regulate their behaviour accordingly.[18] The ambiguity surrounding the definition of terrorism has therefore left the door open for anti-democratic states to violate human rights by going after critics or opposition parties using state security and the fight against terrorism as a justification. Turkey's anti-terror legislation, which has been modelled on anti-terror laws in the United Kingdom, has frequently been used against people as a way to increase the severity and so the penalties for actions that would normally not fall under the umbrella of 'terrorism'.

European states have also adopted vague anti-terror legislation which, although aimed at increasing security, has had the effect of in some cases criminalising legitimate free expression and have had a chilling effect on debate and opposition. UK anti-terror laws have adopted a definition of terrorism that is vague and broad in its reach. The definition, as stated in section 1 of the Terrorism Act 2000 and later amended in the Terrorism Act 2006, can be interpreted as including legal demonstrations and gatherings as well as activities that, while illegal, would have never before have been considered serious enough to fall under anti-terror legislation.[19]

Kongra-Gel, formerly Kurdistan Workers Party (PKK), Kurdistan Freedom and Democracy Congress (KADEK), was listed as a Specially Designated Global Terrorist in 2001 by the US State Department's Office of the Coordinator for Counterterrorism, thus making it illegal for anyone under US jurisdiction to 'knowingly provide "material support or resources" [to the organisation]' and making its members 'inadmissible to and, in certain circumstances, removable from the United States'.[20] In addition, President George W Bush in 2008 designated the PKK under the Foreign Narcotics Kingpin Designation Act thereby allowing the US government to freeze any assets of the organisation and prohibiting US citizens from conducting financial or commercial transactions with the group. In 2009 the US Department of Treasury's Office of Foreign Assets Control announced it had designated three leaders of Kongra-Gel, Murat Karayilan, Ali Riza Altun and Zübayir Aydar, as significant narcotics traffickers. The PKK, in response, accused the US government of attempting to exclude the organisation from the Turkish government's Kurdish initiative. According to a statement released by the executive council of the PKK, 'Everyone knows that a long-lasting solution to the Kurdish issue can only be reached through beginning of a dialogue in between the both parties. Attempts made at excluding the PKK from this process will not bring a solution and, in fact, will only lead to a conflict'.[21]

On 14 September 2001, the US Congress passed a joint resolution authorising President George W Bush to 'use all necessary means and appropriate force' against those suspected of taking part in the 11 September attacks.[22] The resolution did not contain a time limit, nor did it state any geographic limit to the use of force, allowing the Executive branch unprecedented power and discretion. Using the authority granted by Congress' resolution, and with international support, the United States commenced operating 'Enduring Freedom' in Afghanistan on 7 October 2001. After months of debate the United States launched a military attack on Iraq on 20 March 2003.

By casting its counter-terror response as a 'war against terror', the United States initiated a necessary search for allies. This approach instigated an adversarial approach to US foreign relations, casting states as either allies, or state sponsors of terrorism.[23] On 15 September 2001, the US Assistant Secretary of State for Near East Affairs William Joseph Burns met with 15 Arab envoys to deliver them the following message: 'the time has come to choose sides'.[24] As noted earlier, on 20 September, President George W Bush publicly reiterated this message in his address to a joint session of Congress. Once a state had qualified as an 'ally', many demanded reciprocation in their own wars against terror, often conflicts with complex domestic or regional dimensions that the US administration did not fully understand but now had to pay lip-service, at the very least, to supporting.

Turkey is a prominent example of this type of reciprocal relationship. The US terrorism report of 2001 calls Turkey a 'staunch counterterrorism ally'.[25] This relationship was tested at the outset of the 'war on terror'. Due to Turkey's geo-strategic location it became an important part of the US military's war plans with Turkey allowing the US military basing and fly over rights and contributing troops to train the local military in Afghanistan. However, by 2003, Turkey feared domestic backlash and was re-positioning its foreign policy alignment. Turkey therefore refused these privileges in relation to the war in Iraq.[26] As is discussed later, Turkey was able to use the use of these privileges and its strategic location as Iraq's neighbour to its advantage by gaining vital US intelligence regarding PKK locations in Kurdistan, Iraq. This intelligence was not only used in determining targets of Turkey's cross-border operations ostensibly aimed at rooting out PKK bases, but was shared with other states with a long history of discrimination against their Kurdish populations, notably Iran.[27]

In September 2006 the United States appointed a military general and former Vice Chairman of the Joint Chiefs of Staff to be the US Special Envoy for countering the PKK. In a speech in Istanbul a month later General Joseph Ralston asserted: 'the US will not negotiate with the PKK. We will not ask Turkey to negotiate with the PKK. And I pledge to you that I will never meet with the PKK'.[28]

The United States allowed Turkey to cast the conflict with the PKK as a part of the wider 'war on terror'. In a press statement following their meeting in November 2007, President George W Bush and Turkish Prime Minister Erdogan referred to their joint fight against the PKK and international terrorism, and agreed to share intelligence on the PKK.[29] President George W Bush repeatedly called the PKK 'a common enemy of Turkey, the United States and Iraq'.[30] However, when the conflict was enlarged to Kurdistan, Iraq, where the United States was the occupying force, interests complicated the simple allegiance. One US Congressman noted: 'Given America's leading role in Iraq, there is a perception in Turkey that America has not done enough to remove the threat of PKK terrorists based in Kurdistan, Iraq. Perceived inaction on the American side has lead to a nationalist backlash in Turkey against the US'.[31] When Turkey began planning its most recent military incursions into Kurdistan, Iraq, the United States provided Turkey with intelligence on the PKK's location, and stressed that the operation needed to be as targeted and fast as possible. The last thing the United States wanted was a lasting military presence by Turkey in Iraq, further complicating the domestic and regional dynamics of the conflict. President George W Bush urged Turkey to 'move quickly, achieve their objective and get out'.[32]

In recent years the United States has started to emphasise the need for a more comprehensive approach to the Kurdish conflict between Turkey and the PKK. After the start of the ground invasion into Kurdistan, Iraq, US Defense Secretary Robert M Gates sounded a cautionary note: 'It should be clear that military action alone would not end this terrorist threat. While it is certainly part of the equation, there must be simultaneous efforts made with non-military issues such as economic programs'.[33] Following a visit by Turkish President Abdullah Gul in January 2008, the White House stressed that 'working politically and improving the lives of the Kurds within Turkey to make sure that there isn't a disaffected minority that would be a recruiting pool for the PKK is also part of a long-term solution to that issue'.[34] However, despite these promising statements the United States has long failed to pressure the Turkish state to cease military operations against its Kurdish population and the PKK and to instead highlight a political solution that would help to ensure a resolution of the conflict and strengthen long-term stability in the region.

The United Kingdom has been a prominent partner with the United States in combating terrorism and has provided both political and military support for the wars in Afghanistan and Iraq. As France and Germany had from the outset openly opposed the war in Iraq (resulting in their being branded by the US Secretary of Defense Donald Rumsfeld as being 'Old Europe' and so out of touch with the opinions of many European countries[35]) tense divisions erupted in Europe. A further blow to the US coalition was when Spain, as a result of elections shortly following the Madrid train bombings, decided to withdraw its troops from Iraq.

However, while friction remained regarding the use of military action in Iraq, there was, as remains today, greater coherence between countries regarding the introduction of domestic legislation and security procedures in the fight against terrorism. Following the Madrid bombings, a number of European countries incorporated a military component into domestic security arrangements: the

French government used the army to reinforce police security for public transport and Greece sought NATO support for security at the 2004 Olympic Games in Athens.[36] Domestic anti-terror legislation was introduced or updated in many European states, including Portugal, Spain, the United Kingdom, Germany, Italy, Austria and Poland following the 2001 attacks. The European Union also tried to systematise a regional counter-terror framework, including the introduction of a European Arrest Warrant, which would allow member states to arrest and transfer suspects between member states without having to use formal extradition procedures.[37] Additionally, the European Council adopted The EU Action Plan to Combat Terrorism on 21 September 2001, which was aimed at guiding and co-ordinating counter-terror policy in Europe.[38] The Council Framework Decision on combating terrorism of 13 June 2002 further allowed 'the definition of terrorist offences should be approximated in all Member States, including those offences relating to terrorist groups'.[39] This has enabled member states to target groups it perceived to be threatening without recourse to international principles. Those groups then could face international sanctions, if the state is able to internationalise the 'terrorist' label by exploiting diplomatic channels. As Mark Muller QC, Chairman of the Bar Human Rights Committee of England and Wales has noted in relation to the national and international proscription regimes: 'whether a group is on or off a proscription list has more to do with geo politics and diplomatic relations between states than with genuine threats to a particular countries national security and the strict application of law in relation to terrorism'.[40]

For instance, the European Union proscribed the PKK as a terrorist organisation in 2002 with KADEK and Kongra-Gel having been proscribed as aliases of the organisation in 2004. Both proscriptions were annulled on legal grounds in 2008.[41] According to a spokesperson for the European Court of Justice, the ruling annulling the proscription had been made 'on procedural grounds' because the Council of the European Union had 'failed to give the PKK an adequate statement of reason as to why they are on the list, which they are required to do'.[42] The PKK was also proscribed by the United States as previously noted and in the United Kingdom under the Terrorism Act 2000. This had profound implications for the Kurdish diaspora community living in the United Kingdom. In 2003 a number of Kurdish activists were prosecuted for supposedly raising funds for the PKK. Although all were eventually acquitted, reports of UK police using anti-terror 'stop and search' powers to question Kurdish activists in the United Kingdom continues even now.[43] The United Kingdom's approach to counter-terrorism also has an international impact. One such example of this is its influence in tabling the criminalisation of 'incitement to terrorism' throughout the world at the UN Security Council. This measure has raised frequent problems as the definition of what constitutes 'incitement' is in dispute. Under the Turkish penal code, the glorification of terrorism is frequently used as a basis to arrest journalists and human rights advocates, which has been a serious concern in relation to free expression in the country. While UK political leadership has consistently referred to the PKK as a terrorist organisation,[44] there has been increasing recognition, as there has been within the United States, that a comprehensive political solution is needed. This is due in large part to the dawning realisation that finding a peaceful political solution to Turkey's Kurdish issue is essential, not only to Turkey's stability but to the stability of the region as a whole. Despite this realisation neither the United Kingdom, the United States, nor the international community has found the political will to recognise the armed conflict between Turkey and the PKK and push for conflict resolution.

7.1.2 Turkey and the war on terror

Following the attacks on the United States on 11 September 2001, Turkey rushed to express its empathy as well as to draw parallels between the attacks and its own conflict with the PKK.[45] As a member of NATO, Turkey endorsed and contributed troops to the mission in Afghanistan[46] and lead the International Security Assistance Force (ISAF) from June 2002 for 6 months. The logistical support Turkey was able to offer to the mission in Iraq, due to its geographic location, has also been critical to the US military's efforts in Iraq. The use of the cargo hub at Turkey's Incirlik Air Base, through which United States shipped 74 per cent of all air cargo to Iraq was extremely important to keeping troop supplies moving into the country. Additionally, tankers operating out of Incirlik have flown 3,400 sorties and delivered 35 million gallons of fuel to US fighter and transport aircraft on missions in Iraq and Afghanistan. The then Deputy Prime Minister of the conservative ANAP (Motherland Party), Mesut Yilmaz, stated at the time that the 'world will understand the determined and rightful struggle of Turkey against terrorism … The terrorist attacks in the United States will be an important opportunity for the world to realise the facts'.[47] The 'war on terror' gave Turkey a way to validate its military approach to the PKK and to legitimise not only its expansive anti-terror legislation but also its historical denial of Kurds. Turkey's anti-terror legislation has almost exclusively been used towards those who challenge state policy and disproportionately so against religious and ethnic minorities. Amendments to Turkey's anti-terror law in 2006 increased the number and range of crimes that may be considered terrorist offences.[48] Additionally, punishments were increased and due process limited for the offences related to the distribution of 'terrorist propaganda'.[49] The legislation criminalised the carrying of emblems or signs, or shouting slogans, that are associated with a terrorist organisation.[50] The law retained the broad definition of terrorism[51] that has resulted in its arbitrary application over the past decade.

Moreover, the keenness of the United States to cooperate and participate in Turkey's 'war on terror' has led to the US military directly contributing to Turkey's military activity against the PKK. When Turkey initiated its military incursion into Kurdistan, Iraq the United States provided intelligence on the region and allowed Turkish aircraft into Iraqi airspace. The Chief of General Staff Yasar Büyükanit argued that this amounted to US approval of the operation.[52] Masoud Barzani, President of the Kurdistan Regional Government (KRG), agreed, and blamed the United States for air strikes conducted by Turkey in Kurdistan, Iraq.[53] US military personnel set up centres for sharing intelligence in Ankara, providing real-time information gathered from US aircraft to the Turkish military. As one US military official was quoted as saying, the United States is 'essentially handing' Turkey their targets.[54]

7.1.3 Regional responses to terrorism

Relationships between the states with significant Kurdish populations have always been complicated, but the war on terror has added a further dimension to allegiance making. The KRG is under pressure from its neighbours to fight the PKK in order to prove it will not be held hostage to one organisation and to establish its legitimacy by demonstrating that it has reach throughout its territory to maintain security. The pressure is compounded for the KRG by the United States's casting of Turkey's conflict with its Kurdish population as part of the global 'war on terror'. The United States plays a important role in the KRG's security, not only due to its military presence in Iraq, but its historical support for autonomy in the Kurdish region of Iraq since the establishment the safe haven in Kurdistan, Iraq in 1991.

There is increasing pressure on the KRG to push the PKK out of Kurdistan. Cooperation with its neighbours, particularly Turkey, is important to the region's economic development and overall stability. During an interview with Dubai's Al-Arabiya Television on 26 October 2007, Kurdistan President Masoud Barzani noted, 'the PKK members are not in the Kurdistan region at the invitation of the Kurdistan Region and they are not welcome here'. He further said that the PKK does not have any premises in any area in the Kurdistan region, and if 'the PKK has any presence, it is in remote areas where there are no villages or peshmerga forces'.[55] Recognising the complexity of Turkey's Kurdish issue, Barzani stated that that the Kurdish region will not support a military solution to the conflict. He noted that the PKK would not be defeated by using conventional military tactics as it engages in guerrilla warfare and because the PKK issue is essentially a political issue.

However unwelcome the PKK may be in Kurdistan, Barzani does not yet seem willing to label it a terrorist organisation. In a November 2007 news conference with the then British Defence Secretary Des Browne in the Kurdistan region, Barzani was asked whether he believed such a label was warranted, 'I don't agree with many activities carried out by the PKK, yet it will be described as a terrorist when it rejects a Turkish peace initiative', he noted.[56] Barzani's comments can be attributed to the general consensus that exists among the Kurdish people and within the KRG that Kurds should not fight amongst each other in this conflict as they have in the past.

The KRG's response to the PKK and to Turkey's cross-border military operations is further complicated by the fact that Iraq's neighbours are highly suspicious of the regional authority, fearing their own Kurdish populations will draw strength from the success of the KRG. Not only Turkey, but also Iran and Syria continue to closely watch the developments in Kurdistan as they have a vested interest in the KRG's inability to bring about positive development in Kurdistan. Fearing that success in Kurdistan, Iraq will further embolden their own Kurdish populations to push for basic rights and greater autonomy, Turkey, Iran and Syria would prefer that the Kurds are not able to achieve stability and economic independence.

Officials both in the Turkish Embassy in Tehran and in the Iranian Embassy in Ankara acknowledge that the two countries regularly share intelligence on the PKK and its Iranian counterpart, the Free Life Party of Kurdistan (*Partiya Jiyana Azad a Kurdistanê* (PJAK)). Both states have noted that intelligence-sharing speeded up following the Turkey-Iran consultation meeting which was held in Ankara from 15 to 17 April 2008.[57]

In April 2008, the meeting of the 12th High Security Commission between Turkey and Iran was held to discuss their mutual fight against terrorism. At the meeting the two countries signed a memorandum of understanding agreeing to increase security cooperation and to exchange intelligence to combat terrorist movement in the regions.[58] As the Turkish Interior Ministry announced, the memorandum should be viewed as both states ' ... expressing their willingness to develop cooperation in security issues'.[59]

In June 2008, General İlker Başbuğ, then commander of the Turkish Land Forces, confirmed that Turkey and Iran were sharing intelligence and coordinating military operations against the PKK and PJAK.

Most of the coordination appears to have involved 'hammer and anvil' operations, in which military units from one country have been deployed to intercept militants attempting to flee across the border in advance of an offensive launched by the second country's military. Although not explicitly confirmed by Başbuğ, Turkey and Iran are also believed to have coordinated some military strikes against PKK and PJAK camps in the Qandil Mountains – these have consisted mainly of shelling by the Iranians and shelling and air raids by the Turks.[60] Although the Turkish Foreign Ministry has assured the United States that it is not the case, Washington has expressed concern that highly valuable real-time intelligence regarding the PKK presence in Kurdistan, Iraq, which has been provided to Turkey since November 2008 is being shared with Iran.[61] These raids not only transgress Iraqi sovereignty in the name of Turkey's Kurdish issue, but also disrupt the security of the Kurdish region, and have caused injury and death to Iraqi Kurdish civilians.[62] As the author witnessed firsthand while travelling in Kurdistan, Iraq, the destruction Iranian shelling causes to villages has had profound effects on the livelihoods of civilians. Further, use of US intelligence in conducting Turkey's cross-border military operations – intelligence it readily admits sharing with Iran – leaves the United States in the awkward position of, in affect, supplying a 'state sponsor of terrorism' with military intelligence.

The United States has good reason to want to maintain its strong relations with the KRG and therefore faces competing allegiances within the war on terror 'with us or against us' paradigm. The Kurds in Iraq have long been allies of the United States. Before the invasion in March 2003, Kurdish leaders prefaced their support on US support for a federal structure where they would retain the considerable degree of self-rule that had been established since 1991.[63] The Peshmarga, the Kurdish region's security forces, fought alongside the US military when they invaded Iraq in 2003.[64] The United States responded in kind by cooperating with Kurdish forces to launch military operations against the group Ansar Al-Islam, an Islamist militant group operating in the Kurdish region, which had long been a threat to the PKK and KDP.[65] Further, it has been argued that the presence of the PKK in Kurdistan, Iraq prevents other terrorist organisations from obtaining a foothold in the area. Additionally, Kurdistan, Iraq has been one of the few areas in Iraq that have remained politically stable and secure from the violence seen elsewhere in the country. The United States is mindful that Turkey's cross-border military operations in Kurdistan, Iraq could threaten this stability and so must walk a fine line between the two states.

The KRG finds itself under pressure from the Iraqi central government in addition to US command in Iraq due to its extensive border with Iran, through which it is suspected that Iran has allowed several groups thought to have launched insurgent attacks throughout Iraq safe passage.[66] The United States therefore faces a dilemma in its war on terror narrative: pressure the KRG too hard to fight against the PKK, and it may reduce the regional government's political capital and security capability to deal with other terrorist groups, those operating in central and southern Iraq and sheltering in Iran and Syria, that are a more direct threat to United States interests and to stability in the whole region.

7.2 International responses to conflict in the Kurdish regions of Turkey and Kurdistan, Iraq

This part of the chapter reviews the different approaches of the major international and regional bodies to the conflict in the Kurdish region of Turkey and the Turkish military operations into Iraq. International and regional bodies have the capacity and means for resolution; however, they have lacked the political will and public pressure to apply them towards Turkey's ongoing conflict with the PKK.

International institutions, particularly the UN Security Council, the European Union, the Organization for Security and Co-operation in Europe (OSCE), the Council of Europe and NATO have shown varying degrees of interest and involvement in the conflict in Turkey and its extension into Kurdistan, Iraq. They have struggled to define the conflict, interweaving the labels of 'terrorism', 'domestic insurgency' and 'self-determination'. This has led to confusion about the role the international community can and should play in resolving the conflict, as its humanitarian concern is in a fine balance with the principle of national sovereignty and domestic security.

The attention Turkey's conflict with the PKK, and by extension its Kurdish population, received by international and regional institutions heightened when the conflict crossed the border into Kurdistan, Iraq. Not only does this reflect the unease among the international community regarding what qualifies as an armed conflict, a question that has been constantly equivocated about. It also reflects the political pressures that come to bear on such institutions. Despite Turkey's historical state policy of denial of the existence of the Kurdish people and the gross human rights violations committed by the state against them the international community has not found the political will to act in relation to Turkey's Kurdish issue, regardless of Turkey's existing obligations under international law. However, as has been seen time and again conflicts gain greater attention when the dominant world powers have a stake in their outcome, such as the United States interest in creating a 'stable' Iraq.

7.2.1 The UN Security Council

The United Nations' foremost commitment is to maintain international peace and security and it therefore wields the most power in terms of conflict resolution. One of the functions of the United Nations is to investigate any dispute which might lead to an international conflict. The UN Security Council holds the primary responsibility for maintaining peace and security and within its powers is the ability to undertake investigations and mediation in the pursuance of a peaceful agreement. The UN Security Council also has the power to appoint special representatives or it may request that the Secretary General do so. Measures are also in place to deal with conflict prevention, peace building and development. If a dispute escalates into a conflict then the UN Security Council can issue cease fire directives, send peacekeeping forces or take direct action by imposing economic sanctions or enforcing collective military action.[67]

The UN Security Council has a continuing obligation to act in relation to matters involving peace and security, therefore its involvement in resolving the Kurdish issue should have been ongoing and forceful throughout. In relation to Sadaam Hussein's treatment of the Kurds in Iraq, the UN Security Council did act forcefully in condemning the many human rights violations that occurred.

The United Nations used a multidisciplinary and 'creative strategy' with regards to intervening in Kurdistan, Iraq. Reliance was placed on 'lightly armed Guards and humanitarian relief capabilities to support and protect the vulnerable population of refugees who fled the Iraqi government's military attacks'.[68] The United Nations stated in 1991 that it was 'gravely concerned by the repression of the Iraqi civilian population in many parts of Iraq, including most recently in Kurdish populated areas ... '.[69] The United Nations passed Resolution 688 which concluded that the internal repression in Iraq was a threat to international peace and security. The Resolution was restrictive and vague as there was no provision for a steady political solution.

The United States and allied forces established safe havens in Kurdistan, Iraq for the Kurds. The objective of the safe havens was to hold back the Iraqi army in order to allow the safe passage of the refugees for their return journey home. The creation of the safe havens was successful in that a few months after their establishment, the Iraqi government withdrew its forces from Kurdistan. The Kurdish administration in Kurdistan, Iraq, although somewhat unstable, has been perceived as a success due to the involvement and support of the United Nations, the United States and its allies.

Other UN resolutions have attempted to address the Kurdish issue further. France unsuccessfully attempted to insert a provision into UN Security Council Resolution 687 regarding the Kurdish issue.[70] The final Resolution did not make reference to the plight of the Kurds but instead focused on the destruction and removal of Iraq's weapons of mass destruction. Subsequent Resolution 986 (1995) allowed Iraq to use $260 million of oil proceeds to buy humanitarian supplies for Kurdish-controlled Kurdistan, Iraq. In Resolution 1546 (2004)[71] the United Nations welcomed 'the commitment of the Interim Government of Iraq to work towards a federal, democratic, pluralist and unified Iraq, in which there is full respect for political and human rights'.[72]

Following Turkey's decision to again begin cross-border military action in Iraq in 2007, ostensibly to target PKK bases located in the Qandil area, UN Secretary-General Ban Ki-moon urged 'all sides to demonstrate restraint at this delicate juncture'.[73] Yet the United Nations' involvement into the conflict going on in the Kurdish region of Turkey has been different from that in Kurdistan, Iraq. The lack of involvement by the UN Security Council in the conflict in southeast Turkey is indicative of the political nature of the Security Council. In past situations the collective interests of the UN Security Council have determined a certain course of action.[74] UN members are unwilling to exert pressure on Turkey to cease the conflict when their best interests would not have been served. Also, the Kurdish issue in Turkey presents the members of the UN Security Council with a dilemma as the issues are essentially political in nature and deal with contentious issues such as self-determination.

Article 53(1) of the United Nations Charter provides that 'no enforcement action shall be taken under regional arrangements or by regional agencies without the authorisation of the Security Council, with the exception of measures against any enemy state'. Article 53(1) has not, however, prevented unilateral action being taken by independent state actors. We can then infer that individual state involvement is consequently of a political nature. This may offer an indication of why there remains a lack of state actors involved in the Turkish-Kurdish conflict. Despite evidence that Turkey's cross-border operations are a clear violation of the human rights of people living in the area, the UN Security Council member states did not act. However, a proactive stance could have been taken in the Turkish conflict by the UN Security Council such as was taken in Kosovo.[75]

The United States, as one of Turkey's most powerful and influential allies and as a permanent member of the UN Security Council, has consistently failed to exert real pressure on Turkey to cease its repression of its Kurdish population. This is consistent with the United States past acquiescence where

Turkey is involved. The United States blocked enforcement of UN Security Council Resolutions 353 and 354 which called for Turkey to withdraw its forces from northern Cyprus, it failed to condemn the Turkish government for widespread human rights violations against its own population, and Washington, until recently, refused to even acknowledge the Turkish state's role in the Armenian genocide.[76] In addition, during the 1990s, US military aid and arms sales totalled about $10.5 billion.[77] As the civilian population has borne the brunt of Turkey's cross-border operations, this lack of political will and refusal to act has weakened the credibility of the United Nations.

As was previously mentioned, the UN Security Council has various options when dealing with international disputes. The methods used in the conflict in Kurdistan, Iraq have been coercive and active with the establishment of the safe havens, however, silence is resounding in relation to the conflict in Turkey. The UN Security Council being a political organ reflects the reluctance of states to become involved in the Kurdish conflict in southeast Turkey. Article 2(7) of the United Nations Charter may be cited by some states as justification for not getting involved in the domestic affairs of states.[78] However, as Turkey has taken its conflict with the PKK across the border into Iraq it can be argued that the conflict should be one of international concern. Turkey has not only violated the sovereignty of the Iraqi state but has created a situation that has significant ramifications for the peace and stability of the entire region.

It has been argued that the military action by the United States and the United Kingdom in Iraq has led to a shift in the UN Security Council's role and to the increasing decentralisation of powers and enforcement action of member states.[79] Individual state actors have acted unilaterally by reinterpreting the United Nations Charter provisions.

The United Nations could, and under the provisions of its charter has a duty to, play an important role in the Kurdish conflict. Its unparalleled reservoir of experience in conflict resolution and post-conflict peace-building means that it could be a key player in providing options for the parties to the conflict to bring about a peaceful and lasting resolution.

7.2.2 NATO

The role of NATO is to safeguard the freedom and security of its members through politics and the use of force. NATO aims to protect and promote the member states' shared values of democracy, individual liberty, the rule of law and the peaceful resolution of disputes. The North Atlantic Treaty of 1949 reaffirmed the signatory states commitment to the purposes and principles of the United Nations Charter. The heart of NATO is expressed in Article 5 of the treaty which states, 'an armed attack against one or more of them in Europe or North America shall be considered an attack against them all … '. Other Articles set out member states' commitment to settling international disputes peacefully (Article 1), that member states contribute toward the further development of peaceful and friendly international relations by strengthening their free institutions (Article 2) and that member states will maintain and develop their individual and collective capacity to resist armed attack (Article 3).[80]

NATO had been vocal in its condemnation of Saddam Hussein's actions, both internally and regionally. Speaking of the regimes treatment of Iraq's Kurds, NATO's Secretary General stated that:

> Iraq has once again blatantly and gravely violated UN Security Council Resolutions and mounted an aggressive attack against civilians inside the exclusive zone in Kurdistan Iraq. Against this background, the U.S. action this morning was a justified, measured and proportionate attack. I hope that this clear message will be heeded by Saddam Hussein and that he will immediately withdraw his forces from the area, stop any further brutal attacks and comply fully with UN resolutions.[81]

Following the March 2003 US invasion of Iraq and the fall of Saddam Hussein, the NATO Secretary General, Lord Robertson, issued a press statement regarding the NATO-European Union Informal Working Luncheon in April 2003, which involved discussions on how best to assist the Iraqi people after the demise of Saddam Hussein's regime.[82] In that statement, George Papandreou the Greek Foreign Minister stated that:

> we also reiterated our position that we want to see stability in the region, the territorial integrity of Iraq. We acknowledged and welcomed the statements of Prime Minister Erdogan and Foreign Minister Gul that they were not to get involved with Kurdistan Iraq and this is an important statement that they've made. And we are ready, of course, to assist with problems in the neighbouring countries, particularly the candidate country Turkey of the European Union in dealing with humanitarian problems.[83]

This statement makes clear that NATO understood the importance of Turkey's cooperation in achieving and sustaining stability in Kurdistan, Iraq. Turkey's ceasing of its cross-border military operations and internal handling of the Kurdish issue were recognised to be of vital importance to the region.

Although Turkey is a member of NATO, in terms of chastisement of its members NATO's actions are restrictive, particularly since the United States has backed its ally Turkey by providing real-time intelligence on PKK movements in Iraq which was used in the planning of cross-border military operations. This intelligence assisted the Turkish military in targeting numerous attacks on suspected PKK camps resulting in the displacement and loss of livelihood for many Kurdish and non-Kudish civilians living in the area.[84] NATO has not, however, actively or publicly intervened in the Kurdish conflict in southeast Turkey. Again, it is necessary to look at the political nature of NATO's involvement in certain conflicts and its reluctance to become involved in other, equally important, conflicts.

7.2.3 The Council of Europe

The role of the Council of Europe is to protect rights and freedoms whilst also promoting human rights and demonstrating a commitment to democracy and the rule of law. The Council has achieved its objectives by adopting conventions, recommendations and conducting research into the areas of human rights and fundamental freedoms.[85] The Council considers the protection and promotion of human rights as one of its primary functions. Article 8 of the Council of Europe Statute 1949 states that if a member state seriously violates its obligations in relation to the observance of human rights and fundamental freedoms it can be suspended or expelled from the Council.[86]

The Council of Europe places emphasis on the protection of minorities. The European Charter for Regional and Minorities Languages was created to protect regional and minority languages. The Charter has been ratified by 23 member states, however, Turkey has yet to ratify it.[87] The Framework Convention for the Protection of National Minorities entered into in 1995 by 39 member states emphasised that it was one of the fundamental roles of international institutions to protect national minorities and promote their rights.[88] Turkey has also yet to ratify this Convention. Article 9 of the Council of Europe's Framework Convention for the Protection of National Minorities states: 'In the legal framework of sound radio and television broadcasting, [State Parties] shall ensure, as far as possible, and taking into account the provisions of paragraph 1, that persons belonging to national minorities are granted the possibility of creating and using their own media'. Turkey has not signed the Framework Convention, but the Council of Europe Parliamentary Assembly has urged it to do so.[89]

The Parliamentary Assembly has no legislative powers but can make recommendations to the Committee of Ministers who are the decision-making body of the Council of Europe. The Committee can then make recommendations to governments on a course of action, or, recommendations in relation to conventions and agreements that are binding on the states that have ratified them.[90]

Like NATO, the Council of Europe strongly vocalised its disapproval of the repression of the Kurds in Kurdistan, Iraq under Saddam Hussein. Recommendation 1150 was passed in 1991 by the Council of Europe on the situation of the Iraqi Kurdish population and other persecuted minorities.[91] The Recommendation noted that the Iraqi army had 'launched a brutal, deadly campaign to crush the insurgents, especially in the Kurdish provinces of Kurdistan, Iraq'. The Assembly also associated 'itself with the unequivocal condemnations by the international community including those issued on 9 April 1991 by its President and the Committee of Ministers, of the brutal repression … against some two million Iraqi Kurds'. The Recommendation also supported the creation of the safe havens in Kurdistan, Iraq and of the speedy deployment of UN forces. The Assembly importantly then went onto state that it:

> welcomes in this connection the departure from international doctrine on non-interference in a country's internal affairs and approves the establishment

of the right of interference, as implied in the United Nations Security Council Resolution 688 and in the United Nations Convention on the Prevention and Punishment of the Crime of Genocide[92] ratified by Iraq in 1959.

The Assembly also strongly urged 'the Iraqi authorities to comply scrupulously with the fundamental humanitarian principles set out in the 4th Geneva Convention on the Protection of Civilians in Time of War, which also apply in the event of a domestic conflict'.[93]

As it had with regards to Saddam Hussein's treatment of the Kurds in Kurdistan, Iraq, the Council of Europe passed Recommendation 1266 in 1995 that commented on Turkey's military intervention in Kurdistan, Iraq and on Turkey's respect of commitments concerning constitutional and legislative reforms. The recommendation stated that the Assembly was deeply concerned about human rights violations in Turkey, particularly in the southeast, following armed conflict between central government forces, the PKK and Kurdish nationalists, and noted the right of Turkey to fight within the limits of international law and the European Convention on Human Rights against terrorism. There was condemnation of the PKK's use of terrorism as well as Turkey's military interventions into Kurdistan, Iraq. The recommendation also called for Turkey to immediately withdraw its troops from Kurdistan, Iraq and to seek a peaceful solution to the Kurdish problem.[94]

From as far back as 1992 the Parliamentary Assembly stated that although Turkey had accepted many international agreements, there was still a 'considerable' increase in political violence, torture and extra-judicial killings. The Assembly called upon the Turkish government to improve the human rights situation and recommended that Turkey accept a number of additional protocols to the European Convention on Human Rights.[95] A further report published in 1994 dealt with issues of arrest and detention in Turkey and focused on the arrest of six members of the Turkish Grand National Assembly.[96] Resolution 1030 (1994) called on the Turkish government to withdraw the existing charges against the six members of the Parliament all of whom were members of the Democracy Party (DEP) and were of Kurdish origin. In Resolution 1041[97] the Assembly again urged the Turkish Grand National Assembly, the Turkish authorities and the parliamentary delegation from Turkey to comply with its proposals as set out in Resolution 1030 (1994). The Resolution also stated that it desired Turkey to receive delegations from the Commission on Security & Cooperation in Europe (CSCE), which preceded the OSCE until 1995 (when the name was changed to OSCE), to implement the human rights mechanisms accepted by Turkey.

An additional report was issued in 1995 on Turkey's military intervention in Kurdistan, Iraq and on Turkey's respect of commitments concerning constitutional and legislative reforms.[98] The Assembly considered Turkey to be in violation of its obligations under the Council of Europe Statute. The Assembly also called upon the Committee of Ministers to consider suspending Turkey's right of representation unless it could report significant progress on amending its constitution to bring it in line with the standards of the Council. The Council also called for the abolition of Article 8 of Turkey's anti-terrorism law in its report.[99]

An information report detailing Turkey's honouring of its commitments was produced from a visit to Turkey in November 1997. The report called on the Turkish authorities to 'engage in a dialogue on cultural rights of Turkish citizens of Kurdish origin; and to make legislative changes in relation to fundamental freedoms and torture'.[100] The Council of Europe has commented on the Kurdish conflict on various occasions but all reports have been purely recommendatory, leaving the Council unable to enforce change in the Turkish regime.[101] Although the Council of Europe, like other international organisations, should fulfil its obligations to assist to resolve the conflict between Turkey and its Kurdish population, it appears that the lack of political will of individual member states is yet again placed before the need for peaceful political solutions to the conflict. The Turkish authorities have not felt compelled to alter their human rights practices and have continued to ignore the calls for dramatic reforms. The forcefulness of the Council of Europe has been limited and has not resulted in the Turkish authorities dramatically amending their actions and protocols.

Despite past recommendations leading to little practical reform, there was a desire for the Council of Europe to play an 'active and constructive role in consolidating democratic stability and restoring security and rule of law'. So the Parliamentary Assembly made further recommendations in 1998 in regards to the humanitarian situation of Kurdish refugees and displaced persons in southeast Turkey and Kurdistan, Iraq,[102] and again in 2002 commenting on the humanitarian situation of the displaced Kurdish population in Turkey.[103] Although Turkey has been unwilling to implement the many years of recommendations from the Council of Europe aimed at encouraging the state to fulfil its human rights obligations, the Council recommended ending monitoring of the state in June 2004, declaring that the country had 'achieved more reform in a little over two years than in the previous decade'.[104]

The role of the Council of the Europe is to ensure that member states are complying with the Council's principles and standards. The Council of Europe assists in reinforcing structures that implement and promote human rights.[105] The Council of Europe could play a more stringent monitoring role regarding forced displacement, compensation and the right of return in terms of cases brought before the European Court of Human Rights. The Committee of Ministers passed an Interim Resolution on the execution of the judgments of the European Court of Human Rights actions of the security forces in Turkey. The resolution detailed the progress achieved by Turkey and other outstanding issues.[106] General measures may also be introduced to ensure compliance with the judgments of the European Court of Human Rights in cases against Turkey concerning actions of members of the security forces.

The Council of Europe has expressed concern that, in the international climate following the terrorist attacks of 11 September 2001, some Council member states have violated the Council's principles and standards by combating terrorism without fully respecting human rights and the rule of law. In 2002 the Council of Europe Committee of Ministers adopted the 17 Guidelines on Human Rights and the Fight against Terrorism, which reminded member states of their obligations as members of the Council and as parties to the European Convention on Human Rights.[107] In recent years the Parliamentary Assembly has called member states to task for active involvement in the US Central Intelligence Agency's (CIA's) transfer and detention of terror suspects in secret detention centres[108] and has cautioned the application of targeted sanctions against individuals or specific groups (such as travel restrictions and freezing of assets) in combating terrorist organisations.[109] Only recently, in November 2009, did the Council of Europe Commissioner for Human Rights, Thomas Hammarberg, write that 'there is an urgent need to improve the democratic oversight of intelligence and security agencies and to regulate cross-border co-operation between them'.[110] Despite these general condemnations regarding the use of terrorism as an excuse to ignore human rights obligations, the Council of Europe has not forcefully addressed Turkey's use of anti-terror legislation in silencing opposition parties or those who dare to speak for the rights of Kurds.

While almost all of the resolutions passed by the Council of Europe refer to human rights issues, the Council, along with the other international bodies discussed in this chapter, have failed to publicly acknowledge the real consequences of allowing Turkey to continue ignoring its human rights obligations. Regional stability is threatened and a resolution to the conflict between Turkey and the PKK will remain elusive unless a political solution is pursued. This will require dialogue between the Turks and Kurds, as well as support and pressure from the international community. While the judgments of the European Court of Human Rights in effect put an obligation on the shoulders of Council of Europe member states to pressure the Turkish state to comply, those states have so far failed to do so.

7.2.4 The European Union

The European Union has stated that it is 'committed to working with Iraq and international partners in order to bring about a secure, stable, unified, democratic and prosperous Iraq'.[111] The European Union has passed various Resolutions in relation to Kurdistan, Iraq all of which have highlighted the ongoing violence and its relationship with international law.[112] This involvement has not unfortunately gone much further than verbal condemnation of Turkey's actions in Kurdistan, Iraq.

In 1995 Turkey invaded Kurdistan, Iraq in one of its largest organised operations. Up to 35,000 troops entered Kurdistan, Iraq. The US government was sympathetic to the Turkish action after assurances were provided that the invasion would be limited and reportedly expressed 'understanding for Turkey's need to act decisively'.[113] There was condemnation by the French President of the European Union who held Turkey in breach of international law. In April 1995 the Council of Europe Parliamentary Assembly subsequently voted to 'suspend Turkish membership of the Assembly because of its human rights policies and the invasion of Iraq'.[114]

The European Union Troika passed a Resolution in 1995 on the Turkish military intervention in Kurdistan, Iraq after their visit to Ankara.[115] The resolution stated that the European Union was 'gravely disturbed' by the increased violence between Turkey and the PKK in Kurdistan, Iraq. It went on to highlight that Kurdistan, Iraq is a UN-protected area and that Turkey's military intervention violated human rights laws. The Resolution[116] further stated that the 'Turkish Army's bombardment of Kurdish villages in Kurdistan Iraq constitutes a violation of the territorial integrity of Iraq and of international law'. It called upon the Council and Commission to highlight that Turkey must respect human rights, the rule of law and international law if it wished to join the European Union. Finally, the Resolution went on to urge fellow member states to follow the example of Germany, which made military aid to Turkey conditional on its withdrawal of troops from Kurdistan, Iraq.

The resolution of the European Union on this issue, however, failed to involve all available mechanisms to prevent the aggression of the Turkish state. Therefore, the Turkish Parliament again authorised the military to conduct cross-border military action against the PKK in Kurdistan, Iraq in 2007. This initial authorisation was set to expire in October 2008. After the vote, the European Commission said it hoped Turkey would decide to respect the territorial integrity of Iraq. Instead, Turkey went on to carry out air strikes against the PKK in Mount Qandil, Kurdistan, Iraq in July 2008.[117] Again, the European Union Presidency called for Turkey to show restraint in its attacks. The European Union expressed its concern to Ankara in a statement from the Portuguese presidency: 'The presidency calls on the Turkish authorities to exercise restraint, to respect the territorial integrity of Iraq and refrain from taking any military action that could undermine regional peace and stability', it said, according to the AFP news agency. These calls for restraint, however, have fallen on deaf ears as the Parliament voted on 6 October 2009 to extend this authorisation for one more year.[118]

The involvement by the European Union in the Kurdish conflict in Turkey has been vocal, but not active. There have been calls for restraint and for compliance with human rights laws, however no strategy for resolution of the conflict has been put forward. The importance of dialogue and cooperation between the governments of Turkey and Iraq has been stressed but no long-term agreement has been sought.[119] Further, calls for dialogue between Turkey and the PKK and other representatives of the Kurdish population have been very few.

The European Union has an influential and powerful role to play in Turkey's human rights reform process due to Turkey's strong desire to join the European Union and its willingness to abide by and fulfil the European Union's demands. However, the European Union needs to understand and acknowledge that resolution of the Kurdish issue in Turkey cannot come solely from reform and vice versa, the reform cannot fully be implemented without resolution of the conflict. It is necessary that the European Union, arguably one of the most influential international organisations in terms of enforcing change in Turkey, calls for substantial legal reform and practise. The reforms that have taken place so far are important and should not be completely discounted as they can, if implemented freely, provide a platform for democratic discussion of possible solutions. It may be argued that the European Union's scrutiny in relation to human rights can be interventionist as it imposes pressure on candidate states to comply with European Union standards.[120]

It was in 1997 that the European Union decided to involve Turkey in the enlargement process and a report was produced in 1998 by the Commission detailing Turkey's implementation of the Copenhagen criteria. The report documented cases of torture, disappearances and limitations of freedom of expression and association.[121] There are various conditions or 'accession criteria' which a state must fulfil before it can become a member of the European Union. Those accession criteria, which were decided upon in 1993 at the Copenhagen European Council, are referred to as the Copenhagen criteria. The Copenhagen criteria outline standards in relation to the stability of institutions guaranteeing democracy, the rule of law, human rights and respect for and protection of minorities that each candidate state must meet.

Since Turkey became a candidate of the enlargement process, the European Commission has prepared reports every 12 months on the progress made by Turkey in order to monitor its implementation of the European Union's recommendations and its compliance with its standards. The Commission's progress reports and accession partnership documents stress the requirement to guarantee non-discrimination, women's and children's rights and freedom of thought, expression, association, peaceful assembly and religion. The European Union has regularly appealed to the Turkish state to find a political solution to the Kurdish issue without giving specific guidance regarding what the solution should look like. The European Union has failed to assist either Turkey or the state's Kurdish population in resolving the armed conflict. Instead, the European Union has been satisfied with small, cosmetic reforms, failing either to understand or acknowledge that, as the conflict is political, substantive and far-reaching political solutions are necessary.

In the European Commission's 1998 Regular Report on Turkey's Progress towards Accession,[122] the Commission asked for a 'political and non-military solution to the problem of the south-east'. The report also made a vague and broad provision for a civil solution that included the 'recognition of certain forms of Kurdish cultural identity and greater tolerance'.[123]

In the European Commission's 2004 Regular Report on Turkey's Progress towards Accession,[124] the Commission stated that 'the normalisation of the situation of the south-east should be pursued through the return of displaced persons, a strategy for socio-economic development and the establishment of conditions for the full enjoyment of rights and freedoms by the Kurds'. The report was vague and open ended as per the 1998 report. The 2004 Report did, however, acknowledge that there 'has been greater tolerance for the expression of Kurdish culture in its different form … (however) There are still considerable restrictions, in particular in the area of broadcasting and education in minority languages'.[125]

Since 1989 the European Parliament has passed many resolutions that have been openly critical of Turkey's actions and addressing the Kurdish issue.[126] A Resolution passed in 1991 on the situation of the Kurds[127] welcomed 'Resolution 688 of the UN Security Council on the situation of the Kurds in Iraq and hopes that the Security Council will take all necessary measures to guarantee the security of the Kurdish population ... ' and also likened the treatment of the Kurdish people to that of the crime of genocide. The European Parliament[128] has repeatedly emphasised the importance of cultural autonomy for the Kurds in Turkey.

The European Parliament's Report on Turkey's Progress Towards Accession in 2005[129] indicated that Turkey had made insufficient progress in the areas of freedom of expression, minority rights, corruption and violence against women. It also noted the Parliament 'strongly condemns the resurgence of terrorist violence on the part of the PKK', and called upon the 'Turkish Government to pursue a democratic solution to the Kurdish issue ... '. Likewise the 2008 Accession Partnership for Turkey Report[130] urges the state to 'develop a comprehensive approach to reducing regional disparities, and in particular to improving the situation in southeast Turkey, with a view to enhancing economic, social and cultural opportunities for all Turkish citizens, including those of Kurdish origin' and also asks that the village guard system in the southeast be abolished.[131] The Reports calls upon Turkey to make vague reforms, but by not addressing the underlying causes they indicate a distinct lack of understanding as to the core issues that prevent resolution of the conflict.

The European Union has continually called upon the Turkish authorities to resolve the conflict with the Kurds by finding political, rather than military solutions. In this spirit the European Parliament voted in 1997 for the Turkish government to grant a general amnesty to the PKK, and in 2004 the EU's Enlargement Commissioner, Guenter Verheugen noted that 'Turkey must do more to improve the cultural rights of its Kurdish minority'.[132] Turkey has in turn responded to these calls by making some positive developments in the area of human rights that have been driven by its desire to join the European Union. The economic and political incentives that come with EU membership are reason for the state's human rights reforms, but Turkey has often done just enough and has accomplished neither the reforms necessary to bring it in line with the Copenhagen criteria nor the overarching political changes necessary to resolve the armed conflict.

In January 1999 after Turkey had been officially recognised as a candidate for the European Union, a number of reforms were announced by Mehmet Ali Irtemcelik, the State Minister with Responsibility for Human Rights. Very few of these reforms have been implemented. The reforms that Turkey has made include abandoning Article 8 of the anti-terror law which made it an offence, punishable with imprisonment, to publish separatist propaganda. The National Programme for Adoption of the Acquis was introduced in March 2001 in which 89 new laws were created and 94 laws amended.[133] Three reform packages were introduced in February, March and August 2002: Act Nos 4744, 4748 and 4771.

Turkey also went on to sign the 1969 UN Convention on the Elimination of All Forms of Racial Discrimination.

Despite these reforms, Turkey has not been willing to enter into meaningful dialogue or offer political solutions aimed at resolving the conflict in Turkey. There is a great deal that must be done on both sides before the conflict can be resolved. The Kurdish people deserve equality and the right to democratic governance, which has been denied to them in Turkey. Kurds still face an inordinate amount of discrimination and face retribution for seeking justice and equality. It is these inequalities and the state's refusal to acknowledge that its Kurdish population can be both Kurdish and Turkish that prohibits a dialogue between the parties to the conflict. The Turkish state would do much to unify the country and to resolve the Kurdish issue by entering into honest and open dialogue.

Acknowledging the possible implications of Turkey's cross-border operations, the Presidency of the European Union expressed 'great concern over the operation of the Turkish Army in the territory of Iraq, undertaken on 21 February 2008'. 'While recognizing Turkey's need to protect its population from terrorism', the Presidency called on 'Turkey to refrain from taking any disproportionate military action and to respect Iraq's territorial integrity, human rights and the rule of law'. The statement also called on 'Turkey to limit its military activities to those which are absolutely necessary for achieving its main purpose – the protection of the Turkish population from terrorism'. The Presidency encouraged the Turkish authorities to pursue dialogue with its international partners, particularly with the government of Iraq. Finally, the Presidency reiterated its call on the Iraqi government and the KRG to take appropriate measures and ensure that the Iraqi territory is not used for violent action against Iraq's neighbours.[134]

The European Union designated the PKK a terrorist organisation on 15 September 2003. The European Court of First Instance in Luxembourg ruled, based on procedural issues, on 3 April 2008 that the PKK should not be included on the list of terrorist organisations although this had no practical application as to how European states viewed the organisation. What effect does this designation have on the possibility that the European Union will ever communicate with the PKK in the hopes of working towards a solution to the conflict?[135] Ironically, at the time the PKK was placed on the European Union's list of terrorist organisations the organisation had declared a ceasefire in the hope that Turkey would respond positively. In an interview with EurActiv, EU Enlargement Commissioner Olli Rehn gave his support to Turkish military operations against PKK guerrillas on the Iraqi border, saying Brussels understands the government's need to protect its citizens from 'continual cross-border terrorist attacks'.[136]

While there are arguments on either side concerning the PKK's label as a terrorist organisation, the fact remains that it is a party to the conflict and so must be engaged if there is to be any hope of negotiating a peaceful resolution. It is only through open dialogue and engagement with all parties to the conflict that a sustainable political solution can be found. The reality is that the European institutions, in particular the European Union, have not fully taken advantage of the opportunity that enlargement provides. It is not possible for the European Union to welcome Turkey as a full member without the resolution of the conflict. It is time that the European Union publicly acknowledges this to both Turkey and the European public so that the European Union can play a substantial role in guiding Turkey towards resolution of the Kurdish issue.

7.2.5 *The OSCE*

The OSCE plays a strategic role in intervention in the areas of human rights, democracy, rule of law and national minorities. The OSCE does not consider these areas to be internal affairs of the state and is therefore committed to openly criticising member states on their actions or lack of commitment to the OSCE's shared values.[137] The Moscow Document of 1991 highlighted this point by stating that the 'commitments undertaken in the field of the human dimension of the OSCE are matters of direct and legitimate concern to all participating States and do not belong exclusively to the internal affairs of the State concerned'. This allows the OSCE to intervene in human rights areas and prevents member states from citing the principle of non-intervention.[138] In theory, this could offer the OSCE an opportunity to pressure Turkey to live up to its human rights obligations in regards to the Kurds and to move towards a political solution to the state's ongoing armed conflict.

The OSCE considers the primary responsibility of guaranteeing human rights and fundamental freedoms to lie with the OSCE member states themselves.[139] The OSCE may, however, call upon member states to adhere to international mechanisms to ensure that they are complying with the standards of other international organisations.[140] There is an emphasis on maintaining a continuous dialogue with member states whose compliance with OSCE standards is being investigated. Regularly held conferences and meetings allow member states to build upon their OSCE commitments and take part in open discussions on the implementation of OSCE standards by fellow member states.

In addition to regular conferences and meetings, the OSCE has created two mechanisms that supervise the implementation of human rights standards and commitments by member states by allowing individual member states to invoke the mechanisms on an ad hoc basis. The first of these is the Vienna Mechanism, which was adopted at the Vienna Follow-up meeting in 1989. This allows a state to ask questions of another member state in relation to their human rights obligations. It consists of four separate phases where the participating states may, first, respond to requests for information made by other participating states and exchange information relating to the human dimension; second, hold bilateral meetings (should these be requested by other participating states) with a view to examine and resolve situations and specific cases relating to the human dimension; third, notify all participating states of situations and cases in the human dimension; and, finally, discuss the issues raised under the Mechanism, at the Review Conference, Human Dimension Implementation meetings, meetings of the Senior Council or Permanent Council.

The second mechanism, the Moscow Mechanism, is an extension of the Vienna Mechanism. The Moscow Mechanism provides for the possibility of sending ad hoc missions to member states with the intention that independent experts would be able to assist in the resolution of human rights issues. In exceptional circumstances it may be possible to send a mission without the consent of the member state.[141] The OSCE itself has admitted that these mechanisms have fallen into abeyance as member states take political consequences into consideration before invoking them.[142]

The OSCE may also implement what is known as a 'long duration mission' which requires (10) member states to go to the region in order to monitor the conflict. The OSCE has utilised this mechanism in a number of conflicts including in Kosovo, Sandjak and Vojvodina in 1992, although the mission was closed by Slobodan Milošević in 1993. The use of a 'long duration mission' in Turkey, however, is not simply a question of whether the OSCE has the political will to push for such a mission. Missions can neither be established nor their mandate extended without the agreement of the receiving state. In some cases the mission must actually be invited into the state. Given Turkey's historical denial of Kurdish identity and the belief that the conflict can be won through military means, it is difficult to see the state inviting the OSCE to establish a mission of long duration.

While the OSCE has gotten involved in Turkey's cross-border operations into Kurdistan, Iraq, it has been vocal in its criticism regarding the Kurdish conflict in southeast Turkey. Turkey became a member of the OSCE in 1973 and was one of the OSCE's founding member states thereby committing itself to pursuing and upholding the OSCE's objectives of conflict prevention, crisis management and the protection of minority rights. Importantly, OSCE members are entitled to check whether member states are observing and following the OSCE objectives and standards and may also criticise fellow member states for non-compliance.

The Copenhagen Document signed in 1990 by the OSCE member states stated that it is a basic function of government to protect and promote human rights. The Copenhagen Document introduced provisions in relation to national minorities which committed the member states to guaranteeing 'full respect for human rights and fundamental freedoms, equal rights and status for all citizens, the free expression of all their legitimate interests and aspirations, political pluralism, social tolerance and the implementation of legal rules that place effective restraints on the abuse of governmental power'.[143]

There was a further affirmation by member states that it is essential for peace and stability that the rights of national minorities are upheld. The OSCE indicated its emphasis on the protection of national minorities by establishing a post of the OSCE High Commissioner on National Minorities in 1992. High Commissioner Van der Stoel[144] remarked in his keynote address at the opening of the OSCE Minorities Seminar in Warsaw in 1994 that 'the existence of a minority is a question of fact and not of definition. (...) First of all, a minority is a group with linguistic, ethnic or cultural characteristics, which distinguish it from the majority. Secondly, a minority is a group which usually not only seeks to maintain its identity but also tries to give stronger expression to that identity'. Turkey has been unwilling to accept the definition of a national minority and inserted a reservation to the effect that the term national minorities can only be used in relation to national minorities recognised in international treaties.

As stated in the OSCE commitments which member states agree to:

> the participating States, in their efforts to protect and promote the rights of persons belonging to national minorities, will fully respect their undertakings under existing human rights conventions and other relevant international instruments and consider adhering to the relevant conventions, if they have not yet done so, including those providing for a right of complaint by individuals.[145]

The requirements under the Copenhagen Document are, however, declaratory and no repercussions exist for a member state breaching them. The commitments made by each member state are essentially politically binding as opposed to legally binding.[146] The ability of the OSCE to enforce commitment to its shared values is therefore strictly limited. The OSCE, however, has stressed that this does not mean that the commitment entered into by each member state is not binding. The OSCE draws a distinction 'between "legal" and "political" and not between "binding" and "non-binding"',[147] thereby implying that a political 'promise' is made to abide by standards. There is no court or independent body that monitors and enforces the implementations of OSCE standards and shared values, there is only the shared political commitment and the pressure of fellow member states on those who fail to meet their commitments.

Switzerland initiated the Moscow Mechanism against Turkey in 1992 in relation to the Kurdish issue. The proposal, however, failed to maintain support from other nation states and was abandoned.[148] In the same year, Austria invoked the mechanism with respect to Turkey's treatment of its Kurdish citizens in southeastern Turkey.[149]

In 1993, after Turkey refused to invite a CSCE team of experts to the country, Switzerland again began to look at whether other states would support a continuation of the Moscow Mechanism. Following the 4th OSCE Annual Session held in Canada in July 1995, a member of the Canadian Parliament wrote to the OSCE expressing his regret that a resolution was not drawn up to address the freedom of the Turkish Grand National Assembly. A petition signed by 92 OSCE delegates calling for the release of Kurdish MPs from the DEP who had been arrested was forwarded to the OSCE with the intention that the Turkish delegation would be made aware of the petition. The letter also highlighted the importance of the role played by the OSCE in ensuring that human rights and democracy are upheld, given Turkey's desire to join the European Union.[150]

The US mission to the OSCE made a statement on national minorities on 29 September 2005, in which it stated that it remained 'concerned about the situation of the Kurds of Turkey. Despite laws to the contrary, Kurds face obstacles in broadcasting or publishing in their own language. Those who advocate Kurdish cultural and language rights may be branded in public opinion as members and supporters of the terrorist PKK'.[151]

Within the OSCE, which is not a legal treaty but a politically binding process, member states have not only an obligation but also a duty to consider the situation of the Kurds in Turkey and the ongoing armed conflict with the PKK. As noted, the OSCE commitments as well as the Copenhagen Principles clearly state that persons belonging to national minorities must be provided the right to freely express themselves and to maintain and develop their cultural, linguistic and religious identities free from any attempts at involuntary assimilation. The situation of national minorities is a matter of legitimate international concern particularly in Turkey as the states policy on Kurds is directly related to and the underlying cause of the ongoing conflict.

As discussed earlier, there are relevant procedures under the OSCE whereby member states can diplomatically take initiatives to complain against Turkey in regards to the military operations in Kurdistan, Iraq. To ensure the peace and stability of the Kurdish region, OSCE member states should consider establishing a mission of long duration in Turkey as there is a fundamental conflict between the constitution of Turkey and the principles the state has signed. The mission would give the governments of the OSCE the information necessary to act not only in protecting the Kurdish population but also to assisting all parties in the conflict in finding a lasting resolution.

7.3 International engagement with 'terrorists': a comparative analysis

This part of the chapter looks at different armed conflict situations where parties to the conflict have been designated as terrorist organisations and examines the differing approaches utilised by local and international actors that have resulted in either peace building measures or a continuation of conflict. Comparisons will be drawn between the conflict in Northern Ireland and that of *Euskadi Ta Askatasua* (ETA), the Basque separatist organisation whose stated aim is independence for the Greater Basque Country in Spain, with the ongoing Kurdish conflict in Turkey in order to highlight possible modes of engagement. By looking at past conflicts and their progress in moving towards resolution, recommendations can be made concerning which methods would best be utilised by parties in the Kurdish conflict in order to work towards peace-building in the Kurdish regions. A more detailed look at the conflict in Northern Ireland and peace process and the valuable lessons learned that can be utilised in resolution of the Kurdish conflict is dealt with in Chapter 9.

The conflict in Northern Ireland represents an example of a peaceful, negotiated resolution that offers the parties to the Kurdish conflict potentially valuable tactics and lessons in conflict resolution. That officials from the United Kingdom took part in both unofficial and official talks with unionist and republican parties helped to build trust and confidence in the peace process. The government of Spain, on the other hand, has had limited dialogue with ETA about resolving the conflict in the Basque region. The result of this has been a continuation of the conflict and should be viewed as a cautionary tale by Turkey. Taking a deeper look at how the 'terrorist' label has or has not affected efforts made towards resolution can provide helpful guidelines to Turkey, the PKK and the international community regarding what approaches may or may not result in open dialogue, political solutions and, eventually, peaceful resolution.

Some scholars have criticised the over enthusiasm with which the 'Northern Ireland model' has been abstracted to different contexts, stressing the uniqueness of each conflict situation, and stressing the importance of specific regional, historical, socio-economic and political factors.[152] While it can be agreed that each conflict is unique, the conflict in Northern Ireland and the process through which it was resolved can offer many opportunities to witness the implementation and outcome of various resolution mechanisms. As an example, The Mitchell Principles can be seen as one of the important developments to come out to the Northern Ireland negotiations and could be potentially the most useful to the Kurdish conflict. This is not to say that the process in Northern Ireland has been a complete success. Factions of the militant republican movement have remained sceptical towards the peace process and over a decade after the Good Friday Agreement, dissident republicans still engage in sporadic terrorist activity.[153] Nevertheless, the Northern Ireland negotiations are widely viewed as successful and can offer lessons in other conflicts. They can provide a neutral set of guidelines for Turkey and the PKK to build upon.

Both the conflict in Northern Ireland and ETA's struggle for an independent Greater Basque Country have long histories. Like the Kurdish issue in Turkey, these conflicts have lasted decades and have seen their respective states attempt to end the conflict through military means. The governments of Spain and the United Kingdom, as well as the international community, labelled ETA and the Irish Republican Army (IRA) as terrorist organisations which was viewed by some as a reason to exclude them from efforts at negotiation. However, while both the governments of Spain and the United Kingdom have taken part in negotiations aimed at creating a lasting peace, only the United Kingdom's dialogue with the parties to the conflict in Northern Ireland resulted in a successful peace process. Why this has been the case and what, if any lessons, can be applied to the Turkey's Kurdish conflict is what this section hopes to make clear.

One of the most important differences between the Northern Ireland and Basque conflicts is that the parties involved in Northern Ireland saw negotiation as the best and only means to resolving the conflict. The conflict was costing the government financially, as well as in terms of international reputation, while the IRA and the republicans came to the realisation that more could be achieved through engagement than through violence.[154] Statements from the late 1980s, when talks between the parties began, support this. Discussing Sinn Féin's position regarding ongoing conflict, Gerry Adams, leader of Sinn Féin, the political wing of the IRA, stated in 1987, 'There's no military solution, none whatsoever ... There can only be a political solution ... an alternative, unarmed struggle, to attain Irish Independence'. The Secretary of State for Northern Ireland, Peter Brooke, echoed this sentiment in 1989, 'it is difficult to imagine a military defeat of the IRA'.[155]

Certainly, there was opposition on both sides to opening dialogue, particularly with groups like the IRA who had taken part in violence. As well many have argued that the IRA, unlike other organisations linked to terrorist activity such as the African National Congress (ANC) in South Africa, did not have the backing of the majority of people who they claimed to represent.[156] However, the understanding that these tactics and the military response that inevitably ensued would achieve little helped to make negotiation the more attractive option. Only once both parties to the conflict believed that dialogue offered the best chance at resolution were they willing to move towards ending the use of armed force.

In the case of ETA and Spain this has not been the case. It has been argued that the Spanish government has no compelling reason to open further negotiations with ETA. ETA likewise seems unlikely to abandon its armed struggle for negotiation as its younger leadership are reluctant to give up arms and have less incentives for an agreement.[157] Following the attacks of 11 September 2001 in the United States and the Madrid train bombings on 11 March 2004, the Spanish government has been able to take advantage of international acceptance in applying stricter security measures in the name of national security. In the case of ETA, its label as a terrorist organisation helps to take pressure off the government of Spain to work towards a negotiated settlement. The Spanish government's hardline approach and uncompromising attitude towards ETA is preventing meaningful peace talks from taking place. The official government stance is that until ETA fully pledges to withdraw all its arms, there will be no cooperation on the part of the Spanish state.[158]

Turkey has taken a similar approach with the PKK, using the 'terrorist' label as justification for pursing a military rather than a political solution to the conflict. This strategy does nothing to ease the underlying causes and tension of the conflict and the necessary increase in use of military operations and strict security legislation can only lead to a continuation and escalation to the conflict. Turkey should instead model its solution on the Northern Ireland process by bringing all parties of the conflict into negotiations and working towards a democratic political solution.

Negotiations do not necessarily have to entail face-to-face talks with armed groups directly. For example, unionists refused face-to-face talks with Sinn Féin until well after the Good Friday Agreement, instead working through a third party. Additionally, the government may prefer secret talks so as not to enable its internal or external opponents to discredit the process before it has had a chance to achieve tangible results. In Northern Ireland this tactic helped the government to get a ceasefire without admitting it was talking. The system of backchannel talks that ran through the 1980s and 1990s, used proxy negotiators ranging from priests to intelligence officers, passed messages back and forth between the negotiating parties. Backchannel communications can be essential for successful negotiations with groups labelled as terrorist, as they provide a system which is free from public attention, political scrutiny and the threat of face-to-face exposure.[159]

Another factor that can affect the success of a conflict resolution process is the imbalance of power between the parties to the conflict. For negotiations to succeed there must be some balance in the relationship between the parties. Following the establishment of a formal peace process, the state can undertake some confidence-building measures to achieve this balance of power, including, although not limited to, lifting the ban on organisations deemed as unlawful or terrorist, suspending stringent security laws, ensuring no undue harassment of opposition forces by members of the security forces, and releasing key political prisoners, particularly those in leadership positions whose participation in the process is essential.[160]

In Northern Ireland most of these issues were addressed in the Good Friday Agreement, which was endorsed by most parties to the conflict in 1998. The Spanish government by contrast has historically done all it can to weaken the pro-independence movement including banning Batasuna, the Basque nationalist political party, and preventing pro-independence leaders from forming a new party. For these reasons, it appears that the balance of power lies in favour of the Spanish state. Turkey, like Spain, has done everything in its power to weaken Kurdish prospects for political representation. Using anti-terror legislation, the state has prosecuted and imprisoned members of political parties who address Kurdish concerns publicly, closed and banned political parties by claiming they were associated with the PKK and stifling legitimate political opposition and demonstrations.

Finally, for any peace process to achieve a lasting peaceful resolution of conflict there must be meaningful and impartial international support. As is discussed in the previous section of this chapter, there is much the international community can do to pressure Turkey to end military operations and seek a democratic solution to the Kurdish conflict. However, this is not enough. The international community must support all parties to the conflict and encourage and foster open and constructive dialogue on substantive issues. Despite the fact that Northern Ireland does not enjoy strategic importance, there was great international assistance for the peace process. However, in the case of Spain there has been little international engagement. The conflict that has been taking place in Turkey, a state with strategic military and economic links to the United States, Europe and the Middle East, has worryingly also received little international attention aimed at bringing the parties together in a peaceful resolution.

The PKK's designation as a terrorist organisation must be seen as a factor in the lack of international attention the conflict has received. 'Once a group is labelled "terrorist", its grievances, legitimate or not, are usually viewed as invalid, reducing international pressure on governments to work towards a negotiated settlement'.[161] As noted, this is especially the case following the attacks of 11 September 2001. This lack of international pressure has allowed Turkey, until very recently, to continue its policy of denial and its pursuit of a military solution to the conflict. Another explanation is the lack of international political will, discussed in the previous section. International organisations and important allies to Turkey have refused to call attention to the real causes of the conflict in Turkey, allowing the state to make cosmetic reforms while ignoring the larger, constitutional issues that prevent the process of resolution from even beginning.

The international community should urge Turkey to engage with representatives of the Kurds, stressing the need for a negotiated, rather than a military solution, to the conflict. While there can be no denial that the PKK has used violence in the past, Turkey's refusal to negotiate on the grounds that it is a terrorist organisation does nothing to resolve the underlying political issues that perpetuate the conflict. Both sides must commit to ending the armed conflict and, as was the case in Northern Ireland, begin the long, painstaking process of conflict-resolution through dialogue and substantive political reforms.

Conclusion

Engagement with all parties to the conflict, working towards a political and not a military solution, is the most effective way towards conflict resolution. The label of 'terrorist' complicates this engagement and can prove to be a detrimental obstacle to peace. Marginalising a group or movement by giving it the 'terrorist' label can backfire and result in an escalation in the conflict, as the group may have nothing to lose if excluded from the process. On the other hand, states and the international community do not want to be seen as rewarding bad behaviour by giving 'terrorist' organisations a place at the negotiating table. The government of Norway alluded to this when it refused to include the PKK on its list of terrorist organisations. The government's reasoning was that it may, in the future, wish to engage the PKK in an effort to assist to resolve the conflict and that such a designation would prevent it from doing so. Looking at the peace process in Northern Ireland, and in other conflicts, it can be inferred that negotiating with organisations that have been given the 'terrorist' label can produce positive results if conducted with the commitment of both sides, international support and an efficient system for conducting negotiations.

It is important to note that the international community has never effectively called Turkey to account for the treatment of the state's Kurdish population. The Council of Europe, European Union, OSCE, United Nations and NATO all have an obligation to pressure Turkey to abide by its international obligations and to make the political changes necessary to ensure a peaceful resolution to the conflict. Now is the time for Europe and the international community, including the United States and Russia, to acknowledge and act on their responsibilities and to assist both the Turkish and Kurdish people to end the present armed conflict by finding a peaceful, democratic solution through structured dialogue. Without seriously and honestly tackling the Kurdish conflict and the issue of democracy in Turkey, the public order of Europe and the stability of the Middle East are at risk.

8 Self-determination
Models for a political solution

Introduction

> The proposition ... that every people should freely determine its own political status and freely pursue its economic, social and cultural development has long been one of which poets have sung and for which patriots have been ready to lay down their lives.
>
> John P Humphrey[1]

This definition of self-determination by the drafter of the Universal Declaration of Human Rights begins the discussion of possible solutions to the Kurdish crisis. To complete this study, the right of self-determination, a peremptory norm of public international law, is the one crucial final area crying out for legal analysis. Establishing the scope of this right will undoubtedly inform any political settlement. The debate with respect to groups seeking national liberation represents the other side of the coin of the terrorism debate discussed in Chapters 6 and 7, as many nations seek to have persons who are members of self-determination movements excluded from any definition of terrorists as freedom fighters. We have previously discussed the *jus ad bellum* and *jus in bello* applicable to these types of insurgencies but we need finally to place this discussion within the self-determination framework.

Hannum argues that the meaning and content of self-determination is vague and imprecise.[2] According to Higgins the concept is 'difficult, extraordinarily intertwined with other norms of international law, controversial, topical, and well illustrates the complexities of the law-creating process'.[3] This chapter makes a start at unravelling some of the definitional problems by, first, outlining the history of the development of the term, discussing the components of the concept, viewing the jurisprudence that has further amplified the term, and applying this definition to recent developments, particularly the declaration of independence of Kosovo. The major difficulty in the definition of self-determination is in ascertaining whether it allows an ethnic, cultural or religious group to secede from a nation state in a post-colonial context.

The long-term situation of the Kurds in Turkey and denial of the Kurdish claim for self-determination necessitates a political solution to the legal issues involved in the denial of their status. This chapter examines two possible models for a political solution to the legal claims to self-determination, federalism and secession, and argues that within international law and politics both models provide solutions to the claims of the Kurdish people of Turkey. Therefore, after discussion of the legal content of the principle of self-determination, the second part of this chapter considers two possible political models for settlement of the armed conflict in southeast Turkey based on the legal principles discussed above. First, we discuss the possibility of secession and the debate within the Kurdish movement with respect to separation from the Turkish state. Second, and most importantly, we discuss the federalism model used in other situations such as Canada and Belgium which provides a special constitutional status for major minority groups. This is also the model being used for the situation of the Kurdish people in northern Iraq. There are as many models of federalism as there are countries which employ this political arrangement and this chapter can only begin to sketch out a general framework.

8.1 Self-determination

8.1.1 Legal context of the self-determination principle with the context of statehood

In the contemporary international system, the entity possessing the primary legal personality is the state. As Higgins states 'States are, at this moment in history, still at the heart of the international legal system'.[4] Crawford asserts that although individuals and companies can bring claims in international forums, it is states and international organisations that create and control these forums and these entities 'remain the gatekeepers and legislators of the international system'.[5] It is for this reason that statehood is often the goal of many insurgencies in order that they may secure full membership in the international community. However, the international system, supposedly based upon a community of so-called *nation*-states, is in reality an inter-*state* system, made up of what are often *multi-national* policies.[6] Often in these types of political arrangements, there exists a desire amongst a beleaguered minority (such as the Kurdish minority) to secede from an existing state and acquire statehood of their own. These minorities are driven by the belief that only in this way can they achieve effective protection, maintain and develop their collective identity and ensure the human rights of their members. Many groups seeking statehood justify their secession on the basis of an apparent universal right of self-determination,[7] as Kosovo and Abkhazia/South Ossetia have done. Historically, this has been the position of the Kurdish rebel groups in southeast Turkey and in other regions of historic Kurdistan, as is discussed in Chapter 1.

Castellino argues that the genesis of self-determination can be traced back to the American Declaration of Independence and the declaration of the French National Assembly during the French Revolution.[8] However, within modern international history, the 'father of modern self-determination' is United States

President Woodrow Wilson.[9] The history of the Kurdish people is interwoven with this modern development of self-determination as this case within the collapse of the Ottoman Empire was one that occupied the debate within the post-First World War period, again, as is recounted in Chapter 1. President Wilson stated that self-determination was not 'a mere phrase, but it is an imperative principle of action that statesmen will henceforth ignore at their peril'.[10] Wilson's famous Fourteen Points speech did not have a clear statement of self-determination but two of his points were clearly relevant to the Kurdish situation. He demanded:

5.   A free, open-minded, and absolutely impartial adjustment of all colonial claims, based upon a strict observance of the principle that in determining all such questions of sovereignty the interests of the population concerned must have equal weight with the equitable claims of the government whose title is to be determined.

...

12.   The Turkish portions of the present Ottoman Empire should be assured a secure sovereignty, but the other nationalities which are now under Turkish rule should be assured an undoubted security of life and an absolutely unmolested opportunity of autonomous development, and the Dardanelles should be permanently opened as a free passage to the ships and commerce of all nations under international guarantees.[11]

It is evident that Wilson promoted the idea of self-determination with the idea of promoting de-colonisation and a settlement of European territorial disputes, which evidently included significant minorities within the Ottoman Empire including the Kurdish people. Castellino contends that Wilson was concerned about the oppression of, and adequate representation of, minorities making this principle his guiding ethos.[12]

It can be argued therefore, that after the First World War, self-determination was used as a tool in the reconfiguration of Europe, justifying the breakdown of its large multinational empires, including the Austro-Hungarian and Ottoman Empires, into smaller units, referred to as *nation*-states.[13] Despite Wilson's efforts to expound it as a universal principle[14] and for it to be included within the League of Nations Covenant,[15] it was regarded as a *political* concept rather than a *legal* rule.[16] This view of self-determination was upheld by a first and second body appointed to examine the Åland Islands dispute. First, the International Commission of Jurists report stated:

Although the principle of self-determination of peoples plays an important part in modern political thought ... it must be pointed out that there is no mention of it in the Covenant of the League of Nations. The recognition of this principle in a certain number of international treaties is not considered sufficient to put it upon the same footing as a positive rule of law of the Law of Nations.[17]

Second, the Commission of Rapporteurs in its report on the *Åland Islands* case (1921) were as direct stating that the principle of self-determination was not 'properly speaking a rule of international law' but rather it was a 'principle of justice and of liberty, expressed by a vague and general formula which has given rise to the most varied interpretations and differences of opinion'.[18] Interestingly, the report suggested that there should be protections for the Åland Islanders guaranteeing their cultural autonomy but if this was not implemented, the Commission would advise the separation of the islands from Finland.[19] This was an early statement pointing to a contrast between internal autonomy and secession which is known in international law as the debate between internal versus external self-determination.

Another development in the years between the First and Second World Wars was consideration of the conditions necessary for a political unit to be considered a sovereign state. Article 1 of the Montevideo Convention of 1933 cites the international law criteria for statehood, its provisions are:

> The State as a person of international law should possess the following qualifications: (a) a permanent population; (b) a defined territory; (c) government; (d) capacity to enter into relations with other States.[20]

This statement is the authoritative description of the constitutive elements of statehood and not only forms part of customary international law in itself,[21] but is regarded as a codification of pre-existing customary international law.[22] It is evident that these criteria do not include the concept of self-determination which makes sense based on the post-First World War interpretation of self-determination as a political concept. However, development since the Second World War may have modified these criteria. Harris has argued that there is evidence 'to suggest that [the Montevideo] requirements, which are concerned solely with the effectiveness of the entity claiming the rights and duties of a state, have been supplemented by others'.[23] The most important of these is statehood achieved through self-determination.[24] Shaw also agrees stating that '[i]n addition to modifying the traditional principle of effectiveness of government in certain circumstances, the principle of self-determination may also be relevant as an additional criterion of statehood'.[25] This change in the status of this concept took place after the Second World War and the development of human rights instruments.

The development of self-determination as a legal concept commenced with the decolonisation movement ushered in at the end of the Second World War. It was officially included in the key international treaty, the United Nations Charter. Initially, the Dumbarton Oaks proposal for the United Nations Charter made no reference to self-determination and it was only included as a result of support of the concept by the Union of Soviet Socialist Republics (USSR).[26] As a result of USSR intervention, one of the purposes of the United Nations set out in Article 1(2) was set out to be: 'To develop friendly relations among nations based on respect for the principle of equal rights and self-determination of peoples, and to take other appropriate measures to strengthen universal peace'. The second reference to self-determination was in Article 55, which stated:

With a view to the creation of conditions of stability and well-being which are necessary for peaceful and friendly relations among nations based on respect for the principle of equal rights and self-determination of peoples, the United Nations shall promote:

a. higher standards of living, full employment, and conditions of economic and social progress and development;
b. solutions of international economic, social, health, and related problems; and international cultural and educational cooperation; and
c. universal respect for, and observance of, human rights and funda-mental freedoms for all without distinction as to race, sex, language, or religion.[27]

This inclusion of 'self-determination' within the United Nations Charter provoked much debate. The Belgian and Colombian representatives voiced their concerns in the debate on its provisions:

If it means self-government, the right of a country to provide its own government ... we would certainly like it to be included; but if it were interpreted ... as ... the right of ... secession, then we should regard that as tantamount to international anarchy ... [and] desire that it should [not] be included in the text of the Charter.[28]

Britain and France, as colonial powers, were fearful that the elevation of self-determination to a legal rule would call into question the integrity of their own Empires. These objections presented an early indication of the tense relationship that would exist between the principle of self-determination and the right of a state to have its territorial integrity respected (a corollary of state sovereignty)[29] which continues to resonate today. The worry about the emergence of international anarchy, if external self-determination is confirmed in international law, has never abated.

For the purposes of the claims of the Kurdish peoples to self-determination the critical issue raised in the objections above is whether these brief references in the United Nations Charter represent a substantive legal right. It is evident that not every statement of a political aim in a treaty can be regarded as automatically creating legal obligations[30] and at the time, several of the colonial powers resisted the idea that there was a legal right of self-determination, stating it was merely a 'political aspiration'.[31] Articles 1(?) and 55 refer to self-determination in the context of friendly relations among nations and in conjunction with the 'equal rights' of peoples.[32] Higgins supports the idea that it is a legal obligation and maintains that within this context it is 'clearly the rights of peoples of one state to be protected from interference by other states or governments. It is revisionism to ignore the coupling of 'self-determination' with 'equal rights' '.[33] She further contends that it is the equal rights of *states* that are being provided for, not of individuals.[34] Cassese regards the linkage with friendly relations and peace as a limitation, in that self-determination must be set aside 'when its fulfilment would give rise to tension and conflict among states'.[35] He also argues that the principle of self-determination in the United Nations Charter is formulated 'only as a goal, a political policy ... not as a definite obligation'.[36] In spite of this debate between two prominent international law scholars, the inclusion of this concept within the United Nations Charter has allowed for a subsequent interpretation of the principle both in terms of its legal effect and consequences with regard to its definition in two respects; as a legal criterion for statehood, and, as a free standing human right.[37] Through custom and treaty, its elucidation and standing as a principle and more particularly its perceived application in specific instances has conclusively established self-determination as a doctrine of public international law.[38]

There was another article in the United Nations Charter which has bearing on this discussion of legality, particularly as a legal criterion for statehood. Chapter XI is entitled 'Declaration Regarding Non-Self-Governing Territories'. Article 73 states:

> Members of the United Nations which have or assume responsibilities for the administration of territories whose peoples have not yet attained a full measure of self-government recognize the principle that the interests of the inhabitants of these territories are paramount, and accept as a sacred trust the obligation to promote to the utmost, within the system of international peace and security established by the present Charter, the well-being of the inhabitants of these territories, and, to this end ...
>
> b.   to develop self-government, to take due account of the political aspirations of the peoples, and to assist them in the progressive development of their free political institutions, according to the particular circumstances of each territory and its peoples and their varying stages of advancement;
>
> ...
>
> e.   to transmit regularly to the Secretary-General for information purposes, subject to such limitation as security and constitutional considerations may require, statistical and other information of a technical nature relating to economic, social, and educational conditions in the territories for which they are respectively responsible other than those territories to which Chapters XII and XIII apply.

This Chapter together with Chapter XIII on the Trusteeship system (continuing the League of Nations mandate system) provided for the gradual independence of colonial territories and ushered in the era of decolonisation. With the increase in Afro-Asian membership throughout the 1950s and 1960s, there was growing agreement that it was obligatory to bring forward dependent peoples to independence if they so chose, even though Article 73 above, had only mentioned 'self-government'.[39] This was confirmed in the ruling in the *Namibia Advisory Opinion* as the court held that can be 'little doubt that the ultimate objective of the sacred trust was the self-determination and independence of the peoples concerned'.[40] The international practice of decolonisation culminated in the passing of two UN General Assembly Resolutions within 24 hours of each other, Resolutions 1514[41] and 1541,[42] which together provide the clearest statements of self-determination within international law.[43] Both resolutions were passed unanimously, suggesting that for the purpose of international law, they constitute a customary norm.[44] Resolution 1514 on the Declaration on the Granting of Independence to Colonial Countries and Peoples stated that 'all peoples have the right to self-determination by virtue of that right they freely determine their political status and freely pursue their economic, social and cultural development'.[45] Resolution 1541 on the 'Principles which should guide Members in determining whether or not an obligation exists to transmit the information called for under Article 73(e) of the Charter' contained the steps needed towards self-government for a dependent territory. First of all, Principle IV indicated that there was an obligation to transmit information in respect of a territory which is geographically separate and is distinct ethnically and/or culturally from the country administering it. Principle VI indicated that a non-self-governing territory was said to have reached a full measure of self-government by: (a) emergence as a sovereign independent state; (b) free association with an independent state; or (c) integration with an independent state.[46] Although self-determination was not stated as an aim in this resolution, together with the previous resolution it was clear that the goal was independence of geographically separate and distinct ethnic or cultural groups.

Besides these international declarations, the international practice in decolonisation supported the emergence of self-determination as a *legal* requirement for statehood. Examples of this practice are the Southern Rhodesia and the South African Homelands situations, as these respective political entities would have met the traditional Montevideo criteria and qualified as states under international law.[47] In spite of that fact, in both cases, these entities' claims to statehood were condemned by the membership of the United Nations as having no legal validity; no state extended recognition to any of these entities. The main reason cited for non-recognition was the failure to meet the requirement of self-determination as these regimes would perpetuate an apartheid system.[48] These examples illustrate the importance of self-determination as a legal requirement for statehood: even where the Montevideo criteria were fulfilled, statehood for these entities at least was blocked by the absence of self-determination.

There is another significant declaration that has confirmed as customary a series of fundamental rules of public international law: the Declaration on Principles of International Law, Friendly Relations and Co-operation among States in Accordance with the Charter of the United Nations, which was passed in the UN General Assembly in 1970.[49] One of the major principles in this resolution was on equal rights and self-determination of peoples and the text stated:

> By virtue of the principle of equal rights and self-determination of peoples enshrined in the Charter of the United Nations, all peoples have the right freely to determine, without external interference, their political status and to pursue their economic, social and cultural development, and every State has the duty to respect this right in accordance with the provisions of the Charter.
>
> Every State has the duty to promote, through joint and separate action, realization of the principle of equal rights and self-determination of peoples, in accordance with the provisions of the Charter, and to render assistance to the United Nations in carrying out the responsibilities entrusted to it by the Charter regarding the implementation of the principle, in order:
>
> (a)   To promote friendly relations and cooperation among States; and
> (b)   To bring a speedy end to colonialism, having due regard to the freely expressed will of the peoples concerned; and bearing in mind that subjection of peoples to alien subjugation, domination and exploitation constitutes a violation of the principle, as well as a denial of fundamental human rights, and is contrary to the Charter.
>
> ... Every State has the duty to refrain from any forcible action which deprives peoples referred to above in the elaboration of the present principle of their right to self-determination and freedom and independence. In their actions against, and resistance to, such forcible action in pursuit of the exercise of their right to self-determination, such peoples are entitled to seek and to receive support in accordance with the purposes and principles of the Charter.[50]

As Vanda argues, the Declaration is imprecise as it grants several options for self-determination including: (a) the establishing of a sovereign and independent state; (b) the free association or integration with an independent state; or (c) the emergence into any other political status, provided these entities were freely determined by a people.[51] It seems to provide for either internal or external self-determination depending on the circumstances, and how it would apply in a manner that would not dismember the territorial integrity of existing states formed subsequent to decolonisation remains unclear. Notwithstanding the difficulty in interpretation, this Declaration has been viewed as a listing of important principles of customary international law, including this principle of self-determination.

Given the declarations and the practice, it is quite clear that, despite its absence from the Montevideo criteria, self-determination may well be legal requirement for statehood but the question remains as to whether self-determination as a legal criterion for statehood applies beyond the colonial context. Prior to continuing this discussion, it is important to note that the international law regime for the creation of states is not the only context in which self-determination is debated, its meaning and content is also heavily debated within human rights discourse. However, the inclusion of the self-determination as an important human right – an international legal norm – strengthens the argument that this norm is far more than a political ideal.

8.1.2 Legal context of the self-determination principle within human rights law

The concept of self-determination is an important human rights doctrine. It is contained in both the International Covenant on Civil and Political Rights and the International Covenant on Economic Social and Cultural Rights.[52] Article 1 is common to both Conventions and states:

Article 1

1. All peoples have the right of self-determination. By virtue of that right they freely determine their political status and freely pursue their economic, social and cultural development.
2. All peoples may, for their own ends, freely dispose of their natural wealth and resources without prejudice to any obligations arising out of international economic cooperation, based upon the principle of mutual benefit, and international law. In no case may a people be deprived of its own means of subsistence.
3. The States Parties to the present Covenant, including those having responsibility for the administration of Non-Self-Governing and Trust Territories, shall promote the realization of the right of self-determination, and shall respect that right, in conformity with the provisions of the Charter of the United Nations.

The importance of this right was confirmed in the Vienna Declaration and Programme of Action of 1993 which stated:

2. All peoples have the right of self-determination. By virtue of that right they freely determine their political status, and freely pursue their economic, social and cultural development. Taking into account the particular situation of peoples under colonial or other forms of alien domination or foreign occupation, the World Conference on Human Rights recognizes the right of peoples to take any legitimate action, in accordance with the Charter of the United Nations, to realize their inalienable right of self-determination. The World Conference on Human Rights considers the denial of the right of self-determination as a violation of human rights and underlines the importance of the effective realization of this right.[53]

The case law of the International Court of Justice has considered the legal status of self-determination. Any remaining doubts as to its legal standing as a human right has been dispelled by successive International Court of Justice judgments,[54] culminating in the unequivocal *East Timor* case in which the judgment stated:

> The right of ... peoples to self-determination, as it has developed from the Charter and practice of the UN, is a right that is enforceable *erga omnes*. The principle of the right of self-determination of peoples has been recognised by the Charter of the UN and in the jurisprudence of the Court. ... This is one of the essential principles of contemporary international law.[55]

The most recent case in the International Court of Justice to consider this issue was the *Legal Consequences of the Construction of a Wall in the Occupied Palestinian Territory* Advisory Opinion.[56] Discussing self-determination in a colonial context again, the International Court of Justice observed that since the wall constructed by Israel violated the '*erga omnes*' obligation of self-determination binding on all nations, it resulted in an international legal obligation for all states 'to see to it that any impediment [...] to the exercise by the Palestinian people of its right to self-determination is brought to an end'.[57] The court, however, did not explore how all the other states were to accomplish this task. In the process of assessing the impact of the location of the wall on the right of the Palestinian people to self-determination, the court further observed that the construction of the wall 'severely impedes the exercise by the Palestinian people of its right to self-determination'.[58] Judge Kooijmans argued that it would have been better had the court left the issue of self-determination to the political process and that the issue was embedded in the wider context of the political settlement.[59] Kooijmans cannot be correct. Although the wall forms only part of the impediment of the Palestinian claim for self-determination, their right is nevertheless legally enshrined in aforementioned instruments. On that basis therefore the court was correct to have considered this substantial hindrance to the exercise of the Palestinian right to self-determination.[60]

It is evident then, that self-determination has a legal status as a human right but the meaning and content of the right is not that clear. Thornberry's first question in his analysis of this right is who are the peoples that are entitled to claim self-determination?[61] He asks whether this means that minorities are justified in 'appropriating self-determination to state their claims and aspirations?'.[62] The International Covenant on Civil and Political Rights has a separate article concerning the protection of minorities. Article 27 states:

> In those States in which ethnic, religious or linguistic minorities exist, persons belonging to such minorities shall not be denied the right, in community with the other members of their group, to enjoy their own culture, to profess and practise their own religion, or to use their own language.[63]

Thornberry confirms that neither the articles on self-determination, nor the article on minorities contains a definition of the term peoples or a minority. He cites a definition by the Special Rapporteur of the UN Sub-Commission on the Prevention of Discrimination and Protection of Minorities Professor Caportorti who proposed that a minority would be:

> ... a group numerically inferior to the rest of the population of a State, in a non-dominant position, whose members – being nationals of the States – possess ethnic, religious or linguistic characteristics differing from those of the rest of the population and show, if only implicitly, a sense of solidarity, directed towards preserving their culture, traditions, religion or language.[64]

Buchheit argues that as a minimum 'selfness' in self-determination could include elements of a religious, historic, geographic, ethnic, economic, linguistic, and racial character.[65] This is a much broader definition than a minority group. No legal analysis brings together the definition of minorities to those of 'peoples' within the language of self-determination. Even though a more restrictive definition of minority might suit a definition of 'people' this is not confirmed as such in any international instrument. Crawford argues that self-determination is a collective rather than individual right, even though individuals will benefit from retaining or achieving self-government in accordance with their wishes or preferences. It is also a right of 'peoples' rather than governments.[66] This concept of the peoples is confirmed in the *Legal Consequences of the Construction of a Wall in the Occupied Palestinian Territory* Advisory Opinion, as the court held that Israel had violated the right of the Palestinian 'people' to self-determination.[67] We are left with a general concept of a 'people' entitled to self-determination although it could be argued that the history of self-determination movements harkens back to the Wilsonian argument of those who are distinct from the majority group by reason of culture, ethnicity, religion or language.

The second difficulty is the legal meaning of 'determination'. The International Court of Justice in the *Western Sahara* case argued that 'the right of self-determination leaves the General Assembly a measure of discretion with respect to the forms and procedures by which that right is to be realised'.[68] This ruling fails to provide any real clarification as to what the right entails. The critical part of this discussion then is the debate over how this human right might be realised. None of the human rights instruments discussed above clarifies how self determination might lawfully be realised. The key debate, then, is whether determination can be realised within a sovereign state or without. Therefore, we turn now to the legal debate between absolute autonomy and some sort of special status as a means to obtain 'determination'.

8.1.3 External versus internal self-determination

The issue of how self-determination might be realised has occupied a great deal of international law debate which can only be briefly summarised in this book.[69]

The major legal issue is how within the United Nations Charter framework and the corpus of human rights instruments, self-determination can be achieved. This has become particularly acute after the end of the decolonisation period where various groups such as Biafrans, Eritreans and Bangladeshis argued for self-determination even though they were within post-colonial independent states. There were two broad positions, one that self-determination should be realised within the territorial boundaries, and the other that called for autonomy and the legal right to secede. On the side of secession, Vanda argues that a state has to meet the requirement of a government representing a whole people before it is entitled to protection from 'any action which would dismember or impair' its territorial integrity or political unity.[70] He proposes that under special circumstances that the principle of self-determination is to be according priority over the opposing principle of territorial integrity.[71] He supports this position by quoting the Preamble of the Declaration on Friendly Relations that states that 'the subjugation of peoples to alien subjugation, domination and exploitation constitutes a major obstacle to the promotion of international peace and security'.[72] This is not agreed by all commentators, and from the preservation of sovereignty perspective, Higgins asserts that 'contrary to popular mythology', the notion of self-determination bestowing a right of independence 'does not find its origins in the UN Charter' and in fact constitutes 'a retrospective rewriting of history'.[73] She goes on to contend that 'there is no legal right of secession where there is a representative government'.[74] Tomuschat agrees with Higgins and in a recent contribution argues, 'the armed conflict in Chechnya provides ample proof that the international community flatly denies a right to self-determination of ethnic groups included in the population of a sovereign State'.[75]

This stalemate may never be resolved. Buchheit is indeed accurate in stating that '[n]othing in the principle of self-determination itself demands … absolute autonomy or even a Western-style democracy'.[76] Nevertheless, if self-determination is to be regarded as predominantly an internal right, it can be assumed that it would have a close relationship with the rights of minorities as discussed above. Article 27 of the International Covenant on Civil and Political Rights[77] and Article 1 of the Declaration on the Rights of Persons Belonging to National or Ethnic, Religious and Linguistic Minorities[78] both provide that minorities have the right to enjoy their own culture, practise and profess their own religion and use their own language in private and public without hindrance; such persons also have the right to participate effectively in cultural, social, economic and public life.[79] In 2007, the Declaration on the Rights of Indigenous Peoples was adopted. Article 3 provides that indigenous peoples – those minorities that have a close relationship with a particular territory – must have the right to self-determination and in exercising this, have the right to autonomy or self-government in matters relating to their internal and local affairs, as well as ways and means for financing their autonomous functions (Article 4). They further have the right to maintain and strengthen their distinctive political, economic, social and cultural characteristics, as well as their legal systems, while retaining the right to participate in the life of the state (Article 5).[80]

In spite of her position on internal autonomy, Higgins leaves the door open for other interpretations. Although self-determination as a means of independence 'is *not* provided for by the text of the UN Charter', she crucially notes that:

> [i]nternational law does not develop from written words alone.[…]In the case of self-determination, the term originally had a rather limited and state-based meaning. But there was nothing in the Charter that actually *prohibited* the emergence of a norm that required states … to provide to dependent peoples the right to determine their own destiny.[81]

Despite the Charter's drafters' and contemporaries' understanding of 'self-determination' and 'peoples', it appeared that through the adoption of numerous resolutions in the following years such a norm of autonomy developed in the context of decolonisation. With the onset of the Cold War, the USSR began to demand decolonisation by the Western imperialist states in accordance with communist theory, which gained the support of Afro-Asian states.[82] Although self-determination was not mentioned in Chapter XI or Chapter XII, both provided for a *gradual* development of Non-Self-Governing Territories towards self-government or, in the case of Trust Territories, towards independence 'as may be appropriate'. But in the 1950s, this policy of progressive and gradual development towards increased self-government came under greater pressure from the UN General Assembly. The UN General Assembly set aside the policy of gradual development and replaced it with a policy which asserted that colonial territories should *immediately* be granted *independence*, culminating in the passing of UN General Assembly Resolutions 1514 and 1541, affirmed 'the necessity of bringing to a speedy and unconditional end colonialism in all its forms and manifestations'. This process saw the evolution of self-determination from being interpreted as solely applying to the 'internal' dimension, to one of an 'external' application, ie the right to independence. This application was strictly within the 'colonial context'. Such a restrictive application was encouraged by UN General Assembly Resolution 1541 which described the subject of self-determination as a 'territory … geographically separate and … distinct ethnically and/or culturally from the country administering it', giving rise to the so-called 'salt-water' test, ie colonies separated from their metropoles by salt-water[83] could exercise *external* self-determination.[84] However, once the decolonisation process was largely completed, it appeared that the use of self-determination as an instrument to create new states had come to an end as prior to the end of the Cold War only one 'non-colonial' state had emerged following a claim of self-determination – Bangladesh's secession from Pakistan.[85]

The end of the Cold War saw the unthawing of many 'frozen conflicts' and the world's borders began to look a lot more fluid. It was within this context that some cited a resurgence of 'national self-determination', ie the use of self-determination for the purpose of advancing the doctrine of the nation-state. Several new states have succeeded in joining the international state system since the 1990s. This was mainly as a result of the break-up of three communist federations – the USSR, Yugoslavia and Czechoslovakia, although Eritrea and Timor-Leste have also obtained self-determination but at the price of the loss of thousands of lives.[86] Recognition was granted in two of these cases because there was no central government willing to resist the break-up as both Prague and Moscow assented to the break-up of their federations. In Yugoslavia, the Badinter Commission pointed out that the federation was breaking apart, ie it was not a matter of a region seceding.[87] It rather considered that 'the answer to the question should be based on the principles of public international law which serve to define the conditions on which an entity constitutes a State; that in this respect, the existence or disappearance of the State is a question of fact; that the effects of recognition by other States are purely declaratory'. Furthermore; it found that 'the existence of a federal state, which is made up of a number of separate entities, is seriously compromised when a majority of these entities, embracing a greater part of the territory and population, constitute themselves as sovereign states with the result that federal authority may no longer be effectively exercised'.[88] However, the Commission made clear, that on the basis of *uti possidetis*, only Yugoslavia's federal republics had the right to independence and not regions within these republics, such as the Republika Srspka or Kosovo.[89] Eritrea and Timor-Leste left with some degree of consent from the central authorities in Ethiopia and Indonesia respectively and both are examples of decolonisation rather than secession as they had been at one time distinct colonies.[90] These developments have marked a continuation of self-determination as it had been applied in the colonial context, ie along civic lines and as a furtherance of internal self-determination, rather than any significant departure.

Some, such as Buchheit, have highlighted the apparent unfairness in the way the law of self-determination has developed:

> [such a] distinction [between colonial and non-colonial situations] is ... easily explicable in terms of the political interests of the world community, ... but [o]ne searches in vain ... for any principled justification ... why a colonial people wishing to cast off the domination of its governors has every moral and legal right to do so, but a manifestly distinguishable minority ... must forever remain without the scope of [(external)] self-determination.[91]

Although wary of the consequences of extending 'external' self-determination beyond the colonial context it would appear that the current law on self-determination leads to some strange logical conclusions: for example, Newfoundland, which had been a separate colony from Canada until 1949, might be able to claim the right to external self-determination on the same lines as Eritrea or Timor-Leste, whereas Quebec, having always been an integral part of Canada, could not. In the pivotal domestic case on self-determination, *Reference Re Secession of Quebec*,[92] the Supreme Court of Canada struggles with the question of whether a unilateral secession by Quebec from Canada would be legal for the purposes of international law.[93] The Supreme Court declared that:

[t]he recognised sources of international law establish that the right of self-determination is normally fulfilled through internal self-determination – a people's pursuit of its political, economic, social and cultural development within the framework of an existing state.[94]

This appears to support the assertion that beyond the colonial context, self-determination is primarily an internal right. Self-determination should, *in the main*, be based upon a civic conception and exercised as an internal right; however, there may be occasions in which a group finds itself completely blocked from meaningful *internal* exercise of its right to self-determination. The Canadian Supreme Court significantly outlines three tenets of a successful claim of external self-determination.[95] First, the grouping must be a 'peoples', second, there must be serious human rights abuses, and finally the would-be secessionists must have exhausted all domestic remedies.[96] The Supreme Court of Canada defines secession, as: 'the effort of a group or section of a state to withdraw itself from the political and constitutional authority of that State, with a view to achieving statehood for a new territorial unit on the international plane'.[97] This means that the collective will of the majority is taken under consideration, therefore an expression of qualitative evaluation takes precedence over quantitative evidence of consent. In the opinion of the Supreme Court of Canada, international law does not specifically grant component parts of sovereign states the legal right to secede unilaterally from their 'parent' state.[98] The court focuses on the implied duty of states to recognise the legitimacy of secession brought about by the exercise of the well-established international law: the right of 'a people' to self-determination.[99]

The Quebec opinion continues to place great importance on territorial integrity, stating that: 'There is no necessary incompatibility between the maintenance of the territorial integrity of existing states, including Canada, and the right of a "people" to achieve a full measure of self-determination'.[100] Key portions of the judgment support this position:

(Para.130) A state whose government represents the whole of the people or peoples ... and respects the principles of self-determination in its own internal arrangements, is entitled to ... protection under international law of its territorial integrity.

(Para.134) The Vienna Declaration requirement that governments [must] represent 'the whole people belonging to the territory *without distinction of any kind*' adds credence to the assertion that such a complete blockage may potentially give rise to a right of secession.

Therefore, a state whose government represents the whole of the people or people's resident within the territory, on a basis of equality and without discrimination, and respects the principles of self-determination in its own internal arrangements, is entitled to the protection under international law of its territorial integrity. Therefore, the case does not establish the border line between internal and external self-determination and as a domestic case it only adds to the debate, it does not resolve it. As Macklem asserts:

> Notwithstanding the Supreme Court of Canada's decision in the *Quebec Secession Reference*, the field remains divided on whether the right of external self-determination extends beyond the contexts of colonization and foreign occupation to include and to legitimate certain secessionist movements.[101]

Despite this progressive jurisprudence, there had been little direct evidence that customary international law supports the right to secession;[102] there was rather a wealth of evidence against it: for instance, recognition has not been forthcoming for those, like the Turkish Cypriots, who have established the realities of statehood on the ground;[103] on the basis of *uti possidetis*, the whole of Bosnia-Herzegovina was recognised as one state rather than its internal ethnic cleavages (the Bosniac-Croat part and the Serb Republika Srpska); and even in the velvet divorce of Czechoslovakia, European Union spokesmen warned the Czech and Slovak leaders that their impending divorce could mean isolation outside the Europe family.[104] In 1994, Liechtenstein attempted to clarify the right of self-determination by circulating in the UN General Assembly's Social, Cultural and Humanitarian Affairs Committee a draft Convention on Self-Determination through Self-Administration, which recognised a right of internal autonomy for all 'peoples', where peoples were explicitly defined to include not only indigenous peoples but also homeland national minorities.[105] However, as Kymlicka recounts, this draft was never debated seriously and quickly disappeared from view.[106] Within the disintegration of the Republic of Yugoslavia, among the entities which sought the Badinter Commission's endorsement were Kosovo and the Serb Krajina in Croatia. The Commission would not consider their applications on the basis that the rule of *uti possidetis* bound its hands. These two were excluded because they were not Federal States of the Socialist Federal Republic of Yugoslavia (SFRY).[107] However, Antonio Cassese writing in the middle of the Yugoslav conflict states:

> Allowance should nevertheless be made for exceptional cases where factual conditions render internal self-determination impracticable. When, in a multinational State, armed conflict breaks out and one or more groups fight for secession, it may be that it is too late to plead for a peaceful solution based on internal self-determination. Similarly, when the central authorities of a multinational State are irremeably oppressive and despotic, persistently violate the basic rights of minorities and no peaceful and constructive solution can be envisaged, it seems difficult to imagine that those central authorities would be willing to grant autonomy, or participatory rights.
>
> ... one might thus envisage the intervention of the international community with a view to promoting some sort of independent statehood for the minorities at issue.[108]

Cassese may well have been prescient, as academic opinion, state practice and the relevant treaty provisions have been thrown into question as a result of the declaration of independence of Kosovo. The break-up of the Soviet Union, Yugoslavia and Czechoslovakia took place within the context of recognised boundaries of former constituent republics or provinces. It is the situation of Kosovo in 1999 which begins to take this debate into a wider and even more controversial context.

Kosovo independence 2008 – a change in the law of self-determination?

In 2007, Marti Ahtisaari[109] proposed a 'supervised independence' as the only viable option for the resolution of the status of Kosovo, which has remained unresolved since the NATO intervention of 1999 based on the disputed grounds of humanitarian intervention.[110] UN Security Council Resolution 1244 dated 10 June 1999, following the end of hostilities introducing international administration for Kosovo, confirmed the territorial integrity of the Federal Republic of Yugoslavia.[111] In February 2008, Kosovo made a unilateral declaration of independence and – unlike its previous attempt in October 1991 in which its claim was recognised solely by Albania[112] – gained recognition from a number of states, including the United States, France and Britain (a total that now stands at 56[113]). Prima facie, this appears to be at odds with previous developments: as discussed above the Badinter Commission determined that, unlike the Yugoslav republics, Kosovo was not a 'nation' but an autonomous province of Serbia and thus not entitled to exercise a right of self-determination on the basis of *uti possidetis* – a position then accepted by the international community.[114] Subsequently, some of the states that have recognised Kosovo's claim to statehood via self-determination have done so on the basis that 'there was a legal and factual similarity between Kosovo and the other republics, deriving from the 1974 constitution',[115] suggesting that Kosovo is akin to the more conventional colonial situations of the past. The constitutional difference between republics and autonomous provinces under the 1974 Constitution did, however, have real legal and political consequences. It cannot be argued that the two were essentially coterminous and moreover no state (particularly no NATO member state), either before or after the 1999 Kosovo War, seriously invoked this argument as a justification for intervention or for the independence of Kosovo.[116] On this basis, to justify Kosovo's claim to statehood via self-determination on the basis that it is a '*de facto*' colonial situation appears rather artificial.

It would seem more accurate to recognise Kosovo as the first example of statehood being achieved on the basis of self-determination outside the colonial context. It would appear that those states that have accorded recognition to Kosovo have done so as a result of the three factors set out above in the *Quebec Secession* case and it conforms to the Cassese view of external self-determination.[117] There may be such a right to secession along these lines, but such a right could only be exercised in 'the most extreme of cases and, even then, under carefully defined circumstances'.[118] This appears to have set the threshold that a denial of internal self-determination activates the right to secession very high, echoing the findings in the *Åland Islands* case (1921):

> The separation of a minority from the state of which it forms a part ... can only be considered as an altogether exceptional solution, a last resort when the state lacks either the will or the power to enact and apply just and effective guarantees.[119]

Goodwin compellingly applies this point to Kosovo:

> One could reasonably have argued that Milošević's regime lacked the will to ensure just and effective guarantees, but it seems difficult to reach the same conclusion in respect of the democratic government currently in office in Belgrade. Indeed, policing measures taken in respect of Vojvodina give all the appearance of a Serbian regime able and willing to ensure effective guarantees for [the Kosovars]; moreover, it has demonstrated that it is able to provide security and stability in the context of the territory's autonomous status. The abuses ... although severe, are historical in nature and there is no reason at present to suppose, should a solution short of independence be adopted, that these abuses will return. The Serbia of Vojislav Koštunica is not that of Milošević.[120]

In apparently confirming the *Quebec Secession* case threshold, there is a real danger that claims for statehood will result from many secessionist movements, it already appears that the precedent is being seized upon by separatists from Catalonia to Chechnya.[121] Moreover, though Kosovo has received recognition from a number of the world's states, it would appear that the majority of states are cautious in doing so owing to the precedent it would set. Even within the European Union, five states – Spain, Greece, Romania, Slovakia and Cyprus – have refused to extend recognition to Kosovo,[122] despite the European Parliament's adoption of a Resolution urging them to do so,[123] principally over concerns the precedent it would set regarding their own border disputes or rebellious regions.[124] Russia's President Putin posed the question, 'If people believe that Kosovo can be granted full independence, why then should we deny it to Abkhazia and South Ossetia?'.[125] Furthermore, the Deputy Foreign Minister of Abkhazia stated, regarding Kosovo's then imminent independence, just 'because Russia does not want Kosovo to be recognised, it does not mean that we do not want it'.[126]

To try to limit its use as a precedent in this regard, many of those states that have recognised Kosovo claimed to have done so on the basis that it was a 'special' or '*sui generis*' case.[127] The features Warbrick refers to are mainly the repression of the Kosovars up to the year 2000 which stands out, and the indictments of the Serbs for crimes against humanity and war crimes by the International Criminal Tribunal for the Former Yugoslavia (ICTY).[128] But Goodwin submits, 'it is unlikely that the precedent set will be ... contained within a secure box marked "*sui generis*"'.[129] The double standard of this position has been highlighted by those opposed to Kosovo's independence, including the Russian President Medvedev who stated, 'Each case of recognising independence is a special case ... A special case in Kosovo, a special case in Abkhazia and South Ossetia'.[130] It appears that to argue Kosovo as a '*sui generis*' is superficial and this case may well be the beginning of confirmation of external self-determination under the *Quebec Secession* case criteria. Cvijic accurately predicted in 2007 that:

> the imposition of self-determination of Kosovo on Serbia by the international community, by bypassing the UNSC, in the case of a potential Russian or Chinese veto, will represent ... a revolutionary challenge to established fundamental international norms ... Such a political and legal development would be a radical departure from the slow evolutionary adaptation of international law to [a] new geopolitical situation, and amount to a funda-mental shift in the post-ww2 order that none of the major international players involved in the negotiating the process on the future status of Kosovo (including the US and NATO) desires.[131]

Although some sought to play down or dismiss Kosovo as a major development of international law, such notions were dispelled when, on 26 August 2008, the Russian President signed Decrees recognising the independence of Abkhazia/South Ossetia, declaring that the decision had been taken on grounds almost identical to those cited by states recognising Kosovo (indeed, the two were explicitly linked).

On this basis, it is clear that the Kosovo precedent has presented a revolutionary challenge to established international law[132] – particularly the law of self-determination – and created a situation for which no state in the interna-tional community seems willing to take responsibility;[133] it has formed the basis of Russia's recognition of Abkhazia/South Ossetia. Nevertheless, it cannot be said that the issue of external self-determination in a post-colonial setting is resolved as one case is not determinative of customary international law. Furthermore, the suggestion that this case might apply to Kurdistan has not been raised and so therefore, both an internal and external solution to the Kurdish crisis must be considered in the political context as international law has been thrown into turmoil as a result of Kosovo.

8.2 Political solutions to the crisis

The above discussion on self-determination has revealed that there is not a clear international law solution to claims of minority groups who do not have their cultural, religious or ethnic rights guaranteed. One cannot state unequivocally that there is a right of external self-determination. International law always works hand in hand with political processes and in this case with the lack of clarity in the legal regime the political process is critical.

Within the literature of political science are two models that largely conform to the international law proposals of either internal or external self-determination.

The first political model that results from successful claims of external self-determination is the constitution of a new political entity by consensual or non-consensual secession. However, the second long-standing political model of federalism seems to be a political arrangement that best suits international law requirements of internal self-determination. We consider both models in the next section.

8.2.1 The formation of a new state by secession[134]

In political terms if a right to external self-determination is recognised, it results in a new state being formed from a secessionist movement. Even though, as Buchheit argues, the international community did not 'intend the enthronement of a right of secession exercisable by any minority group within an independent State as a canon of international law',[135] it is a political reality that secession often results from movements of self-determination. Secession is defined for the purposes of this analysis as the 'withdrawal from a state or society through the constitution of a new sovereign and independent state'.[136] The growth in the number of states from 151 in 1990 to 192 at present has been largely due to secession.[137] As can be seen from Chapter 1, the stated aim of the Kurdistan Workers Party (PKK) for much of its history has been the constitution of a separate state, a Kurdistan divorced from the Turkish polity. However, as Kohen asserts secession is not an instant fact but rather 'a complex series of claims and decisions, negotiations and/or struggle, which may – or may not – lead to the creation of a new State'.[138]

The legal and political model of secession is predicated on two models, a consensual model of state succession and a model based on non-consensual armed conflict, with the secessionist movement winning the battle for separation and the necessity for a peace agreement or UN Security Council or UN General Assembly resolution setting out the terms of the new political arrangement. The conflict model was very much the case for Bangladesh, Kosovo and Eritrea. The situation of Kosovo is very much unresolved as the international community as a whole has not recognised the new state of Kosovo and as a result the state will not be able to assume membership of the United Nations or any other international organisation. On the other hand, Bangladesh was recognised within 3 months by over 90 states after the forcible intervention by India,[139] and Ethiopia conceded Eritrean independence after a long-standing armed conflict.[140]

Buchanan in his study of secession proposes conditions that would have to be satisfied if a political argument of cultural preservation would justify secessions. Among these conditions are:

(1) the culture in question must in fact be imperilled
(2) less disruptive ways of preserving the culture must be unavailable or inadequate
(3) the culture in question must meet minimal standards of justice
(4) the seceding cultural group must not be seeking independence in order to establish an illiberal state – there must be basic civil and political rights.[141]

These conditions lead to an argument that there should be a constitutional right to secede which could be based on a substantive model which would specify all and the only moral justifications for seceding. Chief among these would be that the group wishing to secede had been treated unjustly such as: its territorial sovereignty had been violated; it had suffered discriminatory redistribution; its members had been denied equality of opportunity; or their individual or states' rights had been violated; and other forms of redress other than secession were not available.[142] This is very similar to the discussion in the *Quebec Secession* case discussed above. Both the moral cultural conditions and these substantive conditions could be met when we consider the situation of the Kurds in southeast Turkey. Buchanan also proposes a procedural model for secession based on a vote of three-quarters of the eligible voters in the region. This procedural model was followed in the dissolution of the Yugoslav federation. A domestic constitution in the current state (in this case Turkey) could propose both the substantive and procedural process of secession.[143]

Although secession is often considered within an internal constitutional framework, since the end of the Cold War there has been much more international involvement in this process.[144] Many of the cases where new states have emerged entail a substantial element of international oversight. Examples are the Badinter Commission with respect to Yugoslavia, and the NATO/European Union process in Kosovo. In the circumstances of the Kurds and Turkey, the dialogue has been taking place within the context of the Turkish wish to become part of the European Union. Yet it must be emphasised that there seems to be a lack of international will for a separate Kurdish state, the Wilsonian support for such an entity as set out in the Treaty of Sèvres has never been repeated.

Besides the political process, there is also a legal regime involved in the evolution of a new state which emerges from an existing state and that is the process of state succession. According to the Badinter Commision, Opinion No 1, the expression 'state succession' means the replacement of one state by another in the responsiblity for the international relations of a territory.[145] Brownlie further defines the concept a 'definitive replacement of one state by another in respect of sovereignty over a given territory in conformity with international law'.[146] As a result of this definition, instances of secession can constitute cases of state succession, if the secessionist movement is in a position to constitute a new state.[147] This new state, even if originating with a secessionist movement, can be resolved by a consensual process of negotiation. According to the Badinter Commission, the peremptory norms of general international law and, in particular, respect for the fundamental rights of the individual and the rights of peoples and minorities, are binding on the parties to the succession.[148] Zimmermann suggests that there are two types of legal succession: separation and dismemberment. Eritrea is viewed as a case of separation, whereas, the SFRY as dismemberment.[149]

The most important example of state practice dealing with the legal process of succession is the Badinter Commission (also known as the European Commission Peace Conference on Yugoslavia) which convened following the eruption of civil war in the SFRY. The conference asked the five members of the Badinter Commission to act as an arbitration panel and as such they handed down Opinion Nos 1–10, three opinions are relevant to the situation of extinction and succession of states and represent important examples of state practice in this complex area. Opinion No 1 stated that the SFRY was in the process of dissolution and that the various constituent republics has an obligation to settle problems of state succession in keeping with the principles and rules of international law in particular with regard to human rights and rights of minorities.[150] Opinion No 8 indicated that the dissolution of a state meant that it no longer had legal personality, and in this case the SFRY no longer existed.[151] In Opinion No 3 the Commission dealt with the territorial repercussions of the break-up of the SFRY. In this opinion the Commission found that all external frontiers had to be respected and that the former internal boundaries between Croatia and Serbia and Bosnia-Herzegovina and Serbia now became international frontiers in compliance with the principle of *uti possedetis*. This legal rule means that existing boundary delimitations have the protection of international law, and it is now recognised as a rule of customary international law outside of the colonial context.[152]

There are also examples of legal contractual dissolutions of state such as the break up of the Former Soviet Union which instead of an extinction of a state was treated as a partial succession with the Russian Federation, by agreement, becoming the successor to the rights and obligations of the USSR, including its retaining the permanent seat on the UN Security Council. The European Commission Guidelines on the Recognition of the New States in Eastern Europe and the Soviet Union also confirmed respect for existing frontiers.[153] This practice confirms that respect for the former provincial boundaries is an important part of state succession. In the Kurdish situation this could conceivably represent a distinct area representing southeast Turkey.

Another example of consensual dissolution in state practice is the extinction of the Democratic Republic of Germany and its merger into the unified state of the Federal Republic of Germany, which assumed all the international rights and responsibilities of the former state. Another example is the consensual break-up of Czechoslovakia into the two states of the Czech Republic and Slovakia. In keeping with the peaceful nature of the 'velvet revolution' this dissolution was peaceful and the territorial boundaries of the former parts of the republic were respected. In addition, the two new states agreed on issues such as treaty obligations and division of public property and debts. The last example reveals that a country can negotiate 'a friendly divorce', with all legal arrangements being negotiated in an international treaty. This is supported by the case of Eritrea which, after a long conflict, eventually separated with the explicit prior consent of the central government of Ethiopia.[154]

If there is no contractual agreement, and a state secedes through conflict, there are two treaties governing the succession of states, the Vienna Convention on Succession of States in respect of Treaties and the Vienna Convention on Succession of States in respect of State Property, Archives and Debts.[155]

The second treaty is not yet in effect and its provisions are long and complex but Lowe neatly summarises the law in this area.[156] He argues that states are not automatically bound by the treaties of their predecessor states except in the case of provisions defining borders.[157] Zimmermann expands upon this and suggests that there is a distinction between newly independent states and those which are formed from dismemberment or separation not in a decolonisation process. The former are not bound but latter may well be according to Article 34 of the Vienna Convention on Succession of States in Respect of Treaties which provides that any treaty in force in respect of the entire territory continues in force in respect of the successor state. Therefore, former colonies were not bound by treaties but state practice particularly with respect to Yugoslavia was that existing treaties did devolve upon the seceding state.[158]

There is a broad principle of succession to public property and debts which oblige the new state and the former state to agree to apportion the public property and debts. As Brownlie asserts succession to the public property of the annexed of ceding state is a principle of customary international law as confirmed in the *Peter Pázmány University Case*.[159] The successor state also has the right to take up fiscal claims belonging to the former state including the right to collect taxes.[160] With respect to debt, Articles 36 to 37 and 39 to 41 of the Vienna Convention on Succession of States in respect of State Property, Archives and Debts provides for the passing of state debt to the successor state with a reduction according to an equitable proportion in case of transfer of part of a state.[161] However, if this is a newly independent state, no state debt shall be apportioned accept by agreement according to Article 38 of the same Convention.[162] According to Article 2(1) (e) a newly independent state means a successor state the territory of which had been 'a dependent territory for the international relations of which the predecessor state was responsible'. As Brownlie asserts, distinguishing between newly independent states and successor states is problematical.[163] The status of an independent Kurdistan could only be determined on the basis of negotiation with the assistance of the international community or the problem of the settlement of debts, assets and treaty obligations will occupy the new state and the rump state of Turkey for generations to come.

This political model for the settlement of the Kurdish conflict in southeast Turkey, based on secession seem to be fraught with serious obstacles. First, there is the absolute opposition for such an arrangement in Turkey and indeed within the rest of the international community, including the European Union. Second, there are the serious and unresolved international law difficulties in apportioning assets, debts and international treaties between Turkey and any new Kurdish state. Third, the Kurdish people are spread over several countries and this arrangement would not resolve the long-standing claim for self-determination. Fourth, there is the simple fact that up to this time neither party is the clear victor in this long-standing war of secession. The possibility of this armed conflict going on for even more generations than it already has is a real one with no end in sight.

There is another political model that could provide a lasting solution to this long-standing armed conflict and that is a new constitutional arrangement based on a federal structure. It is to this model that we now turn.

8.2.2 The federalism model

The political solution that has been used in other situations where a significant minority group exists, such as Canada and Quebec, is the model of federalism. This part of the chapter reviews the political literature concerning the applicability of federalism in cases of self-determination. The particular context of the Kurdish people of northern Iraq is reviewed within this model. Federalism has emerged as a major issue on the political agenda of the post-Cold War world due to the resurgence of both nationalist and ethnic tensions.[164] Although the Kurdish struggles for autonomy pre-dates the end of the Cold War it is a model well worth reviewing as a possible solution to this long-standing armed conflict.

Federalism is defined by the noted Canadian scholar Ronald Watts as a normative term referring to 'the advocacy of multi-tiered government combining elements of shared-rule and regional self-rule'.[165] In another more provocative definition, Smith argues that federalism can be considered as an ideology which holds that the ideal organisation of human affairs is best reflected in the celebration of diversity through unity.[166] He proposes that the federal ideal is a compromise, conveyed by the image of checks and balances between the national and the regional, autonomy and sovereignty and unity and diversity.[167] Burgess asserts that this dual goal of unity and diversity gives federalism as a political concept its special appeal.[168]

The political unit that implements the ideology of federalism is a federation. Federations have in common the following structural characteristics:

- Two orders of government each acting directly on their citizens;
- A formal constitutional distribution of legislative and executive authority and allocation of revenue resources between the two orders of government ensuring some areas of genuine autonomy for each other;
- Provision for the designated representation of distinct regional views within the federal policy-making institutions, usually provided by the particular form of the federal second chamber;
- A supreme written constitution not unilaterally amendable and requiring the consent of a significant proportion of the constituent units;
- An umpire (in the form of courts or provision for referendum) to rule on disputes between governments;
- Processes and institutions to facilitate intergovernmental collaboration for those areas where governmental responsibilities are shared or inevitably overlap.[169]

It is the constitutional process that is particularly important in establishing a federation. The literature on the topic described the particular form of political institutionalisation which reflects and acknowledges diversity as a federation. This is defined by King as having four essential features:

1. Its representation is predominantly territorial
2. This territorial representation is characteristically secured on at least two sub-national levels (local and regional government)
3. The regional units are incorporated electorally, or perhaps otherwise, into the decision procedure of the national centre
4. The incorporation of the regions into the decision procedure of the centre can only be altered by extraordinary constitutional measures.[170]

Barendt states that a federal constitution distributes power between central or federal legislatures and governments on the one hand, and state (or provincial) authorities on the other.[171] Critically neither the federal nor the state authority may trespass into the legislative or executive competence of the other.[172] The earliest modern federations were the United States in 1787, Switzerland in 1848, Canada in 1867, Germany in 1871 and Australia in 1901.[173]

An important aspect of this review is that Watts indicates that there is no pure model of federation that is applicable everywhere and he discusses various types of federalism including decentralised union, federation, confederation, federacy, associated statehood, condominium and league.[174] The variations in federations include: the character and significance of the underlying economic and social diversities; the number of constituent units and the degree of symmetry or asymmetry in their size, resources and constitutional status; the scope of the allocation of legislative, executive and expenditure responsibilities; the allocation of taxing power and resources; the character of federal government institutions and the degree of regional input to federal policy making; the procedures for resolving conflicts and facilitating collaboration between interdependent governments; and the procedures for formal and informal adaptation and change.[175] Although this may cause difficulty for a comparative analysis of various models of federalism, in the case of the Kurdish conflict it allows great flexibility in arriving at a post-conflict federal arrangement. As Smith argues, federalism offers possibilities and opportunities for constructing more democratic and possibly less nation-state bound communities.[176]

Barendt, however, identifies some features in common, arguing that it is standard for some important powers to be reserved for the federal authorities, particularly the conduct of defence and foreign affairs, the raising of income and other taxes, the regulation of interstate commerce, and the printing of currency.[177] On the other hand social affairs such as education, health services, social welfare and labour services, maintenance of law and security and local government have usually been assigned to the regional government.[178] This is particularly important to secure the cultural, religious and ethnic identity of major minority groups that live in distinct provinces or regions such as the Kurdish peoples.

Another common feature of federations is that disputes between the central and regional institutions about their respective legislative and other competencies are resolved by a supreme or constitutional court.[179] In the case of Turkey a Constitutional Court is already part of the judicial apparatus and so it would be given power to adjudicate the constitutional disputes over competence that inevitably arise in federal structures. The extensive case law in such institutions as the European Court of Justice and the US and Canadian Supreme Courts provide examples of peaceful resolution of disputes between regional and central power.

There are of course difficulties in introducing a federal structure in the 21st century. The first of these is globalisation, with the blurring of the territorial boundaries of the nation-state with internationalisation of capital, the greater mobility of labour, the growth of inter-continental trading blocks.[180] Second, there is the challenge of nationalism to federalism.[181] Finally, there is the fact that federalism is a territorial and non-majoritarian form of government which can be criticised as challenging the rights of the majority.[182] It can be argued that all of these criticisms can be addressed in constitutional arrangements guaranteeing regional participation in the global economic and social community, preserving the rights of the disparate national groups and, finally, ensuring all citizens have equal access to human rights mechanisms and political participation. As King asserts 'the history of federation is at least as much a history of success as of dissolution ... they can often be said to have succeeded where no imagined alternatives would have done'.[183]

As we see from the discussion in this and earlier chapters, the Kurdish people's claims for internal autonomy cannot be guaranteed save for a type of federal structure as it is the culture's connection with a particular part of the Turkish territory that needs protection. King argues that federations are arrangements that focus on the retention or entrenchment of local identities, common religion, common language, or common culture and that the regions these peoples inhabit may be demarcated with reference to such desires.[184] Although there will certainly be difficulties in holding together such a federation, it is the only political model that will suffice in this context. This is also a model that is being used with respect to the Kurdish peoples in Iraq, the region in which this conflict has spilled over.

Iraq and Kurdistan

The newest federal state in the international community is Iraq. Its constitution states in Article 1:

> The Republic of Iraq is a single federal, independent and fully sovereign state in which the system of government is republican, representative, parliamentary, and democratic, and this Constitution is a guarantor of the unity of Iraq.

Brancati has argued that dividing power between two levels of government in Iraq resulting in giving ethnic groups contained in Iraq including the Kurdish people greater control over their own political, social, and economic affairs offers 'the only viable possibility for preventing ethnic conflict and secessionism as well as establishing a stable democracy in Iraq'.[185] The Kurds in Iraq have been strong supporters of the political model of federalism due to their pragmatic view that independence is not feasible due to Turkey's adamant opposition to it. The model of federalism would give the Kurds control over many political and social issues and the ability to protect their cultural identity.[186] Although the Iraqi federal experiment is just beginning and strong ethnic conflict still exists, it could in the future provide an example of a model for settlement of the conflict in southeast Turkey.[187]

Another basic feature of a federal state is the constitutional guarantees of the minority groups' language, religious, educational and cultural rights. The Canadian Charter of Rights and Freedoms is just such an instrument but individual human rights are also guaranteed in these constitutional arrangements with the American Constitution being the first of such pivotal instruments. Therefore, no matter what political arrangement is negotiated, for the sake of completion, it is important to highlight the necessity for a constitutionally guaranteed regime of protection of human rights, which is discussed in Chapter 9.

Conclusion

This chapter concludes by reviewing the political solutions to legal claims to self-determination, and stresses the importance of human rights protections in Iraq and Turkey for peaceful resolution of the Kurdish conflict.

Comprehensive study of self-determination that had been undertaken over years by many international law academics and by judicial consideration has failed to resolve the key controversy, whether or not it allows a people to secede from a sovereign state. The authors of this book cannot unequivocally state that self-determination as a human right '*erga omnes*' allows for a separate state to be established by the Kurdish peoples. Chapter 9 proposes a path for peace including a federal structure with a degree of autonomy that ensures that the Kurdish people have their important minority rights respected. It is clear from the above discussion that some degree of autonomy has to be granted within this right of self-determination. It can be argued that the model of federalism might be ideally suited to provide such guarantees. It is also useful to examine the political negotiations that have taken place, and the solutions proposed for other self-determination conflicts. However, the negotiators ought to bear in mind this statement issued from the Supreme Court of Canada:

(Para.126) [T] he international law right to self-determination ... generates a right to external self-determination in situations of former colonies; where a people is oppressed ... ; or where a definable group is denied meaningful access to government to pursue their political, economic, social and cultural development. In all three situations, the people in question are entitled to a right to external self-determination because they have been denied the ability to exert internally their right to self-determination.

(Para.134) when a people is blocked from the meaningful exercise of its right to self-determination internally, it is entitled, as a last resort, to exercise it by secession.[...][188]

The Turkish government has to be willing to grant the minority rights protections and constitutional guarantees of diversity that are incorporated in a model of federalism or else the only other possible result of this conflict is a continuing struggle for secession. Chapter 9 reviews negotiations in other peace processes as examples for possible settlement of the conflict.

9 International humanitarian law

Recognition of the conflict as a basis for constructive political dialogue and peace-building

9.1 Recognition of the conflict

Having endured over 25 years of conflict, the people of Turkey have experienced immense suffering. Likewise, in Kurdistan, Iraq, lives have been blighted by the conflict between the Turkish military and the Kurdistan Workers Party (PKK): to date, an estimated 40,000 lives have been lost in the Kurdish conflict.[1] There are over 3 million people displaced from their homes by the fighting.[2] Conflicts in the 20th and 21st centuries have increasingly had a disproportionate effect on the civilian population,[3] and the Kurdish conflict has been no exception. Thousands have lost their lives, and untold numbers have experienced violence, torture, intimidation, loss of livelihood, disappearance of relatives, and the psychological impact of living through war.[4] The experiences of combatants who directly engaged in hostilities have also been severe. There are hundreds of thousands of Turkish soldiers and tens of thousands of PKK combatants who have engaged in hostilities and viewed each other as bitter enemies for several decades. For such vast numbers of civilians and combatants to engage across the dividing lines of the conflict, and to trust that an end to conflict is in their interest, it will be necessary to openly acknowledge the full extent of these experiences during the conflict. The public recognition by both parties that the conflict has risen to the level of an armed conflict under international humanitarian law would be a first step in recognition of these experiences. Only if both parties acknowledge the severity of the conflict and the impact that it has had on both Turks and Kurds, can a durable and deep-rooted peace be established.

An initial note should be made about the relevance of the distinction between international and non-international armed conflict to this discussion. Part 1 of this book demonstrates that the legal criteria for each classification apply to the conflict between the Turkish armed forces and the PKK. Deciding which legal classification applies may not be crucial to the application of humanitarian protections; we demonstrate that most of the rules of international conflict have customary status with regards to non-international armed conflict. However, Part 1 also notes the important differences between the legal regimes. Jurists have struggled over the appropriate regime in a number of modern conflicts with both internal and international characteristics. The International Criminal Tribunal for the Former Yugoslavia (ICTY), for example, had to determine whether the conflict was international or non-international as the Yugoslav federation had disintegrated, but then its constituent units, between whom fighting was taking place, had not all been internationally recognised as states in their own right.[5] In the *Tadić* case, the ICTY appeals chamber reversed the tribunal's initial judgment that the conflict was non-international, and therefore outside of the tribunal's jurisdiction over 'grave breaches' of the Geneva conventions.[6] Likewise, the International Court of Justice (ICJ) found Uganda responsible for violating the rule of international humanitarian law[7] despite the judgment of the UN Special Rapporteur on the Situation of Human Rights in the Democratic Republic of Congo that despite the internationalisation of the conflict, it was essentially an internal conflict.[8] In the future, a formal legal body may have to apply this complex jurisprudence to violations of international humanitarian law in the Kurdish context, and it is hoped that the arguments advanced in this book would be an aid to the elucidation of the appropriate law. However, for the purposes of establishing conditions conducive to peace through recognition of the conflict, acknowledgement that armed conflict has taken place may be of greater initial importance than classifying it within the legal typology.

Turkey, however, has been reluctant to acknowledge that an armed conflict governed international humanitarian law has been taking place, either within its border or in the cross-border operations into Kurdistan, Iraq. As is noted in earlier chapters, classification of armed conflict of a non-international character is a politically charged topic. Generally, states remain reluctant to acknowledge the existence of an armed conflict under international humanitarian law within their borders, preferring the characterisation of rebellion, terrorism or criminal conspiracies, which can be governed by domestic criminal law and law enforcement, and does not require the involvement of the international community.[9] Turkey has also resisted the characterisation of an international armed conflict governed by humanitarian law with regards to its cross-border operations into Kurdistan, Iraq. Instead, it has been keen to associate the operations with the US war on terror, with all the associated legal obfuscation in order to avoid the protections of human rights and humanitarian law, as Chapter 7 demonstrates.

A number of reasons may be suggested to explain this general reluctance to acknowledge the presence of armed conflict. First, the recognition places obligations on the state party to ensure adherence to international humanitarian law. This places logistical burdens on the state, such as ensuring compliance with the protections of prisoner of war status. Although the conduct of operations that violate international humanitarian law, such as the targeting of civilians, are likely also to be violations of domestic criminal and military codes and international human rights law, the acknowledgement of the application of international humanitarian law may compound legal arguments and attract the attention of legal experts, and become an inconvenience for the state, particularly where the aforementioned legal systems were quietly circumvented. This reluctance is a reluctance to implement the law, and thus should not be countenanced.

Second, the recognition of armed conflict may be felt to confer undue legitimacy to the non-state party,[10] when the participation of the state in the conflict
entails that this party is regarded as a threat. It is probably the case that a non-
state actor is more likely to acknowledge the existence of an armed conflict due to
the parity implied by the reciprocity of obligations on both parties. However, the
formulation of the law on non-international armed conflict was heavily influenced
by these state concerns and contains a number of safeguards for the state party.
As is noted in Chapter 3, Common Article 3 to the Geneva Conventions explicitly
states that its provisions do not affect the legal status of the parties to the conflict.
Criminal and anti-terror law may still be applied to the non-state party at the
state's behest. In addition, as is noted in Chapter 2, international humanitarian
law regarding non-international armed conflict is restricted to *jus in bello* and does
not address the lawfulness of use of force. Thus the legitimacy of the aims and
agenda of the non-state party are explicitly not addressed by international
humanitarian law in non-international armed conflict. Were the conflict to be
recognised as international, the rules of *jus ad bellum* would apply to the parties,
and the legality of the use of force would have to be addressed. However, for the
purposes of establishing peace, recognition that an armed conflict has been taking
place could initially focus on the *jus in bello* common to international and non-
international armed conflicts, with further issues of classification and *jus ad bellum*
to be clarified by an appropriate body at a suitable time in the future. Generally,
the state's nervous association of humanitarian law with impractibility and conferral of legitimacy does not appear to be supported once its provisions have been
clarified.

These factors have certainly influenced the disparity between the state and the
non-state party in recognising the conflict in the Kurdish context. To date, the
PKK has been much keener to recognise the situation as an armed conflict
and the application of international humanitarian law. Historically, the Turkish
state has denied this characterisation, insisting instead that the situation is
solely one of terrorism, and the state fulfilling its duty to combat terrorism.[11]
The Turkish Chief of General Staff has also referred to the situation as 'low-
intensity armed conflict',[12] which is generally used to characterise conflict
situations where international humanitarian law does not apply, defined in
Additional Protocol II as 'internal disturbances and tensions'.[13] However, since
2005 Turkish Prime Minster Erdogan has acknowledged that the conflict
has more facets than a simple problem of terrorism or internal disturbance, and
made steps towards addressing the multi-dimensional nature of the conflict as
a problem of discrimination and democratisation.[14] In contrast to the state
policy, the PKK has consistently denied the label of 'terrorism', and in the first
phase of the conflict insisted that they intended to engage in a 'war' with the
Turkish state. Since the early 1990s this has also informed its approach to the
conduct of the conflict. In January 1995, the PKK communicated to the Swiss
government its commitment to observe the Geneva Conventions and Protocol 1
of 1977 in its conduct of hostilities. More recently, this framework appears
to have informed PKK's approach to how the conflict should be resolved.

For example Murad Karayilan, head of the Kurdish Con-Federal System (KCK) Presidential Council, stated in May 2009:

> There has been a war. Both Turkish and Kurdish societies have been damaged. Both sides have to forgive one another. Everyone should participate in that, including Abdullah Öcalan. Forgiveness is necessary for peace. Kurds and Turks must open a new white page.[15]

Recognition of the conflict by both parties will set the groundwork for peace. Recognising an armed conflict under international humanitarian law activates rules governing the conduct of hostilities that are binding on non-state actors and entail an international responsibility for their implementation; they are thus more likely to be observed than other legal regimes, and reduce levels of violence (due to the emphasis on necessity, proportionality and distinction). As is demonstrated in Chapter 3, humanitarian law clearly binds non-state, as well as state actors that are party to the conflict. Generally, human rights treaties have exclusively bound state actors, although it has been demonstrated that evolving human rights law does apply legal obligations to non-state actors.[16] States, such as Turkey, have argued that national criminal law is the best framework for governing behaviour in conflict as it is directed at non-state actors as individuals and is likely to have a more restrictive framework than international humanitarian law (for example in not allowing the capture of state forces, which international humanitarian law might allow through regulating the treatment of captured members of the opposing party during hostilities). However, aside from the argument that international humanitarian law may be more appropriate (and possibly the *lex specialis*) in a situation where hostilities have risen to the level of an armed conflict, there is a pragmatic argument about practicalities of implementation of each body of law. In a situation of ongoing armed conflict where the non-state party has extensive control over part of the state territory, the non-state party may doubt the state's ability to implement domestic criminal law in this territory, rendering these rules ineffective in modifying the behaviour of the non-state party. By contrast it is clear that international humanitarian law is intended to be implemented by the party to the conflict themselves. In case of violations, the onus of implementation does not fall onto the other party to the conflict, the state, but to the international community as a whole, and thus is harder for the non-state party to disregard. Bugnion has argued for the codification of accountability of non-state actors at the international level in order circumvent the legitimacy problem at the national level.[17]

In addition, recognising an armed conflict under international humanitarian law provides the parties with a basis for engagement that may lead to peace, without giving parity to the parties' goals or tactics. This confers a further pragmatism to the international humanitarian law framework. The practical and legal difficulties of defining terrorists and terrorism are discussed in Chapters 6 and 7. Chapter 7 also notes that once a group or individual is classified as terrorist, there are immense legal and political obstacles to the state engaging with it.

In Turkey the government has long pursued an overt policy of refusing to meet or to talk to the PKK, and even a legal political party such as the Democratic Society Party (DTP) that has not publically denounced the PKK as terrorists,[18] even though there are recent suggestions of internal debate and external pressure to pursue such dialogue.[19] This is supported by claims that engagement would confer undue legitimacy to a group's goals or tactics. However, international humanitarian law presents a pragmatic case for engagement, entirely separate to evaluation of a group's goals and tactics. For example, customary international humanitarian law prohibits acts of terror,[20] but does not prevent engagement with those who perpetrate them. Instead, a party to the conflict is identified by a 'certain level of organisation and command structure, as well as the ability to implement international humanitarian law'.[21] This provision probably grew out of a pragmatic interest by the state that the non-state party be able to reciprocate good treatment of their combatants. However, it can be suggested that the ability to implement humanitarian law implies that the non-state party would also have the ability to enforce provisions of a peace agreement, and thus the state has a pragmatic interest in engaging the opposite party as a partner in any peace negotiations. While this is certainly not foreseen in any of the provisions of humanitarian law, which exclusively focuses on the conduct of war rather than its cessation, it might be suggested that humanitarian law does envisage engagement within these confines (for example by obliging parties to try to bring about a fuller application of the Geneva Conventions by means of a bilateral agreement, as is discussed in Chapter 3), and thus might be a useful basis for the beginning of dialogue between parties to a conflict.

Finally, recognising an armed conflict under international humanitarian law triggers an international obligation to respond in the interests of international peace and security. We set out the legal basis for the collective responsibility of the international community to respond to situations of armed conflict in Chapter 2. Thus, the recognition that the situation has risen to the level of an armed conflict would encourage individual states and multi-lateral organisations to use the mechanisms for promoting peace in the region that are outlined in Chapter 7.

Turkey also has the opportunity to strengthen the international legal regime regulating the conflict, by ratifying the two 1977 Additional Protocols to the Geneva Conventions. The Protocols have been widely ratified by parties to the Geneva Conventions,[22] however Turkey is among the few states nervous that the provision of 'wars of national liberation' in Additional Protocol I, and elucidation of the law of non-international armed conflict in Additional Protocol II, will curtail their use of force in specific types of internal conflict. Non-parties include most of the countries that have been involved in major armed conflicts over the last 30 years;[23] it is not difficult to surmise that avoiding the legal regulation of conflict has not been an effective way to deal with instances of conflict. We argue in earlier chapters that many of the protections afforded by the Additional Protocols form customary rules in international law in any case. Yet Turkey, by its refusal to ratify the Protocols, sends a signal that it is not committed to the international legal regime regulating armed conflicts, and is among a group of states that would prefer to deny the existence of an armed conflict rather than recognise it and seek its resolution.

9.1.1 Obstacles to recognition of the conflict

This section of the chapter looks at the historical development of the main political parties in Turkey and how this has inhibited the formation for a political platform for recognition and peaceful resolution of the conflict. It then considers the political system in Turkey, and whether it is conducive to the representation of diverse voices within society, which will be necessary for meaningful political discussions on how peace may be achieved in Turkey.

Political parties in Turkey first arose as a way of implementing Kemalist one-party rule, and have subsequently been shaped by the continued overbearing presence of the military, and in the atmosphere of stringent nationalism in the political arena. The 'People's Party' was founded on 9 September 1923 by Kemal Ataturk, renaming itself Republican People's Party (*Cumhuriyet Halk Partisi* (CHP)) on 10 November 1924. Although there were attempts to create a multiparty system, CHP ruled the country as the sole political party until 1950.[24]

However, from 1946 to 1980, a multi-party system began to materialise, yet at the same time the military role was so powerful in Turkish political life that it carried out three coups, one in 1961, another in 1971, and the final one in 1980. The 1961 coup resulted in Turkey's second constitution and despite being formulated in the context of military rule, it is widely seen as a positive step towards constitutional rights. The constitution established parliamentary democracy in Turkey. None of the four parties who contested the 1961 election secured an overall majority, but CHP and the Justice Party (*Adalet Partisi* (AP)) – formed in 1961 – formed a ruling coalition as the largest two parties in parliament. The Workers' Party of Turkey (*Türkiye İşçi Partisi* (TIP)) was also founded in 1961 as the first socialist party in Turkey, winning 3 per cent of the votes in 1965 national elections. The TIP was banned in July 1971 for recognising the Kurds, the first legal party to have done so.[25] In the late 1960s agitation on the left and right of the political spectrum compounded Turkey's economic and social problems, and the military intervened to pressure the AP government's resignation in 1971, in the 'coup by memorandum'. Elections were re-instituted in 1973. The CHP, now presenting itself as a party of social democracy, strengthened its position by gaining 44 per cent of seats.

As a result of transition to multiparty political system, the Democrat Party (DP) was founded in 1946 and won the 1950 parliamentary election. A military coup on 27 May 1960 ousted the DP government, and the Turkish military took over the administration of the country. Turkey's second constitution was adopted in 1961; due to the international political atmosphere, the rise of the left in Turkey, and its developing economy, the constitution marked a positive step towards constitutional rights,[26] despite being formulated in the context of military rule. The constitution established parliamentary democracy in Turkey and the 1961 election which was contested by four parties. No party secured an overall majority, but CHP and AP formed a ruling coalition as the largest two parties in Parliament. The coalition broke down the following year, and was followed by a succession of failed coalition governments and the establishment of an interim administration to serve until the next election. In 1965 elections the AP increased its share of seats in the National Assembly from 35 per cent to 53 per cent.

Between 1971 to the military coup in 1980, there were two general elections and 10 different governments in Turkey. None of the parties represented a majority party in the Turkish Parliament and only five of them constituted coalitional majorities formed from the parties represented in the Assembly. The others were technocratic cabinets indirectly installed by the military (1971–74) or minority governments.[27] Following the 1980 military coup, a new constitution was drawn up and severe restrictions were placed on political participation. Parties considered successors to the CHP and AP were banned from participating, and in the event, only three political parties contested the election, leading to a government of the newly-founded Motherland Party (*Anavatan Partisi* (ANAP)).[28]

The first party to openly advocate for Kurdish issues in Turkey was established in 1990 under the name of People's Labor Party (*Halkin Emek Partisi* (HEP)). For the general elections of 1991, HEP formed an alliance with the Social Democratic People's Party (*Sosyaldemokrat Halk Partisi* (SHP)) and secured 22 seats in Parliament. One of the deputies, Leyla Zana, took her swearing-in oath in the Kurdish language, although speaking Kurdish was against the law. This served as the spark that started the closure case against the party. On 1 April 1992, 18 Kurdish deputies left the SHP and joined the HEP, but the HEP was closed down on 14 July 1993. From 1993 to 2003, politicians advocating for Kurdish issues regrouped under various parties, including OZDEP, DEP and HADEP. All were prosecuted and forced to close. In 2005, the more recent incarnation, the Democratic Society Party (*Demokratik Toplum Partisi* (DTP)) was formed.

The days of coups were not, and indeed may not yet be, over. The 1995 elections were marked by sudden rise of the Welfare Party (*Refah Partisi* (RP)) by obtaining 21 per cent of Parliamentary seats.[29] A coalition government was established between the RP and True Path Party (*Doğru Yol Partisi* (DYP)) – both parties had religious roots – which lasted only a year and a half. The coalition government was overthrown by the military as a result of 'post-modern coup' in 1997. As is discussed in Chapter 1, the military claimed that the secular nature of the state was under threat, and has continually intervened in politics in this regard. Many of the Virtue Party members joined the Justice and Development Party (*Adalet ve Kalkınma Partisi* (AKP)), which won the 2002 elections by a majority. The AKP has deliberately sought to target the Kurdish region for votes, with some measure of success in the 2007 elections. At the same time, another 20 DTP deputies stood as independent candidates, later forming a DTP group in Parliament, thereby circumventing the 10 per cent threshold for political parties. The first party with predominant support in the Kurdish region to enter Parliament in 14 years, the DTP has faced much of the same harassment in office as did its predecessor parties. In November 2007 the Chief Public Prosecutor of

Turkey's Constitutional Court filed a case of party closure against the DTP. DTP members have faced continual judicial harassment, and in 2009 the DTP Congress had to replace 55 of its 80 Council members who had been jailed.[30] However, as is discussed in Chapter 1, it has not only been the DTP which has been targeted. There has been no love lost between the military and the AKP, and as recently as 2007, the military has made noises about its responsibility to protect the constitution and inferring that another coup was not out of the question.[31] In addition, there have been closure cases brought against the party, because of the military establishment's discomfort with the party's religious roots.[32]

The AKP escaped closure but not sanction, and it is widely believed this is due in large part to Turkey's bid for EU accession. Formal talks opened in 2004 and the legislative reforms required from this process have provided new political spaces in Turkey by applying pressure for reform and a reduced role of the military in politics. In addition, the AKP is regarded as having a strong alliance with the business class, who have a financial interest in peaceful resolution of the conflict.[33] TÜSIAD (the Association of Industrialists and Businessmen in Turkey) has long advocated for settlement of the conflict on the basis that stability is a precondition for successful market growth.

In August 2009, the AKP launched a programme of public engagement to develop proposals for the resolution of the conflict and political reform, variously named the 'Democratic Initiative', the 'Kurdish initiative' or the 'Kurdish opening'. The AKP brought the initiative to parliamentary debate in October 2009, and the significance of its openness to discussing the conflict in the context of parliamentary debate rather than security strategy cannot be overstated. However, the AKP initiative does not appear to include opportunities for consultation or more imaginative solutions to the conflict than those reforms already required by the EU accession process.

The other largest parties in the 2007-elected Parliament have been primarily obstructive to pursuing a peaceful resolution of the Kurdish conflict. CHP leader, Deniz Baykal has voiced opposition to the AKP initiative, stating that there are two 'red lines' his party will not cross: regional autonomy and the Kurdish language in schools.[34] However, recently CHP parliamentarians and leaders of its local branches acknowledged that there is currently a historic opportunity to finally resolve the Kurdish question. For instance, the CHP's Istanbul branch chairman, Gursel Tekin, said that the steps taken by the government on the Kurdish issue should be fully supported, contradicting his party's official stance. Tekin stated: 'one should either support the efforts to resolve the Kurdish issue, or share the responsibility for its failure. Whoever resolves it will be remembered in history: that is a fact'.[35] This suggests that there may be internal tensions within the party over engagement in a peace initiative, and Baykal's 'red lines' may not be as absolute as he likes to portray.

The MHP has been hostile to engagement and the peace initiative, with MHP leader Devlet Bahçeli refusing to meet Prime Minister Erdogan to discuss the AKP's 'Democratic Initiative'[36] and reacting virulently to AKP attempts to recognise the history and importance of the Kurdish character of parts of Turkey.[37] The MHP parliamentary group deputy chairman Oktay Vural said in August 2009: 'I do not see this as a social problem. To me, it is a problem created by those who want to see Turkey partitioned based on political arguments. Western countries make reference to this problem by linking it to human rights. The only thing going on here is a fight between armed terrorists and legitimate security forces'.[38] However, the MHP's rhetoric does not preclude some flexibility in its position. The MHP has put some distance into its historic relationship with the Turkish military since the election of the AKP.[39] Academic Tanju Tosun argues that the MHP does appreciate the need for democratisation to bring peace to the region, but is trapped in a discourse of populist rejectionism as the party is concerned about losing its support base.[40] Since the decline of the two centre-right parties, the ANAP and the DYP, in the 1990s, the MHP has been trying to capture the centre-right vote.[41] They are responsive to their electorate, and may be challenged over their lack of proposed solution that in any way differs to that of the unsuccessful attempts of the last 25 years – military defeat and prosecutions.

The current political system in Turkey contains a number of obstacles to representation of diversity within the polity and thus peaceful engagement in issue of conflict, peace and political reform across the breadth of Turkey's society. One such obstacle is the provision in Turkish electoral law which states that a political party must obtain at least 10 per cent of the national vote in parliamentary elections in order to win seats in the National Assembly.[42] The 10 per cent threshold is widely regarded as discriminating not only against smaller parties, but parties whose support is heavily weighted in one area of the country, such as the pro-Kurdish DTP. In the European Court of Human Rights judgment in the case of *Yumak and Sadak v Turkey*[43] the Court found that the threshold did not violate the right to fair election, but noted that it would be desirable for the threshold to be lowered in order to ensure optimal representation, while preserving the objective of achieving stable parliamentary majorities. The Turkish threshold is by far the highest in Council of Europe. The nearest comparable European electoral thresholds are Poland's Sejm and Germany's Bundestag at 5 per cent, both also considered to be relatively high. Many countries use proportional representation systems without any threshold, such as Portugal, Finland, the Netherlands and Ireland.

There are other restrictions on political parties, including Turkey's political parties law (LPP), which prohibits parties from recognising the existence of minorities,[44] use languages other than Turkish[45] or question Turkey's current political structure.[46] Turkey's Constitution gives the Constitutional Court power to dissolve political parties and ban their deputies from politics from politics. With such restrictions, the political space for activists advocating for the rights of the Kurdish population have little space to operate.

A significant obstacle to the capacity of Turkey's political system to give air to a truly representative breadth of views of the electorate, is the systematic politicised closure of parties and removal of parliamentary immunity by unelected proponents of a strongly secularist, nationalist ideology. Parliamentary immunity is designed to protect the electorate, allowing the candidates they have selected to talk openly and to adopt policies without fear of prosecution, and is therefore a practice in most democratic countries. The system of parliamentary immunity is intended to balance the need to protect electoral choice with the need to ensure that members of Parliament are held accountable for criminal behaviour. In Turkey, however, politicians are more likely to be prosecuted for their political opinions and policies than for activity in other spheres of their life. Parliamentary immunity can be removed by a closure case by the Constitutional Court. The system of party closure itself presents particular vulnerabilities for parties in Turkey who represent Kurdish interests. Party closure is presented as being a legal safeguard designed to protect national interests from politicians' subversion, however 'national interests' in this case are defined in this context by the 1982 Constitution and its interpretation by the 11 judges of the Constitutional Court. The degree of power that the system of party closure and removal of parliamentary immunity affords to an unelected body, the Constitutional Court, is unprecedented in similar democratic countries. In a number of European Court of Human Rights cases[47] the Court found that the deprivation of DEP MPs parliamentary mandate was in breach of the right to free elections under Article 3 of Protocol 1 to the European Convention on Human Rights. Politicised party closure cases tend also to prefigure targeted prosecutions of MPs. In addition, Article 83 of the Constitution allows investigations that begun prior to an MP taking office based on Article 14 of the Constitution – which prohibits 'violating the indivisible integrity of the state with its territory and nation, and endangering the existence of the democratic and secular order of the Turkish Republic' to continue after election. In practice, the scope of the Article paves the way for politically-motivated prosecutions. Since 1963, 24 political parties have been closed, on charges of extremism, anti-secularism, or separatism.[48]

The political parties in Turkey and the political system in which they operate, arose from a common historical legacy of Kemalist nationalism and prominence of the military in politics. While civil society and public debate has moved on, parties are restricted by their institutional inertia, ideological hostility and a system which restricts the representation of a full diversity of voices in Turkish society. This has presented a major obstacle to recognition of conflict in Turkey. This chapter argues that such recognition, within the framework of international humanitarian law, will enhance prospects for peaceful resolution of conflict in the region. In order to demonstrate how such obstacles might be overcome, the chapter now turns to another conflict which once appeared intractable, but today experiences relative peace.

9.2 Comparison with the Northern Ireland peace negotiations

Peace in Northern Ireland once seemed impossible to each of the parties to the conflict, and the rest of the world. Yet by 2007 irreconcilable enemies were sharing power in formal governing institutions, and violence had greatly diminished in the region. This success heralded hopes that 'lessons to be learned'[49] from the process will presage successful peace negotiations elsewhere. Secretary of State for Northern Ireland, Peter Hain, stated in June 2007: 'if one of the longest running conflicts in European history can be resolved, then there is hope for even the most bitter and seemingly intractable disputes across the globe'.[50] This section highlights similarities and differences between the Northern Ireland conflict and peace negotiations, and the Kurdish context. First, we give an overview of the conflict and peace process, before discussing how the parties to the conflict began a process of engagement, and illustrate parallel possibilities for the Kurdish conflict. Parallels also emerge in the main themes of opposition to negotiations, and we examine how the players in Northern Ireland were able to overcome repeated moments of impasse. We suggest that many shared features indicate that a peace process in Turkey could have similar success, but that there are two key differentials between the two contexts that have impeded peace in the Kurdish context thus far. First, is the Turkish government's failure to recognise the conflict and thus openly address lasting solutions that could bring violence to an end between the parties. Second, international engagement has been a crucial support to the Northern Ireland peace process, but sorely lacking towards resolution of the Kurdish conflict.

9.2.1 The Northern Ireland conflict and peace process: an overview

Divisions between the Protestant and Catholic communities in Northern Ireland reach back as far as the 1600s,[51] when all of Ireland was dominated by Protestant mainland Britain, before being formally incorporated into the United Kingdom in 1801. In the midst of growing resistance to British rule, the island was divided by the UK's Government of Ireland Act 1920, partitioning six counties in the northeast from the remaining 26, with separate Parliaments in Belfast and Dublin.[52] While the north continued under UK sovereignty, the south formed an independent Republic, joining the United Nations as an independent state in 1955. Between 1920 and 1972 Northern Ireland's devolved Parliament exercised a considerable degree of autonomy, although ultimately subject to UK sovereignty represented by the Governor of Northern Ireland. During this period, Northern Ireland's two thirds Protestant majority dominated the political sphere, and widespread civil, political and socio-economic rights violations led to unrest. The Catholic population had lower educational standards, were discriminated against in employment, public housing and regional development. Local government boundaries were redrawn to ensure Unionist domination in Catholic-majority areas.[53] Catholic discrimination against the Protestant population was also pervasive, but due to the marginalisation of the Catholic population had a lesser impact.[54] The Ulster Unionist Party (UUP) formed a majority in every parliament and thus the Prime Minister of Northern Ireland, the highest executive office, was always chosen by the Governor from the UUP. Broadly, the

Protestant community favoured maintaining the union with the United Kingdom, hence the epithet of Unionists, and the Catholic community favoured uniting with the Catholic majority Irish Republic, and thus are often referred to as Nationalists or Republicans. This disparity in political representation contributed to the rise of Sinn Féin and other Catholic nationalist parties, at the expense of a more moderate opposition.[55] It also fomented growing hostility between Protestant and Catholic communities, as the political institutions failed to address injustice, unrest and exclusion in Northern Ireland. Violent communal clashes erupted in 1966, and British troops were deployed to the region to restore order in 1969. Repressive military tactics compounded conflict, further exacerbated by the introduction of internment in 1971 and the 'in depth' interrogation of prisoners, including substantiated claims of torture.[56] The 1960s saw a proliferation of paramilitary organisations. The historic Irish Republican Army split into the Provisional Irish Republican Army (PIRA) and Official Irish Republican Army (OIRA) in 1969; the OIRA declared a ceasefire in 1972, before splintering again, with one faction, the Irish National Liberation Army, renewing violence. The PIRA emerged as the dominant group within the Republican movement,[57] and is often referred to today simply as the IRA (although this book retains the full acronym). Sinn Féin is often referred to as the 'political wing' of the IRA. Certainly there were strong links between the two, and during the peace process this relationship was absolutely crucial to the importance of Sinn Féin as a party to negotiations. Unionist paramilitaries were also established during this period, the Ulster Volunteer Force (UVF) in 1966 and the Ulster Defence Association (UDA) in 1971. Two new political parties also emerged: the moderate nationalist Social Democratic and Labour Party (SDLP) and the Democratic Unionist Party (DUP), founded by Reverend Ian Paisley in opposition to perceived UUP accommodation of nationalists.

In the late 1960s a period of intense conflict, often referred to as 'the Troubles', broke out in Northern Ireland. In 1972, 496 people were killed, the highest annual death toll during the conflict.[58] The same year, Britain suspended the Northern Ireland Parliament and instigated direct rule over the region. Increased security measures were enforced by the British government during the 1970s and Republicans expressed outrage at their perceived 'criminalisation' by British media, politicians and security personnel.[59] Britain became a target of paramilitary attacks, including PIRA bombings of Hyde and Regents Parks in London in 1982 and the ruling Conservative party conference in 1984. Violence persisted during the 1990s, and by the end of the decade over 3,600 people – civilians, paramilitaries, security forces and soldiers – had been killed during 30 years of conflict.[60] Relations between the Republic of Ireland and the UK government developed during this period, as bilateral agreements were reached in order to try and stem the bloodshed. The 1973 Sunningdale Agreement approved a Northern Ireland Assembly, Executive, and a cross-border 'Council of Ireland' but the agreement collapsed due to opposition from Republican and Unionist communities. The Anglo-Irish Agreement of 1985 gave the Republic an advisory role in Northern Ireland, but stipulated that its constitutional relationship to the

United Kingdom could not be changed without majority endorsement by the people of Northern Ireland. It too faced wide opposition in the Republican and Unionist communities, and was accused of circumventing popular discontent by making the agreement non-consultative and between elites.[61] It was not until the 1993 Downing Street Declaration, which included a commitment by the British and Irish governments that all political parties that renounced violence would be involved in the political process, that a degree of success emerged. The Declaration was followed by ceasefire announcements by the PIRA and several unionist paramilitary groups. This collapsed when the PIRA bombed London's Canary Wharf in 1996, citing the continued exclusion of Sinn Féin from political processes. However through ongoing contacts the ceasefire was re-established in July 1997, signalling the way for Sinn Féin involvement in negotiations over the Good Friday Agreement.

The 1998 Good Friday Agreement (GFA), also known as the Belfast Agreement, signalled a historic compromise between Irish nationalism and Irish unionism. The agreement was endorsed by Sinn Féin, the SDLP and the UUP and put to a referendum in both Northern Ireland and the Republic of Ireland in May 1998. In Northern Ireland it was endorsed by a vote of 71 per cent (with an 81 per cent turnout), and in the Irish Republic, by 94 per cent (with a 56 per cent turnout).[62] The DUP opposed the GFA, but having won a majority in the 2003 Northern Ireland Assembly election was eventually brought into a power-sharing executive with Sinn Féin following the St Andrews Day Agreement (detailed below). The GFA addressed a broad number of issues from devolution, decommissioning, to criminal justice and policing reforms. It established the Northern Ireland Assembly, its Executive, and a consultative Civic Forum, to which substantial powers were devolved from the UK government in the Northern Ireland Act 1998. It also established the North-South Ministerial Conference (NSMC) and British-Irish Council, to facilitate cooperation on issues affecting north-south and east-west relations respectively. The Agreement founded independent commissions to review policing, and to monitor and advise on the issues of equal opportunities and human rights in Northern Ireland.

The implementation of the GFA was problematic from the start. In November 1999 devolved Parliament returned to Northern Ireland, with a power-sharing agreement between the UUP and the SDLP, but issue of arms and the activities of militant groups continued to restrict the progress of the newly established assembly.[63] In October 2002, devolution was once again suspended, due to persistent allegations of non-cooperation and lack of trust on both sides. Assembly Elections were held in 2003 despite the suspension, with the DUP now the majority unionist party. It was becoming apparent that the DUP and Sinn Féin were now the two largest parties in Northern Ireland, but the DUP refused to meet Sinn Féin in person. The October 2006 St Andrews Day agreement represented the culmination of extensive negotiations conducted through shuttle diplomacy. It led to the restoration of the Northern Ireland Assembly, the establishment of a new Executive, and all-party endorsement of the new Police Service of Northern Ireland (PSNI).[64] Elections to the Executive in 2007 saw further

DUP and Sinn Féin electoral gains. In March 2007 Sinn Féin and the DUP met for the first time, and in May they formed a joint executive with DUP leader Ian Paisley as First Minister, and Sinn Féin's Martin McGuinness, as Deputy First Minister.

Lest the grand sweep of history imbue the Northern Ireland peace process with an air of inevitability, the views of the participants in the process clearly vouch otherwise. At every stage the process appeared fragile and uncertain. Jonathan Powell, who was Tony Blair's Chief of Staff during his terms as Prime Minister, compared it to keeping a bicycle upright: 'you have to keep the process moving forward, however slowly. Never let it fall over'.[65] In Turkey, the current political climate and systemic obstructions to meaningful political dialogue (as detailed in the previous section) confer a similar sense of fragility on prospects for peaceful resolution of the Kurdish conflict. By looking at the evolving attitudes of participants in the process, and key developments and obstacles along the path to the relative peace of 2007, we will demonstrate that peaceful resolution of the Kurdish conflict is possible, should the parties commit to this path.

9.2.2 Starting negotiations

Behind the public glare of formal agreements and the establishment of new institutions, much of the peace process in Northern Ireland was conducted in private between individuals acting on behalf of the parties to the conflict. The UK government had secret backchannel contacts with the PIRA from 1972.[66] Publically deniable, the contacts enabled parties to gain an appreciation of the motives, capacity and direction of the other, away from the media gaze. The channel provided a forum where contentious issues could be discreetly negotiated; for example backchannel contacts facilitated an agreement by which the first hunger strike conducted by PIRA prisoners was called off in 1981.[67] From that point onwards, the IRA and the British government pursued both direct contact, primarily conducted by Secret Intelligence Service (SIS) officers, and unofficial 'indirect' links, that were maintained by unconnected individuals who relayed messages between the two sides.[68] Irish priest Father Alec Reid, for example, served as an interlocutor between Sinn Féin and the British government from 1986. The existence of the channel itself sent a clear message to the PIRA that the British government were not principally opposed to a negotiated route out of the conflict. It also allowed parties to begin a process of confidence-building by communicating their willingness to explore new options in the pursuit of peace. While the talks were being held in secret, public statements were used to reinforce expressions of good will. In 1989, for example, the Secretary of State for Northern Ireland Peter Brooke stated to the press that the British government would respond 'flexibly and imaginatively' to a PIRA ceasefire.[69] The building of confidence is particularly fragile, however, when it has not been publically affirmed and endorsed. When the backchannel was leaked to a journalist in November 1993, both parties rushed to publish their own versions of the conversations that had taken place in order to reassure their constituencies, leading to renewed antipathy.[70] Yet these talks had laid the foundations for the Downing Street Declaration, announced the following month, which marked the beginning of open talks between the British government and the PIRA.[71] The backchannel paved the way to ceasefires and public negotiations in the 1990s. Indeed the success of the GFA has been credited to the backchannel 'groundwork' that preceded it.[72]

Throughout the 1970s and 1980s the official policy of the British government was that they would not contact, talk or meet with the PIRA as a designated terrorist group, or Sinn Féin as PIRA's political wing. Sinn Féin had long faced restrictions on its political activities, including access to the media, government representatives, and the arrest of its leaders.[73] This is echoed in the approach of the Turkish government. Official policy prohibits any contacts with the PKK. However, the restrictions on political activities, as is noted earlier in this chapter, are even more draconian as any political parties representing Kurdish interests has faced alienation, closure and arrests. Following the DTP's representation in Parliament Prime Minister Erdoğan refused to meet with the party until they made a public statement renouncing the PKK as a terrorist group; before finding a compromise position by meeting them in his capacity as AKP chairman rather than Prime Minister.[74] Yet every government of Turkey since the early 1990s has made similar discreet contacts with the PKK. Under Turgut Özal's government Iraqi Kurdish leader Jalal Talabani acted as a mediator between the PKK and Turkey. These contacts led to the PKK's declaration of a unilateral ceasefire in 1993, before breaking down a short time later when the Turkish government missed its opportunity to initiate reciprocal measures.[75] During Prime Minister Necmettin Erbakan's tenure (1996 to 1997) 'private local channels' were used to engage with the PKK.[76] In his trial in Turkey, Abdullah Öcalan stated that Erbakan had sent him two letters offering economic and social reforms in response to an end to violence.[77] According to a recent publication by the Turkish National Intelligence Organisation, regular contacts took place between Turkish state representatives and the PKK in 2006 and 2007,[78] surrounding the 2006 unilateral ceasefire by the PKK, again breaking down as another opportunity to stem violence in the region was lost. Beyond these limited disclosures, it is likely the government in Turkey has pursued extensive exploratory contacts with the PKK, akin to those of the British government and the PIRA. However, the Turkish government has failed to capitalise on these contacts to make progress in building the conditions for peace in the region thus repeated ceasefire declarations by the PKK have dissolved back into violence. International precedents, including the Northern Ireland peace process, demonstrate what can be achieved when the political will is there.

9.2.3 Opposition to negotiations

During the peace negotiations in Northern Ireland, all parties in Northern Ireland issued dire warnings that the process would presage national disaster.

Participation in governing bodies within the region of Northern Ireland, often referred to as the 'six counties' by Republicans, was seen as 'partitionist' within parts of the PIRA and Sinn Féin,[79] and agreement with Unionists regarded as the end of united Ireland. Meanwhile DUP members claimed that the British negotiators were consorting with terrorists and sacrificing wishes of the Unionist community. In a statement following the collapse of PIRA's 1996 ceasefire, DUP's Ian Paisley Junior stated: 'all decent human beings want peace but the reality is that peace has got to be won. If you accept is as a gift from terrorists it is not free – it is enslavement … now it the time for short sharp shock military tactics against the leadership of IRA/Sinn Féin'.[80] Overwhelmingly, the DUP's discourses about the peace process were framed in terms of 'giving in to the demands of the pan-nationalist front' – Sinn Féin, the IRA, the Republic of Ireland, and the SDLP were often characterised as a unitary opponent, which would inevitably lead a united Ireland and the division of Northern Ireland from Great Britain.[81]

A similar belligerent rejection of negotiated settlement has been espoused by army figures in Turkey, and even supported by high profile US academics, such as Professor Henri J Barkey of the Carnegie Endowment for Peace, who advocates for US military assistance to decisively disarm the PKK.[82] Such opposition has drawn on similar themes of catastrophe and division to those expressed in the context of Northern Ireland. As noted above, the AKP government's forays into discussing peaceful resolution of the conflict has triggered a vitriolic response in certain areas of Turkey's political class. CHP leader Deniz Baykal has accused the AKP of betrayal, claiming 'the government doesn't combat terror, but negotiates with those responsible for the terror activities'.[83] Hints of a growing openness to the recognition that denial of Kurdish identity and ethnic discrimination has played a role in the conflict, have been portrayed as a threat to the unity of the Turkish state. Responding to the AKP's 'Kurdish Initiative', MHP Deputy Chairman Mehmet Şandır warned 'if you try to discuss these problems on the basis of a single ethnic identity, you will divide the country'.[84]

The reluctance of parties to enter the peace process is likely to hinge on a number of interlocking factors: pursuit of political interests, institutional intransigence, and real fears amongst the different parties' constituencies. Turkey's military and sections of the judiciary and civil service continue to associate the public expression of ethnic difference as denial of the integrity of the nation. The historical legacy of Kemalist ethnic nationalism has yet to be aligned with modern theories of the democratic pluralist state, and thus public discourse, political positioning, and security policy remains rooted in the past. In the Northern Ireland peace process, the DUP continually tried to outflank the UUP in capturing the unionist constituency who were uneasy with the fact of negotiations and with their outcomes. On the eve of the signing of the GFA, Ian Paisley led protests against the UUP and its leader David Trimble, for its participation in negotiations.[85] However, this was not all politicking, as DUP's supporters and many Unionists had genuine concerns about their security situation before

PIRA and other Republican groups disarmed – the release of prisoners, the reform of policing and the RUC, reductions in the British Army presence, and the disbanding of the Royal Irish Regiment (RIR) was all felt to come too soon.[86] They also perceived the GFA to disproportionately benefit the Republican community, arguing that there was discrimination against Protestants joining the PSNI, and that the Catholic community receives more peace funding than the Protestant community.[87] Republicans also had their own concerns. Wary about British policy in the region and perception that the Unionists were waiving a 'veto' over British strategy in the negotiations, Sinn Féin negotiators faced considerable opposition within their ranks. In the lead up to the GFA the members put forward a motion of no-confidence in the leadership of the PIRA based on their strategy in negotiations.[88]

Despite vocal opposition to negotiations, by the 1990s it was increasingly clear to all parties to the Northern Irish conflict that containment and stalemate was all that could be achieved militarily.[89] Scholars posit this recognition as a key factor underpinning productive peace negotiations.[90] The recognition that violence was no longer in any parties' interest led to the negotiations between the African National Congress (ANC) and the de Klerk government to end apartheid in South Africa.[91] In contrast, the continued pursuit of a military solution in the Spanish conflict with ETA has undermined a number of attempts at engagement between the parties. Further, the government and ETA have not built up the confidence and awareness during a pre-negotiation period[92] that so benefited the Northern Ireland peace process. Having participated in extensive negotiations with all parties – both in secret and openly – in Northern Ireland, Powell argues: 'It is very hard for democratic governments to admit to talking to terrorist groups while those groups are still killing innocent people. But on the basis of my experience I think it is always right to talk to your enemy, however badly they are behaving'.[93]

Parties to the Kurdish conflict are not unaware that a military solution, elusive for over a quarter of a century, is not a viable path to peace. The costs of pursuing a military strategy have been openly recognised by Prime Minister Erdoğan, who questioned: 'If Turkey had not spent its energy, budget, peace and young people on [fighting] terrorism, if Turkey had not spent the last 25 years in conflict, where would we be today?'.[94] However, the implications of this recognition have yet to be realised in changes to Turkey's policy of denial. Rather, Erdogan continues to insist: 'neither the state nor the government of the Republic of Turkey will sit down with terrorists or treat a terrorist organization as a party to negotiations. This can never, ever be a subject for discussion'.[95] These comments are difficult to align with the history of government contacts with the PKK stated above. Confining rhetoric to the politics of the past, and to the eliciting of support from narrow constituencies, may become a self-fulfilling policy. Recent years may present a unique opening for applying the lessons of Northern Ireland. Murat Karayilan, head of the PKK Presidential Council, stated in May 2009: 'I've studied Irish history and talked with people who participated in it. I know the development and stages of that struggle. Turkey needs to solve our problem in the way that the British solved that problem'.[96] Turkey continues to miss the opportunity to take advantage of the transformative impact of peace negotiations, which led to confidence building and eventually lasting ceasefires and demobilisation in the case of Northern Ireland.

The evolution of the Republican opposition, from the paramilitary strategy of the IRA to Sinn Féin's role in the Northern Ireland Executive, attests to the impact of inclusion in peace negotiations on an armed movement. PIRA hostility to ever renouncing its military tactics was epitomised in the slogans daubed on the walls of Belfast declaring 'not a bullet, not an ounce'.[97] From this, PIRA began to ease towards a more conciliatory approach through ongoing dialogue with the 'moderate' Republican party SDLP, and the leadership of the Republic of Ireland.[98] Sinn Féin President Gerry Adams has publically acknowledged that without SDLP's John Hume there would have been no peace process.[99] In the early 1980s, as channels of contact with the British government and Republican parties developed, the PIRA followed a dual strategy of war and politics, the latter via its influence in Sinn Féin.[100] This strategy was symbolised by Republican spokesman Danny Morrison at Sinn Féin's 1983 annual conference, who asked: 'Who here really believes we can win the war through the ballot box? But will anyone object if, with a ballot paper in one hand and the Armalite in the other, we take power in Ireland?'.[101] Despite continued IRA attacks, the republicans recognised that diplomatic contact was essential in order to resolve the conflict. For example, Gerry Adams, the leader of Sinn Féin, stated in 1987 that 'There's no military solution, none whatsoever. ... There can only be a political solution ... an alternative, unarmed struggle, to attain Irish independence'.[102] By 2002, Gerry Adams announced that he could 'imagine a future without the IRA',[103] and in 2005, the IRA Army Council formally announced an end to its armed campaign, stating that its commitment to using 'purely political and democratic programmes through exclusively peaceful means'.[104] Entering into dialogue also impacted the British government's approach to the conflict. Following its ongoing engagement with the PIRA, the government was 'not able to return to promoting a straight "anti-terrorist" line'[105] even after the PIRA ceasefire collapsed in 1996. Through talking to the IRA, the British government was exposed to the triggers of conflict, and began to recognise violence as a symptom, rather than a cause, of deeply rooted grievances. This encouraged the government to formulate a more imaginative and nuanced strategy to ending the conflict than the simple, but inadequate, formula of combating terrorism. Even the DUP, which had been most vehement in its casting of the PIRA as irredeemable terrorists, was brought into the process of power-sharing by the enticement of realising executive authority.[106] By contrast, Turkey's alleged contacts with the PKK for over two decades have failed to build confidence between the parties and each unilateral PKK ceasefire has in time collapsed into renewed violence. Talking is a necessary, but not sufficient, condition for peace. Without structured engagement, political will, and international support, Turkey's limited contacts with the PKK have yet to develop into open talks, heralding the crucial peace dividend of the Northern Ireland process.

9.2.4 Common difficulties in a peace process

Negotiations in the Northern Ireland peace process repeatedly hit precarious junctures.

A recurrent impasse has been a fundamental disagreement between the parties over the sequencing of disarmament and inclusion into political institutions. The UUP and DUP both initially refused to enter into government with Sinn Féin until the PIRA was disbanded, at a time when the PIRA declared disbandment 'unrealisable'.[107] In turn, Sinn Féin argued that its inclusion in the political process without preconditions was necessary to build confidence preceding disarmament. Sinn Féin's role in political institutions was presented as an essential guarantee for their Republican constituents of the efficacy of the political process, and thus a prerequisite to the dissolution of the PIRA. Thus while the PIRA ceasefire of 1994 was intended to presage Sinn Féin entry into political talks, the Unionist parties and British government insisted they decommission before entry into institutions. The PIRA viewed decommissioning at this stage as 'surrender' and as doubts crept in that the British government was serious about engaging with it, the ceasefire collapsed.[108] In an interesting parallel, similar 'conditions-led' approaches have been argued to undermine US and European engagement with Islamist political parties in the Arab world, such as Hamas, as by focusing on surface rhetoric they have failed to open channels that would explore the group's deeper motivations and opportunities for strategic evolution.[109]

The British Labour government has argued that a key innovation of its approach was the crafting of the GFA as a way out of this impasse in Northern Ireland. Powell contends that UK Prime Minister John Major's insistence on the precondition of PIRA decommissioning prior in the early 1990s magnified the importance of the issue of weapons, and precluded compromise solutions through exploratory dialogue by excluding Sinn Féin from talks. In contrast, he argues, the 'creative ambiguity' in the GFA allowed the political process to be established, leaving ambiguous issues to work themselves out as distrust dissipated between the parties.[110] Yet even with ambiguous wording, some of the more controversial issues had to be solved by unconventional means: Prime Minister Tony Blair gave Gerry Adams a private oral assurance that he would try to expedite the release of PIRA prisoners before the 2-year period stated in the agreement,[111] and sent a side letter to David Trimble pledging his support for changes to the provisions for excluding parties from the Shadow Assembly after 6 months should they be ineffective, in order to mitigate the GFA's lack of a decommissioning precondition.[112] Moreover, following the GFA the Northern Ireland Assembly was suspended by the British government in February 2000, August and September 2001, and again in October 2002, as these issues continued to recur.[113]

Attitudes of the parties to the Kurdish conflict towards disarmament and political inclusion indicate prospects of a comparable impasse. Turkish government and army officials repeatedly state their aim as the 'eradication' of the PKK, and have linked the cease of military operations to the total dissolution of the armed group.

Shortly before becoming the Turkish army's Chief of General, Yasar Buyukanit vowed: 'as long as the PKK exists our operations will continue in ever-increasing intensity'.[114] Yet the PKK leadership regard their military capacity as a crucial guarantee in the face of a hostile state. Murat Karyilan in 2008 stated that the PKK 'have no other way to defend ourselves against the might of Turkey'.[115] While the Turkish state continues with this zero-sum mentality towards the PKK, and the PKK remains highly mistrustful of the state's motives, it is likely that an impasse over de-militarisation and cessation of hostilities will persist.

Yet the relative peace and DUP-Sinn Féin power-sharing in Northern Ireland today demonstrate that this impasse is not, as it were, impassable. Currin identified the lack of progress in the aftermath of the GFA with the 'positional' negotiating style of the political parties in Northern Ireland, and advocated for a shift to 'needs-based negotiation' where demands are explained, rather than asserted, allowing parties to address the real grievances that lie beneath demands.[116] The skills of individual negotiators play no small part in the progress of a peace process, as do their personal foibles and sensitivities, including perceptions of humiliation and 'face-saving'.

The Northern Ireland peace process also suggests that a certain structural formula can be used to break through an impasse. Leaving a measure of ambiguity in formal agreements is one example. However, as noted above, establishing an ambiguous common ground is not without difficulty; all parties to the GFA pushed for further guarantees that were only resolved through private communications. In time the GFA's ambiguity came to be detrimental to the peace process, as distrust grew between the parties when implementation did not match what they believed had been agreed.[117] Its ambiguity has also been viewed as an 'elitist' construction to allow political parties to capture power through cementing their position with the British government, while disenfranchising the populace and their grievances in the conflict.[118] In the event, however, Republican and Unionist parties were under pressure to reflect the views of their constituencies in their negotiating position. All parties referred to the intransigence of their communities to underline their positions on demilitarisation and inclusion in institutions. The SDLP and the UUP faced the growing electoral success of Sinn Féin and the DUP, respectively, absorbing their constituencies in response to dissatisfaction with the process. Further, paramilitary groups also faced internal dissent over their relationship to the peace process. Unionist paramilitaries became highly fragmented, and PIRA hardliners splintered off into new organisations: the Continuity IRA in 1986 and Real IRA in 1997. Critics have argued that the PIRA exploited the threat of division as a bargaining tactic, when in fact Adams and McGuinness had almost total control over the PIRA throughout the process.[119] Judgment as to the extent of the constraints experienced by the parties to the negotiations is beyond our scope here, but suffice to say that the ambiguities in the GFA offered a path out of an impasse, but was not able to counter the broader roots of the disagreement at its heart.

Many critiques of the peace process in Northern Ireland point to a lack of integration of the wider community into the process. Yet there is a tension in every peace process between expanding participation, and thus legitimacy and stake-holders, and the increasing difficulty of cooperation and decisive action as the number of players at the negotiating table increases. A number of strategies to balance these factors have been employed in different scenarios. Parallel negotiation processes, often referred to as 'track two' negotiations, aim to provide a forum for civil society input, while maintaining a separate space for the principal parties to negotiate. Towards the end of apartheid in South Africa, civil society engagement was established through the National Peace Accord (NPA), signed in September 1991 by politicians, security forces, and civil society leaders. The NPA set up a network of peace committees throughout the country as forums for dispute resolution, widely engaging society in the process of peace and formulating channels of engagement between previous adversaries.[120] Other peace negotiations have relied on strong public communications strategies to foster inclusion in the process, such as opinion polls, discussion forums, and regular report back meetings with constituencies with designated communicators from the parties.[121] Studies have shown that negotiations with high civil society involvement tend to lead to sustained peace, whereas low society involvement leads most often to the converse.[122] The example of Northern Ireland has been used to demonstrate that civil society engagement can impact the character of the debate, moving away from confrontational positioning. In the GFA referendum Sinn Féin campaigned on a platform of securing Irish unity and the UUP on securing a place within the union, whereas an independent civil-driven 'yes' campaign was able to focus on the more inclusive aspects of the GFA.[123] The prominent role played by civil society in developing support for the recognition of the Kurdish conflict and building a culture of peace has already been noted. Inclusion of civil society actors in the building of peace is essential for lasting resolution of the conflict.

The Northern Ireland peace process did not just need to overcome initial obstacles, but repeatedly respond to acts of violence that threatened to derail the process. The bombing of Omagh in August 1998 by the Real IRA, the PIRA splinter group, killed 29 people, and could have sparked renewed communal hostility and a return to circular reprisals and spiralling violence. Immediately condemned by the Sinn Féin leadership, the bomb failed to derail the process when the people of Northern Ireland responded by strengthening their resolve for peace.[124] Yet the continued presence of the PIRA put strain on the process throughout the early 2000s. In March 2002 a raid on the Special Branch office in Northern Ireland, for example, was attributed to the PIRA.[125] While the political atmosphere was turning against the paramilitary violence, the British government sought concrete assurances to stabilise the process. In October 2002, Prime Minister Tony Blair called on paramilitaries to move from ceasefires to 'acts of completion'. It is likely that moments of communal tension and even violence will occur during any peace process. In the event of negotiations, it will be important for parties to the Kurdish conflict to appreciate this and carefully respond to ensuing outrage in order to sustain momentum for peace.

9.2.5 Independent third parties in the peace process

Through initial talks, the parties to the conflict in Northern Ireland developed awareness that the road to peace would be fraught and complicated; and thus sought the assistance of international interlocutors to bring an independent presence to the working out of the most complex issues. One of the first was US Senator George Mitchell, who headed a commission to assess how decommissioning might take place in Northern Ireland. The commission report, released in January 1996, suggesting a set of 'principles of democracy and non-violence' that all participants in negotiations should affirm their commitment to: democratic and exclusively peaceful means of resolving political issues; the total disarmament of all paramilitary organisation, verifiable by an independent commission; the end of 'punishment' killings and beatings.[126] The 'Mitchell principles' offered a way forward to both parties without reneging on their seemingly incompatible stances. By affirming the principles, parties could proceed along both tracks – decommissioning and negotiations – in parallel, with the assurance that violence had been publically renounced and would not be used to pressure negotiations. They had some success in this regard. By July 1997, the PIRA had declared a ceasefire and the British government responded by requesting a 6-week quarantine period to ensure genuine compliance, and endorsement of the Mitchell principles. On the basis of their observance of these requests, Sinn Féin was invited to participate in the talks leading up to the GFA. Jonathan Powell has argued that 'as a device they are applicable in other similar disputes where there is no confidence in the permanence of the ceasefire called by a terrorist movement'.[127] Indeed, a similar approach had already proved effective in the negotiations leading to the end of apartheid in South Africa. The 'Groote Schuur Minute' agreed between the ANC and the de Klerk government in 1990 set the scene for substantive discussions, as both parties pledged to 'agree on a common commitment towards the resolution of the existing climate of violence and intimidation from whatever quarter as well as a commitment to stability and to a peaceful process of negotiations'.[128]

It seems likely that at the point of entry into negotiations, confidence would be low on both sides of the Kurdish conflict, particularly related to the use of military force. The PKK has declared a number of unilateral ceasefires, which Turkey asserts have been poorly observed, and the PKK maintains were followed by an intensification of hostilities by the Turkish army. A similar set of principles, with international backing and monitoring, could be a significant confidence-building measure between the parties to the Kurdish conflict. Principles that might be applicable in this context include: commitment to democratic and exclusively peaceful means of resolving political issues, formal recognition of the Kurds in Turkey by the state, and recognition of the territorial integrity of Turkey by the PKK.

The Mitchell principles prefaced agreement in substance with agreement in principle, and established the basis upon which negotiations, the forum in which substantive issues were to be addressed, could be entered. However, the success of the Mitchell principles was limited in other respects. They brought some parties to the table, but as unenforceable commitments they did not establish firm confidence between all parties. The UUP did not meet directly with Sinn Féin until January 1999; the DUP refused to meet with Sinn Féin until March 2007. Most of the negotiations preceding agreements were conducted through 'shuttle diplomacy' by British and international interlocutors. The principles were also unsuccessful in bringing violence to an end. Independent bodies established to monitor paramilitary decommissioning (to be discussed further in the following section) continued to find PIRA involvement in violence until after the St Andrews Day agreement in 2006.[129] It was not until the 19th report of the Independent Monitoring Commission (IMC) in September 2008 that an independent assessment found that the PIRA was no longer a 'threat to peace or to democratic politics'[130] and that the IRA's Army Council was 'no longer operational or functional'.[131] Nor did the principles allay mutual mistrust over parties' motives. Unionists alleged that persistent violence by the PIRA increased the relative strength of their bargaining position with the British government after the GFA.[132] In turn, it was alleged that the principles were in practice applied more stringently to Republican paramilitaries than those associated with Unionists.[133] Yet despite their limitations, the Mitchell commission forged a new approach to the establishment of negotiations.

The international role in the Northern Ireland peace process continued throughout negotiations. Following the appointment of George Mitchell in 1995, the US continues to appoint a Special Envoy to Northern Ireland. In 2006, US Special Envoy Mitchell Reiss refused to grant Sinn Féin President Gerry Adams a US visa, placing pressure on Sinn Féin in the negotiations leading to the St Andrews Day Agreement. International commissioners have validated the independence of bodies overseeing decommissioning.[134] In a quagmire of conflicting motives and alleged agendas, the international presence contributed to building confidence in the process amongst the parties, while confidence in each other was elusive. Promises of international aid, particularly from the United States, also incentivised resolution of the conflict. In 1977, Jimmy Carter delivered a public statement promising US aid to Northern Ireland should a political settlement be reached.[135] Following the Anglo-Irish Agreement of 1985, substantial US capital was injected into Northern Ireland.[136] USAID set up the International Fund for Ireland in 1986, which to date has received $457 million from the US government.[137]

The parties to the Kurdish conflict face a comparable atmosphere between them. Yet Turkey, as noted above, is reluctant to openly recognise the conflict, and insistent that it is addressing a solely domestic issue. Yet the opening of negotiations for Turkey's accession to the European Union in 2004 vouches otherwise. Annual reports documenting Turkey's progress towards the accession criteria have given violence in the Kurdish region a prominent focus within the human rights criteria, establishing the conflict as a matter of international concern.[138] Yet, as is detailed in Chapter 7, the international community has been far from outspoken regarding the Kurdish conflict. Historically, the context of Northern Ireland within the international community has been very different to the Kurdish region. The United States, for example, has a large Irish community and its relationship with Ireland dates back to its very roots. Kurdish diaspora communities in the United States and Europe, although significant in number, may not be able to exert comparable political pressure due to their less influential and structured political role. However, there are a number of compelling reasons for an enhanced international role in resolution of the conflict, beyond the obligations under international law that are outlined in this book. The United States and Europe have close military ties with Turkey, and the OSCE, Council of Europe, and EU members already have significant diplomatic and economic ties that make peaceful resolution of the conflict in their interest as is detailed in Chapter 7. In addition, the European Union has a strong interest in Turkey's accession; an impossible prospect until Turkey has peace within and at its borders. Moreover, the stability of the southeast of Turkey is important to the international community due to its geostrategic location at the crossroads of Europe and the Middle East.

9.3 Post-conflict arrangements

This section examines post-conflict mechanisms that might be established in Turkey in order to prevent the conflict from re-emerging. Approximately half of post-conflict states return to conflict within a decade;[139] in order to establish a lasting peace in Turkey all citizens will need to be galvanised in the project of peace, confident that both the causes and effects of the conflict are being addressed. This entails a hard-headed examination of the root causes of the conflict, and tackling the multi-dimensional problems Turkey now faces following decades of violent conflict. First, we examine different political models that may be useful in addressing the political roots of the conflict. Then we turn to the complex issues arising from the conflict, including opportunities for justice and reconciliation, and disarmament, demobilisation and reintegration (DDR) of combatants.

This chapter concludes by proposing a path to peaceful resolution of the Kurdish question. While the authors regard it as a highly positive development that there is now a platform for openly addressing the Kurdish issue amongst civil society in Turkey, and the issue is even discussed in the Turkish Parliament, a previously unthinkable prospect, to date there has been no structured guide for the parties to chart a way out of the conflict. We hope the post-conflict arrangements suggested here may be instructive when parties are examining the various options available for post-conflict Turkey. The path provides a framework by which they might engage, negotiate and decide these arrangements.

9.3.1 Political models for post-conflict Turkey

As is demonstrated in Chapter 1, at its roots the Kurdish conflict is a political disagreement concerning the governance of the Kurdish region, and its relationship to central power, since 1923 embodied in the state of Turkey. Parties committed to a lasting resolution of the conflict must address these political questions, acknowledging the political dimension to the conflict and seeking a consensus solution. A political compromise between the parties may not be as impossible as it first appears. The previous section demonstrates that practical compromise arrangements have helped diffuse fundamental disagreements over political sovereignty in Northern Ireland. Moreover, even in the last 25 years the political approaches of both parties to the Kurdish conflict have evolved, with the Turkish government easing its denial of Kurdish identity in Turkey, and the PKK abandoning references to independent Kurdistan in its manifesto by the early 1990s, and concentrating on the idea of a 'democratic republic'. This is not to underestimate the complexity of the issues that will have to be tackled for consensus to be reached between the parties. In Chapter 8, we examine the basis in international law for claims of self-determination, and how the right to external self-determination as secession, and internal self-determination as federalism, have been realised. Yet while a practical solution for the political dispute at the heart of the conflict must be grounded in international law, it will also have to take into account factors such as resource distribution, regional politics, and the political will and capacity in Turkey. The Kurdish conflict is particularly complicated due to the division of Kurdish-inhabited lands across several nation states with varying regime types, and the different relationships of the international community with those states. However, disputes over sovereignty are not unique to the Kurdish region, and have been addressed using a range of political models in different international contexts. This section will look at a range of political models that have utilised complex and various forms of power distribution and sharing, which might provide instructive examples as the parties to the Kurdish conflict try to establish political arrangements for post-conflict Turkey.

Devolution

The United Kingdom has devolved significant powers to three constituent regions: Scotland, Northern Ireland and Wales. Certain powers had been devolved to the regions for over a century by the time political devolution was formalised in government legislation in 1998.[140] The UK government created a Scotland Office with regional administrative powers in 1885,[141] and in the Government of Ireland Act 1920 established a legislature in Northern Ireland.[142] The process of establishing and extending devolution of executive and legislative functions through the creation of regional assemblies in the 1998 legislation was intended to make regional administration more accountable to the population of the region. The new arrangements also arose out of a combination of political pressures from the regions and political will of central government. The New Labour government was elected in 1997 with a manifesto commitment to enhancing devolution, a policy to which the previous Conservative government had been opposed. Increasing nationalism in Scotland and Wales,[143] and the acknowledgement of the political dimension to the conflict in Northern Ireland gave added impetus to formalising devolution arrangements.

Although devolution across the regions was re-invigorated at a common point in history, the arrangements for each region vary substantially, such that devolution in the United Kingdom is usually characterised as 'asymmetric'. This has allowed devolution arrangements to respond to distinctive features of each region. Scotland and Northern Ireland have distinct bodies of law from England and Wales. Thus, the Scottish Parliament has power over criminal justice, criminal law and policing, and while these powers were retained in the GFA for the UK Secretary of State for Northern Ireland, it was envisaged in the agreement that they would be transferred in time to the Northern Ireland Assembly. Scotland and Northern Ireland also have separate legislative and executive bodies, whereas the Welsh Assembly combines legislative and executive functions. All the devolved legislatures can enact law in areas that are not reserved to the UK Parliament such as defence, national security and foreign affairs. The Scottish Parliament and Northern Ireland Assembly can initiate primary and secondary legislation in non-reserved areas, whereas the Assembly of Wales can only initiate secondary legislation in these areas.[144]

Spain provides another example of the ability of the devolution model to react to historical and regional contingencies. Devolution arrangements in Spain grew out of the democratisation process following the death of General Franco, and thus granted significant powers to local regions in an attempt to re-build processes of participation and accountability. The 1978 Spanish Constitution divided the territory into 17 autonomous communities and two autonomous cities, each with its only legislature elected by proportional representation, president, regional ministers and set of arrangements on the sharing of power with the central government. Yet much of the devolution arrangements were established through various regional parties bargaining with the central government for decentralisation in their territory, resulting in uneven measures across the regions. For example, Catalonia, Galicia and the Basque Country, which have a long history of a distinct identity and possessed medieval privileges of self-governance, have greater autonomy than the other regions, including an autonomous police force that is part of the Spanish National Police and Guardia Civil. Two regions, the Basque Country and Navarre, collect their own taxes and pay the government for centrally provided services; all other regions are allocated their budgets from the centre. Devolution in Spain demonstrates that historical claims to regional autonomy, such as that of the Kurds, can be incorporated into modern constitutional arrangements.

Devolution arrangements in Northern Ireland were inexorably shaped by the peace process from which they arose, and therefore might be particularly instructive for the Kurdish context. One particular feature of devolution in Northern Ireland is the institutionalisation of power-sharing between parties to the conflict in the central executive. The Northern Ireland Executive guarantees the distribution of power across different communities by allocating ministerial portfolios to all the major parties under the d'Hont method which assigns positions to broadly reflect party strength. The First Minister and Deputy First Minister are elected by the agreement of a majority of Unionist and Republican Assembly members. This model of power-sharing, often referred to as consociationalism,[145] has been utilised in the aftermath of inter-communal conflict in order to guarantee an agreed form of power allocation between communities, for example in South Africa since 1994 and Bosnia-Herzegovina since 1995. Post-Ba'athist Iraq chose not to formalise consociationalism in its Constitution but through negotiations between political parties the Presidential Council is composed of members from each of the three largest communities in Iraq.[146] Consociational arrangements have not been without criticism. It is argued that in the long-term consociationalism entrenches communal division, encourages elite-led politics and fails to respond as demographic balances evolve.[147] However, consociational arrangements have been defended as a more realistic guarantor of pluralism than integration in the short-term aftermath of conflict.[148] There remains international regard for their potential despite past failures, as demonstrated by the UN Secretary-General's report on settlement of the Cyprus problem, which recommends a Presidential Council of six members with at least two from Turkish and Greek communities,[149] despite previous power-sharing agreements having broken down in the territory. Thus consociationalism might merit consideration, whether on a temporary or permanent basis, at the central and regional government level in Turkey; were parties to be concerned about representation of Kurds in the central government, or non-Kurdish minorities in a Kurdish regional government in Turkey.

The devolution arrangements in the United Kingdom also varied in the institutional frameworks regulating relations between the regional bodies and central government. Relations between the UK government and Scottish and Welsh administrations were elucidated in non-enforceable 'memorandum of understanding'. However, the GFA in Northern Ireland specifically institutionalised three strands of relations for Northern Ireland,[150] in recognition of the complexity and contestation over Northern Ireland's constitutional status. Strand one concerned relationships within Northern Ireland, and lead to the creation of the Northern Ireland Assembly, Executive, and a consultative Civic Forum. Strand two concerned relationships between Northern Ireland and the Republic of Ireland, and lead to the creation of the North-South Ministerial Conference (NSMC) which brings together members of the Northern Ireland Executive and the Irish Government to oversee the work of six cross-border implementation bodies. Strand three concerned relationships with Britain in the context of devolution, and lead to the creation of the British-Irish Council, a body that facilitates meetings between representatives of the devolved administrations of the United Kingdom, the Irish government, the Isle of Man, Jersey and Guernsey, in order to cooperate over areas of common interest.[151] The relations of the Kurdish region in Turkey with both the Turkish state and neighbouring Kurdish regions might benefit from similar arrangement into formal strands, each with their own consultative and advisory institutions to manage the relationship and shared areas of interest.

Devolution arrangements are typically less formalised than federal models, although they will usually be codified in national law and agreements between the central government and regional governments. Unlike federal models of government, they are infrequently constitutionally enshrined and thus, technically at least, subject to repeal or withdrawal at the centre. In the UK regional assemblies remain constitutionally subordinate to the UK Parliament under the doctrine of parliamentary sovereignty, even though they in practise do function with a great deal of autonomy. Devolution arguably provides considerable flexibility, but where there is uncertainty about the enduring commitment of central government to retain devolution arrangements, this might be at the expense of stability. Thus, federalism may also be considered as a potential political model for post-conflict Turkey.

Federalism

As is briefly outlined in Chapter 8, federalism is a constitutional arrangement in which each federal unit formally possesses an equal relationship with the central government and participates in central decision-making. Federalism is a widespread model of government; today over 40 per cent of the world's population live in a federation.[152] Federal arrangements vary considerably; in terms of size and number of units, division of powers and incorporation of units in central government procedures. Illustrative of this diversity is the federation of Bosnia-Herzegovina, composed of two constituent units and Russia, composed of 83. In this sense, federal arrangements demonstrate considerable flexibility to reflect specific geographical, cultural and historical characteristics. Yet federalism also confers stability through its constitutional entrenchment. As the main features of a federation are constitutionally codified, the procedures for constitutional amendment usually provide significant protection for all those with an interest in the federal arrangement, for example by requiring authorisation of a federal upper house. Federalism thus tends to be pursued when nations have an interest in a stable, codified system with restrictions on the withdrawal or extension of powers, including in the aftermath of regional conflicts where trust has eroded between parts of the country. Several countries emerging from such conflict have adopted federalism, including Iraq, Sudan and Ethiopia.

The example of federalism in neighbouring Iraq may be of particular interest to Turkey. The predominantly Kurdish north has developed a comprehensive administrative and security apparatus that could present examples of best practice to a Kurdish federal region in Turkey. The Kurdish regions in Iraq and Turkey share a legacy of repression by the central government, including military operations, forced displacement and widespread human rights abuses. In recognition of this past, the Iraqi constitution, approved by a national referendum on 15 October 2005, gives explicit expression to the pluri-national character of Iraq, as a federal state of 'multiple nationalities, religions and sects'.[153] The constitution designated Iraq as a bi-lingual state with Kurdish and Arabic both official languages, and enshrines protections for minority languages, including Turkish,

Syriac, and Armenian-speaking Iraqis.[154] In addition the constitution envisages significant devolved power to self-governing regions. Regions are empowered to set up their own constitutions and establish internal security forces.[155] The national government reserves powers over national security, fiscal and customs policy, planning policy regarding external water sources, citizenship, general and investment budget, mail, broadcast frequencies, population statistics, standard weights and measures.[156] Shared powers between the national and regional government include: customs, energy distribution, environmental, planning, water resources, public education and public health policies.[157] Revenue-sharing is according to regional needs rather than strictly per capita.[158] Regional representation in central government is to be safeguarded through a bicameral legislature along the lines of that in the United States: a council of representatives with members allocated proportional to the population,[159] and a federation council intended to bring together the representatives from the regions.[160] The precise specifications of the federation council are to be established by the council of representatives, which had yet to do so at the time of this books publication.

Many facets of Iraqi federalism have yet to be established. How an 'equitable' share of oil revenues will be distributed between the regions, as, mandated in the constitution,[161] is still a matter of political contention.[162] The Iraqi constitution envisages a multi-regional Iraq, setting out provisions for the establishment of other regions,[163] which were further elucidated in a regional autonomy law of October 2006.[164] Yet at the time of this books publication, Kurdistan remained the only region in Iraq. In this respect, it is important to note significant differences in the political context in Iraq to that of Turkey. The federal Iraqi constitution arose out of an international conflict that abruptly brought to an end several decades of brutal dictatorship and one party rule. The transformation of Iraq into a federal, democratic state is taking place in the context of multi-dimensional inter-communal conflict. The difficulties faced in Iraq's constitutional arrangements are likely to be different to those that Turkey is likely to face.

A further difference to the Iraqi context is that the institutional framework in Kurdistan, Iraq has developed over more than a decade. Following the 1990 Gulf War, international forces oversaw a no-fly zone and withdrawal of Iraqi troops from Kurdistan, Iraq, providing an opportunity for Kurdish self-government. In October 1992 the Kurdish Parliament in Iraq unilaterally declared Iraqi Kurdistan as a constituent state in a federal Iraq. Following the 2003 collapse of the Ba'ath regime, the Kurdish leadership were in a position to codify their *de facto* status, and the Iraqi constitution explicitly recognises the Kurdistan region in its text.[165] Yet during the intervening period some of the benefits of self-government had been blighted by ongoing conflict between the two largest political parties in Iraq, the PUK and KDP, de-escalated when the parties agreed to share power in 2002. The Kurdish region of Turkey does not possess Kurdistan, Iraq's institutional legacy, but neither does it share the blight of internecine struggles. In considering the political framework for post-conflict, the distinctive experience of the Kurdish region in Turkey must take precedence over international models.

However, it may be that Kurdistan, Iraq evolves into a regional example of the protection of Kurdish identity and self-determination within a nation state, with significant protections for internal minorities and strong human rights standards. Steps have been taken, for example, to encourage an active and inclusive civil society in Kurdistan, Iraq, with the creation of Human Rights and Civil Society ministries.[166] Kurdistan's draft regional constitution includes further guarantees of the region's status, including a provision that if the constitution 'is changed without the consent of the Kurdistan Regional Assembly ... this shall afford the people of the Kurdistan Region the right to self-determination'.[167] The draft includes protections for minorities within the region: allowing non-Muslim minorities jurisdiction over personal status law, and Turkmen and Syriac minorities linguistic rights in the education system and the compulsory teaching of Arabic in the region. A draft constitution was approved by the regional Parliament, the Kurdistan National Assembly, in June 2009,[168] but has yet to be ratified after a planned regional referendum in July 2009 was indefinitely postponed.

Yet Kurdistan, Iraq and the Kurdish region in Turkey share a central feature: that attitudes towards them are underpinned by the fear that distinctively 'Kurdish' self-government will presage conflict and state dissolution. Neighbouring states with Kurdish populations have been hostile to the development of self-government in Kurdistan, Iraq, and scholars have argued that Iraq's federal units should follow the boundaries of the 18 pre-existing governates from the Ba'athist regime, in order to dilute the strength of any one community in Iraq and encourage inter-communal cooperation.[169] Pluri-national federations are supposed to be inherently unstable, and the dissolution of the former Soviet Union, Yugoslavia and Czechoslovakia are cited as demonstrative examples.[170] Yet these examples all possessed features conducive to fragmentation that were entirely separate to the composition of their federal units, including weak democratic practices and representation of federal units in central decision making. There are several examples of well-functioning democratic federalism where federal units reflect distinctive communities. Switzerland, for example, is divided into 20 full cantons and six half cantons, most of which are unilingual and have a Protestant or Catholic majority. Moreover, pluri-national federations have successfully devolved asymmetric powers between regions in response to specific regional characteristics. In Canada, for example, Quebec is the sole majority French-speaking province, and Quebecois, comprising a fifth of Canada's population, consider themselves a distinct nation with their own language, culture and history.[171] Thus Quebec possesses distinctive powers, including over immigration and income tax collection,[172] and uses French as the official language of the province. Such examples undermine the fatalism about pluri-national federalism that has been applied to both Iraq and Turkey.

Special autonomy arrangements

In some cases, the distinctive character of a region necessitates further provisions than those of asymmetric devolution or federalism. This is particularly the case where the religious, ethnic or linguistic characteristics of a sub-national unit are shared with one or more adjacent territory, and thus might be considered in the case of the Kurdish region in Turkey, where neighbouring Iraq, Iran and Syria all have significant Kurdish populations. In such cases, special autonomy arrangements have been formulated to respond to the complexity of the region's relationship with the state, and neighbouring territories. Frequently, the arrangements aim to formalise these overlapping relations, in order to alleviate tensions regarding sovereignty of the region. Multiple claims to sovereignty over a region by bordering states has been a principle source of inter-state conflict in the 20th and 21st centuries, such as that between Russia and Georgia regarding Abkhazia and South Ossetia in August 2008. However, there are examples of states coming to an agreement of joint sovereignty over a region. One such is the Co-Principality of Andorra, a region in the Pyrenees ruled for centuries by the Bishop of Urgel from Spain and the French head of state as co-princes. In 1993 the Constitution of Andorra formalised the 'co-princes' as joint heads of state, with powers to call general elections, accredit diplomatic representatives, sanction laws and give consent to entering international treaties.[173] Many of these duties are largely ceremonial, and Andorra exercises considerable '*de facto*' autonomy. A parallel arrangement exists internally in Bosnia-Herzegovina, where the two federal entities – Federation of Bosnia and Herzegovina and Republika Srpska – share sovereignty of the Brčko District. The District is a multi-ethnic and geo-strategic region in Bosnia-Herzegovina whose disputed status threatened to scupper implementation of the 1995 Dayton Peace Accords,[174] but was agreed to be held in condominium (joint sovereignty) following the recommendation of an international arbitration tribunal.[175] As in the case of Andorra, Brčko District largely manages its own internal affairs. Brčko elects a legislative District Assembly, and has an independent judiciary and police force.[176] Joint sovereignty arrangements allow parties to compromise over internal governance, without losing their sovereignty claim to a territory. Should Turkey countenance sharing sovereignty over the Kurdish region within the framework of regional autonomy, the above agreements might provide instructive precedents.

Where a neighbouring state is not recognised as joint sovereign, special autonomy arrangements may institute another third party role, for example as guarantor of kin rights. This is the case regarding South Tyrol, a German-speaking autonomous region on the Italian-Austria border. In the 1915 Treaty of London the Triple Entente agreed to back Italian claims to South Tyrol, which was under Austrian sovereignty, in exchange for Italian support for the Entente in the First World War.[177] Austria conceded Italian sovereignty over the region following the end of the Second World War, but sought guarantees of the ethnic, cultural and linguistic character of the region in the Paris Agreement of 1946. When Italy broke these guarantees, Austria sought the mediation of the United Nations in 1960, and a package of autonomy measures was passed in 1972, with Austria taking on an active guarantor role. Implementation of the package was declared satisfactory by both parties in 1992, and Austria and Italy agreed to resolve any further disputes via the International Court of Justice.[178] This model might be considered with regards to Turkey in order to provide external guarantees of autonomy status and cultural and linguistic rights in the Kurdish region. The complexities of regional politics might impact which entity could fulfil the guarantor role. Bordered by repressive regimes in Iran and Syria, and fledgling post-conflict democracy in Iraq, an effective guardian of Kurdish autonomy in Turkey might need to be drawn from an international organisation such as the United Nations.

The parties to the Kurdish conflict have a broad array of political models before them in charting a peaceful political solution to the conflict. Each political context is unique, and the Kurdish conflict will not be solved by mechanical transplantation of one model outlined above. However, the wide diversity of political arrangements that have been pursued, whether devolution, federalism or autonomy, and the many variants amongst them, demonstrate that innovative solutions to a political crisis are not unreachable. Indeed, the political arrangements depicted above illustrate that pluralism can be a celebrated part of the national polity, and seemingly intractable disputes over territory can reach an appropriate accommodation.

9.3.2 Justice and reconciliation in post-conflict Turkey

This chapter argues that recognition of an armed conflict under international humanitarian law by both parties is a critical step on the path to peace. It emphasises the importance of such a step in acknowledging the collective suffering of Kurdish and Turkish people over several decades. However, in order to build a durable and inclusive peace, it might be prudent to go further than this and address individual, as well as collective, grievance and trauma. On his presentation of the UN fact-finding mission on the Gaza conflict before the Human Rights Council, Richard Goldstone emphasised this point, stating: 'it has been my experience in many regions of the world, including my own country, South Africa, that peace and reconciliation depend, to a great extent, upon public acknowledgement of what victims suffer'.[179] Recognition of the conflict could be the basis of establishing formal mechanisms to acknowledge personal experiences under armed conflict. It has been suggested that individualising guilt in this way helps undermine the potential for collective reprisals and the persistence of communal tension down generations.[180] This section outlines different possible mechanisms for justice and reconciliation and highlights considerations that may influence choosing between them.

Recent years have seen heightened debate over the extent to which the interests of peace and justice come into conflict or complement each other. This is likely to be a key issue in devising such mechanisms in the Kurdish context. Those negotiating peace agreements have argued that the spectre of prosecutions have raised obstacles to peace.[181] For example, it has been argued that the prosecutions against high officials and the head of state in Sudan not only de-incentivised the pursuit of peace, but undermined the authority of key players who are crucial to the implementation of a peace agreement.[182] This has been a particularly prominent question for a number of African countries, largely due to the focus of prosecutions of the International Criminal Court (ICC) being on that continent to date. The African Union has issued resolutions condemning universal jurisdiction and international justice as a threat to efforts towards peace in the region.[183] However, there have also been strong statements from the continent about the complementarity of peace and justice. The Waki Commission on violence following Kenya's December 2007 election, for example, emphasised the role of justice to tackle impunity and recurring cycles of violence.[184] Justice plays a crucial role in deterrence and channelling trauma and desire for retribution into formal institutions, arguably reducing the likelihood of a resumption of violence. If peace and justice reinforce each other in the long term, but may conflict in the short term, perhaps the question rests on the timing and design of peace and justice mechanisms, rather than a zero-sum choice between the goals. The Waki Commission recommended a three-track system within differing time periods, including ICC investigation, a national process, such as a Special Tribunal set up by the Kenyan Parliament, and a Justice, Truth and Reconciliation Commission to establish the full course of events and recommend preventative mechanisms.[185] In fact, there is recognition in international law that mechanisms of peace or justice may take predominance at certain time periods without jeopardising the interests of either. Article 16 of the Rome Statute, for example, allows an ICC prosecution to be deferred by the UN Security Council for a renewable period of 12 months,[186] in recognition of the UN Security Council's mandate to promote international peace and security.

A carefully sequenced combination of different mechanisms may also be applicable to the Kurdish conflict. When violations have been systematic and/ or widespread, a broad programme of 'transitional justice' is often implemented, the term 'transitional' emphasising the wider objective to transform society.[187] Within this framework a selection or combination of justice mechanisms may be used, including criminal prosecutions, truth commissions, reparations programmes, gender justice, security system reform and memorialisation efforts.[188] Each of these could play a role in the transition of the Kurdish regions from conflict. This section looks in more detail at the first two mechanisms, and particularly whether lessons from other contexts could be applied to the Kurdish conflict.

Prosecutions

Formal adversarial justice mechanisms serve a range of purposes in the aftermath of conflict: delegitimisation of perpetrators or regimes, retribution, incapacitation, rehabilitation, truth telling, norm institutionalisation and deterrence.[189] In some cases, it may be beneficial to a peace process for certain actors to be marginalized or excluded. For example, it has been argued that the inability of Radovan Karadžić to participate in the Dayton accords, due to his indictment in 1995 by the International Criminal Tribunal for the former Yugoslavia, was important to their success in bringing peace to the region.[190]

Formal justice mechanisms may take place at the national or international level. According to the principle of complementarity,[191] domestic justice mechanisms are generally regarded as preferable. The ICC's Rome Statute specifies that a national investigation or prosecution that is 'genuinely' carried out renders cases inadmissible before the Court. Similarly international human rights courts, such as the European Court of Human Rights, require the exhaustion of domestic remedies before admitting a case. Domestic trials often have enhanced legitimacy and a greater impact on strengthening the rule of law within a country, however they often do not possess the capacity and resources of an international trial. In some contexts, a middle-ground may be sought, such as the establishment of locally-based but internationally-sponsored justice mechanisms, such as the UN-administered local courts in East Timor and Kosovo, and hybrid tribunals in Sierra Leone and Cambodia.[192]

Formal justice mechanisms could draw from international criminal law, humanitarian law, and human rights law in the Kurdish context. Part I of this book establishes that both parties have committed violations of international humanitarian law. Although breaches of Common Article 3 applying to non-international armed conflict are not considered 'grave breaches' and therefore obligatory for state parties to criminalise in domestic courts, violations of Common Article 3 have been recognised as war crimes in the Statutes of the International Criminal Tribunals for Yugoslavia and Rwanda, the Special Court for Sierra Leone and the International Criminal Court (based on Article 8 2(f) of the Rome Statute).[193] Although Turkey is not yet a party to the Rome Statute, it is possible for the ICC to exercise jurisdiction over crimes committed by Turkish nationals or on Turkish territory. In such cases, a referral by the UN Security Council,[194] as was the case with the prosecution of the President of Sudan Omar al-Bashir[195] or the acceptance of the state,[196] activates the jurisdictional competence of the Court. However, the Court does not have jurisdiction over crimes committed before the entry into force of the Rome Statute in 2002.[197] In 2004, Article 38 of the Turkish Constitution was amended to allow for the extradition of Turkish nationals to the ICC, and Prime Minister Erdogan and other high-ranking officials have expressed their support for ratification of the Rome Statute.[198] However, Turkey has yet to incorporate into domestic law all the crimes under the jurisdiction of the court.[199] It is not the reach of the ICC alone that may encourage this step, but that many states have already instituted universal jurisdiction over these crimes in their domestic legislation.[200] Some violations of international humanitarian law, then, may be treated as international crimes, and should Turkey develop its national legislation in line with current trends, also tried domestically.

In addition to the possibility of prosecutions based on international humanitarian law, there is considerable jurisprudence that establishes that international human rights law applies in situations of conflict,[201] and therefore a formal justice mechanism in the case of the Kurdish context could also address violations of human rights law. The advisory opinion on the *Legal Consequences of the Construction of a Wall in the Occupied Palestinian Territory* set out three possibilities that a body considering the relationship between international humanitarian law and human rights law in a particular situation of armed conflict should countenance: 'some rights may be exclusively matters of international humanitarian law; other may be exclusively matters of human rights law; yet others may be matters of both these branches of international law'.[202] In the latter case, while norms will usually be complementary as they are both concerned with the dignity of the person, the principle of *lex specialis*, that is the application of the body of law that is more specific to the situation at hand, should adjudicate disparities between them. Generally, human rights bodies have regarded the direct application of international humanitarian law as exceeding their mandate. However, by interpreting the American Convention on Human Rights in light of the Geneva Conventions, the Inter-American Court has applied humanitarian law (in *Bámaca Velázquez v Guatemala*).[203] Due to the underdevelopment of a supervisory mechanism or system of remedies under humanitarian law in many jurisdictions, lawyers have made use of the stronger supervisory framework of human rights law mechanisms to establish violations in situations of armed conflict.[204]

However, using the framework of human rights law may be seen to lose some of the benefits of humanitarian law, due to its state-centric focus. Rather than prosecutions, human rights bodies primarily address the damage done to the individual in the power of a state, and usually award individual reparations where a violation is found. Although human rights law has more developed procedural rights, it is possible that victims will not find reparation from the state sufficient to hold individuals (even if they have been acting under the state's control) accountable for their violation of human rights and humanitarian law. In addition, human rights are primarily applicable within the territory of the state party, although the UN Human Rights Committee, the European Court of Human Rights and the American Commission of Human Rights have all ruled that human rights apply extra-territorially when the state has 'effective control' over the territory or person associated with the complaint. The European Court of Human Rights confirmed the extra-territorial application of the European Convention on Human Rights where Turkish state agents operated in Kurdistan, Iraq in the case of *Issa and Others v Turkey*[205] and a case currently before the Court aims to establish the extra-territorial application of the Convention where indiscriminate aerial bombing and shelling by Turkish forces violated the rights of civilians in Kurdistan, Iraq.[206] This is an evolving body of law, as is the application of human rights law obligations to non-state actors, as mentioned above. Sassòli argues that international humanitarian law is thus always the *lex specialis* regarding the obligations of non-state armed groups.[207] However, the human rights obligations of non-state actors during conflict has been affirmed by a number of UN Security Council resolutions condemning human rights violations by a faction, party to a conflict or armed opposition group.[208] A final distinction offered between the bodies of law is the availability of derogation. Human rights law allows derogations in certain circumstances, including situations of armed conflict, whereas humanitarian law is non-derogable.[209] Turkey has derogated from the European Convention on Human Rights several times due to conflict in southeast Turkey. Yet derogations are strictly confined to the extent and duration of the circumstance at hand, and may not conflict with other obligations under international law, or the principle of non-discrimination,[210] although there is some leeway for the state to define these conditions. Certain articles, such as the right to life and the prohibition of torture, are non-derogable in any circumstances. Despite practical differences between the two bodies of law, both the developed procedural framework and jurisprudence of human rights law, and the evolving procedures of international humanitarian law at the international and national levels, could be utilised in formal judicial processes addressing violations during the Kurdish conflict.

Reconciliation

There is a fear that the pursuit of criminal prosecutions could interfere with the political agreements that are necessary to end, and prevent the reoccurrence of, fighting among parties to the conflict and further violations of the human rights of civilians.[211] The question then becomes one of peace versus justice. Each state and each conflict will necessarily call for differences in approach though the model of the South African Truth and Reconciliation Commission (TRC) is often heralded as an example of the power of wide-scale restorative justice, bringing together victims and perpetrators. It may also be a valuable point of reference in the Turkish conflict as the ANC, like the PKK in Turkey, existed as an opposition movement and armed resistance group before coming to power and initiating the Commission to investigate past human rights abuses, carried out by itself as well as the government.

Many claim that forms of restorative justice are more culturally appropriate in certain settings, than the adversarial set up of Western justice mechanisms and the ICC.[212] There are also concerns that specific dispute resolution mechanisms or peace building mechanisms must have wide enough legitimacy to embrace all victims. For example the LRA-Acholi settlement in Uganda had no meaning for non-Acholi peoples.[213] Clearly, a major prerequisite is for the restorative mechanism to have wide legitimacy, and it is often likely that it will be implemented alongside other measures, including prosecutions, as mentioned above. TRCs usually come at a time of regime change or political transition within a state and, by their nature, necessitate that those parties responsible for violations are no longer in positions of power. In regards to Turkey, the utilisation of a TRC would not regime change per se, but would necessitate comprehensive democratic constitutional reform so that the existence and rights of Kurds were recognised.

Reconciliation has been formalised as a set of cumulative stages: recognition, restorative justice, redress and reconstruction; and the TRC criticised for focusing on the first, without developing the latter stages.[214]

The most widely used definition for truth commissions comes from transitional justice expert Priscilla Hayner. Hayner describes four primary elements of truth commissions: first, a truth commission focuses on past human rights violations;

second, the body attempts to illustrate an overall picture of violations of human rights or international humanitarian law over a period of time and does not focus on one event; third, truth commissions usually exist for a pre-defined period of time; and finally a truth commission is vested with some authority that allows it access to information, the ability to dig into sensitive issues giving greater impact to its report.[215] All of these criteria mean that important questions must be addressed before a truth commission can be established. Parties must agree on the time period to be covered, the scope of the commission's mandate and whether its findings should be published.

In the case of South Africa, the TRC's success was based not just on the above elements but also on the qualities that made it unique to past TRCs. The process began by engaging civil society and opening a national dialogue, which lasted 16 months, to determine the nature of the TRC. The South African TRC had been approved by Parliament,[216] establishing governmental support for its work, and possessed subpoena powers making it possible to force parties to testify. It was also given the power to grant amnesty, when appropriate, to individuals who came forward. Conversely, those who refused to come forward could be prosecuted *sine die*, or indefinitely. It was well funded, both nationally and internationally and well staffed. During its 3-year tenure, the Committee on Human Rights Violations held over 120 hearings across the nation, listening to approximately 4,000 victims' testimonies.[217] The TRC held public hearings all over South Africa so that by the time the Commission's report was released in 1998 the process had become far more important and cathartic than the product.[218]

For the reasons noted, the South African TRC is often credited with playing a key role in the transformation of South African society and a reconciliation with its past. The commission was premised on the understanding that more than vengeance or retribution would be needed for society to reconcile after suffering through years of brutal injustice. Amnesties and prosecutions could only take place after the TRC had concluded its business. However, scholars point out a number of shortcomings to the TRC in South Africa; subsequent evidence revealed that truth disclosure was only partial and the TRC had limited mechanisms to ensure full disclosure, restitution intended to follow the TRC has been slow and limited in implementation, and actions supporting apartheid were placed on a par with actions pursuing democracy in South Africa.[219] Some have asserted that it was the very fear of prosecution that gave the TRC its effectiveness, citing the tailing off of applications to the TRC once high-ranking officials were acquitted and the threat of prosecution was lessened.[220] This may highlight the importance of pursuing a dual track consisting of formal justice and truth and reconciliation mechanisms.

For all its shortcomings, the TRC is still upheld and studied across the world as a model for post-conflict reconstruction. Restorative justice mechanisms particularly appear to be appropriate to non-international armed conflict. Because opposing parties live in closer proximity and it can be difficult to establish combatants from non-combatants, truth-telling and establishing a historical record of human rights violations may be more important than simply punishing guilt in many cases. It may also be more practical when violence has been widespread. For example it is estimated that in Rwanda casework to bring all perpetrators to justice would take approximately 90 years.[221] In a conference in Turkey in 2007, a number of intellectuals supported the truth and reconciliation framework as most suitable for Turkey to come to terms with its past.[222] Law professor Turgut Tarhanlı emphasised that mediation between 'victim' and 'perpetrator' might be a better model to build a peaceful future in Turkey.[223] Abdullah Öcalan has also suggested that the PKK is in favour of a truth and justice commission.[224]

In a case such as the Kurdish conflict, when mutual mistrust and marginalisation of a people's historical, ethnic, linguistic and cultural background have a long history, establishing a public record of events during the conflict will be even more important. One benefit of formal justice in this regard is that the evidentiary rules confer legitimacy on documentary evidence collected, preventing revisionist history that might reignite conflict in the future. However, the benefit of a TRC is that a much wider record can be taken as prosecutions will necessarily only address a small subset of crimes, and with robust evidentiary rules should be able to support a legitimate documentation of the conflict.[225]

Following the peace process in Northern Ireland there has been much discussion as to whether a truth commission is appropriate, and the form it might take. Community-led efforts, such as the membership organisation 'Healing Through Remembering',[226] have begun to form discussion groups and opened consultation across society as to how best to acknowledge, commemorate and learn from the experiences of the conflict. Its 2002 report made a number of recommendations, including a truth commission akin to South Africa, collection of testimony, and a national day of remembering.[227] In 2007, the Northern Ireland Office formed the 'Consultative Group on the Past' to make recommendations on these issues.[228] The central recommendation of its 2009 report, the establishment of an independent Legacy Commission of three members including an international chair, was positively received. The commission would be tasked with re-investigating killings during the conflict, coordinating information recovery and fostering reconciliation through broad engagement with society.[229] It would take over the remit of a number of ongoing public enquiries, the Police Ombudsman and the Police Historical Enquiries team, amalgamating all justice and reconciliation in one body. The experience of Northern Ireland demonstrates both the continuing importance of addressing the past in a post-conflict society, and the desire for diverse but effective procedures of truth-telling and remembrance.

Justice and reconciliation can also be channelled through engagement in political reform. It is important to note that the TRC in South Africa was held in parallel with citizen participation in the writing of a new national constitution. By establishing a forum that was inclusive, participatory, and forward looking, the justice debate in South Africa was complemented by a focus on securing social justice for current and future generations, and the South African constitution is recognised as pioneering in its enshrinement of socio-economic rights. We note above the restrictions on fundamental human rights and the obstacles to peaceful resolution of the conflict in Turkey's current constitution.[230] After the 2007 elections, the AKP initiated the drafting of a 'civilian constitution' centred on individual rights.[231] However the preparation of the draft constitution solely by the AKP, without consultation with civil society, has been heavily criticised by the opposition parties.[232] The implementation of amending the constitution has been suspended since 2007, apart from some minor amendments to the electoral procedure (including the popular, rather than parliamentary, election of the President) that were passed by popular referendum in October 2007.[233]

Participatory constitution-writing was a crucial tool of post-conflict reconstruction in South Africa. Over 4 years, more than 2 million people participated in the writing of the constitution, giving strength and legitimacy to the constitutional document and all citizens a renewed sense of confidence in the judicial process.[234] Historical precedent suggests the importance of consensus and societal engagement in formulating an enduring democratic constitution. Thus German, Spanish and Italian constitutions have endured due to their inclusive and compromise character, whereas the 1946 French constitution, which failed to find consensus agreements, led to government instability, and the 1976 Portuguese constitution was prepared unilaterally and thus had to be revised in 1982 and 1989.[235] Major civil society institutions such as DISK, TÜSIAD, the Turkish Confederation of Employers Unions, the Press Council and two major unions, Türk-Is and Hak-Is have expressed their support for a more liberal, pluralist and participatory constitution.[236]

This is not to say that TRCs are a cure-all. With all their limitations and their virtues, TRCs are ultimately the product of the needs of statesman and politicians as commissions can be established by a government to manipulate public perception or to promote a favourable view of the country's human rights policies.[237] Further, there is debate on whether truth commissions indeed help to promote reconciliation or, as some would argue, they divide rather than unite society by failing to move from a divided past of perpetrators versus victims to a united future of all survivors of conflict.[238] The success or failure of a TRC in Turkey will ultimately be dependent on the level of consultation with civil society, the level of support (both financial and political) given domestically and internationally and the political will present to implement any recommendations made by the Commission.

9.3.3 Disarmament, demobilisation and reintegration

The discussion of the Northern Ireland peace process, in this and previous chapters, helps to illustrate how issues regarding weapons and combatants can potentially delay and complicate the peace process. These issues have already proved obstructive to engagement between the PKK and Turkey.[239] We have argued that routes out of this impasse are possible by de-linking disarmament from entry into negotiations, and instead using negotiations, underpinned by commitment to non-violent principles, in order to formulate a comprehensive peace plan where progressive disarmament can be independently monitored, and coordinated with other peace objectives. Additionally, the disarmament and demobilisation process must have a civilian focus, as the main aim of disarmament, demobilisation and reintegration (DDR) is to prepare ex-combatants for civilian life. Below, we formulate a suggested model for such a path to peace for the Kurdish conflict. Here, we give some consideration to what the DDR process would entail in the Kurdish context, including addressing issues of security sector reform and amnesties.

The first stage of DDR requires a thorough and independent assessment of the extent of weapons and combatants that will be involved in the process. The United Nations has taken the lead role in this stage of DDR in a number of conflicts, through a formal process of post-conflict needs assessments (PCNAs).[240] The reliability of information at the start, and throughout, the disarmament process will be enhanced by the presence of a body that can conduct independent verification, such as the Independent Monitoring Commission in the case of Northern Ireland. The collection, monitoring and destruction of weapons may have to be carefully sequenced due to the symbolic importance of weapons as noted above. For example, a 'step-by-step' approach of phased withdrawal linked to reciprocal disarmament or political objectives can build confidence at a time when parties may feel insecure giving up weapons. In the case of Northern Ireland, the IRA was worried about being taken for granted in negotiations if it gave up armed violence, and thus the GFA linked demilitarisation to other developments in the peace process. Reform of government security structures was also incorporated into the GFA. Reciprocal disarmament measures by both parties may also increase confidence. For example, at the end of the Salvadoran civil war the FMLN armed group demobilised in concert with the Salvadoran army significantly reducing numbers, submitting to a process of doctrinal reform, and being placed under civilian authority.[241] Although these examples of DDR initiatives were particular to these conflicts, they represent possible solutions in the Turkish conflict.

Security sector reform

Security sector reform is fundamental to the DDR process as it provides for fair and impartial lawmaking and enforcement for the entire population. In the case of Turkey, mutual respect for each other's rights, in particular the protection of minority rights, is fundamental to the success of the DDR process. As is documented in Chapter 1, the Turkish Armed Forces have an extensive presence in the Kurdish region, have a broad range of structures directed specifically at the fight against the PKK, and have exerted considerable influence in Turkish politics. As part of the DDR process in Turkey, it might be prudent to conduct a strategic review of the armed forces to assess how the military might function most effectively in post-conflict Turkey, and in the context of a process of democratisation. Reform may be a strategic benefit to the army in the long term, as its permanent conflict footing has demonstrably left the modernisation process of Turkish army lagging behind its NATO allies.[242] Some reform measures have already been broached. In October 2008, the National Security Council announced restructuring measures for the institutions engaged in fighting the PKK. These changes, which were also addressed in a summit on terrorism held in Turkey, included the creation of an anti-terrorist unit within the Ministry of the Interior to coordinate all the agencies involved in anti-terrorist matters. This change represents a shift of leadership to civilian power in the approach to the PKK.

Demobilisation refers to the process by which parties to the conflict disband their military structures and combatants begin to transition back into civilian life. Very generally the process entails the registration of combatants, assistance to help them meet basic immediate needs such as food, shelter and medical care. In the context of demobilisation, some ex-combatants could be absorbed into the formal security sector, such as the police force. The problems of the village guard system, as is outlined in Chapter 1, have rendered this scheme a security threat rather than asset, and proposals for an inclusive, accountable and regulated local security sector may be a useful way to promote sustainable peace in the region. Through his lawyers, Öcalan has communicated from İmralı Island his ideas regarding demobilisation. He has proposed a regional 'self defence force', essentially an elected municipal police, to include former PKK combatants.[243] The Independent Commission on Policing for Northern Ireland, established by the GFA, provides an interesting model for re-formulating a security service that was once a key marker of communal division. The Commission's final recommendations envisaged a proactively inclusive police force, re-named from the Royal Ulster Constabulary to the PSNI and a new badge and symbols without associations with the British or Irish states. Accountability mechanisms were extended, and police recruitment was tasked to ensure 50:50 composition of Catholic and non-Catholics in the service.[244] The implementation of these reforms was crucial in obtaining the Sinn Féin PIRA endorsement and engagement with the police service.

The issue of security forces reform where there is a history of abuses, impunity, and a discriminate population is highly pertinent to the Kurdish conflict. It is likely that a report on the issue in the Kurdish context would differ to the above, for example, symbolism may not be as pressing an issue as building a security force in the region that is seen as locally accountable, engaged, and effective. As is described in Chapter 1, the Turkish armed forces have a long and fraught history of engagement in the Kurdish region, and it may be valuable to commission an independent assessment along these lines as to how this history might be mended while delivering effective security in the region.

The main objective of reintegration is to transition ex-combatants into civilian life. While disarmament and demobilisation are meant to be confidence building measures, easing the way for dialogue and negotiated resolution to the conflict, reintegration focuses on helping ex-combatants to be absorbed back into society, by assisting with housing, training and employment. A successful reintegration process is one which enables those who had previously been involved in the conflict to become responsible, contributing members of society.

Any reintegration process will have to address issues of amnesty and accountability for conduct during the hostilities. This chapter addresses the thorny debate about formal and restorative justice in the context of peace-building. Amnesties have been opposed by advocates of formal justice mechanisms[245] but were used as a tool in South Africa's TRC, in an attempt to reconcile the aims of justice and peace. Other conflict situations have struck a different balance by giving amnesties to lower-level combatants, but distinguishing those with a command function, or those who could be charged with international crimes, such as crimes against humanity, as ineligible for amnesties. The Inter-American Court of Human Rights has restricted blanket amnesty provisions in Chile and Argentina, on the basis that they remove the right to a remedy for victims.[246] However, Additional Protocol II to the Geneva Conventions calls for 'the broadest possible amnesty' following the resolution of armed conflict, demanding serious consideration from the state party to the conflict of the benefits of amnesties for reintegration and reconciliation.

Turkey has issued a number of amnesty laws in the past, which have all been highly unsuccessful and could discredit similar attempts in the future. Under previous 'amnesties' PKK fighters had to 'buy' their amnesty by giving the government information on the PKK or by joining forces against them. In this context it may be useful to distinguish any future amnesty programme by explicitly linking it to the peace process and the desire to aid the reintegration of all PKK fighters. However, the issue of amnesties, as in many peace processes, remains highly controversial in Turkey. In January 2008 the Turkish Prime Minister clarified previous statements on amnesties by declaring that current law would be enforced, rather than the passing of new laws.[247] However, in a statement in August 2009 Minister of the Interior Beşir Atalay left the issue more open, stating: 'We did not mention the concept of pardon and we will not do so. But a starting point is to put down the weapons and get rid of them. We have to work a lot for that. In this context we work on all possible alternatives'.[248]

The reintegration phase of DDR vitally underpins the disarmament and demobilisation of the PKK. Delays and deficiencies with reintegration programmes can undermine demobilisation, for example in the case of Mozambique, Angola and Liberia in the 1990s.[249] However, there are examples of how such problems can be addressed: such as 'stopgap projects' to provide short-term employment to ex-combatants before entering the formal re-integration process as instituted in Sierra Leone. The perception that armed groups are benefiting from special status in income or employment projects, leading to friction between parts of the community, can be offset by directing re-integration efforts at community projects where the whole community will see the benefit of the ex-combatants' re-integration.[250] Long-term and community-wide arms control strategies may be necessary in situations where conflict has been ongoing and endemic, such as strengthening national weapons controls and measures against arms trafficking and public awareness campaigns about violence in the community, as was successfully carried out in Cambodia.[251] However, as the South African experience illustrates, when society is able to come together and participate in a transparent and democratic process and engage in a dialogue concerning the fate of perpetrators of crimes, some of whom may be prosecuted while others are not, those decisions should be respected.[252]

9.4 Starting on the path to peace

Whether described as a 'democratic initiative', as the government of Turkey describes its plan for reform or as a 'roadmap to peace', the term, though most commonly associated with the Israeli-Palestinian conflict, which Abdullah Öcalan uses to describe his proposal for ending the conflict between Turkey and the PKK, it is essential that there be an agreed-upon basis from which a peaceful dialogue between the parties can begin. Laying the foundations for lasting peace and security in Turkey will be a complex process, and it is important that designing conflict resolution and post-conflict programmes involve all parties, start early within the peace process and take an integrated approach to the political, civil, social, cultural and economic context in Turkey. The exclusion of a range of political voices and regional civil society groups from any formal negotiation process threatens the sustainability and durability of any peace agreement reached. Peace processes need to be complimented by and connected with initiatives that reach out to wider constituencies so that they too become stakeholders in any peace settlement.

As is discussed in this and previous chapters, significant steps have been taken by the international community to develop integrated approaches to conflict resolution and post-conflict security building within recent peace processes. However, implementing such integrated approaches into practice in complex armed conflicts, like Turkey, are often fraught with significant challenges. Without addressing the historical suppression of Kurdish culture and identity, the Turkish state and its Kurdish population will find it ever more difficult to resolve the ongoing Kurdish issue. Since the early years of the republic, Turkey's overall goal has been to assimilate the Kurds and to generally eradicate Kurdish cultural identity. Generations of Turks have been raised, and indoctrinated, with the belief that recognition of minority identities represents a threat to the unity and security of the state of Turkey. Kurds living in Turkey have suffered forcible relocation, economic and cultural deprivation and other ill treatment at the hands of state authorities. The ongoing use of armed violence by both sides has further complicated the issue. Both Turks and Kurds are divided over what resolution of the Kurdish issue should look like and serious divisions remain on both sides in regards to questions of self-determination, constitutional reform, amnesty and disarmament.

As was the case in Northern Ireland backchannel negotiations between the parties may be necessary to prepare for and determine the parameters of formal peace negotiations. The use of backchannel negotiations could be useful in that it helps to keep the fledgling peace process free from public scrutiny or political opposition until the two sides can mutually agree on a way forward to peace. This time is useful as well in helping to prepare society for peace since, particularly in the case of prolonged conflict such as the one in Turkey, there will be strong emotions on both sides regarding the actions of the other.

A 'roadmap' to the resolution of the Kurdish conflict will provide the basis for formal engagement between the parties, establishing the initial common ground of recognition of the conflict, and commitment to its peaceful and democratic resolution. The 'roadmap' will go further than merely laying out recommendations for reform to be implemented by the Turkish state, by giving a platform for the mutual exploration of disputed parties, and mutual advances on the road to peace. Such a plan should explicitly focus on building good faith between the parties, and developing mechanisms to reach settlement of the contentious issues that currently divide them. In addition, it will be necessary to broaden the base of political support for the dialogue process. By engaging journalists, civil society organisations and opinion makers the parties can help to shape public opinion in favour of political engagement and dialogue. This process can often take years and, as noted, may call for the parties to develop both secret and open channels of communication before holding direct meetings, implementing confidence-building measures, or negotiating post-conflict arrangements. Here the authors briefly provide suggestions regarding possible elements of a 'roadmap' that could structure developing engagement between the parties and establish forums for a negotiated path out of the conflict.

The 'roadmap' for the Kurdish conflict should be divided into phases, outlining a timeline in which certain benchmarks will be met, allowing progress to the next phase. As a performance-based plan, the 'roadmap' will build confidence between the parties, as obligations must be complied with at each stage before progressing to the next. The 'roadmap' will also help ensure that all political and cultural dimensions of the Kurdish conflict are addressed within the peace process. Setting up parallel negotiating tracks, that adhere to the multi-dimensional 'roadmap' benchmarks, integrates the inter-locking aspects of the conflict, ensuring that no issue or group of people are sidelined in the process. A multi-track process also establishes the basis for technical working groups to focus on the development of key issues, and include national and international experts and advisors on these groups. Parties may find it useful to submit position papers on topics to these committees, as was utilised in the Northern Ireland case. The 'roadmap' must be comprehensive, clear, and goal-driven. The ultimate goals being, of course, a complete end to violence and the substantive constitutional reform necessary to address the issues in Turkey that are the cause of and have arisen as a result of the conflict. Achieving these goals will require discussion of, among other issues, restitution for internally displaced persons (IDPs), military and security sector reform, and institution of post-conflict arrangements addressing the roots of the conflict, to prevent violence from re-emerging in Turkey.

Before any formal processes can begin the parties must agree to a number of basic measures. As is noted in Chapter 7, both sides must accept and express its commitment to finding a resolution to the conflict through peaceful dialogue. Both Turkey and the PKK will need to recognise the reality that a military solution will not bring lasting peace. In addition, both parties must keep the lines of communication open, particularly if there are continued clashes as this will be when the process is most vulnerable to collapse. Finally, both parties will have to make efforts to prepare their constituencies for peace. The people of Turkey, both Kurds and non-Kurds, have suffered greatly throughout the conflict. Without public support any peace process, no matter how carefully planned, is doomed to failure.

Additionally, issues that can be addressed in this preliminary phase of negotiations may include an overall airing of the main Turkish and Kurdish concerns or issues; the possible steps that can be taken to reduce both PKK attacks and Turkish military operations; and the obstacles to ceasefire declarations. Although understandably the government of Turkey may not explicitly agree to a ceasefire agreement, it might agree to halt offensive military operations as long as the PKK abided by its ceasefire obligations in order to provide an opportunity for the process for peacefully move forward.

The parties can then begin to establish a time period in which they can develop and review the structure of the 'roadmap', and identify and agree upon procedures, timetables, negotiating tracks and key substantive issues. As these issues will demand re-visiting throughout the 'roadmap' process, one specific track could be designated a 'procedural track', to work alongside the other negotiating tracks to deal with the practical issues arising from the negotiations. The practical issues surrounding the 'roadmap' demand considerable attention. For instance, questions such as whether Turkey will allow armed groups a place at the table to negotiate on both military and political issues and, if only the latter, then who will represent the political interests of the Kurds throughout the process will need to be addressed. This track will thus benefit from international assistance, in particular technical and logistical assistance, which could play a coordinating role for the contribution of independent expertise for each track. The parties might find it helpful at this stage to introduce a third party mediator to the process. Mediators work impartially with the parties to help them talk through options and voluntarily reach an agreement to end the armed conflict and secure a just and sustainable peace. Typically, mediation involves a range of activities such as setting up initial bilateral contacts with each party alone; one-way message carrying to a party; backchannel communications with one party via an additional intermediary, or capacity-building work with one party to the process. Such capacity-building may include negotiation support, logistical help or introducing a party to civil society and international organisations. Additionally, a set of principles similar to the Mitchell principles might be endorsed at this stage to demonstrate the parties' commitment to non-violence during the negotiations.

Following this the parties can begin negotiations over substantive issues, according to the negotiating tracks agreed in the preceding phase. Within the two broad tracks that will be essential to a successful peace process, the political and military tracks, there are issues of enormous importance that will need to be honestly and openly addressed. Constitutional reform, the disarmament, demobilisation and reintegration of not only PKK cadres but of the village guards, issues of Kurdish self-determination and prisoner issues, including the status of Abdullah Öcalan on İmralı Island will take patience and considerable political will and require mutual committed solutions.

Initial negotiations could entail the submission of position papers by the par with a mediator facilitating the best solution agreeable to the parties. Concurrently, measures will be taken in this phase towards withdrawal of forces and disarmament measures, as a demonstrable step towards final cessation of hostilities. This phase should also continue to focus on broadening the base of support for peace. The parties can issue periodic public statements expressing their commitment to the process and may engage in private advocacy with opinion and policy makers. Media and dialogue initiatives aimed at reaching wider society should be undertaken to keep the process transparent and allow the public to see that progress towards peace is being made.

The final phase of the roadmap marks the major phase of implementation of the agreed upon measures, which must include DDR and security sector reform, and may, in addition to, include the granting of amnesties and the initiation of a justice and reconciliation process. A constitutional reform process will necessarily follow in order to implement the terms of political reform agreed upon between the parties. This phase marks the permanent cessation of hostilities, accompanied by public statements along these lines confirming the end of the conflict, and the commitment of all parties to a more democratic post-conflict Turkey.

While this final phase may mark the end of formal peace process, it is by no means an end to the work that will need to be completed to ensure that the conflict in Turkey does not re-emerge. The constitutional reform discussed will take time and require continued political will. In addition, the justice and reconciliation process agreed upon will take time and the commitment of the state if there is hope for it to be successful in addressing human rights violations and healing some of the wounds of the conflict suffered by the people of Turkey.

Conclusion

As this chapter shows, much work and many contentious issues will need to be addressed before peaceful conclusion can be found to Turkey's Kurdish conflict. All parties will need to not only express their commitment to dialogue aimed at securing a peaceful resolution but to exhibit the continued political will necessary for success. While only briefly mentioned in this chapter, previous chapters make clear that there will need to be both pressure and support from the international community in order to move the peace process forward. The parties will need to develop a comprehensive and detailed strategy, one with both international and domestic backing, to end the conflict and begin the reconciliation process. While the prospects for peace seem daunting, the success of peace processes in both Northern Ireland and South Africa, states where conflict had raged for decades, proves that with continued commitment, political will and international support, peace, security and a unified Turkey can be possible.

Notes

Chapter 1

1 Kurdish demographic figures have become a politicised issue, as state authorities' desire to understate their numbers mar official census data, but these figures are based on the estimates of regional authorities. See K Yildiz and M Muller, *The European Union and Turkish Accession: Human Rights and the Kurds* (London: Pluto Press, 2008), pp 4–6.

2 Kurdish Human Rights Project (KHRP), *The Safe Haven in Northern Iraq* (London: KHRP, 1995), p 6.

3 V Saeedpour, *Meet the Kurds* (London: Cobblestone Publishing, 1999).

4 D McDowall, 'The Land of the Kurds', in *The Encyclopedia of Kurdistan*, available at <http://www.kurdistanica.com/english/geography/geography-frame.html>.

5 K Yildiz, *The Kurds in Iraq: Past, Present and Future* (London: Pluto Press, 2004), p 8.

6 <http://www.culturalorientation.net>, 'Language Issues, Iraqi Kurds: Their History and Culture, Refugee Fact Sheet No 13.

7 Foreign and Commonwealth Office, 'Turkey Fact Sheet', May 1994.

8 Yildiz, op. cit., fn 5, p 7.

9 Minority Rights Group International (MRG), Summary of the MRG Report by D McDowall, 'The Kurds', September 1997.

10 See above, fn 1.

11 M Gunter, *The Kurds in Turkey: A Political Dilemma* (Boulder, CO: Westview Press, 1990).

12 The territorial boundaries of the Kurdistan Regional Government's (KRG's) jurisdiction and, linked to this, the areas of Kurdish demographic predominance in Iraq, are fiercely disputed. Plans to hold a nationwide census in Iraq were postponed indefinitely in August 2009. See Appendix B, 'Disputed Territories claimed by the KRG' to the International Crisis Group report, *Turkey and Iraqi Kurds: Conflict or Cooperation?*, 13 November 2008, p 24.

13 Historical sources on this period include N and H Pope, *Turkey Unveiled: A History of Modern Turkey* (Woodstock, NY: Overlook Press, 2000); B Lewis, *The Emergence of Modern Turkey* (Oxford: Oxford University Press, 2001); S Kinzer, *Crescent and Star: Turkey Between Two Worlds* (New York, NY: Farrar, Straus and Giroux, 2001).

14 The Republican People's Party, the CHP, remains a key political player today.

15 The 1923 Treaty of Lausanne followed the Turkish War of Independence and superseded the 1920 Treaty of Sèvres, which had been signed with the Ottoman government. Crucially, Sèvres provided for the autonomy of Kurds and other minorities, whereas Lausanne recognised only religious minorities and ignored Kurdish claims to self-determination. See K Yildiz, *The Kurds in Turkey* (London: Pluto Press, 2005), p 7.

16 WL Cleveland, *A history of the modern Middle East* (Boulder, CO: Westview Press, 2004), p 283.

17 F Ahmad, *The Making of Modern Turkey* (London: Routledge, 1993), p 148.

18 On 29 June 1981 the military junta appointed an Advisory Assembly to draft a new Constitution. It rescinded what limited liberal developments had been incorporated into the 1961 Constitution, and was based fundamentally on the notion of military control. On 7 November 1982 the new Constitution was accepted by referendum of almost 92 per cent in favour.

19 Article 118 of the Constitution, available at <http://www.constitution.org/cons/turkey/turk_cons.htm>.

20 A recent court case has been heralded as an opportunity to bring some of these activities to light. On 10 July 2008, 86 individuals, including generals, heads of police departments, businessmen and persons from the secular press, were indicted on charges of conspiracy before the Istanbul Court of Assize for Organised Crimes and Terror Crimes: Case no 2007/1536. According to the indictment, the group, a clandestine organisation in Turkey which used to call itself 'the deep state', has a long history; it restructured and renamed itself 'Ergenekon' in 1999.

21 See M Gunter and YM Hakan, 'Turkish Paradox: Progressive Islamists versus Reactionary Secularists', (2007) 16 *Middle East Critique* 289–301.

22 The Constitutional Court determined that the Parliament was not able to gather the required 367 MPs to vote.

23 The 10 per cent threshold is widely regarded as discriminating not only against smaller parties, but parties whose support is heavily weighted in one area of the country, such as the pro-Kurdish DTP.

24 The Court decided against the closure of the AKP in July 2008. The case against the DTP was still open at the time of writing.

25 KHRP, 'Protecting Politicians or Protecting Democracy? Parliamentary Immunity and Party Closure in Turkey: Briefing Paper', 27 July 2008.

26 For example, the Socialist Party (SP, 1992), the Socialist Unity Party (SBP, 1995), the Party for Democracy and Change (DDP, 1996), the Labour Party (IP, 1997) and the Democratic Mass Party (DKP, 1999).

27 Founded in 1991.

28 *Sadak and Others v Turkey (No 2)*, Application Nos 25144/94, 26149/95 to 26154/95, 27100/95 and 27101/95, Judgment of 11 June 2002. See also <http://bianet.org/english/human-rights/10742-13-dep-deputies-won-the-case-v-turkey>.

29 Cases in which the European Court of Human Rights found Turkey in violation of Article 11 (freedom of association) for its banning of political parties include *United Communist Party v Turkey*, Application No 19392/92, Judgment of 30 January 1998; *Socialist Party and others v Turkey*, Application No 21237/93, Judgment of 25 May 1998; *Freedom and Democracy Party (Ozdep) v Turkey*, Application No 23885/94, Judgment of 8 December 1999; *Yazar, Karatas, Aksoy and the Peoples' Labour Party (HEP) v Turkey*, Application No 22723-25/93, Judgment of 9 April 2002; *Sadak and Others v Turkey (No 2)*, Application Nos 25144/94, 26149/95 to 26154/95, 27100/95 and 27101/95, Judgment of 11 June 2002.

30 D McDowall, *The Kurds: A Nation Denied* (London: Minority Rights Publication, 1992), p 27.

31 G Chaliand, M Pallis and D McDowall, *A People Without a Country: The Kurds & Kurdistan* (New York, NY: Olive Branch Press, 1993), p 5.

32 Chaliand, Pallis and McDowall, ibid, p 5.

33 President Woodrow Wilson's Fourteen Point Programme for World Peace (1918), available at <http://www.ourdocuments.gov/doc.php?flash=falseanddoc=62>.

34 The Treaty of Peace Between The Allied and Associated Powers and Turkey, Signed at Sèvres on 10 August 1920, Section III, 'Kurdistan'.

35 Yildiz, op. cit., fn 5, p 10.

36 D McDowall, *A Modern History of the Kurds*, 3rd edition (London: IB Tauris, 2004), p 191.

37 McDowall, ibid, p 195.

38 McDowall, op. cit, fn 37, p 207.

39 Yildiz and Muller, op. cit., fn 1, p 14.

40 Ahmad, op. cit., fn 17, pp 148–9.

41 Ahmad, op. cit., fn 17, pp 150–1.

42 Ahmad, op. cit., fn 17, p 152.

43 MA Lee, *The Beast Reawakens: Fascism's resurgence from Hitler's Spymasters to Today's Neo-Nazi Groups and Right Wing Extremists* (London: Routledge, 1999), p 98.

44 <http://www.info-turk.be/349.htm>.

45 Amnesty International, *Turkey: Human Rights Denied* (London: Amnesty International, 1988), p 1.

46 Law 2932 of 19 October 1983 was enacted 'in order to protect the indivisible unity of the state, with its land and nation; the national sovereignty, the national security, and public publication of ideas other than the first official language of each country which recognizes the Republic of Turkey' (Article 2). 'The mother tongue of the Turkish citizen is Turkish. It is forbidden: (a) to develop any form of activity in which a language other than Turkish is used and disseminated as the mother tongue; (b) at gatherings, or demonstration to carry posters, banners, signs or other such objects written in another language … or to broadcast in records, tapes or video-cassettes, or other objects of the media in another language, without the consent of the highest official in the region' (Article 3).

47 For example, newspaper Özgür Gündem was repeatedly closed and its journalists harassed, with Istanbul State Security Court ruling that the use of the words 'Kurd' and 'Kurdistan' was a breach of the Constitution in which Turkey is defined as a unitary State (*Özgür Gündem v Turkey*, Application No 23144/93, European Court of Human Rights). The Freedom and Democracy Party (ÖZDEP) was closed down in 1983, with the Constitutional Court citing the use of the words 'Kurd', 'Kurdish people', 'minority' and 'peoples' in the party's programme as evidence of the threat to the unity of the nation (*ÖZDEP v Turkey*, Application No 23885/94, European Court of Human Rights).

48 Yildiz and Muller, op. cit., fn 1, pp 106–7.

49 Yildiz and Muller, op. cit., fn 1, pp 6–8.

50 Yildiz and Muller, op. cit., fn 1, p 17.

51 The southeast was under military law during the period of the state of emergency legislation (OHAL) from 1987–2002, filing reservations to the European Convention on Human Rights (ratified by Turkey in 1989) to the rights of liberty and security of persons, to a fair hearing, to respect for private and family life, to an effective remedy, and to freedoms of expression and association. Yildiz and Muller, op. cit., fn 1, p 155. Since 2002, the state has used the designation of 'high security zones' to implement many of the same restrictions, KHRP, 'Return to a state of emergency? Fact-finding mission report' (KHRP, London, June 2008), p 14.

52 140,000–150,000 belonged to the Army, 10,000 to the Air Force, 40,000–50,000 to the Jandarma, 40,000 to the national police, and some 67,000 to village guards, see Human Rights Watch (HRW), *Weapons Transfers* (New York, NY: HRW, 1995), p 24, available at <http://www.hrw.org/legacy/reports/1995/Turkey.htm>.

53 KHRP, 'Promoting Conflict – the Şemdinli Bombing' (KHRP, London, September 2006), p 18.

54 <http://www.scribd.com/doc/2059095/asker>.

55 Article 117 of the Constitution of the Republic of Turkey.

56 Larry J Smith, *Condensed World Paramilitary Forces 2006*, available at <http://orbat.com/site/gd/cwpf_2006/cwpf_display%20version.pdf>.

57 Article 118 of the Constitution of the Republic of Turkey.

58 Article 72 of the Constitution, available at <http://www.constitution.org/cons/turkey/turk_cons.htm>.
59 Article 2 of the Law on Military Service, No 1111, available at <http://www.unhcr.org/refworld/docid/3ae6b4d020.html>.
60 Article 4, No 1111.
61 Article 5, No 1111.
62 Military criminal law is established in the Military Penal Code (No 1632) of 22 May 1930, as last amended by the law (No 3970) of 19 May 1994.
63 Article 45 of the Military Penal Code (No 1632).
64 UN Commission on Human Rights Resolution 1998/77.
65 Turkish Constitutional Court 467/1991 and 422,343/1993 (Netherlands Department of Foreign Affairs) 2003.
66 Article 45 of the Military Penal Code (No 1632).
67 UK Home Office Border & Immigration Agency, *Country of Origin Information Report, Turkey 22 June 2007*, p 40, available at <http://www.homeoffice.gov.uk/rds/pdfs07/turkey-120907.doc>.
68 Article 87/1 of the Penal Code.
69 *Ulke v Turkey*, Application No 39437/38, Judgment of 24 January 2006, para 46, European Court of Human Rights.
70 Quaker Council for European Affairs (QCEA), *The Right to Conscientious Objection in Europe: A Review of the Current Situation. Country Report: Turkey*, April 2005, available at <http://www.quaker.org/qcea/coreport/turkey.pdf>.
71 War Resisters International, Turkey 2008, p 4, available at <http://wri-irg.org/system/files/Rrtk-update-2008-Turkey.pdf>.
72 Passed in 2005 reforms to the Turkish Penal Code.
73 Amnesty International Annual Report 2009, Turkey, available at <http://report2009.amnesty.org/en/regions/europe-central-asia/turkey>.
74 Amendment to Article 74 of the 1924 Law of Temporary Village Guards.
75 KHRP, 'The Internally Displaced Kurds of Turkey: Ongoing Issues of Responsibility, Redress and Resettlement' (KHRP, London, September 2007), p 92.
76 Turkish Economic and Social Studies Foundation (TESEV), 'A Roadmap for a Solution to the Kurdish Question: Policy Proposals from the Region for the Government' (Istanbul: TESEV, 2008), p 33.
77 Batman Petrol, 'Koruculuk Sistemi ve Turkiye', 1 August 2006, available at <http://www.petrolgazetesicom/Default.Asp?Action=Haberler&HID=1405&Haberler=Detay> (last accessed 3 August 2009).
78 Batman Petrol, ibid.
79 BBC News, 'Many Die in Turkey Wedding Attack', 5 May 2005, available at <http://news.bbc.co.uk/1/hi/world/europe/8032970.stm>.
80 McDowall, op. cit., fn 36, p 427.
81 Provision to Turkey of US Intelligence on PKK highlights Policy Shift, 7 November 2007, available at <http://www.jamestown.org/single/?no_cache=1&tx_ttnews%5Btt_news%5D=4520>.
82 A Manes, *Profiles in Terror: The Guide to Middle East Terrorist Organizations* (Boston, MA: Rowman & Littlefield, 2004), p 181, A Marcus, *Blood and belief: the PKK and the Kurdish fight for independence* (New York, NY: New York University Press, 2007), p 4. Marcus also estimates that there were around 50,000 civilian activists loyal to the PKK during this period, carrying out non-combatant duties for the organisation.
83 HJ Barkey and GE Fuller, *Turkey's Kurdish Question* (New York, NY: Rowman and Littlefield, 1998), Chapter 2, p 28, available at <http://www.wilsoncenter.org/subsites/ccpdc/pubs/kur/kurfr.htm>.
84 Marcus, op. cit., fn 82, p 242.
85 KR DeRouen, Uk Heo, *Civil Wars of the World: Major Conflicts since World War II* (Santa Barbara, CA: ABC-CLIO, 2007), p 783.

86 As part of Turkey's legal reforms to facilitate accession to the European Union it revoked the death penalty in 2002. Marcus, op. cit., fn 82, p 296. (The European Court of Human Rights ruled in 2005 that Turkey had violated the right to a fair trial and recommended a retrial for Öcalan: *Öcalan v Turkey*, Application No 46221/99, Judgment of 12 March 2003.)

87 Application PKK and KNK v Council of the European Union. Case C-229/05P *PKK and KNK v Council* [2007] ECR I-439 (judgment of 18 January 2007).

88 Yildiz and Muller, op. cit., fn 1, p 107.

89 <http://www.kurdistan.org/Current-Updates/kadek.html>.

90 Yildiz and Muller, op. cit., fn 1, p 107.

91 G Jenkins, *PKK Changes Battlefield Tactics to Force Turkey into Negotiations* (The Jamestown Foundation), available at <http://www.jamestown.org/single/?no_cache=1&tx_ttnews%5Btt_news%5D=4494>.

92 Marcus, op. cit., fn 82, p 47.

93 Marcus, op. cit., fn 82, p 286.

94 Marcus, op. cit., fn 82, p 108.

95 Marcus, op. cit., fn 82, p 173.

96 Ergil Dogu, 'PKK: Partiya Karkaren Kurdistan', in Marianne Heiberg, Brendan O'Leary and John Tirman (eds), *Terror, Insurgency and the State* (Philadelphia, PA: University of Pennsylvania Press, 2008), p 330.

97 Marcus, op. cit., fn 82, p 108.

98 <http://www.hpg-online.com/eng/news/2008_news_2.html>.

99 Marcus, op. cit., fn 82, p 1. Figures provided to the UN Special Rapporteur on extrajudicial, summary or arbitrary executions during her mission to Turkey by the Governor of the Emergency District in 2001, broke down the number of wounded and killed since the imposition of the state of emergency in 1987 as follows: over 23,000 suspected PKK militants killed, more than 4,400 unarmed civilians killed and 5,400 wounded, more than 5,000 police officers and gendarmes killed and 11,000 injured. (Special Rapporteur on extrajudicial, summary or arbitrary executions, 'Civil and Political Rights, including the Question of Disappearances and summary executions', Report of the Special Rapporteur, Ms Asma Jahangir, submitted pursuant to Commission on Human Rights resolution 2001/45, 18 December 2001, UN Doc E/CN.4/2002/74/Add.1, para 36).

100 Yildiz and Muller, op. cit., fn 1, p 106.

101 Yildiz, op. cit., fn 15, p 2.

102 Marcus, op. cit., fn 82, p 50.

103 Marcus, op. cit., fn 82.

104 A Kahraman, *Uprising, Suppression, Retribution: The Kurdish Struggle in Turkey in the Twentieth Century* (London: Garod Books Ltd, 2007), p 245.

105 McDowall, op. cit., fn 36, p 423.

106 The amendment (# 3175) to Article 74 of the Law of Temporary Village Guards, enacted in 1924, was passed on 26 March 1985. A civilian militia had first been established under this law at the dawn of the Turkish republic, but had been repealed in the 1960s. Marcus, op. cit., fn 82, p 98.

107 KHRP, op. cit., fn 75, p 91.

108 The 14 provinces were Bingol, Hakkari, Tunceli, Bitlis, Van, Mus, Elazig, Adiyaman, Agri, Diyarbakir, Batman, Siirt, Mardin and Sirnak. KHRP, 'The Lifting of State of Emergency Rule: A Democratic Future for the Kurds?' (London: KHRP, November 2002), p 6.

109 Chapter II of the 1982 Constitution, Articles 119–22 empower Parliament to introduce a state of emergency where serious indications of widespread acts of violence aimed at the destruction of the free democratic order or serious deterioration of the public order existed.

110 HRW Briefing Paper, *Turkey and War in Iraq: Avoiding Past Patterns of Violation* (New York, NY: HRW, March 2003), p 3.

111 *Akdivar and others v Turkey*, Judgment of 16 September 1996; *Menteş v Turkey*, Judgment of 28 November 1997; *Selçuk v Turkey*, Judgment of 24 April 1998; *Asker v Turkey*, Judgment of 24 April 1998; *Bilgin v Turkey*, Judgment of 17 July 2001; *Dulas v Turkey*, Judgment of 30 January 2001; *Orhan v Turkey*, Judgment of 18 June 2002; *Akdeniz and others v Turkey*, Judgment of 31 May 2001; *Kurt v Turkey*, Judgment of 25 May 1998; *Çakıcı v Turkey*, Judgment of 8 July 1999; *Ertak v Turkey*, Judgment of 9 May 2000; *Timurtaş v Turkey*, Judgment of 13 June 2000.

112 That the commission of human rights abuses occurred during these state security operations has recently been attested to by the European Court of Human Rights in cases brought by the London-based KHRP, including *Yöler v Turkey*, Application No 26973/95 and *İpek v Turkey*, Application No 25760/94.

113 K Yildiz and J McDermott (KHRP and Bar Human Rights Committee), *Torture in Turkey* (London: KHRP, January 2004), p 28.

114 N Gur, 'Forced Displacement and Destruction of Human Settlements in Turkey', United Nations HABITAT Conference, June 2001.

115 KHRP, op. cit., fn 75, p 25.

116 See *The Independent*, 24 and 31 January and 6 June 1989.

117 See above, fn 20.

118 After preliminary excavations of graves in Şırnak in which human remains were found Nuşirevan Elçi, the chairman of the Şırnak Bar Association, stated his hope that the remains of up to 200 missing people might be found with further investigation of similar sites. *Today's Zaman*, 'New excavations start at death wells of Ergenekon', 17 March 2009, available at <http://www.todayszaman.com/tz-web/news-169804-new-excavations-start-at-death-wells-of-ergenekon.html>.

119 McDowall, op. cit., fn 36, p 427.

120 McDowall, op. cit., fn 36, p 429.

121 In August 1992, the government reported that the PKK had attacked Şırnak in large numbers and thus, the government military were forced to wage random house raids to rout out the PKK. HRW report, *Kurds of Turkey: Killings, Disappearances and Torture* (New York, NY: HRW, March 1993), p 7.

122 HRW, op. cit., fn 121, p 6.

123 HRW, op. cit., fn 121, p 17.

124 For example, in *Akdivar and others v Turkey*, Application No 21893\93, and *Azize Mentes and others v Turkey*, Application No 23186/94.

125 Yildiz and Muller, op. cit., fn 1, p 155.

126 Marcus, op. cit., fn 82, p 214.

127 *Akdeniz and others v Turkey*, Application No 23954/94, Judgment of 31 May 2001.

128 *Orhan v Turkey*, Application No 25656/94, Judgment of 18 June 2002.

129 *Orhan v Turkey*, ibid, para 298.

130 Joost Jongerden, *Settlement Wars*, PhD thesis on file with author, p 46.

131 *Orhan v Turkey*, above, fn 128, para 224.

132 *Orhan v Turkey*, above, fn 128, para 276.

133 HRW, op. cit., fn 110, p 10.

134 For example, see *Tanis and Others v Turkey*, Application No 65899/01.

135 See, for example, *Kurt v Turkey*, Application No 24276/94, Judgment of 25 May 1998, (1998) 27 EHRR 373; *Çakıcı v Turkey*, Application No 23657/94, [1999] ECHR 43; *Ertak v Turkey*, Application No 20764/92, Judgment of 9 May 2000, *Reports of Judgments and Decisions* 2000-V; *Timurtaş v Turkey*, Application No 23531/94, Judgment of 13 June 2000, *Reports of Judgments and Decisions* 2000-VI; and *Taş v Turkey*, Application No 24396/94, Judgment of 14 November 2000.

136 KHRP, op. cit., fn 75, p 92, Internal Displacement Monitoring Centre, *Village guards are a key obstacle to safe returns* (2005), available at <http://www.internal-displacement.org/idmc/website/countries.nsf>.

137 *Mentes and others v Turkey*, Application No 58/1996/677/867, Judgment of 28 November 1997; *Akdivar and others v Turkey*, Application No 21893/93, Judgment of 16 September 1996; *Selçuk and Asker v Turkey*, Application Nos 23184/94 and 23185/94, Judgment of 24 April 1998.

138 *Mentes and others v Turkey*, ibid, para 76. HRW report, 'Turkey: Human Rights and the European Union Accession Partnership', chapter entitled 'Contributing to Stability in the Southeast' (New York, NY: HRW, 30 September 2000).

139 Yildiz and Muller, op. cit., fn 1, p 93.

140 Application PKK and KNK v Council of the European Union. Case C-229/05P *PKK and KNK v Council* [2007] ECR I-439 (judgment of 18 January 2007).

141 Manes, op. cit., fn 82, p 182.

142 In a statement made on 19 December 2000, Prime Minister Bülent Ecevit defended the operation, stating: 'All our security forces are performing their duties in harmony and patience. They do whatever the can to ensure that lives are saved without killing anyone. For this reason, it may take some time in certain prisons, especially in Bayrampaşa and Umraniye, since the problem is dealt with as peacefully as possible, without resorting to violence.' See, KHRP, 'The F-type Prison Crisis and the Repression of Human Rights Defenders in Turkey: Observer Mission Report' (London: KHRP, October 2001), p 16.

143 KHRP, ibid, p 17.

144 Special Rapporteur on extrajudicial, summary or arbitrary executions, op. cit., fn 99, para 54.

145 Marcus, op. cit., fn 82, p 288.

146 PKK becomes KADEK, 15 April 2002, see <http://www.kurdistan.org/Current-Updates/kadek.html>.

147 LE Cline, 'From Öcalan to Al Qaida: The Continuing Terrorist Threat in Turkey', (2004) 27 *Studies in Conflict & Terrorism* 321, p 327.

148 <http://www.ihd.org.tr/eindex.html>.

149 'Bomb in Istanbul kills 4 ahead of NATO summit', *International Herald Tribune*, 25 June 2004; 'Freedom Calls', The Turkish police blamed PKK for two bomb attacks in Istanbul's tourist districts and further gas plant bombing on 10 August 2004, which together killed two and injured 11; PKK denied involvement; in separate incidents violence in southeast Turkey claimed 14 lives: see *The Economist*, 10 June 2004; BBC, 'Fatal blast rocks Turkish resort', 23 August 2004; Reuters AlertNet, 'Separate blasts in Turkey wound 11 people', 29 August 2004. Troops killed 11 PKK southeast Turkey end August 2004 in biggest offensive against PKK for 5 years; further incidents killed approximately five security personnel and four rebels: see AFP, 'Turkish Kurd rebels call for unity after losing support', 21 September 2004.

150 Reuters AlertNet, 'PKK says open to bilateral truce with Turkey', 25 August 2004.

151 October 2004 sporadic clashes in Tunceli, Diyarbakir and Bingol provinces killed 12: see Reuters AlertNet, 'Two Turkish soldiers killed in separatist violence', 24 October 2004; CNN, 'EU Commission back Turkey talks', 6 October 2004.

152 PKK were blamed for a landmine that hit a military convoy in Sirnark province, killing a civilian; two PKK members killed by security forces in Batman province in two separate incidents on 19 November 2004: see Reuters AlertNet, 'Women killed, 10 hurt by mine in southeast Turkey', 19 November 2004.

153 December 2004 clashes occurred in Hatay province: see Reuters AlertNet, 'Kurdish rebel killed in clash in southeast Turkey', 11 December 2004; *The Economist*, 'A date with Turkey', 17 December 2004.

154 'Five Kurdish rebels killed in southeast Turkey', Reuters AlertNet, 20 January 2005. Turkish security operation in southeast near Pervari town killed 21 PKK; further operation near Diyarbakir resulted in one death: see AlertNet, 'Rebel Kurd group claims bloody blast at Turk resort', 1 May 2005; BBC, 'Turkey kills 21 Kurdish fighters', 15 April 2005.

155 'Turkey beefs up forces for Kurdish rebels', *The Washington Post*, 20 May 2005.
156 Alertnet, 'Turkish police, Kurds clash on Öcalan anniversary', 15 February 2005; 'The coming clash over Kirkuk', *International Herald Tribune*, 10 February 2005.
157 PKK kidnapped mayor of Yayladere, eastern Turkey on 28 July 2005; three Turkish soldiers, 33 PKK killed in clashes near Iraqi border; two police killed by car bomb on 29 July 2005: see *International Herald Tribune* (NYT), 'Turkey grows impatient with Europe', 11 June 2005.
158 'Turkey, Kurdish rebels exchange threats', AFP, 20 July 2005; 'Rebel Kurds may have new enemy', *International Herald Tribune*, 20 July 2005; 'Kurds "deny" Turkey resort bomb', BBC, 17 July 2005.
159 Six soldiers and five PKK were killed; further clashes killed four in Sirnak: see *Washington Times*, 'Turkey's Western ways', 28 October 2005; BBC, 'Turkey sentences Armenian writer', 7 October 2005.
160 Army killed seven PKK: see 'Dozens wounded in Istanbul blast', ISN, 14 February 2006.
161 Suspected PKK attacks killed at least 10 including three in suicide bombing outside governor's office in Van 9 March 2006: see 'Turkish police break up widening Kurdish rioting', *International Herald Tribune*, 31 March 2006; 'Turkish military rejects call to probe general', AlertNet, 20 March 2006.
162 'Turkish police break up widening Kurdish rioting', *International Herald Tribune*, 31 March 2006; 'Turkish military rejects call to probe general', AlertNet, 20 March 2006.
163 BBC, 'Turkish army rejects rebel truce', 2 October 2006.
164 'Three Kurdish rebels killed in Turkey-officials', AlertNet, 12 October 2006.
165 AlertNet, 'Down but not out, Turk generals warily eye polls', 13 December 2006.
166 Yildiz and Muller, op. cit., fn 1, p 94.
167 KHRP, op. cit., fn 53, p 14.
168 Southeast clashes continued with at least five soldiers and 15 militants reportedly killed: see AP, 'Clash in southeast Turkey leaves 10 Kurdish rebels, 2 soldiers dead', 25 August 2007.
169 Clashes between armed forces and PKK continued through to September, including military operation in Sirnak, Hakkari and Siirt provinces in which 11 PKK militants reported dead 14–21 September and suicide attack on Tunceli gendarmerie station which killed one soldier 25 September; PKK minibus attack in Sirnak left 12 dead 29 September; visiting Iraqi Interior Minister Bolani signed security agreement 28 September; provisions allowing Turkish troop cross-border 'hot pursuit' dropped after sides unable to agree conditions: see 'Turkey, Iraq sign terrorism deal amid border row', Reuters, 28 September 2007; 'Turkey PM wants headscarf ban eased', Al Jazeera, 19 September 2007.
170 <http://news.bbc.co.uk/1/hi/world/europe/7500282.stm>.
171 <http://www.institutkurde.org/en/info/latest/berlin-demands-pkk-release-of-german-hostages-1419.html#>.
172 <http://www.spiegel.de/international/world/0,1518,566930,00.html>.
173 *Today's Zaman*, '2008 not a year of progress in human rights', 28 December 2008, available at <http://www.todayszaman.com/tz-web/news-162503-2008-not-a-year-of-progress-in-human-rights.html>. See also <http://www.hurriyet.com.tr/english/domestic/10164663.asp>.
174 HRW, op. cit., fn 110, p 1.
175 Yildiz and Muller, op. cit., fn 1, p 110.
176 Yildiz, op. cit., fn 5, p 67.
177 KHRP, Fact Finding Mission Report 'The Civilian toll of Cross Border Operations in Iraq' (London: KHRP, August 2009), p 13.
178 KHRP, ibid, p 13. The 'hot-pursuit' agreement was signed in 1984, and despite it remaining officially unrenewed and a 'legally grey area' since the late 1980s, is invoked by Turkey on a regular basis.

179 Yildiz and Muller, op. cit., fn 1, p 109.
180 HRW, op. cit., fn 110, p 4.
181 KHRP, op. cit., fn 177, p 13.
182 Yildiz and Muller, op. cit., fn 1, p 109.
183 Yildiz and Muller, op. cit., fn 1, p 109.
184 HRW, *Weapons Transfers* (New York, NY: HRW, 1993), Case 22, p 68; (1994), Case 13, p 53.
185 HRW, ibid (1993), Case 22, pp 68–9.
186 HRW, ibid (1994), Case 13, pp 53–4.
187 Yildiz and Muller, op. cit., fn 1, p 109.
188 Yildiz and Muller, op. cit., fn 1, p 109.
189 Yildiz and Muller, op. cit., fn 1, p 109.
190 *Issa and Others v Turkey*, Application No 31821/96, Judgment of 16 November 2004. The European Court of Human Rights found that Turkish troops had been carrying out cross-border military operations 'aimed at pursuing and eliminating terrorists who were seeking shelter in northern Iraq'.
191 Yildiz and Muller, op. cit., fn 1, p 109.
192 Yildiz and Muller, op. cit., fn 1, p 109.
193 BBC News, 10 January 2001, cited in Armed Conflict Report 'Iraq – Kurds'.
194 Radio Free Europe/Radio Liberty, 'Turkish Incursion', 22 December 2000.
195 HRW, op. cit., fn 110, p 4.
196 HRW, op. cit., fn 110, p 4.
197 HRW, op. cit., fn 110, p 4.
198 KHRP, op. cit., fn 177, p 13.
199 Associated Press, 'Turkey bolsters forces along Iraqi border: U.S. cautions against action outside of coalition', 7 March 2003.
200 Speech by Prime Minister Bulent Ecevit to the US Chamber of Commerce, Washington DC, 15 January 2002.
201 'Turkey denies troops entered Iraq but tough on Kurds', AlertNet, 26 April 2006; 'Resurfacing in Turkey: Deadly old hatreds', *International Herald Tribune*, 6 April 2006.
202 At least 14 soldiers, two police, one pro-government village guard and eight PKK rebels killed in fighting in southeast: see 'Security hawk seen taking over Turkish military', AlertNet, 31 July 2006; 'Turkey signals it's prepared to enter Iraq', AP, 18 July 2006.
203 'Turkey sharpens response to upsurge in Kurd violence', *Christian Science Monitor*, 29 August 2006.
204 'Turk PM asserts right to intervene in Iraq, raps US', AlertNet, 12 January 2007.
205 Casualties in clashes between armed forces and PKK continued, including seven soldiers in mine explosion 24 May 2007 and 10 PKK on 29 May 2007: see 'Turkey-Iraq border tension grows', BBC, 30 May 2007; 'Turkey asks US not to violate its airspace again', AlertNet, 29 May 2007.
206 'Turkish general says can hit Kurd rebels in Iraq', AlertNet, 10 March 2007; 'Kurd jailed for honouring Öcalan', BBC, 6 March 2007.
207 'The next battle', *The Economist*, 30 August 2007; 'Clash in southeast Turkey leaves 10 Kurdish rebels, 2 soldiers dead', AP, 25 August 2007.
208 'Turkey Authorizes Iraq Incursion; Parliament Permits Cross-Border Attacks on Kurdish Rebels', *The Washington Post*, 18 October 2007.
209 KHRP News release, 'KHRP Urges Calm in Wake of South-East Turkey Violence', 9 October 2008.
210 *The Guardian*, 'Families seek redress for Turkish incursions', 9 June 2008. KHRP has filed an application against Turkey before the European Court of Human Rights, claiming that its aerial strikes against the PKK in northern Iraq caused civilian deaths and injuries, and damage to livelihood, farmland and property.
211 KHRP, op. cit., fn 177, p 17.

212 UN Assistance Mission for Iraq, Human Rights Report: 1 July – 31 December 2007 (15 March 2007), p 20.
213 'Turkish army fires on PKK in Iraq', BBC, 1 December 2007; 'Turkey charges troops captured by rebels with neglecting their duty', AP, 12 November 2007.
214 US denies backing Turkey PKK raid, BBC News, 17 December 2007.
215 'Turkey again hits Kurdish hide-outs in Iraq', *International Herald Tribune*, 26 December 2007; 'For Turkey and U.S., delicate cooperation issue in combating Kurds', *International Herald Tribune*, 20 December 2007.
216 Turkish soldiers cross into Iraq, BBC News, 18 December 2007 and Turkey in new Iraq air strikes, BBC News, 23 December 2007.
217 'Turkey again bombs Kurdish rebels in Iraq', AP, 15 January 2008.
218 EC, 8 November 2006; BBC, 8 June 2007.
219 'Turkey warns of plans to invade northern Iraq', *The Guardian*, 30 June 2007.
220 KHRP News release, 'Turkish military forces cross Iraqi border resulting in heavy clashes and casualties', 25 February 2008.
221 *New York Times*, 'After 8 days, Turkey pulls its troops out of Iraq', 1 March 2008; *The Economist*, 'Trouble for Turkey?', 13 February 2008.
222 Turkey withdraws from Northern Iraq, PKK claims victory, *The Times* (London), 1 March 2008, available at <http://timesonline.co.uk>.
223 Turkey launches raids on N Iraq, BBC News, 26 April 2008, available at <http://news.bbc.co.uk/1/hi/world/europe/7368541.stm>.
224 Turkish planes bomb rebel Kurds, BBC News, 2 May 2008, available at <http://news.bbc.co.uk/1/hi/world/europe/7378927.stm>.
225 Iran shells Iraqi Kurd border Villages, BBC News, 19 March 2008. Iranian forces carried out artillery attack on Shinawa, Maradu, Sura Gula and Basta villages.
226 Top Turkish General Says Turkey, Iran Coordinating on Strikes Against Kurds, 5 June 2008, available at <http://www.globalsecurity.org/wmd/library/news/iraq/2008/06/iraq-080605-voa03.htm>.
227 KHRP, op. cit., fn 177, p 13.
228 Armed Conflict Reports, Turkey 2009, available at <http://www.ploughshares.ca/libraries/ACRText/ACR-Turkey2.htm>.
229 KHRP, op. cit., fn 177, p 11. In 2008, KHRP provided support for 76 new applicants to the European Court of Human Rights who have suffered as a direct result of Turkish operations in Iraq. Over the past year, air strikes and ground assaults by Turkish forces in northern Iraq have had a devastating impact, killing and injuring civilians and destroying property.

Chapter 2

1 Protocol I Additional to the Geneva Conventions of 12 August 1949, and relating to the Protection of Victims of International Armed Conflicts, 1125 UNTS 3, 8 June 1977.
2 See JM Henckaerts and L Doswald-Beck, *Customary International Humanitarian Law, Volume 1: Rules* (Cambridge: Cambridge University Press, 2005) where the majority of the customary rules of humanitarian law are argued to be the same for international and internal armed conflict – this is discussed in detail in Chapter 3.
3 Geneva Conventions I–IV of 1949, Common Article 3, 75 UNTS 31, 85, 135 and 287.
4 These treaty regimes include: 1907 Regulations Respecting the Laws and Customs of War on Land, to the 1907 Convention (IV) Respecting the Laws and Customs of War on Land, The Hague, 18 October 1907, (1910) UKTS 9; the Geneva Conventions of 1949, ibid; and 1977 Protocol Additional to the Geneva Conventions of 12 August 1949, and Relating to the Protection of Victims of International Armed Conflicts, Geneva, 8 June 1977, 1125 UNTS 3; 1977 Protocol Additional to the Geneva Conventions of 12 August 1949, and Relating to the Protection of Victims of

Non-International Armed Conflicts, Geneva, 8 June 1977, 1125 UNTS 609; and various other Weapons and Environmental Conventions.

5 See Article 51 and Chapter VII of the United Nations Charter, 26 June 1945, (1945) TS 993.

6 L Moir, *The Law of Internal Armed Conflict* (Cambridge: Cambridge University Press, 2002), p 1.

7 Common Article 3, op. cit., fn 3.

8 J Peijić, 'Status of armed conflicts', in E Wilmshurst and S Breau (eds), *Perspectives on the ICRC Study on Customary International Law* (Cambridge: Cambridge University Press, 2007), p 78.

9 Peijić, ibid, p 79 and Moir, op. cit., fn 6, pp 127–32 for his discussion on Chechnya and the Decision of the Constitutional Court of the Russian Federation on the constitutionality of the Presidential Decree No 2137 of 30 November 1994.

10 D Schindler, 'The Different Types of Armed Conflicts According to the Geneva Conventions and Protocols', (1979) 163(ii) *Recueil des cours* 117, in which he summarises the legal literature on the threshold of armed conflict.

11 Peijić, 'Status of armed conflicts', op. cit., fn 8, pp 85–86 and Moir, op. cit., fn 6, p 36.

12 Peijić, 'Status of armed conflicts', op. cit., fn 8, p 86.

13 Schindler, op. cit., fn 10, p 147.

14 ICTY, Appeals Chamber, *Prosecutor v Tadić*, Decision on the Defence Motion for Interlocutory Appeal on Jurisdiction, IT-94-1-A, 2 October 1995, para 70.

15 1977 Protocol Additional to the Geneva Conventions of 12 August 1949, and Relating to the Protection of Victims of Non-International Armed Conflicts, Geneva, 8 June 1977, 1125 UNTS 609.

16 Moir, op. cit., fn 6, pp 91–96 for a history of the negotiation of this Protocol.

17 *Military and Paramilitary Activities in and against Nicaragua (Nicaragua v USA)*, Merits, (1986) ICJ Rep 4, paras 118–20.

18 *Juan Carlos Abella v Argentina*, Case 11.137, Report N 55/97, Inter-Am CHR, OEA/Ser.L/V/II.95 Doc 7 rev at 271 – 18 November 1997.

19 Statute of the International Criminal Court, 2187 UNTS 90.

20 Peijić, 'Status of armed conflicts', op. cit., fn 8, p 89.

21 CNN, 'Turkey launches major Iraq incursion', 22 February 2008 (an estimated 10,000 Turkish troops were involved), available at <http://www.cnn.com> (accessed 4 August 2008).

22 Kurdistan Workers Party (PKK) Statement to the United Nations Geneva, 24 January 1995.

23 F Hampson, 'Other Areas of Customary law in relation to the Study', Wilmshurst and Breau, op. cit., fn 8, p 62.

24 *Military and Paramilitary Activities in and against Nicaragua (Nicaragua v United States of America)* Merits, Judgment of 27 June 1986, [1986] *ICJ Reports* 14.

25 MN Schmitt, CHB Garraway and Y Dinstein, 'The Manual on the Law of Non-International Armed Conflict With Commentary', in Yoram Dinstein and Fania Domb (eds), *Israel Yearbook of Human Rights (Special Supplement)*, Volume 36 (Dordrecht: Martinus Nijhoff, 2006).

26 International Committee of the Red Cross Opinion Paper March 2008, available at <http://www.icrc.org/web/eng/siteeng0.nsf/htmlall/armed-conflict-article-170308/$file/Opinion-paper-armed-conflict.pdf> (accessed 4 August 2008).

27 Statute of the International Court of Justice, 26 June 1945, (1945) TS 993, Article 38 of the Statute states:

1. The Court, whose function is to decide in accordance with international law such disputes as are submitted to it, shall apply:

   a. international conventions, whether general or particular, establishing rules expressly recognized by the contesting states;

b. international custom, as evidence of a general practice accepted as law;
c. the general principles of law recognized by civilized nations;
d. subject to the provisions of Article 59, judicial decisions and the teachings of the most highly qualified publicists of the various nations, as subsidiary means for the determination of rules of law.

28 Peijić, 'Status of armed conflicts', op. cit., fn 8, p 78.
29 ICRC, op. cit., fn 26.
30 Geneva Conventions I–IV of 1949, Common Article 3, op. cit., fn 3.
31 J. Pictet, *Commentary on the Geneva Convention for the Amelioration of the Condition of the Wounded and Sick in Armed Forces in the Field* (Geneva: International Committee of the Red Cross, 1952), p 32.
32 Schindler, op. cit., fn 10, p 131.
33 HP Gasser, 'International Humanitarian Law: an Introduction', in H Haug (ed), *Humanity for All: the International Red Cross and Red Crescent Movement* (Berne: Paul Haupt Publishers, 1993), pp 510–11.
34 *Nicaragua v United States of America*, above, fn 24, para 115.
35 *Prosecutor v Tadić*, Appeals Chamber Judgment, 15 July 1999, IT-94-1-A.
36 *Prosecutor v Tadić*, Decision on Defence Motion for Interlocutory Appeal on Jurisdiction, Appeals Chamber, 2 October 1995, IT-94-AR72 and Appeals Chamber Judgment, 15 July 1999, IT-94-1-A.
37 *Prosecutor v Tadić*, Appeals Chamber Judgment, 15 July 1999, IT-94-1-A, para 131.
38 *Prosecutor v Tadić*, ibid, para 162.
39 *Prosecutor v Thomas Lubanga Dyilo*, Decision on the confirmation of charges, 29 January 2007, No ICC-01/04-01/06, International Criminal Court.
40 *Prosecutor v Germain Katanga and Mathieu Ngudjolo Chui*, Decision on the Confirmation of Charges, 26 September 2008, No ICC-01/04-01/07, International Criminal Court.
41 *Prosecutor v Germain Katanga and Mathieu Ngudjolo Chui*, ibid, paras 239–40.
42 *Prosecutor v Thomas Lubanga Dyilo*, above, fn 39, para 209.
43 *Armed Activities on the Territory of the Congo (Democratic Republic of the Congo v Uganda)*, Judgment of 19 December 2005, [2005] ICJ Rep 345.
44 Additional Protocol I, art 1, para 4: 'armed conflicts in which peoples are fighting against colonial domination and alien occupation and against racist regimes in the exercise of their right of self determination, as enshrined in the Charter of the United Nations and the Declaration on Principles of International Law concerning Friendly Relations and Co-operation among States in accordance with the Charter of the United Nations'.
45 Declaration on Principles of International Law, Friendly Relations and Co-Operation Among States in Accordance with the Charter of the United Nations, General Assembly Resolution 2625 (XXV), 1970.
46 Definition of Aggression, United Nations General Assembly Resolution 3314 (XXIX) 1974.
47 BBC Special Report, 'When is a Criminal a Political Prisoner?', 9 January 1998, available at <http://news.bbc.co.uk/1/hi/special_report/46095.stm> (accessed 4 August 2008).
48 YM Lootsteen, 'The Concept of Belligerency in International Law', (2000) 166 *Military Law Review* 109, p 133.
49 V Nanda, 'Self-Determination under International Law: Validity of Claims to Secede', (1981) 13 Case W Res J Int'l L 257, pp 268–70, and see the lengthy dicussion in Chapter 8.
50 J Stewart, 'Towards a single definition of armed conflict in international humanitarian law: A critique of internationalized armed conflict', (2003) 85 *International Review of the Red Cross* 315.
51 Schmitt, Garraway and Dinstein, op. cit., fn 25.

52 *Nicaragua v United States of America*, above, fn 24.
53 Stewart, op. cit., fn 50, p 334.
54 See the discussion of the evolution of the Yugoslav conflict from internal to international in C. Greenwood, 'International Humanitarian Law and the Tadic Case', (1996) 7 *European Journal of International Law* 265.
55 Moir, op. cit., fn 6, p 5, and see A. Cullen, 'Key Development Affecting the Scope of Internal Armed Conflict in International Humanitarian Law', (2005) 183 *Military Law Review* 66, pp 69–78.
56 Moir, op. cit., fn 6, pp 4–5.
57 Cullen, op. cit., fn 55, p 74 discussing *Prosecutor v Tadić*, above, fn 14, para 96.
58 Lootsteen, op. cit., fn 48, p 109.
59 Lootsteen, op. cit., fn 48, see also Hersch Lauterpacht, *Recognition in International Law* (Cambridge: Cambridge University Press, 1947), p 176.
60 Lootsteen, op. cit., fn 48, p 110.
61 Lootsteen, op. cit., fn 48, p 110.
62 Moir, op. cit., fn 6, pp 12–13.
63 Moir, op. cit., fn 6, p 12.
64 Moir, op. cit., fn 6, p 12.
65 Lootsteen, op. cit., fn 48, p 114.
66 General Orders No 100: Instructions for the Government of Armies of the United States in the Field, Prepared by Francis Lieber, promulgated as General Orders No 100 by President Lincoln, 24 April 1863.
67 Lootsteen, op. cit., fn 48, pp 115–16.
68 Cullen, op. cit., fn 55, p 78.
69 Lootsteen, op. cit., fn 48, pp 117–20.
70 Lootsteen, op. cit., fn 48, p 120.
71 Lootsteen, op. cit., fn 48, p 122.
72 Lootsteen, op. cit., fn 48, p 122.
73 Lootsteen, op. cit., fn 48, p 125.
74 Lootsteen, op. cit., fn 48, p 125.
75 J Pictet, *Commentary III Geneva Convention Relative to the Treatment of Prisoners of War* (Geneva: International Committee of the Red Cross, 1960), p 38.
76 Pictet, ibid, p 129.
77 These criteria can be argued to be customary and the fourth condition originates in the Geneva Conventions of 1949, for example Article 13 of Geneva Convention I for the Amelioration of the Condition of the Wounded and Sick in Armed Forces in the Field, 75 UNTS 31 gives criteria for the status of combatant:

(a) That of being commanded by a person responsible for his subordinates;
(b) That of having a fixed distinctive sign recognizable at a distance;
(c) That of carrying arms openly;
(d) That of conducting their operations in accordance with the laws and customs of war.

78 Lootsteen, op. cit., fn 48, p 126.
79 Lootsteen, op. cit., fn 48.
80 Lootsteen, op. cit., fn 48, p 137.
81 Geneva Convention III Relative to the Treatment of Prisoners of War, 75 UNTS 135.
82 Hague Convention II on the Laws and Customs of War on Land, 29 July 1899, available at <http://www.icrc.org>.
83 These are combatants who have ceased being part of the conflict due to surrender, illness or being wounded in combat.
84 Draft Rules of Aerial Warfare, The Hague, February 1923.

85 Geneva Convention IV Relative to the Protection of Civilian Persons in Time of War, 12 August 1949, 75 UNTS 287, Article 4.

86 There is a controversy concerning so called 'dual use targets', those targets which have economic benefits and for discussion of this issue see S. Breau, *Humanitarian Intervention: The United Nations and Collective Responsibility* (London: Cameron May, 2005), Chapter 8, and Articles 51, 52 and 57 of Additional Protocol I of 1977 to the Geneva Convention of 1949.

87 See Henckaerts and Doswald-Beck, op. cit., fn 2, in which many of the rules of international humanitarian law set out in Additional Protocol I are argued to be customary, and the Geneva Protocol for the Prohibition on the Use in War of Asphyxiating, Poisonous or Other Gases and of Bacteriological Methods of Warfare, 17 June 1925, (1925) 94 LNTS 65 (a convention set up as a reaction to the use of gas during the First World War) is clearly customary but Turkey is also a party to that convention.

88 Hague Convention for the Protection of Cultural Property in the Event of an Armed Conflict, 14 May 1954, 249 UNTS 240.

89 1977 United Nations Convention on the Prohibition of Military or Any Other Hostile Use of Environmental Modification Techniques (ENMOD), New York, 18 May 1977, 1108 UNTS 151.

90 Geneva Protocol for the Prohibition on the Use in War of Asphyxiating, Poisonous or Other Gases, and of Bacteriological Methods of Warfare, above, fn 87.

91 For a full discussion of this issue see R. Prevost, *International Human Rights and Humanitarian Law* (Cambridge: Cambridge University Press, 2002).

92 European Convention for the Protection of Human Rights and Fundamental Freedoms, 4 November 1950, 213 UNTS 222, which set up the European Court of Human Rights.

93 International Covenant on Civil and Political Rights, 16 December 1966, 999 UNTS 171.

94 European Convention for the Protection of Human Rights and Fundamental Freedoms, above, fn 92.

95 *Legality of the threat or use of nuclear weapons advisory opinion*, Advisory Opinion of 8 July 1996, [1996] *ICJ Reports* 66, para 25.

96 *Legality of the threat or use of nuclear weapons advisory opinion*, ibid.

97 *Legal consequences of the construction of a wall in the Occupied Palestinian Territory*, ICJ Advisory Opinion of 9 July 2004, [2004] *ICJ Reports* 136, para 106.

98 For criticism of how human rights courts deal with armed conflict, particularly the European Court of Human Rights see Hampson, 'Fundamental Guarantees', in Wilmshurst and Breau, op. cit., fn 8, pp 282–301.

Chapter 3

1 L Moir, *The Law of Internal Armed Conflict* (Cambridge: Cambridge University Press, 2002), pp 91–96.

2 JM Henckaerts and L Doswald-Beck, *Customary International Humanitarian Law, Volume 1: Rules* (Cambridge: Cambridge University Press, 2005), and MN Schmitt, CHB Garraway and Y Dinstein, *The Manual on the Law of Non-International Armed Conflict with Commentary* (The Hague: Brill, 2007).

3 M Ghandi, 'Common Article 3 of the Geneva Conventions, 1949 In the Era of International Criminal Tribunals', [2001] *ISIL Year Book of International Humanitarian and Refugee Law* 11.

4 *Military and Paramilitary Activities in and against Nicaragua (Nicaragua v United States of America)* Merits, Judgment of 27 June 1986, [1986] *ICJ Reports* 14, para 144.

5 A Cullen, 'Key Development Affecting the Scope of Internal Armed Conflict in International Humanitarian Law', (2005) 183 *Military Law Review* 66, p 81, and

Prosecutor v Tadić, Decision on the Defence Motion for Interlocutory Appeal on Jurisdiction, 2 October 1995, IT-94-1-AR72, para 102.

6 See the warrant of arrest against Kony the Commander of Chief of the Lord's Resistance Army in Uganda, available at <http://www.icc-cpi.int/iccdocs/doc/doc97185.PDF> (accessed 21 September 2009).

7 *Prosecutor v Akayesu*, Judgment of Trial Chamber, 2 September 1998, ICTR-96-4-T, para 608.

8 Geneva Convention IV Relative to the Protection of Civilian Persons in Time of War, 12 August 1949, (1949) 75 UNTS 287.

9 Moir, op. cit., fn 1, Chapter 1 for history of the drafting of the article, and International Committee of the Red Cross website commentary to the 3rd Geneva Convention, available at <http://www.icrc.org/ihl.nsf/1a13044f3bbb5b8ec12563fb0066f226/466097d7a301f8c4c12563cd00424e2b!OpenDocument> (accessed 5 August 2008).

10 Geneva Convention for the Amelioration of the Condition of the Wounded and Sick in Armies of the Field, 6 July 1906, (1906) 11 LNTS 440. Moir, op. cit., fn 1, p 22.

11 Moir, op. cit., fn 1.

12 Resolution XIV of the 16th International Red Cross Conference, London 1938.

13 J. Pictet, *Commentary IV Geneva Convention Relative to the Protection of Civilian Persons in Time of War* (Geneva: International Committee of the Red Cross, 1958), p 28.

14 Moir, op. cit., fn 1, pp 23–24, and Pictet, ibid, pp 28–29.

15 Pictet, op. cit., fn 13, p 30.

16 Pictet, op. cit., fn 13.

17 Geneva Conventions I–IV of 1949, (1949) 75 UNTS 31, 85, 135 and 287.

18 Pictet, op. cit., fn 13, p 34.

19 Pictet, op. cit., fn 13.

20 Moir, op. cit., fn 1, p 52.

21 Pictet, op. cit., fn 13, p 37.

22 1968 Vienna Convention on the Law of Treaties, (1968) 1155 UNTS 331.

23 Moir, op. cit., fn 1, p 53, and note the PKK consent to be bound filed with the United Nations.

24 Moir, op. cit., fn 1, pp 53–54.

25 Articles of State Responsibility, Article 11 as incorporated in General Assembly Resolutions 56/83, 28 January 2002, and see J. Crawford, *The International Law Commission's Articles on State Responsibility: Introduction, Text and Commentaries* (Cambridge: Cambridge University Press, 2002), each article includes extensive commentary, see also the various reports of the International Law Commission on the Draft Articles.

26 L Oppenheim, *International Law, Volume II* (London: Longmans, Green & Co, 1906), p 211, fn 3.

27 Moir, op. cit., fn 1, pp 56–58.

28 *International Military Tribunal (Nuremberg) Judgement and Sentences*, reprinted in (1947) 41 AJIL 172.

29 Moir, op. cit., fn 1, p 58 and MN Schmitt, 'Direct Participation in Hostilities and 21st Century Armed Conflict', page proofs supplied by author, and 'The Interpretive Guidance on the Notion of Direct Participation in Hostilities; A Critical Analysis', article supplied by the author, 'Civilians at War: Deconstructing the 21st Century Battlefield', Royal Institute of International Affairs (Chatham House), November 2007, available at <http://www.chathamhouse.org.uk/publications/papers/view/-/id/579/>.

30 Moir, op. cit., fn 1, pp 58–59.

31 Moir, op. cit., fn 1, pp 59–60.

32 For the remainder of the commentary for the wording of Common Article 3 see ICRC website commentary to the 3rd Geneva Convention, above, fn 9; see also Pictet, op. cit., fn 13, and Moir, op. cit., fn 1.

33 Pictet, op. cit., fn 13, p 38.
34 ICRC website commentary to the 3rd Geneva Convention, above, fn 9.
35 Geneva Conventions I–IV of 1949, Common Article 3, (1949) 75 UNTS 31, 85, 135 and 287.
36 International Covenant on Civil and Political Rights 16 December 1966, (1966) 999 UNTS 171, see especially Articles 6, 7, 9 and 10, and European Convention for the Protection of Human Rights and Fundamental Freedoms, 4 November 1950, (1950) 213 UNTS 222, see especially Articles 2, 3, 5 and 6.
37 Moir, op. cit., fn 1, p 61.
38 See the discussion in Part 4 of this chapter.
39 Pictet, op. cit., fn 13, p 39.
40 See particularly *US v List et al* (The Hostages case) (US Military Tribunal) (1948) 13 *Law Reports of Trials of War Criminals* 62.
41 Pictet, op. cit., fn 13, p 40.
42 ICRC website commentary to the 3rd Geneva Convention, above, fn 9.
43 ICRC website commentary to the 3rd Geneva Convention, above, fn 9.
44 ICRC website commentary to the 3rd Geneva Convention, above, fn 9.
45 Pictet, op. cit., fn 13, p 41.
46 ICRC website commentary to the 3rd Geneva Convention, above, fn 9.
47 Pictet, op. cit., fn 13, p 42.
48 ICRC website commentary to the 3rd Geneva Convention, above, fn 9.
49 Pictet, op. cit., fn 13, p 44.
50 Pictet, op. cit., fn 13.
51 Pictet, op. cit., fn 13.
52 Pictet, op. cit., fn 13.
53 T. Farer, 'Humanitarian Law and Armed Conflicts: Towards the Definition of "International Armed Conflict"', (1971) 71 *Columbia Law Review* 37.
54 Moir, op. cit., fn 1, p 189.
55 Statute of the International Criminal Court, 17 July 1998, (1998) 2187 UNTS 90.
56 Henckaerts and Doswald-Beck, op. cit., fn 2, p 568.
57 Henckaerts and Doswald-Beck, op. cit., fn 2, pp 590–91.
58 Amnesty International, *Turkey: No Security Without Human Rights* (London: Amnesty International, 1996), AI Index: EUR/44/84/96, see p 3 where it is reported that since 1980, 400 people had died in police custody as a result of torture, and p 4 where it is alleged there have been over 100 disappearances and a wave of extra-judicial executions claiming hundreds of lives.
59 Amnesty International, ibid, p 14.
60 See the Report on the Committee Against Torture UN Doc A/48/44/Add.1 filed with the General Assembly 15 November 1993 finding that there were 'well-founded indications that torture was practised systematically in Turkey'. See the Report of the European Committee on the Prevention of Torture CPT INF, (2006) 30 on the committee's visit to Turkish detention centres from 7–14 December 2005, available at <http://news.bbc.co.uk/2/hi/middleeast/7382150.stm> (accessed 29 September 2009).
61 The Jandarma are the military forces of law enforcement, also known as security forces in this book.
62 US State Department Country Report on Human Rights Practices in Turkey, March 2009, available at <http://www.state.gov/g/drl/rls/hrrpt/2007/100589.htm> (accessed 24 September 2009).
63 US State Department, ibid.
64 See Kurdish Human Rights Project (KHRP) website and its report on Torture in Turkey, 11 July 2006, and K Yildiz and J McDermot, *Torture in Turkey: The ongoing Practice of Torture and Ill Treatment* (London: KHRP/Bar Human Rights Committee and Human Rights Association, 2004).

65 Amnesty International, op. cit., fn 58, p 3; pp 23 and 24 regarding PKK murders of village guards; and p 25 murders of villagers.

66 Amnesty International, op. cit., fn 58, p 5.

67 Redress Trust, *Not only the State: Torture by Non-State Actors* (London: Redress UK, 2006), available at <http://www.redress.org/publications/Non%20State%20Actors%209% 20 June%20Final.pdf> (accessed 24 September 2009).

68 *Aydin v Turkey*, Application No 57/1996/676/866, Judgment of 25 September 1997, European Court of Human Rights.

69 European Committee for the Prevention of Torture, op. cit., fn 60.

70 Amnesty International, 'Turkey: Justice delayed and denied for victims of sexual violence', 13 February 2003; EUR 44/007/2003, available at <http://asiapacific.amnesty. org/library/pdf/EUR440072003ENGLISH/$File/EUR4400703.pdf> (accessed 29 September 2009), and see Amnesty International, 'Turkey: Torture/Ill Treatment', PUBLIC AI Index: EUR 44/55/00, 20 October 2000, available at <http://asiapacific. amnesty.org/library/Index/ENGEUR440552000?open&of=ENG-TUR> (accessed 29 September 2009).

71 KHRP, 'Trial Observation Report, Turkey's Shame: Sexual Violence without Redress – The Plight of Kurdish Women', December 2003, available at <http:// www.khrp.org/component/option,com_docman/task,doc_view/gid,29/Itemid,47/> (accessed 29 September 2009), and and Yildiz and McDermot, op.cit, fn 64, p 78.

72 BBC News, 'PKK sets German Hostage demands', 10 July 2008, available at <http://news.bbc.co.uk/1/hi/world/europe/7500282.stm> (accessed 24 September 2009), and *The Times* online, 'Turkish soldiers released by PKK ahead of Washington Talks', 4 November 2007, available at <http://www.timesonline.co.uk/tol/news/ world/iraq/article2804007.ece> (accessed 24 September 2009).

73 US State Department Country Report on Human Rights Practices in Turkey, March 2008, available at <http://www.state.gov/g/drl/rls/hrrpt/2007/100589.htm> (accessed 29 September 2009).

74 Amnesty International, op. cit., fn 58, p 3.

75 *Öcalan v Turkey*, Application No 46221/99, Judgment of 12 March 2003, European Court of Human Rights.

76 Amnesty International, op. cit., fn 58, p 3; pp 23 and 24 regarding PKK murders of village guards; and p 25 murders of villagers.

77 Turkey is not a signatory to the Statute of the International Criminal Court, the body exercising supervisory power is the European Court of Human Rights, which is discussed later in this chapter.

78 Henckaerts and Doswald-Beck, op. cit., fn 2.

79 E Wilmshurst and S Breau (eds), *Perspectives on the ICRC Study on Customary International Law* (Cambridge: Cambridge University Press, 2007).

80 Human Rights Watch (HRW), 'Still Critical Prospects in 2005 for Internally Displaced Kurds in Turkey', (2005) March, 17(2)(D) *Human Rights Watch* 5–6, and see Chapter 1.

81 Henckaerts and Doswald-Beck, op. cit., fn 2, pp 3–76, Rules 1–24, and see M Schmitt, 'The Law of Targeting', in Wilmshurst and Breau, op. cit., fn 79, Chapter 6.

82 Henckaerts and Doswald-Beck, op. cit., fn 2, pp 3–76, Rules 1–24, and see Schmitt, ibid, Chapter 6.

83 *Legality of the Threat or Use of Nuclear Weapons*, Advisory Opinion, 8 July 1996, [1996] ICJ Rep 66, para 78. The other principle is 'unnecessary suffering'.

84 Schmitt, op. cit., fn 81.

85 Schmitt, op. cit., fn 81.

86 Professor Michael N Schmitt, George C Marshall European Center for Security Studies, Professor Charles HB Garraway, Royal Institute of International Affairs (Chatham House), Professor Yoram Dinstein, Tel Aviv University – Schmitt, Garraway and Dinstein, op. cit., fn 2.

87 Schmitt, Garraway and Dinstein, op. cit., fn 2, p 8.
88 Trial of the Major War Criminals, 14 November 1945 – 1 October 1946, Nuremberg, 1947, volume I, p 254.
89 *Prosecutor v Tadić*, above, fn 5, para 127.
90 Schmitt, Garraway and Dinstein, op. cit., fn 2, p 10.
91 Y Sandoz (ed), *Commentary on the Additional Protocols of 8 June 1977 to the Geneva Conventions of 12 August 1949* (Geneva: International Committee of the Red Cross, 1987), para 1863.
92 Schmitt, Garraway and Dinstein, op. cit., fn 2, p 11.
93 *Prosecutor v Tadić*, above, fn 5, paras 122 and 127.
94 *Prosecutor v Tadić*, above, fn 5, pp 18–19.
95 *Prosecutor v Tadić*, above, fn 5, p 20.
96 *Prosecutor v Tadić*, above, fn 5, pp 20–21.
97 *Prosecutor v Tadić*, above, fn 5, pp 21–22.
98 ICRC, Commentary to Additional Protocol II to the Geneva Conventions of 1977, available at <http://www.icrc.org/IHL.nsf/COM/475-760019?OpenDocument> (accessed 10 February 2010).
99 Schmitt, Garraway and Dinstein, op. cit., fn 2, p 23.
100 Schmitt, Garraway and Dinstein, op. cit., fn 2, p 24.
101 Schmitt, Garraway and Dinstein, op. cit., fn 2.
102 Schmitt, Garraway and Dinstein, op. cit., fn 2, p 23.
103 Schmitt, Garraway and Dinstein, op. cit., fn 2.
104 Schmitt, Garraway and Dinstein, op. cit., fn 2, p 26 citing *Prosecutor v Tadić*, above, fn 5, paras 111–12, citing UN General Assembly Resolution 2675 (XXV), Basic Principles for the Protection of Civilian Populations in Armed Conflicts, 9 December 1970.
105 Schmitt, Garraway and Dinstein, op. cit., fn 2, pp 26–27. This definition is taken from the Convention of Conventional Weapons, Additional Protocol II, Article 3(10).
106 Schmitt, Garraway and Dinstein, op. cit., fn 2, p 27.
107 HRW, op. cit., fn 80, see p 5 for a description of the village clearances of the 1990s where security forces would surround and destroy villages, and see KHRP, 'The Civilian Toll of Cross-Border Operations in Iraq', August 2009, available at <http://www.khrp.org/component/option,com_docman/task,cat_view/gid,45/Itemid,47/> (accessed 10 February 2009).
108 HRW, op. cit., fn 80, pp 5 and 9 where the report indicates the destruction of villages and infrastructure was 'total'.
109 *Doğan and others v Turkey*, Application Nos 8803-11/02, 8813/02 and 8815-19/02, Judgment of 18 November 2004.
110 KHRP, op. cit., fn 107.
111 Declaration of Minimum Humanitarian Standards, reprinted in *Report of the Sub-Commission on Prevention of Discrimination and Protection of Minorities on its Forty-sixth Session, Commission on Human Rights*, 51st Sess, Provisional Agenda Item 19, at 4, UN Doc E/CN.4/1995/116 (1995) (Declaration of Turku).
112 Declaration of Minimum Humanitarian Standards, ibid.
113 *Seyfettin Acar and others v Turkey*, Application No 30742/03, Judgment of 6 October 2009, European Court of Human Rights, see also *Acar and Others v Turkey*, Application Nos 36088/97 and 38417/97, Judgment of 24 May 2005 concerning the same incident, European Court of Human Rights. For leading cases on the right to life see *McCann and Others v the United Kingdom*, Application No 18984/91, Judgment of 27 September 1995, Series A, No 32, and *Avşar and others v Turkey*, Application No 25657/94, Judgment of 10 July 2001, but note that *McCann* concerns suspected members of the fighting force, the IRA.
114 *Seyfettin Acar and others v Turkey*, ibid, para 7.
115 *Seyfettin Acar and others v Turkey*, above, fn 113, para 32.

116 *Seyfettin Acar and others v Turkey*, above, fn 113, para 34, and see the detailed discussion of the role of village guards in *Avşar and others v Turkey*, above, fn 113, paras 275–81.

117 *Seyfettin Acar and others v Turkey*, above, fn 113, paras 35–36.

118 *Acar and Others v Turkey*, above, fn 113, para 7.

119 *Ergi v Turkey*, Application No 40/1993/435/514, Judgment of 28 July 1998, European Court of Human Rights

120 Hans-Joachim Heintze, 'On the relationship between human rights law protection and international humanitarian law', (2004) 86 IRRC 789, pp 809–10, see also Moir, op. cit., fn 1, p 265.

121 *Ergi v Turkey*, above, fn 119, para 79.

122 Heintze, op. cit., fn 120, p 810.

123 *Gülec v Turkey*, Application No 21593/93, Judgment of 27 July 1998, paras 71 et seq, European Court of Human Rights.

124 *İpek v Turkey*, Application No 25760/94, Judgment of 17 February 2004, European Court of Human Rights, and see an earlier case, *Akdivar and Others v Turkey*, Application No 99/1995/605/693, Judgment of 20 August 1996.

125 *İpek v Turkey*, ibid, para. 137.

126 *İpek v Turkey*, above, fn 124, para 143.

127 *İpek v Turkey*, above, fn 124, para 155.

128 *Orhan v Turkey*, Application No 25656/94, Judgment of 18 June 2002, European Court of Human Rights.

129 *Orhan v Turkey*, ibid, para 3.

130 *Orhan v Turkey*, above, fn 128, paras 379–80.

131 *Altun v Turkey*, Application No 24561/94, Judgment of 1 June 2004, European Court of Human Rights.

132 See also *Mentes and Others v Turkey*, Application No 58/1996/677/867, Judgment of 28 November 1997, and *Dulaş v Turkey*, Application No 25801/94, Judgment of 30 January 2001.

133 *Doğan and others v Turkey*, above, fn 109.

134 *Doğan and others v Turkey*, above, fn 109, para 12.

135 *Doğan and others v Turkey*, above, fn 109, para 154.

136 *Doğan and others v Turkey*, above, fn 109, para 159.

137 Press release 'Chamber Judgment in the case of Doğan and Others v Turkey', 29 June 2004, available at <http://www.echr.coe.int/Eng/Press/2004/June/ChamberJudgmentDoganandothersvTurkey290604.htm> (accessed 20 September 2009).

138 *Aydin v Turkey*, above, fn 68.

139 *Aydin v Turkey*, above, fn 68, para 20.

140 *Aydin v Turkey*, above, fn 68, paras 24 and 25.

Chapter 4

1 G Draper, 'The status of combatants and the question of guerrilla warfare' (1971) *British Yearbook of International Law* 173.

2 General Orders 100, Instructions for the Government of Armies of the United States in the Field (The Lieber Code), reprinted in D Schindler and J Toman (eds), *The Laws of Armed Conflict*, 4th edition (Leiden: Martinus Nijhoff, 2004), p 19.

3 Regulations Respecting the Laws and Customs of War on Land, annexed to Hague Convention (IV) Respecting the Laws and Customary of War on Land, 18 October 1907 (Hague Regulation), reprinted in A Roberts and R Guelff (eds), *Documents on the Laws of War*, 3rd edition (Oxford University Press, 2000), p 73.

4 Geneva Convention III Relative to the Treatment of Prisoners of War, (1949) 75 UNTS 135, see also for example Article 13 of Geneva Convention I for the Amelioration of the Condition of the Wounded and Sick in Armed Forces in the Field,

(1949) 75 UNTS 31 and Article 13 of Geneva Convention II for the Amelioration of the Condition of the Wounded, Sick and Shipwrecked Members of the Armed Forces at Sea, (1949) 75 UNTS 85.

5 A Rogers, 'Combatant Status', in E Wilmshurst and S Breau (eds), *Perspectives on the ICRC Study on Customary International Humanitarian Law* (Cambridge: Cambridge University Press, 2007), p 106.

6 Pictures seen of military formations, weapons and uniforms seen by the authors of this book.

7 Kurdistan Workers Party (PKK) Statement to the Swiss Federal Council, 23 January, 1995, signed by Abdullah Öcalan.

8 Geneva Convention IV Relative to the Protection of Civilian Persons in Time of War, 12 August 1949, (1949) 75 UNTS 287, 'Art. 34. The taking of hostages is prohibited'.

9 Geneva Convention III Relative to the Treatment of Prisoners of War, 75 UNTS 135.

10 See Appendix 1 for provisions on prisoners of war in Geneva Convention III.

11 JM Henckaerts and L Doswald-Beck, *Customary International Humanitarian Law, Volume 1: Rules* (Cambridge: Cambridge University Press, 2005), Chapter 1, pp 3–24 and Chapter 33, pp 384–95.

12 Provided they are not *hors de combat*, see ibid, Vol I, Rule 47.

13 Rogers, in Wilmshurst and Breau, op. cit., fn 5, pp 108–9.

14 Rogers, in Wilmshurst and Breau, op. cit., fn 5, p 102.

15 Rogers, in Wilmshurst and Breau, op. cit., fn 5, p 109.

16 MN Schmitt, CHB Garraway and Y Dinstein, *The Manual on the Law of Non-International Armed Conflict with Commentary* (Leiden: Brill, 2007), pp 4–5.

17 The International Committee of the Red Cross has convened an expert group to study the issue of direct participation in hostilities by civilians, see Interpretive Guidance on the notion of Direct Participation in Hostilities under International Humanitarian Law, Geneva 2009 (ICRC Interpretive Guidance), available at <http://www.icrc.org/Web/eng/siteeng0.nsf/htmlall/direct-participation-report_res/$File/direct-participation-guidance-2009-icrc.pdf> (accessed 24 September 2009).

18 1977 Protocol Additional to the Geneva Conventions of 12 August 1949, and Relating to the Protection of Victims of International Armed Conflicts, (1949) 1125 UNTS 3, Article 53.

19 1977 Protocol, ibid, Article 13.

20 *Prosecutor v Akayesu*, Judgment of Trial Chamber, 2 September 1998, ICTR-96-4-T, para 629, International Criminal Tribunal for Rwanda.

21 M Schmitt, 'Direct Participation in Hostilities and 21st Century Armed Conflict', page proofs supplied by author, p 506.

22 Schmitt, ibid, p 508.

23 The International Committee of the Red Cross (Nils Melzer, author) as drafting committee disassociated themselves from the guidance, see M Schmitt, 'The Interpretive Guidance on the Notion of Direct Participation in Hostilities; A Critical Analysis', draft article provided by Professor Schmitt, see also ICRC Interpretive Guidance, above, fn 17.

24 ICRC Interpretive Guidance, above, fn 17, p 13.

25 Schmitt, above, fn 23, p 12, and *Prosecutor v Akayesu*, op. cit., fn 20, para 629; Rome Statute, arts. 8.2(b)(i), 8.2(e)(i).

26 Melzer, op. cit., fn 23, pp 28–29.

27 Schmitt, above, fn 23, p 12.

28 Melzer, op. cit., fn 23, p 46.

29 Melzer, op. cit., fn 23, p 65.

30 Melzer, op. cit., fn 23, p 70.

31 1899 Hague Convention II Laws and Customs of War on Land, The Hague, available at <http://www.icrc.org/ihl.nsf/FULL.150?OpenDocument> (accessed 1 November 2009).

32 Schmitt, Garraway and Dinstein, op. cit., fn 16, p 13.

33 *Prosecutor v Tadić*, Decision on the Defence Motion for Interlocutory Appeal on Jurisdiction, Appeals Chamber, 2 October 1995, IT-94-1-AR72, para 119, International Criminal Tribunal for Yugoslavia.

34 Schmitt, Garraway and Dinstein, op. cit., fn 16, p 31.

35 Henckaerts and Doswald-Beck, op. cit., fn 11, Part IV, Weapons, pp 237–96.

36 Schmitt, Garraway and Dinstein, op. cit., fn 16, pp 40–45.

37 Henckaerts and Doswald-Beck, op. cit., fn 11, Part III, Specific Methods of Warfare, pp 161–233.

38 Geneva Convention III Relative to the Treatment of Prisoners of War, (1949) 75 UNTS 135.

39 Geneva Convention III, ibid, Article 118.

40 Öcalan the leader of the PKK was initially sentenced to death before his commutation to a life sentence and Nelson Mandela spent 27 years in prison before his release.

41 Kurdistan Workers Party (PKK) Statement to the Swiss Federal Council, 23 January 1995, para 3 and signed by Abdullah Öcalan.

42 Rogers, in Wilmshurst and Breau, op. cit., fn 5, p 125.

43 Rogers, in Wilmshurst and Breau, op. cit., fn 5.

44 For an excellent article on this topic see E Crawford, 'Unequal before the Law: The Case for the Elimination of the Distinction between International and Non-international Armed Conflicts', (2007) 20 *Leiden Journal of International Law* 441–65.

45 1977 Protocol Additional to the Geneva Conventions of 12 August 1949, and Relating to the Protection of Victims of International Armed Conflicts, (1949) 1125 UNTS 3, Article 75.

46 Henckaerts and Doswald-Beck, op. cit., fn 11, p 299.

47 Henckaerts and Doswald-Beck, op. cit., fn 11, p 302.

48 F Hampson, 'Fundamental Guarantees', in Wilmshurst and Breau, op. cit., fn 5, pp 282–301 for her consideration of these rules.

49 Henckaerts and Doswald-Beck, op. cit., fn 11, Chapter 32.

50 Hampson, in Wilmshurst and Breau, op. cit., fn 5, pp 282–301.

51 Hampson, in Wilmshurst and Breau, op. cit., fn 5, p 297.

52 Human Rights Committee, General Comment No 29 on States of Emergency, CCPR/C/21/Rev.1/Add.11, and Hampson, in Wilmshurst and Breau, op. cit., fn 5, p 297.

53 Hampson, in Wilmshurst and Breau, op. cit., fn 5, pp 297–98.

54 Hampson, in Wilmshurst and Breau, op. cit., fn 5, p 299.

55 A Jachec-Neale, 'Status and treatment of prisoners of war and other persons deprived of their liberty', in Wilmshurst and Breau, op. cit., fn 5, Chapter 12.

56 *Öcalan v Turkey*, Case No 46221/99, Judgment of 12 March 2003, European Court of Human Rights.

57 *Öcalan v Turkey*, ibid, para 18.

58 *Öcalan v Turkey*, above, fn 56, para 68.

59 *Öcalan v Turkey*, above, fn 56, para 105, see also *Brogan and others v United Kingdom*, Application Nos 11209/84, 11266/84 and 11365/85, Judgment of 29 November 1988, (1989) 11 EHRR 117, European Court of Human Rights, where detention of suspected terrorists of four days and six hours without judicial review was declared a violation of Article 5(3) of the European Convention on Human Rights, and *Brannigan and McBride v United Kingdom*, Application Nos 1453/89 and 1453/89, Judgment of 26 May 1993, Series A, No 258-B, p 55, §§ 62–63; *Aquilina v Malta*, Application No 25642/94, ECHR 1999-III, § 49; and *Dikme v Turkey*, Application No 20869/92, ECHR 2000-VIII, § 66.

60 *Öcalan v Turkey*, above, fn 56, para 104.

61 *Öcalan v Turkey*, above, fn 56, paras 119–49.

62 *Öcalan v Turkey*, above, fn 56, para 116.

63 *Öcalan v Turkey*, above, fn 56, para 194.
64 *Öcalan v Turkey*, above, fn 56, paras 174–75.
65 *Öcalan v Turkey*, above, fn 56, para 196.
66 *Çiçek v Turkey*, Application No 25704/94, Judgment of 27 February 2001, European Court of Human Rights.
67 *Yasin Ateş v Turkey*, Application No 30949/96, Judgment of 31 May 2005, European Court of Human Rights.
68 *Tanli v Turkey*, Application No 26129/95, Judgment of 28 August 2001, European Court of Human Rights.
69 *Tanli v Turkey*, ibid, para 106.
70 *Tanli v Turkey*, above, fn 68, para 141.
71 *Tanli v Turkey*, above, fn 68, para 147.
72 *Abdülsamet Yaman v Turkey*, Application No 32446/96, Judgment of 2 November 2004, European Court of Human Rights.
73 *Brogan and others v United Kingdom*, above fn 59.
74 *Çelik and İmret v Turkey*, Application No 44093/98, Judgment of 26 October 2004, European Court of Human Rights.
75 *Çolak and Filizer v Turkey*, Applications Nos 32578/96 and 32579/96, Judgment of 8 January 2004, European Court of Human Rights.
76 For other similar cases see *Esen v Turkey*, Application No 29484/95, Judgment of 22 July 2003, para 28; *Yaz v Turkey*, Application No 29485/95, Judgment of 22 July 2003, para 30; and *Ayşe Tepe v Turkey*, Application No 29422/95, Judgment of 22 July 2003.

Chapter 5

1 B Saul, *Defining Terrorism in International Law* (Oxford: Oxford University Press, 2008), p 82.
2 C Gray, *International Law and the Use of Force*, 3rd edition (Oxford: Oxford University Press, 2008), pp 60 and 64.
3 Gray, ibid, p 64.
4 T Honoré, 'The Right to Rebel', (1988) 8 OJLS 34, p 36.
5 Saul, op. cit., fn 1, p 82.
6 Gray, op. cit., fn 2, p 67.
7 Gray, op. cit., fn 2, p 67.
8 H Grotius, *The Law of War and Peace* (F Kelsey Translation, 1925), p 138 and p 148–56 as summarised by A Khan, 'A Legal Theory of Revolution', (1987) 5 *Boston University International Law Journal* 1, p 11.
9 Grotius, ibid, p 150.
10 J Locke, *Second Treatise on Civil Government* (1683) as discussed in L Kutner, 'Due Process of Rebellion', (1972–73) 7 Val U L Rev 1, p 6.
11 E Vattel, *Law of Nations* (English translation by CG Fenwick, 1758; reprinted Dobbs Ferry, NY: Oceana Publications Inc, 1964), Vol III, Chap IV, p 131.
12 LN Cutler, 'The right to intervene', (1985–86) 64 *Foreign Affairs* 96, p 102.
13 Cutler, ibid, p 98.
14 B Sloan, 'General Assembly Resolutions Revisited (Forty Years After)', (1987) 58 BYIL 39.
15 R Lillich, *The Human Rights of Aliens in Contemporary International Law* (Manchester: Manchester University Press, 1984), p 44, and H Hannum, 'Human Rights', in C Joyner, *The United Nations and International Law* (Cambridge: Cambridge University Press, 1997), pp 138 and 149.
16 UN General Assembly Resolution 375 (IV) 6 December 1949.
17 UN General Assembly Resolution 2131 (XX) 21 December 1965.

18 Declaration on Principles of International Law Friendly Relations and Co-operation among States in Accordance with the Charter of the UN, UN General Assembly Resolution 2625(XXV) 24 October 1970.

19 Declaration, ibid.

20 Declaration, above, fn 18.

21 *Military and paramilitary activities in and against Nicaragua (Nicaragua v United States of America)*, Merits, Judgment of 27 June 1986, [1986] *ICJ Reports* 14, para 191, *Armed Activities on the Territory of the Congo (Democratic Republic of the Congo v Uganda)*, Judgment of 19 December 2005, [2005] *ICJ Reports* 168, para 162.

22 1966 International Covenant of Civil and Political Rights (1966) 999 UNTS 171, 1966 International Covenant on Economic, Social and Cultural Rights (1966) 999 UNTS 3.

23 M Reisman, 'Coercion and Self-Determination: Construing Charter Article 2(4)', (1984) 78 AJIL 642, pp 642–43.

24 Cutler, op. cit., fn 12, p 104.

25 J Quigley, 'David v. Goliath: Humanitarian and Human Rights Law in light of the Palestinian Right to Self-Determination and the Right to Recapture Territory Taken by Force', (1988–89) 21 NYU J Int'l L & Pol 489.

26 Quigley, ibid, pp 490–91, and see *Legal Consequences of the Construction of a Wall in the Occupied Palestinian Territory*, ICJ Advisory Opinion of 9 July 2004, [2004] *ICJ Reports* 199, para 155.

27 Quigley, op. cit., fn 25, p 492.

28 UN Commission on Human Rights Resolution 1988/3, *Situation of Occupied Palestine*, para 3, 22 February 1988, UN ECOSOC Official Records Supp (No 2) at 25, UN Doc E/CN.4/1988/88 (Vote : 30-4-8).

29 UN Document A/HRC/12/48 15 September 2009, Human Rights in Palestine and other Occupied Arab Territories, Report of the United Nations Fact Finding Mission on the Gaza Conflict (also known as the Goldstone report), outlining human rights and humanitarian law violations prior to and during Israel's incursion into Gaza, December 2008, see p 54 for Israeli allegations on Palestinian suicide bombers and rocket attacks.

30 M Lippman, 'The Right of Civil Resistance under International Law and the Domestic Necessity Defense', (1989–90) 8 Dick J Int'l L 349, p 354.

31 H Hannum, *Autonomy, Sovereignty, and Self-Determination* (Philadelphia, PA: University of Pennsylvania Press, 1996), p 188.

32 S Breau, *Humanitarian Intervention: The United Nations and Collective Responsibility* (London: Cameron May, 2005), and S Breau, 'The Impact of the Responsibility to Protect on Peacekeeping', (2006) 11 *Journal of Conflict and Security Law* 429.

33 RE Gorelick, 'Wars of National Liberation: *Jus Ad bellum*', (1979) 11 Case W Res J Int'l L 71 p 71.

34 Protocol I Additional to the Geneva Conventions of 12 August 1949, and relating to the Protection of Victims of International Armed Conflicts, (1977) 1125 UNTS 3, 8 June 1977.

35 Gorelick, op. cit., fn 33, p 73.

36 Gorelick, op. cit., fn 33, pp 73–80.

37 Definition of Aggression, United Nations General Assembly Resolution 3314 (XXIX).

38 Honoré, op. cit., fn 4, p 37.

39 Honoré, op. cit., fn 4, p 54.

40 Saul, op. cit., fn 1, p 83.

41 Gorelick, op. cit., fn 33, p 92.

42 Gray, op. cit., fn 2, p 107.

43 Gray, op. cit., fn 2, p 76, and *Nicaragua v United States of America*, above, fn 21, para 191.

44 Breau, op. cit., fn 32.

45 For an excellent analysis of the 2008 operation see T Ruys, 'A Legal Analysis of Turkey's Military Operations against the PKK in Northern Iraq', (2008) 9 *Melb J Int'l L* 334.

46 CNN, 'Turkey launches major Iraq incursion', 22 February 2008 (an estimated 10,000 Turkish troops were involved), available at <http://www.cnn.com> (accessed 4 August 2008).

47 Reuters, 'Iraq protests Turkish incursion into Northern Iraq', 22 February 2008, available at <http://www.reuters.com> (accessed 4 August 2008).

48 Preamble of the United Nations Charter 1945.

49 Gray, op. cit., fn 2, Chapter 3.

50 Y Dinstein, *War Aggression and Self-Defence*, 4th edition (Cambridge: Cambridge University Press, 2005), pp 244–45.

51 States are very reluctant to label another state as an aggressor and the common parlance is an unlawful use of force. The International Court of Justice is equally reluctant, see *The Corfu Channel Case* (Merits), Judgment of 9 April 1949, [1949] *ICJ Reports* 4, *Nicaragua v United States of America*, above, fn 21, and the *Oil Platforms (Islamic Republic of Iran v United States of America)*, Judgment of 6 November 2003, [2003] *ICJ Reports* 161.

52 Al Jazeera (Qatar), 'Turkey "Right to Intervene" in Iraq', 3 December 2007, available at <http://english.aljazeera.net/news/europe/2007/12/2008525143433545716.html> (accessed 4 September 2009).

53 *Note Verbale Dated 26 March 2008 from the Permanent Mission of Turkey to the United Nations Office at Geneva Addressed to the Secretariat of the Human Rights Council*, UN Doc A/HRC/7/G/15 (28 March 2008) ('*Note Verbale*').

54 *Nicaragua v United States of America*, above, fn 21, para 195, and Definition of Aggression, UN General Assembly Resolution 3314 (XXIX) 14 December 1974, para 3(g).

55 *Nicaragua v United States of America*, above, fn 21.

56 *Nicaragua v United States of America*, above, fn 21, para 231.

57 *Islamic Republic of Iran v United States of America*, above, fn 51, para 72.

58 Ruys, op. cit., fn 45, p 349.

59 *Islamic Republic of Iran v United States of America*, above, fn 51, para 195.

60 Ruys, op. cit., fn 45, pp 349–50.

61 See the discussion above with respect to the classification of international armed conflict as it is a different issue in the *jus in bello* context than the Charter prohibition issue.

62 Gray, op. cit., fn 2, p 141.

63 UN Doc S/1995/605.

64 Gray, op. cit., fn 2, p 142.

65 Dinstein, op. cit., fn 50, pp 217–18.

66 *Nicaragua v United States of America*, above, fn 21, para 200.

67 Gray, op. cit., fn 2, p 121.

68 Ruys, op. cit., fn 45, pp 350–51.

69 Ruys, op. cit., fn 45, p 351.

70 S Talmon, 'Changing Views on the Use of Force: The German Position', (2005) 5 *Baltic Yearbook of International Law* 41, pp 52–53.

71 Ruys, op. cit., fn 45, p 353.

72 UN Security Council Resolution 1368, 12 September 2001.

73 Talmon, op. cit., fn 70, p 53.

74 C Greenwood, 'International Law and the Pre-emptive Use of Force: Afghanistan, Al-Qaeda and Iraq', in C Greenwood, *Essays on War in International Law* (London: Cameron May, 2006), p 677.

75 UN Document S/2001/946 Letter dated 7 October 2001 from the Permanent Representative of the United States of America to the President of the Security Council.

76 Gray, op. cit., fn 2, pp 198–202.
77 *Legal Consequences of the Construction of a Wall in the Occupied Palestinian Territory*, ICJ Advisory Opinion of 9 July 2004, [2004] ICJ Rep 136, para 138.
78 *Legal Consequences*, ibid, para 139.
79 *Armed Activities on the Territory of the Congo (Democratic Republic of the Congo v Uganda)*, Judgment of 19 December 2005, [2005] *ICJ Reports* 168.
80 *Democratic Republic of the Congo v Uganda*, ibid, paras 146–47.
81 *Democratic Republic of the Congo v Uganda*, above, fn 79, para 147.
82 Ruys, op. cit., fn 45, p 356.
83 *Islamic Republic of Iran v United States of America*, above, fn 51, para 196.
84 Gray, op. cit., fn 2, p 81.
85 Gray, op. cit., fn 2, p 81.
86 'UK Materials on International Law', (1986) 57 BYIL 614.
87 Gray, op. cit., fn 2, p 85.
88 BBC News, 'Pressure increases on PKK Rebels', 1 November 2007, available at <http://news.bbc.co.uk/1/hi/world/middle_east/7071569.stm> (accessed 7 September 2009).
89 Gray, op. cit., fn 2, p 141, and UN Docs S/23141, 14 October 1991, S/23152, 17 October 1991.
90 L Doswald-Beck, 'Military Intervention by Invitation of the Government', (1986) BYIL 197.
91 Dinstein, op. cit., fn 50, pp 244–45.
92 Dinstein, op. cit., fn 50, pp 246–47.
93 Dinstein, op. cit., fn 50, pp 247–48.
94 Ruys, op. cit., fn 45.
95 BBC News, 'Turkish Troops Pull Out of Iraq', 29 February 2008, available at <http://news.bbc.co.uk/2/hi/europe/7270566.stm> (accessed 7 September 2009), and 'Iraq Warns Turkey over Incursion', 23 February 2008, available at <http://news.bbc.co.uk/2/hi/europe/7260478.stm> (accessed 7 September 2009).
96 Ruys, op. cit., fn 45, p 340.
97 Ruys, op. cit., fn 45, and BBC News, 'Pressure increases on PKK Rebels', 1 November 2007, available at <http://news.bbc.co.uk/1/hi/world/middle_east/7071569.stm> (accessed 7 September 2009).
98 Ruys, op. cit., fn 45, p 341, and BBC News, 'Turkey Must End Iraq Raid – Bush', 28 February 2008, available at <http://news.bbc.co.uk/2/hi/europe/7268345.stm> (accessed 7 September 2009).
99 K Yildiz and M Muller, *The European Union and Turkish Accession* (London: Pluto Press, 2008), pp 117–21 for discussion on the European Union and the conflict.
100 Ruys, op. cit., fn 45, p 343, and Presidency of the European Union, 'EU Presidency Statement on the Military Actions Undertaken by Turkey on Iraqi Territory', Press Release, 17 December 2007, available at <http://www.eu2007.ptfUE/vENfNoticiasDocumentos/DeclaracoesPESC/20071217traque.htm> (accessed 7 September 2009).
101 Presidency of the European Union, ibid, and Presidency of the European Union, 'EU Presidency Statement on the Military Action Undertaken by Turkey in Iraqi Territory', Press Release, 25 February 2008, available at <http://www.eu2008.si/en/News and Documents/CFSPStatements/February/0225MZZturkey.html> (accessed 7 September 2009).
102 UN News Service, 'Secretary-General Concerned at Turkish Move on Attacking Kurdish Targets in Iraq', 19 October 2007, available at <http://www.un.org/apps/news/story.asp?NewsID=24355&Cr=iraq&CrI=turkey> (accessed 7 September 2009); 'Ban Ki-Moon Voices Concern Over Turkish Air Attacks Against Iraq', 17 December 2007, available at <http://www.un.orglapps/news/story.asp?NewsID=25098&Cr=iraq&Crl – turkey> (accessed 7 September 2009); 'Ban Ki-Moon Calls

for "Utmost Restraint" in Turkey-Iraq Border Actions', 22 February 2008, available at <http://www.un.org/apps/news/storyAr.asp?NewsID=25722&Cr-iraq& Crl – turkey> (accessed 7 September 2009).

103 Responsibility of States for internationally wrongful acts as incorporated in UN Doc. A/RES/56/83 (2002).

104 A Cassese, *International Law*, 2nd edition (Oxford: Oxford University Press, 2005), pp 200–1 – Cassese also included obligations to states bound by multilateral treaties.

105 Cassese, ibid, p 201.

106 S Breau, 'The Constitutionalization of the International Legal Order', (2008) 21 *Leiden Journal of International Law* 545.

107 Cassese, op. cit., fn 104, p 263.

108 Cassese, op. cit., fn 104, pp 263–64.

109 *Barcelona Traction Light and Power Company Limited (Belgium v Spain)*, 2nd Phase, 6 February 1970, [1970] *ICJ Reports* 3, *Legal Consequences for States of the Continued Presence of South Africa in Namibia (South West Africa) notwithstanding Security Council Resolution 276 (1970)*, Advisory Opinion, [1971] *ICJ Reports* 12, *Case Concerning East Timor (Portugal v Australia)*, Judgment of 30 June 1995, [1995] *ICJ Reports* 90, *Application of the Convention on the Prevention and Punishment of the Crime of Genocide (Bosnia and Herzegovina v Yugoslavia)*, Order of 8 April 1993, [1993] *ICJ Reports* 3.

110 J Crawford, *The International Law Commission's Articles on State Responsibility* (Cambridge: Cambridge University Press, 2002), pp 18–19.

111 Crawford, ibid, p 242.

112 *Portugal v Australia*, above, fn 109, p 102, para 29.

113 *Application of the Convention on the Prevention and Punishment of the Crime of Genocide, Preliminary Objections* [1996] *ICJ Reports* 595, p 616, para 31.

114 Crawford, op. cit., fn 110, p 243.

115 Crawford, op. cit., fn 110, p 20.

116 Crawford, op. cit., fn 110, pp 203–4.

Chapter 6

1 Office of the Coordinator for Counterterrorism, US Department of State, *Foreign Terrorist Organizations* (2008), available at <http://www.state.gov/s/ct/rls/fs/08/103392.htm> (accessed 9 September 2009); Council of the European Union, *Council Common Position 2008/586/CFSP of 15 July 2008 Updating Common Position 2001/931/CFSP on the Application of Specific Measures to Combat Terrorism and Repealing Common Position 2007/871/CFSP* [2008] OJ L 188/71.

2 For an excellent and comprehensive discussion of this issue see B Saul, *Defining Terrorism in International Law* (Oxford: Oxford University Press, 2006), and see further H Duffy, *The 'War on Terror' and the Framework of International Law* (Cambridge: Cambridge University Press, 2005). For earlier efforts at definition see M Cherif Bassiouni (ed), *Legal Responses to International Terrorism* (Leiden: Martinus Nijhoff, 1988) (particularly the introductory section by Bassiouni).

3 UN Security Council Resolution 1373, 29 September 2001.

4 Council Decision of 28 June 2007 implementing Article 2(3) of Regulation (EC) No 2580/2001 on specific restrictive measures directed against certain persons and entities with a view to combating terrorism and repealing Decisions 2006/379/EC and 2006/1008/EC (2007/445/EC).

5 The current list of Taliban and Al-Qaeda suspects is available at <http://www.un.org/sc/committees/1267/consolist.shtml>.

6 *Osman Öcalan, on behalf of the Kurdistan Workers' Party (PKK) and Serif Vanly, on behalf of the Kurdistan National Congress (KNK) v Council of the European Union*, Case C-229/05P, Judgment of the Court (First Chamber), 18 January 2007 [2007] ECR I-439.

7 R Higgins, 'The General Law of Terrorism', in R Higgins and M Flory (eds), *Terrorism and International Law* (London: Routledge, 1997), p 28.

8 O Gross and F Ní Aoláin, *Law in Times of Crisis* (Cambridge: Cambridge University Press, 2006), p 367.

9 Hans-Peter Gasser, 'Acts of Terror, Terrorism and International Humanitarian Law', (2002) 84 *International Review of the Red Cross* 547, p 547.

10 Gasser, ibid, p 367, and League of Nations, Convention for the Prevention and Punishment of Terrorism, 16 November 1937, (1938) *League of Nations Official Journal* 23.

11 J Dugard, 'International Terrorism: Problems of Definition', (1974) 50 *International Affairs* 67, p 68.

12 Dugard, ibid, p 69.

13 Dugard, op. cit., fn 11, p 68.

14 Dugard, op. cit., fn 11, p 72.

15 Bassiouni, op. cit., fn 2, p xii and Convention at Appendix VI, and 'The United States Draft Convention for the Prevention and Punishment of Certain Acts of Terrorism', UN Document A/C.6/L/850, 25 September 1972.

16 Dugard, op. cit., fn 11, p 74.

17 UN General Assembly Resolution 49/60, 9 December 1994.

18 UN General Assembly Resolution 51/210, 17 December 1996.

19 A Clapham, 'Secession, terrorism and the right of self-determination', in M Kohen (ed), *Secession International Law Perspectives* (Cambridge: Cambridge University Press, 2006), p 46.

20 Clapham, ibid, p 47.

21 Organization of the Islamic Conference, *Convention of the Organisation of the Islamic Conference on Combating International Terrorism*, 1 July 1999, Annex to Resolution No: 59/26-P.

22 Organization of African Unity, *OAU Convention on the Prevention and Combating of Terrorism*, 14 June 1999, available at: <http://www.unhcr.org/refworld/docid/3f4b1f714.html> (accessed 1 October 2009).

23 UN General Assembly Resolution 52/164, International Convention for the Suppression of Terrorist Bombings, 15 December 1997, and UN General Assembly Resolution 54/109, International Convention for the Suppression of the Financing of Terrorism adopted 15 December 1999.

24 International Convention for the Suppression of the Financing of Terrorism, ibid, Article 2(1) (b).

25 Reform the UN.org, 'Ad Hoc Committee Negotiates Comprehensive Convention on International Terrorism, No Consensus Reached', New York, 13 March 2008, available at <http://www.reformtheun.org/index.php/eupdate/3879> (accessed 16 July 2009).

26 Reform the UN.org, ibid; see also the reports from the 6th Committee of the General Assembly on their agenda item, available at <http://www.un.org/ga/sixth/previous_sessions.shtml> (accessed 30 July 2009), which contain the state objections to a Comprehensive Convention.

27 UN Document A/AC.252/2009/L.1/Add.1, Draft Report of Ad Hoc Committee established by General Assembly Resolution 51/210 of 17 December 1996, 30 June 2009.

28 UN Document A/62/100 report of the 6th Committee to the General Assembly.

29 UN General Assembly Resolution A/Res/60/1, para 82, it also called upon the international community to agree on a Comprehensive Convention, para 83

30 UN General Assembly Resolution A/Res/60/288, 20 September 2006.

31 Convention for the Suppression of Unlawful Seizure of Aircraft 14 October 1971, International Convention Against the Taking of Hostages 17 December 1979.

32 Summaries of conventions are taken verbatim from the UN website on terrorism.

33 See Saul, op. cit., fn 2, p 145 for a list of regional conventions.

34 European Convention on the Suppression of Terrorism, Council of Europe, Strasbourg, 27 January 1977.

35 2003 Protocol amending the European Convention on the Suppression of Terrorism (ES No 190 Strasbourg, 15 May 2003), and Saul, op. cit., fn 2, p 148.

36 Council of Europe Convention on the Prevention of Terrorism (CETS No 196, Warsaw, 16 May 2005).

37 Saul, op. cit., fn 2, p 149.

38 Council of Europe Convention on the Prevention of Terrorism, above, fn 36, Preamble.

39 Article 29(2) of the EU Treaty.

40 A Reinisch, 'The Action of the European Union to Combat International Terrorism', in A Bianchi, *Enforcing International Law Norms Against Terrorism* (Oxford: Hart Publishing, 2004), p 122.

41 Reinisch, ibid.

42 Council Framework Decision of 13 June 2002 on combating terrorism (2002/475/JHA), and see also Council Common Position 2001/931/CFSP of 27 December 2001 on the application of specific measures to combat terrorism.

43 Council Framework Decision of 13 June 2002 on the European arrest warrant and the surrender procedures between Member States (2002/584/JHA).

44 Saul, op. cit., fn 2, p 162.

45 Council Framework Decision, above, fn 43.

46 Reinisch, op. cit., fn 40, p 144.

47 Reinisch, op. cit., fn 40, the origin of this phrase is unknown.

48 See Appendix 2 on terrorist conventions.

49 UN Document Press Release, L/2766 dated 27 March 1996.

50 UN Document Press Release, ibid.

51 UN General Assembly Resolution A/Res/60/288, 20 September 2006.

52 UN Security Council Resolution S/Res/1373 of 28 September 2001.

53 Council Regulation (EC) No 2580/2001 of 27 December 2001, Article 2 (1).

54 Council Regulation (EC) No 2580/2001, ibid, Article 3.

55 Council Framework Decision, above, fn 42, Article 2(1).

56 Council Framework Decision, above, fn 42, Article 2(2), and Saul, op. cit., fn 2, p 167.

57 A Clapham, 'Extending international criminal law beyond the individual to corporations and armed opposition groups', (2008) *Journal of International Criminal Justice* 899, p 924.

58 1997 International Convention for the Suppression of Terrorist Bombings, (1997) 1035 UNTS 167, para 19.

59 Clapham, op. cit., fn 19, pp 49–52.

60 Gasser, op. cit., fn 9, pp 565–66.

61 *Italy v Abdelaziz and ors*, Final Appeal Judgment, No 1072, ILDC 559 (IT 2007), Court of Cassation (Italy), summary of decision in English is available at <http://www.adh-geneva.ch/RULAC/national_judical_decitions.php?id_state=114> (accessed 9 September 2009).

62 The following material is taken from a previously published article and updated, see S. Breau, 'United Kingdom Response to Terrorism and the Response of the Courts to these Measures', in 2004–5 11 *Yearbook of Islamic and Middle Eastern Law* 83, pp 83–95.

63 United Kingdom Anti-Terrorism, Crime and Security Act 2001, Chapter 24.

64 Note Verbale from the Permanent Representation of the United Kingdom, dated 18 December 2001, registered by the Secretariat General on 18 December 2001.

65 *A (FC) and others (FC) (Appellants) v Secretary of State for the Home Department (Respondent)*, 16 December 2004, [2002] UKHL 56, House of Lords.

66 *Chahal v United Kingdom*, Application No 22414/93, Judgment of 15 November 1996, (1996) 23 EHRR 413, paras 79 and 80, European Commission on Human Rights.

67 *Chahal v United Kingdom*, ibid, para 113.

68 House of Lords, *Hansard*, volume 376, cols 1203–4, 10 December 2001, cited in: Privy Counsellor Review Committee, 'Anti-terrorism, Crime and Security Act 2001 Review', para 444.

69 Privy Counsellor Review Committee, ibid, Foreword, p 5.

70 Privy Counsellor Review Committee, *Anti-terrorism, Crime and Security Act 2001 Review: Report* (London: House of Commons, 2003), p 4.

71 Privy Counsellor Review Committee, ibid, p 8.

72 See <http://www.hrw.org/backgrounder/eca/uk/4.htm> (accessed 20 May 2006).

73 Privy Counsellor Review Committee, above, fn 68, para 25.

74 Joint Committee on Human Rights, 'Second Report, 2001–2 session', 16 November 2001, paras 30 and 78.

75 Joint Committee on Human Rights, 'Sixth Report, 2003–4 session', 24 February 2004, para 34.

76 Prevention of Terrorism Act 2005, Chapter 2.

77 *Secretary of State for the Home Department v JJ and others*, 31 October 2007, [2007] UKHL 45, House of Lords, *Secretary of State for the Home Department v MB and FC*, 31 October 2007, [2007] UKHL 46, House of Lords, *Secretary of State for the Home Department v E and another*, 31 October 2007, [2007] UKHL 47, House of Lords.

78 Ibid. For example see the Lord Bingham ruling in *Secretary of State for the Home Department v MB and FC*, ibid, para 43.

79 *Guardian*, 'Government Publishes Anti-Terror Bill', 12 October 2005.

80 European Court of Human Rights, *Brannigan and McBride v United Kingdom*, Application Nos 1453/89 and 1453/89, Judgment of 26 May 1993, Series A, 258-B.

81 *Abbasi and Another v Secretary of State for Foreign and Commonwealth Affairs*, 2 February 2003, [2002] EWCA Civ 1598, Court of Appeal (England and Wales).

82 *Abbasi and Another*, ibid, para 1.

83 *Abbasi and Another*, above, fn 81, para 64.

84 *Abbasi and Another*, above, fn 81, para 66.

85 *Abbasi and Another*, above, fn 81, para 69.

86 *Al-Adsani v United Kingdom*, Application No 35763/97, Judgment of 21 November 2001, (2002) 34 EHRR 11, European Court of Human Rights.

87 *Bankovic and Others v Belgium and Others*, Application No 52207/99, Admissibility Decision of 12 December 2001, (2001) 11 BHRC 435, (2002) 41 ILM 517, European Court of Human Rights.

88 *Bankovic and Others*, ibid, para 79.

89 *Bankovic and Others*, above, fn 87, para 106.

90 *Bankovic and Others*, above, fn 87, para 41.

91 J Steyn, 'Guantanamo Bay: The Legal Black Hole', (2004) 53 ICLQ 1, p 11.

92 Steyn, ibid, p 12.

93 Steyn, op. cit., fn 91, p 13.

94 *Hamdi v Rumsfeld*, 28 June 2004, 542 US 507 (2004), US Supreme Court, and *Rasul v Bush*, 28 June 2004, 542 US 466 (2004), US Supreme Court.

95 *Hamdi v Rumsfeld*, ibid, Opinion of Justice Sandra Day O'Connor.

96 *Rasul v Bush*, above, fn 94, Opinion of Mr Justice Stevens.

97 *Hamdan v Rumsfeld*, 29 June 2006, 542 US 507 (2004), US Supreme Court.

98 *Hamdan v Rumsfeld*, ibid, Opinion of Mr. Justice Stevens

99 *Boumediene v Bush*, 12 June 2008, 549 US (2007).

100 *Boumediene v Bush*, ibid, Opinion of Mr Justice Kennedy.

101 *Ireland v United Kingdom*, (1978) 2 EHRR 25, European Court of Human Rights.

102 *A (FC) and others (FC) (Appellants) v Secretary of State for the Home Department (Respondent)*, 8 December 2005, [2005] UKHL 271, House of Lords.

103 *A (FC) and others (FC) (Appellants)*, ibid, para 11.

104 *A (FC) and others (FC) (Appellants)*, above, fn 102, para 80.

105 *The Queen (on the Application of Mazin Mumaa Galteh Al-Skeini and Others) v The Secretary of State for Defence*, 21 December 2005, [2005] EWCA Civ 1609, Court of Appeal (England and Wales), available at <http://www.unhcr.org/refworld/docid/46728cbf2.html> (accessed 22 November 2009).

106 For a more detailed discussion of this case see S Breau, 'The right to life of detainees in armed conflict', in J Yorke, *Orientations of the Right and Value of Life* (Farnham: Ashgate, forthcoming), see also G Simpson, 'The death of Baha Mousa', (2007) 8 *Melbourne Journal of International Law* 311.

107 *The Queen (on the Application of Mazin Mumaa Galteh Al-Skeini and Others) v The Secretary of State for Defence*, 21 December 2005, [2005] EWCA Civ 1609 (CA), Judgment of Baroness Hale of Richmond, para 88.

108 *Italy v Abdelaziz and ors*, Final Appeal Judgment, No 1072, ILDC 559 (IT 2007), Court of Cassation, Italy, summary of decision in English available at <http://www.adh-geneva.ch/RULAC/national_judical_decitions.php?id_state=114> (accessed 9 September 2009).

109 *Italy v Abdelaziz and ors*, ibid, summary of Judgment, date of report: 20 September 2007, reporter: Massimo Iovane.

110 *Italy v Abdelaziz and ors*, above, fn 108.

111 *Ahmed Ali Yusuf & Al Barakaat International Foundation v Council and Commission*, Case 306/01, and *Yassin Abdullah Kadi v Council of the European Union and Commission of the European Communities*, Case T-315/01, both relating to UN Doc S/RES/1267 of 15 October 1999, Judgment of 3 September 2008, European Court of Justice.

112 Summary derived from M Payandeh and H Sauer, 'Case Comment European Union: UN Sanctions and EU Fundamental Rights', (2009) *International Journal of Constitutional Law* 306, pp 306–7.

113 Council Decision of 27 December 2001.

114 Council Decision of 2 May 2002, and Council Common Position of 2 May 2002.

115 Reinisch, op. cit., fn 40.

116 *Osman Öcalan*, above, fn 6.

117 ICRC explanation of these provisions on terrorism, available at <http://www.icrc.org/web/eng/siteeng0.nsf/iwpList575/0F32B7E3BB38DD26C1256E8A0055F83E> (accessed 10 February 2010).

118 Additional Protocol I, Article 51(2), and Additional Protocol II, Article 13(2).

119 The following section is taken completely from those reports for the years including 2008, see US Department of State, Office of the Coordinator for Counterterrorism, *Patterns of Global Terrorism* reports, available at <http://www.state.gov/s/ct/rls/crt/> (accessed 1 August 2009) – the reports are now called *Country Reports on Terrorism*. The website contains the archive on these reports back to 1996.

Chapter 7

1 The UN Security Council passed Resolution 1368 on 12 September 2001, which calls on the international community to redouble their efforts to prevent and suppress terrorist acts. UN Resolution 1373 of 28 September 2001 criminalised terrorism and required member states to deny 'safe havens to those who finance, plan, support or commit terrorist attacks'. The UN Security Council established a Counter Terrorism Committee to oversee the implementation of Resolution 1373. See Chapter 6 for more detail on United Nations work to counter terrorism.

2 Al-Qaeda indicated its involvement in the attacks and formally claimed responsibility in 2002: *The Guardian*, 'Bin Laden voice on video, says TV channel', 10 September 2002, available at <http://www.guardian.co.uk/media/2002/sep/10/alqaida.september112001>, although an international poll in 2008 found large minorities

remain unconvinced of Al-Qaeda involvement, see <http://www.worldpublicopinion. org/pipa/articles/international_security_bt/535.php?nid=&id=&pnt=535>.

3 President George W Bush stated in his address to the Joint Session of Congress on 20 September 2001 that the 'war on terror begins with Al-Qaeda, but it does not end there. It will not end until every terrorist group of global reach has been found, stopped and defeated'. Quoted in US Department of State, Office of the Coordinator for Counterterrorism, *Patterns of Global Terrorism 2001*, May 2002, available at <http://www.state.gov/documents/organization/10319.pdf>.

4 Daniel B Prieto, 'War About Terror: Civil Liberties and National Security After 9/11: A CFR Working Paper', Council on Foreign Relations Press, February 2009, available at <http://www.cfr.org/publication/18373/>.

5 For example the US 2003 'National Strategy For Combating Terrorism' outlines goals to 'defeat terrorist groups' and 'win the war of ideas'; when the document was updated in 2006 the language was amended to reflect the more long-term and limited nature of counter-terrorism goals.

6 The United Nations failed to implement a Comprehensive Convention on International Terrorism (CCIT) due to the problems in defining the term 'terrorism'. The UN General Assembly's Ad Hoc Committee on Measures to Eliminate International Terrorism convened in March of 2008 but was unable to agree on the terms of the draft CCIT. The Ad Hoc Committee concluded the session by recommending that the UN General Assembly establish a Working Group on the CCIT with the aim of concluding a final draft.

7 The lack of definition of the term 'terrorism' ensures that confusion and obscurity persists. If there is no one agreed term then states may apply their own criteria in defining whether an act of terrorism has occurred.

8 *Suresh v Canada (Minister of Citizenship and Immigration)*, [2002] 1 SCR 3, 2002 SCC 1, Supreme Court of Canada, cited in Mark Muller QC, 'Terrorism, proscription and the right to resist in the age of conflict', (2008) 20 *Denning Law Journal* 114.

9 The full text of the President's speech is available at: <http://www.washingtonpost. com/wp-srv/nation/specials/attacked/transcripts/bushaddress_092001.html>.

10 A memo written by Deputy Assistant Attorney General John Yoo and Special Counsel Robert J Delahunty (available at <http://lawofwar.org/Yoo_Delahunty_Memo. htm>) argued that the Third Geneva Convention did not apply to captured members of Al-Qaeda and the Taliban, and was used as the basis of the Presidential decision that detainees in the war on terror were not covered by the Geneva Conventions, nor *habeus corpus* of criminal law. The problems of this legal black hole for detainees in the war on terror led to some scholars to argue for legal reform, bringing the Geneva Conventions and/or criminal law up to date with the current strategic context. See for example, Philip Bobbitt, *Terror and Consent: The Wars for the Twenty-First Century* (London: Penguin Books, 2008), pp 266, 353 and 496–97 who argues that terrorism is the paradigm of a war crime, and the Geneva Conventions should be reformed to account for this and be made enforceable by an international criminal court that answers to the UN Security Council (ie not the current International Criminal Court).

11 *Wall Street Journal*, 'Kill or Be Killed?', 17 July 2009, available at <http://online.wsj. com/article/SB10001424052970204271104574294173544620730.html>.

12 Highlights of the USA Patriot Act are available at <http://www.usdoj.gov/archive/ ll/highlights.htm>. The full text of the USA Patriot Act (HR 3162) is available at <http://thomas.loc.gov/cgi-bin/query/D?c107:4:./temp/~c107NlCUsS:>.

13 American Civil Liberties Union, 'Summary of the US Patriot Act and Other Government Acts', 11 February 2003, available at <http://www.aclu.org/takeaction/ general/18880pub20030211.html>.

14 The Office of the Coordinator for Counterterrorism (S/CT) coordinates and supports the development and implementation of all US government policies and programmes

aimed at countering terrorism overseas. The predecessor organisation to the S/CT was the Office for Combating Terrorism, created in 1972 upon the recommendation of a special committee appointed by President Richard Nixon following the Munich Olympics terrorist attack. The committee determined that an office was needed within the Department of State to provide day-to-day counter-terrorism coordination and to develop policy initiatives and responses for the US government. The Office for Combating Terrorism became the Office of the Ambassador-at-Large for Counterterrorism in 1985, and the Office of the Coordinator for Counterterrorism in 1989. In 1994, Congress officially mandated the Office of the Coordinator for Counterterrorism in Public Law 103–236 (HR 2333). In 1998, Congress further defined the role of the Coordinator for Counterterrorism in Public Law 105–277 (HR 4328). See <http://www.state.gov/s/ct/>.

15 Available at <http://www.state.gov/s/ct/about/index.htm>.

16 Both ODNI and NCTC were established by the December 2004 Intelligence Reform and Terrorism Prevention Act (IRTPA).

17 The US Department of Defense definition, 'the calculated use of unlawful violence or threat of unlawful violence to inculcate fear; intended to coerce or to intimidate governments or societies in the pursuit of goals that are generally political, religious, or ideological': National Military Strategic Plan for the War on Terrorism, 1 February 2006, available at <http://www.defenselink.mil/qdr/docs/2005-01-25-Strategic-Plan. pdf; the FBI definition, 'the unlawful use of force and violence against persons or property to intimidate or coerce a government, the civilian population, or any segment thereof, in furtherance of political or social objectives', available at <http:// jackson.fbi.gov/cntrterr.htm>. The US Code contains longer definitions in Title 22 on Foreign Relations and Intercourse, and Title 18 on Crime and Criminal Procedure (available at <http://www.gpoaccess.gov/uscode>). The USA Patriot Act definition, 'activities that (A) involve acts dangerous to human life that are a violation of the criminal laws of the U.S. or of any state, that (B) appear to be intended (i) to intimidate or coerce a civilian population, (ii) to influence the policy of a government by intimidation or coercion, or (iii) to affect the conduct of a government by mass destruction, assassination, or kidnapping, and (C) occur primarily within the territorial jurisdiction of the U.S.'. The NCTC definition, 'premeditated; perpetrated by a subnational or clandestine agent; politically motivated, potentially including religious, philosophical, or culturally symbolic motivations; violent; and perpetrated against a noncombatant target'.

18 Human Rights Watch, 'Counter the Threat or Counterproductive? Commentary on Proposed Counterterrorism Measures', 22 October 2007, p 23, available at <http:// www.hrw.org/legacy/backgrounder/eca/uk1007/>.

19 Article 19, 'The Impact of UK Anti-Terror Laws on Freedom of Expression' Submission to ICJ Panel of Eminent Jurists on Terrorism, Counter-Terrorism and Human Rights, April 2006, available at <http:ejp.icj.org/IMG/61.pdfejp.icj.org/ IMG/61.pdf>.

20 See the US State Department, Office of Coordinator of Counterterrorism's Current List of Designated Foreign Terrorist Organisations, available at <http://www.state. gov/s/ct/rls/other/des/123085.htm>.

21 Rudaw.net, 'PKK: US Shows it doesn't want a solution', 16 October 2009, available at <http://www.rudaw.net/details.aspx?lang=English&page=articles&c=Rudaw% 20Exclusive&id=13022>.

22 The full resolution stated 'That the president is authorized to use all necessary and appropriate force against those nations, organizations, or persons he determines planned, authorized, committed, or aided the terrorist attacks that occurred on Sept. 11, 2001, or harbored such organizations or persons, in order to prevent any future acts of international terrorism against the United States by such nations, organizations or persons'. *New York Times*, 'After the Attacks', 15 September 2001,

available at <http://www.nytimes.com/2001/09/15/us/after-the-attacks-the-overview-us-demands-arab-countries-choose-sides.html?pagewanted=2>.

23 See the US Department Office of the Coordinator for Counterterrorism List of Designated State Sponsors of Terrorism, available at <http://www.state.gov/s/ct/c14151.htm>.

24 *New York Times*, above, fn 22.

25 US Department of State, above, fn 3, p 41.

26 K Yildiz, *The Kurds in Iraq: Past, Present and Future* (London: Pluto Press, 2004), p 107.

27 Kurdish Human Rights Project (KHRP), Fact Finding Mission Report, 'The Civilian Toll of Cross Border Operations in Iraq' (London: KHRP, August 2007).

28 Speech by Special Envoy to Counter the PKK General (Ret) Joseph Ralston, 'Myths About the PKK and The United States', 19 October 2006, Asam Conference, Istanbul, available at <http://istanbul.usconsulate.gov/ralston_sp_101906.html>.

29 The White House, 'President Bush and Prime Minister Tayyip Erdogan discuss Global War on Terror', 5 November 2007.

30 Background Briefing by a Senior Administration Official on the President's meeting with President Gul of Turkey, 8 January 2008, available at <http://georgewbush-whitehouse.archives.gov/news/releases/2008/01/20080108-8.html>.

31 US-Turkish relations and the challenges ahead: hearing before the subcommittee on Europe of the Committee on Foreign Affairs, House of Representatives, 15 March 2007, available at <http://foreignaffairs.house.gov/110/34040.pdf>, p 3.

32 BBC News, 'Turkey Must End Iraq Raid', 28 February 2008.

33 Secretary Robert Gates, Press Conference with Turkey's Minister of Defense, 28 February 2008, available at <http://www.defenselink.mil/transcripts/transcript.aspx?transcriptid=4162>.

34 Background Briefing by a Senior Administration Official on the President's meeting with President Gul of Turkey, 8 January 2008, available at <http://georgewbush-whitehouse.archives.gov/news/releases/2008/01/20080108-8.html>.

35 BBC News, 'Outrage at "Old Europe" Remarks', 23 January 2003, available at <http://news.bbc.co.uk/1/hi/world/europe/2687403.stm>.

36 BBC News (Barnaby Mason), 'Europe rethinks war on terror', 12 March 2004, available at <http://news.bbc.co.uk/1/hi/world/europe/3500958.stm>.

37 Council of the European Union, Council Framework Decision of 13 June 2002 on the European arrest warrant and the surrender procedures between Member States – Statements made by certain Member States on the adoption of the Framework Decision, available at <http://eur-lex.europa.eu/LexUriServ/LexUriServ.do?uri=CELEX:32002F0584:EN:HTML>.

38 Council Document No SN 140/01.

39 Council Framework Decision 2002/475/JHA of 13 June 2002 on combating terror-ism, available at <http://eur-lex.europa.eu/smartapi/cgi/sga_doc?smartapi!celexapi!prod!CELEXnumdoc&lg=EN&numdoc=32002F0475&model=guichett>.

40 Muller, op. cit., fn 8, p 125.

41 See *PKK und KNK v Council of the European Community*, Case T-229/02, Judgment of 15 February 2005, European Court of Justice, and Judgment of 3 April 2008, Court of First Instance of the European Communities; and *Kongra-Gel and Others v Council of the European Union, United Kingdom of Great Britain and Northern Ireland, Intervener*, Case T-253/04, Judgment of 03 April 2008, Court of First Instance of the European Communities, available at <http://eurlex.europa.eu/LexUriServ/LexUriServ.do?uri=OJ:L:2002:160:0026:0027:EN:PDF>.

42 BBC News, 'EU Court Annuls PKK Terror Ruling', 7 April 2008, available at <http://news.bbc.co.uk/1/hi/world/europe/7328238.stm>.

43 Campaign Against Criminalising Communities (CAMPACC), 'Opposing the UK "Terrorist" List: Persistence as Resistance', February 2009, available at <http://campacc.org.uk/uploads/opposing_uk_terror_list_paper_190209.pdf>.

44 Press conference with the Turkish Prime Minister, 23 October 2007, available at <http://www.number10.gov.uk/Page13609>.

45 Turkey, A Partner in the War on Terror, A briefing by Faruk Loğoğlu (Turkey's former Ambassador to the US, appointed in 2001), 31 May 2002.

46 As of October 2009, Turkey's contribution to the International Security Assistance Force (ISAF) was 820 troops, available at<http://www.nato.int/isaf/docu/epub/pdf/placemat.pdf>.

47 Taken from 'Turkey: "War against terrorism" emboldens fascists and the military', Justus Leicht, 29 September 2001, World Socialist website.

48 KHRP, 'Turkey's Anti-Terror Laws: Threatening the Protection of Human Rights', 11 August 2008, available at <http://www.khrp.org/component/option, com_docman/task,cat_view/gid,40/Itemid,47/>, p 4.

49 KHRP, ibid, p 5.

50 KHRP, above, fn 48, p 7.

51 Defined in the law as 'Terrorism is any kind of act done by one or more persons belonging to an organization with the aim of changing the characteristics of the Republic as specified in the Constitution, its political, legal, social, secular and economic system, damaging the indivisible unity of the State with its territory and nation, endangering the existence of the Turkish State and Republic, weakening or destroying or seizing the authority of the State, eliminating fundamental rights and freedoms, or damaging the internal and external security of the State, public order or general health by means of pressure, force and violence, terror, intimidation, oppression or threat', KHRP, above, fn 48, p 4.

52 BBC News, 'U.S. denies backing Turkey PKK raid', 17 December 2007, available at <http://news.bbc.co.uk/1/hi/world/europe/7147375.stm>.

53 *The Washington Post*, 'U.S. helps turkey hit rebel Kurds in Iraq; Intelligence role could complicate diplomacy', 18 December 2007, available at <http://www.washingtonpost. com/wp-dyn/content/article/2007/12/17/AR2007121702150.html>.

54 *The Washington Post*, ibid. *Today's Zaman*, 'Turkish-U.S. Intelligence Sharing in Northern Iraq Educates Ankara', 26 January 2009, available at <http://www.todayszaman. com/tz-web/detaylar.do?load=detay&link=165076&bolum=101>.

55 BBC Worldwide Monitoring, 'Kurdistan Leader Barzani discusses Iraqi-Turkish dispute over PKK fighters', 27 October 2007.

56 BBC worldwide monitoring, 'Iraqi Kurdish leader rejects calling PKK terrorist organization', 1 November 2007.

57 BBC worldwide Monitoring, 'Turkish paper reports on sharing Intelligence on PKK leader with Iran', 11 May 2008.

58 *Today's Zaman*, 'Absence of trust hinders Turkish-Iranian security cooperation', 21 April 2008.

59 BBC worldwide Monitoring, 'Turkey, Iran sign security cooperation agreement', 17 April 2008.

60 *Terrorism Focus*, 'Turkish Generals Admit Military and Intelligence Coordination with Iran', 10 June 2008.

61 *Today's Zaman*, 'Turkey assures US over Intelligence sharing with Iran', 20 June 2009.

62 KHRP, Fact Finding Mission Report, 'The Civilian Toll of Cross Border Operations in Iraq' (London: KHRP, August 2007).

63 *The Guardian* (Michael Howard), 'Kurdish Leader Shuns US Move to Oust Saddam', 19 June 2003, available at <http://www.guardian.co.uk/international/story/ 0,3604,739786,00.html>.

64 Ali A Allawi, *The occupation of Iraq: winning the war, losing the peace* (London: Yale University Press, 2007), p 89.

65 Kurdistan Regional Government, 'Alleged Terrorist Leader to be Deported from Norway', 2 April 2005, available at <http://www.krg.org/articles/print.asp? anr=2092&lngnr=12&rnr=77>.

66 Statement of Ambassador Ryan C Crocker, US Ambassador to the Republic of Iraq Before a Joint Hearing of the Committee on Foreign Affairs and the Committee on Armed Services, 10 September 2007.

67 See UN Security Council background, available at <http://www.un.org/Docs/sc/unsc_background.html>.

68 David M Malone, 'Creeping Unilateralism: Humanitarian Interventions and No-Fly Zones', in David M Malone, *The International Struggle over Iraq: Politics in the UN Security Council 1980–2005* (Oxford: Oxford University Press, 2007).

69 UN Security Council Resolution 688.

70 Malone, op. cit, fn 68, pp 84–113.

71 UN Security Council Resolution 1546 (2004), adopted 8 June 2004, available at <http://www.uncc.ch/resolutio/res1546.pdf>.

72 UN Security Council Resolution 1546 (2004), ibid.

73 UN News Centre, 'Secretary-General concerned at Turkish move on attacking Kurdish targets in Iraq', 19 October 2007, available at <http://www.un.org/apps/news/story.asp?NewsID=24355&Cr=iraq&Cr1=turkey>.

74 For example 'Operation Iraqi Freedom', see Stahn Carsten, 'Enforcement of the Collective Will after Iraq', (2003) 97(4) *The American Journal of International Law* 809.

75 See UN Security Council Resolution 1199 (1998) which listed the actions that the Security Council was taking under Chapter VII of the Charter of the United Nations.

76 Stephen Zunes, Foreign Policy in Focus Special Report, 'The Continuing Storm: The U.S. Role in the Middle East', available at <http://www.fpif.org/papers/mideast/index.html>. Also published as a chapter in Martha Honey and Tom Barry (eds), *Global Focus: U.S. Foreign Policy at the Turn of the Millennium* (New York, NY: St Martin's Press, 2000).

77 Zunes, ibid.

78 Article 2(7) states that 'Nothing contained in the present Charter shall authorize the United Nations to intervene in matters which are essentially within the domestic jurisdiction of any state or shall require the Members to submit such matters to settlement under the present Charter'.

79 Carsten, op. cit., fn 74.

80 North Atlantic Treaty of 1949, available at <http://www.nato.int/cps/en/natolive/official_texts_17120.htm>.

81 Statement by the Secretary General on Iraq, 3 September 1996, available at <http://www.nato.int/docu/speech/1996/s960903a.htm>.

82 Press Statement by the NATO Secretary General, Lord Robertson, following the NATO-EU Informal Working Luncheon, NATO Headquarters, 3 April 2003, available at <http://www.nato.int/docu/speech/2003/s030403a.htm>.

83 Press Statement, ibid.

84 *The Washington Post,* 'U.S. Helps Turkey Hit Rebel Kurds', 18 December 2007, available at <http://www.washingtonpost.com/wp-dyn/content/article/2007/12/17/AR2007121702150.html>.

85 Donna Gomien, David Harris and Leo Zwaak, *Law and Practice of the European Convention on Human Rights and the European Social Charter* (Council of Europe Publishing, Germany, 1996), p 11.

86 Statute of the Council of Europe, available at <http://conventions.coe.int/Treaty/EN/Treaties/Html/001.htm>.

87 Council of Europe, European Charter for Regional or Minority Languages, available at <http://conventions.coe.int/Treaty/EN/Treaties/Html/148.htm>, and <http://conventions.coe.int/treaty/Commun/ChercheSig.asp?NT=118&CM=1&DF=&CL=ENG>.

88 Council of Europe, Framework Convention for the Protection of National Minorities, available at <http://conventions.coe.int/Treaty/EN/Treaties/Html/157.htm>.

89 Council of Europe Parliamentary Assembly, Recommendation 1377 (1998).

90 Gomien, Harris and Zwaak, op. cit., fn 85, p 13.
91 Council of Europe, Recommendation 1150 (1991) on the situation of the Iraqi Kurdish population and other persecuted minorities, available at <http://assembly.coe.int/Main.asp?link=/Documents/AdoptedText/ta91/EREC1150.htm>.
92 UN Convention on the Prevention and Punishment of the Crime of Genocide, adopted 9 December 1948, available at <http://www.un.org/millennium/law/iv-1.htm>.
93 Council of Europe, above, fn 91.
94 Council of Europe Recommendation 1266 (1995) on Turkey's military intervention in northern Iraq and on Turkey's respect of commitments concerning constitutional and legislative reforms, available at <http://assembly.coe.int/Documents/AdoptedText/ta95/EREC1266.HTM>.
95 See Report of the Parliamentary Assembly of the Council of Europe Doc 6553, Rapporteur Mr Jurgens, published 30 January 1992.
96 Council of Europe Parliamentary Assembly Report, Doc 7067, published 12 April 1994.
97 Resolution 1041 (1994) on the consequences of the dissolution of the Party for Democracy (DEP) in Turkey.
98 Rapporteur Mr Barsony, Doc 7290, 25 April 1995.
99 Council of Europe, Parliamentary Assembly Report on Turkey's respect of commitments to Constitutional and legislative reforms [follow up to Recommendation 1266 (1995)], Rapporteur Mr Barsony, 22 December 1995, Doc 7445.
100 Council of Europe, Doc 8300, 15 January 1999.
101 Humanitarian situation of the displaced Kurdish population in Turkey, Doc 9391, 22 March 2002; Report by Mr Alvaro Gil-Robles, Commissioner for Human Rights on his visit to Turkey in June 2003. The Report acknowledged the constitutional reforms in Turkey and also stressed that protection of human rights must be a top priority for authorities. There was however no reference to the conflict in southeast Turkey.
102 Recommendation 1377 (1998) (GT-MED(2001)1 and CB1, Rec_1377 (1998)), available at   <https://wcd.coe.int/ViewDoc.jsp?id=210727&Site=COE&BackColorInternet=DBDCF2&BackColorIntranet=FDC864&BackColorLogged=FDC864>.
103 Parliamentary Assembly Recommendation 1563 (2002), available at <https://wcd.coe.int/ViewDoc.jsp?id=300467&Site=COE&BackColorInternet=DBDCF2&BackColorIntranet=FDC864&BackColorLogged=FDC864>.
104 Council of Europe Press Release, 'Council of Europe Parliamentarians vote to end monitoring of Turkey', 22 June 2004, available at <https://wcd.coe.int/ViewDoc.jsp?id=1017421&Site=COE&BackColorInternet=DBDCF2&BackColorIntranet=FDC864&BackColorLogged=FDC864>.
105 The Role of the Council of Europe in the New European Architecture and its Competence in the Field of Human Rights, European Commission for Democracy through Law (Venice Commission), Report by Mr Hans Christian Kruger (Special Adviser on the EU Convention), Strasbourg, 5 December 2002, p 7, available at <http://64.233.183.104/search?q=cache:fyGsq3UkWWoJ:www.venice.coe.int/docs/2002/CDL-JU(2002)042-e.pdf+role+council+europe&hl=en&ct=clnk&cd=1&gl=uk>.
106 Council of Europe Interim Resolution CM/ResDH(2008)69.
107 Guidelines on Human Rights and the Fight against Terrorism adopted by the Committee of Ministers on 11 July 2002 at the 804th meeting of the Ministers' Deputies, available at <http://www1.umn.edu/humanrts/.../HR%20and%20the%20fight%20against%20terrorism.pdf>.
108 Council of Europe, Committee on Legal Affairs and Human Rights Report, 'Secret Detentions and Illegal Transfers of Detainees involving Council of Europe Member States: second report', 11 June 2007, available at <http://www.assembly.coe.int/Main.asp?link=/Documents/WorkingDocs/Doc07/EDOC11302.htm>.

109 Council of Europe, Committee on Legal Affairs and Human Rights report, 'United Nations Security Council and European Union Blacklists', 16 November 2007, available at <http://assembly.coe.int/Main.asp?link=/Documents/WorkingDocs/Doc07/EDOC11454.htm>.

110 Council of Europe Commissioner for Human Rights Thomas Hammarberg, 'Viewpoint', 2 November 2009, available at <http://www.commissioner.coe.int>.

111 See <http://ec.europa.eu/external_relations/iraq/index_en.htm>.

112 Resolution on the situation in Iraqi Kurdistan (Official Journal C337, 21/12/1992, p.0201) called upon the Turkish authorities to withdraw from Iraqi Kurdistan and end all armed hostilities.

113 See Reuters, 'Baghdad', 23 March 1995.

114 Council of Europe Parliamentary Assembly Report on Turkey's military intervention in northern Iraq and Turkey's respect of commitments concerning constitutional and legislative reforms, available at <http://assembly.coe.int/Main.asp?link=/Documents/WorkingDocs/Doc95/EDOC7290.htm>.

115 Resolution on the visit of the Troika to Ankara and the Turkish military intervention in northern Iraq, [1995] OJ C109/107, 1 May 1995, available at <http://eur-lex.europa.eu/LexUriServ.do?uri=CELEX:51995IP0636:EN:HTML>.

116 European Parliament resolution on the Turkish bombardment of northern Iraq, [2001] OJ C135/287–88, 5 July 2001.

117 Voice of America, *Turkey Strikes Kurdish Bases in Northern Iraq*, 27 July 2008 Available at: http://www.globalsecurity.org/wmd/library/news/iraq/2008/07/iraq-080727-voa02.htm.

118 *The Washington Post*, 'Turkey Authorizes Iraq Incursion,' 18 October 2007, available at <http://www.washingtonpost.com/wp-dyn/content/article/2007/10/17/AR2007101700967.html>.

119 *The Guardian*, 'EU Calls on Turkey to Halt Strikes in Northern Iraq,' 17 December 2007, available at <http://www.guardian.co.uk/world/2007/dec/17/turkey.iraq>.

120 Andrew Williams, *EU Human Rights Policies, A Study in Irony* (Oxford: Oxford University Press, 2004), p 77.

121 Regular Report From the Commission on Turkey's Progress Towards Accession, 1998, available at <http://www.dpt.gov.tr/DocObjects/Download/2466/1998%20(En).pdf>.

122 Regular Report, ibid, p 20.

123 Regular Report, ibid.

124 2004 Regular Report on Turkey's Progress Towards Accession, Brussels, 6 October 2004 SEC(2004) 1201, available at <http://ec.europa.eu/enlargement/archives/pdf/key_documents/2004/rr_tr_2004_en.pdf>, p 55.

125 2004 Regular Report, ibid.

126 See European Parliament Resolution on the Imprisonment of school children in Turkey (Official Journal C 158,26/06/1989, p.0201) and Resolution on the situation of the Kurds B3-0458/91;B3-0470/91;B3-0477/91 (Official Journal C 106, 22/04/1992, p.0120), available in 'European Parliament resolution on the Kurdish question' (TOHAV, Foundation for Society and Legal Studies, Istanbul, 2008).

127 [1991] OJ C129/141, 20 May 1991.

128 See Resolution on the situation in Turkey and the offer of a ceasefire made by the PKK, [1996] OJ C032/93, 5 February 1996, available at <http://eur-lex.europa.eu/LexUriServ/LexUriServ.do?uri=CELEX:51996IP0060.EN:HTML>, and Resolution of the Committee of the Regions on 'The arrest of Mr Öcalan and the need to find a political solution to the Kurdish problem', cdr 100/99 FIN, [1999] OJ C198/82, 14 July 1999, available at <http://eurlex.europa.eu/LexUriServ/LexUriServ.do?uri=CELEX:51999IR0100:EN:HTML>.

129 European Commission Key Documents concerning Turkey's Accession are available at <http://ec.europa.eu/enlargement/candidate-countries/turkey/key_documents_en.htm>.

130 European Commission, ibid.

131 Council of the European Union, Council decision on the principles, priorities and conditions contained in the Accession Partnership with the Republic of Turkey and repealing Decision 2006/35/EC, 13 February 2008, available at <http://www.avrupa.info.tr/Files/st05815.en08.pdf>.

132 Address by Guenter Verheugen, Member of the European Commission Responsible for Enlargement, 'Turkey and the EU towards December 2004,' 17 June 2004, Brussels, available at <http://europa.eu/rapid/pressReleasesAction.do?reference=SPEECH/04/309&format=HTML&aged=1&language=EN&guiLanguage= en>.

133 Republic of Turkey, Ministry of Foreign Affairs, 'Political Reforms in Turkey', February 2004.

134 European Union Press Release, 'EU Presidency Statement on the military action undertaken by Turkey in Iraqi territory', 25 February 2008, available at <http://www.eu2008.si/en/News_and_Documents/CFSP_Statements/February/0225MZZturkey.html>.

135 European Union Press Release, 'Fight Against Terrorism Updating List of Terrorist Organisations', 15 September 2003, available at <http://europa.eu/rapid/pressReleasesAction.do?reference=PRES/03/264&format=HTML&aged=0&language=EN&guiLanguage=en>.

136 EurActiv, interview with EU Enlargement Commissioner Olli Rehn, 'EU supports Turkey against PKK Terrorists', 23 October 2007, available at <http://www.euractiv.com/en/foreign-affairs/interview-eu-supports-turkey-pkk-terrorists/article-167805>.

137 OSCE/ODIHR, *OSCE Human Dimension Commitments, A Reference Guide* (Warsaw: OSCE Office for Democratic Institutions and Human Rights, 2001), p XV1 (5).

138 OSCE/ODIHR, ibid.

139 OSCE/ODIHR, op. cit., fn 137, p XV1I (B1).

140 Declaration on Principles Guiding Relations between Participating States, principle X, paras 1 and 2, Helsinki, 1975.

141 OSCE/ODIHR, op. cit., fn 137, p XV1II (B3).

142 OSCE/ODIHR, op. cit., fn 137, p XV1 (B1).

143 Organization for Security and Co-operation in Europe, *Document of the Conference on the Human Dimension of the OSCE*, Copenhagen, 29 June 1990, p.18, available at: www.osce.org/item/13992.html.

144 1993–2001.

145 Document of the Copenhagen meeting, above, fn 143, p 20.

146 OSCE/ODIHR, op. cit., fn 137, p XV (4).

147 OSCE/ODIHR, op. cit., fn 137, p XV1 (4).

148 G Gürbey, 'The Kurdish conflict in Turkey – (not a subject for the OSCE?)', (2001) 12(1) *Helsinki Monitor* 7–20(14), p 11.

149 OSCE Mechanisms and Procedures, available at <http://216.239.59.104/search?q=cache:sFMhMJIl89YJ:www.osce.org/item/4056.html+austria+mechanism+turkey& hl=en&ct=clnk&cd=2&gl=uk>.

150 Letter from Andrew Telegdi (MP) to Frank Swaelen (President of the OSCE Parliamentary Assembly), dated 9 August 1995.

151 US Mission to the OSCE, Statement on National Minorities, as preprared for delivery by Felice Gaer, Commissioner, US Commission on International Religious Freedom, to the OSCE Human Dimension Implementation Meeting, 28 September 2005, Warsaw, available at <http://osce.usmission.gov/media/pdfs/statements-at-hdim/hdim_nationalminorities_09_28_05.pdf>.

152 John Bew, Martyn Frampton and Inigo Gurruchaga, *Talking to Terrorists* (London: C Hurst & Co Publishers, 2009), pp 16–17 and 239.

153 BBC News, 'Assembly Condemns Weekend Attacks' 23 November 2009, available at <http://news.bbc.co.uk/1/hi/northern_ireland/8374560.stm> (accessed 25 November 2009).

154 Brian Currin, 'Lessons Learned From Peace Process in South Africa, Northern Ireland and the Basque Country', speech given to the 5th Annual Conference of the EUTCC, January 2009, European Parliament, Brussels.

155 Dean G Pruitt, 'Negotiation with Terrorists', (2006) 11 *International Negotiation* 386–87.

156 Jonathan Stevenson, 'Northern Ireland: Treating Terrorists as Statesmen', (1996–97) 105 *Foreign Policy* 133.

157 Bew, Frampton and Gurruchaga, op. cit., fn 152, p 256.

158 Meredith Moore, 'End of Terrorism? ETA and the Efforts for Peace', (2005) 27(2) *Harvard International Review* 12.

159 Pruitt, op. cit., fn 155.

160 Currin, above, fn 154.

161 Matthew O'Rourke, 'The Impact of the "War on Terrorism" on Internal Conflicts', *The Ploughshares Monitor*, 26:1, Spring 2005, available at <http//www.ploughshares.ca/libraries/monitor/monm05d.htm> (accessed 19 November 2009).

Chapter 8

1 JP Humphrey, 'Political and Related Rights', in T Meron (ed), *Human Rights in International Law: Legal and Policy Issues*, two volumes (Oxford: Clarendon Press, 1984), p 193.

2 H Hannum, *Autonomy, Sovereignty, and Self-Determination: The Accommodation of Conflicting Rights*, revised edition (Philadelphia, PA: University of Pennsylvania Press, 1990), p 27.

3 R Higgins, *Problems and Process* (Oxford: Oxford University Press, 1994), p 111.

4 Higgins, ibid, p 39.

5 J Crawford, *The Creation of States in International Law*, 2nd edition (Oxford: Oxford University Press, 2006). p 29.

6 T Bahcheli, B Bartmann and H Srebrnik (eds), *De Facto States: The Quest For Sovereignty* (New York, NY: Routledge, 2004), p ix.

7 D Raič, *Statehood & The Law of Self-Determination* (The Hague: Martinus Nijhoff, 2002), p 9.

8 J Castellino, *International Law and Self-Determination* (The Hague: Martinus Nijhoff, 2000), p 11.

9 Castellino, ibid, p 13; note, however, A Cassese, *Self-determination of Peoples* (Cambridge: Cambridge University Press, 1995), pp 14–19 in which he discusses the important role of VI Lenin in developing the concept of self-determination.

10 Reply of President Woodrow Wilson to the Addressees of The Imperial General Chancellor and the Imperial and Royal Austro Hungarian Minister for Foreign Affairs (1918), reprinted in James B Scott (ed), *Official Statements of War Aims and Peace Proposals, December 1916 to November 1918* (Washington DC: Carnegie Endowment for International Peace, 1921), pp 256 and 268.

11 President Wilson's Message to Congress, 8 January 1918, Records of the United States Senate; Record Group 46, National Archives of the United States of America.

12 Castellino, op. cit., fn 8, p 13.

13 Raič, op. cit., fn 7, pp 181–82.

14 Raič, op. cit., fn 7, p 182.

15 M Shaw, *International Law*, 6th edition (Cambridge: Cambridge University Press, 2008), p 251.

16 Shaw, ibid.

17 'Report of the International Commission of Jurists entrusted by the Council of the League of Nations with the task of giving an Advisory Opinion upon the Legal Aspects of the Åland Islands Question', (October 1920), *League of Nations Official Journal*, Special Supplement No. 3, p 5.

18 'Report of Commission of Rapporteurs on the Åland Islands Questions', League of Nations Doc B7 21/68/106, 1921.

19 Report of Commission of Rapporteurs, ibid.

20 Montevideo Convention on the Rights and Duties of States, Montevideo, Uruguay, 26 December 1933.

21 Raič, op. cit., fn 7, p 9.

22 Raič, op. cit., fn 7, p 24.

23 DJ Harris, *Cases & Materials on International Law* (London: Sweet & Maxwell, 1997), p 102; and Castellino, op. cit., fn 8, p 77.

24 Castellino, op. cit., fn 8, p 77.

25 Shaw, op. cit., fn 15, p 206.

26 LC Buchheit, *Secession: The Legitimacy of Self-Determination* (London: Yale University Press, 1978), p 73.

27 Charter of the United Nations, TS 993, 26 June 1945.

28 United Nations (UN) Charter Debates, vi United Nations Conference on International Organization (UNCIO) 300, (15 May, 1945) at 20.

29 Raič, op. cit., fn 7, p 23.

30 Shaw, op. cit., fn 15, p 252.

31 Higgins, op. cit., fn 3, p 113.

32 P Thornberry, 'The Principle of Self-determination', in M Akehurst, V Lowe and C Warbrick (eds), *The United Nations & Principles of International Law* (London: Routledge, 1994), p 177.

33 R Higgins, 'Postmodern Tribalism and the Right to Secession, Comments', in C Brölmann, M Zieck and R Lefeber (eds), *Peoples and Minorities in International Law* (Dordrecht: Martinus Nijhoff Publishers, 1993), p 29.

34 Higgins, ibid, p 29.

35 A Cassese, 'The Helsinki Declaration and Self-Determination', in T Buergenthal and J Hall (eds), *Human Rights, International Law and the Helsinki Accord* (New York, NY: Allenheld, 1977), p 84.

36 A Cassese, 'Political Self-Determination – Old Concepts and New Developments', in A Cassese (ed), *UN Law/Fundamental Rights: Two Topics in International Law* (Alphen aan de Rijn: Martinus Nijhoff Publishers, 1979), p 138.

37 Shaw, op. cit., fn 15, p 252.

38 Shaw, op. cit., fn 15, p 252.

39 Higgins, op. cit., fn 3, p 113.

40 *Legal Consequences for States of the Continued Presence of South Africa in Namibia (South West Africa) Notwithstanding Security Council Resolution 276 (1970)*, Advisory Opinion, [1971] *ICJ Reports* 12, para 53, p 19.

41 Declaration on the Granting of Independence to Colonial Countries and Peoples, UN General Assembly Resolution 1514 (XV), 14 December 1960.

42 Principles which should guide Members in determining whether or not an obligation exists to transmit the information called for under Article 73(e) of the Charter, UN General Assembly Resolution 1541 (XV), 15 December 1960.

43 Castellino, op. cit., fn 8, p 22.

44 Castellino, op. cit., fn 8, p 22.

45 UN General Assembly Resolution 1514 (XV), above, fn 41.

46 UN General Assembly Resolution 1541 (XV), above, fn 42.

47 Raič, op. cit., fn 7, p 130.

48 Raič, op. cit., fn 7, p 131.

49 Declaration on Principles of International Law Friendly Relations and Co-operation among States in Accordance with the Charter of the UN, UN General Assembly Resolution 2625 (xxv), 24 October 1970.

50 UN General Assembly Resolution 2625 (xxv), ibid.

51 V Nanda, 'Self-Determination under International Law: Validity of Claims to Secede', (1981) 13 Case W Res J Int'l L 257, pp 268–70.

52 1966 International Covenant of Civil and Political Rights, (1966) 999 UNTS 171, and 1966 International Covenant on Economic, Social and Cultural Rights, (1966) 999 UNTS 3, both 16 December 1966, Article 1 common to both.

53 UN General Assembly Vienna Declaration and Programme of Action, 12 July 1993 (A/CONF.157/23) (VDPA).

54 *Legal Consequences for States of the Continued Presence of South Africa in Namibia*, above, fn 40, para 53, p 19, pp 31–32, paras 52–53; and *Western Sahara*, Advisory Opinion of 16 October 1975, [1975] *ICJ Reports* 12, pp 31–32, paras 54–59.

55 *Case Concerning East Timor (Portugal v Australia)*, Judgment of 30 June 1995, [1995] *ICJ Reports* 90, para 29, p 21.

56 *Legal Consequences of the Construction of a Wall in the Occupied Palestinian Territory*, Advisory Opinion of 9 July 2004, [2004] *ICJ Reports* 136.

57 *Legal Consequences*, ibid, para 159.

58 S Breau, 'International Court of Justice Advisory Opinion on the Legal Consequences of the Construction of the Wall in the Occupied Palestinian Territory', (2005) 54 *International and Comparative Legal Quarterly* 1003, p 1008.

59 Breau, ibid, p 1008.

60 Breau, op. cit., fn 58, p 1009.

61 P Thornberry, 'Self-Determination, Minorities, Human Rights: A Review of International Instruments', (1989) 38 ICLQ 867.

62 Thornberry, ibid, p 868.

63 1966 International Covenant of Civil and Political Rights, op. cit., fn 52, Article 27.

64 Thornberry, op. cit., fn 61, p 878, and F Capotorti, *Study of the Rights of Persons belonging to Ethnic, Religious and Linguistic Minorities*, (1979) UN Sales No E 78, XIV.

65 Buchheit, op. cit., fn 26, p 9.

66 J Crawford, 'The Rights of Peoples: "Peoples" or "Governments"?', in J Crawford (ed), *The Rights of Peoples* (Oxford: Clarendon Press, 1988), p 59.

67 *Legal Consequences of the Construction of a Wall in the Occupied Palestinian Territory*, above, fn 56, p 199, para 155.

68 *Western Sahara*, above, fn 54, p 36.

69 There are many books written on this issue, cited in this chapter, but see particularly Buchheit, op. cit., fn 26, Hannum, op. cit., fn 2, Cassese, op. cit., fn 9, Raič, op. cit., fn 7, and Castellino, op. cit., fn 8.

70 Nanda, op. cit., fn 51, pp 269–70.

71 Nanda, op. cit., fn 51, pp 269–70.

72 Declaration on Principles of International Law Friendly Relations and Co-operation among States in Accordance with the Charter of the UN, UN General Assembly Resolution 2625 (xxv), 24 October 1970, Preamble.

73 Higgins, op. cit., fn 3, p 111.

74 Higgins, op. cit., fn 3, p 117.

75 C Tomuschat, 'Secession and Self-determination', in M Kohen, *Secession International Law Perspectives* (Cambridge: Cambridge University Press, 2008), p 31.

76 Buchheit, op. cit., fn 26, p 11.

77 1966 International Covenant of Civil and Political Rights, op. cit., fn 52, Article 27.

78 Declaration on the Rights of Persons Belonging to National or Ethnic, Religious and Linguistic Minorities, UN General Assembly (A/RES.47/135), 18 December 1992.

79 Shaw, op. cit., fn 15, p 297.

80 Declaration on the Rights of Indigenous Peoples, UN General Assembly Resolution 61/295, 13 September 2007, and Shaw, op. cit., fn 15, p 299.
81 Higgins, op. cit., fn 3, p 113.
82 Raič, op. cit., fn 7, p 201.
83 Bahcheli, Bartmann and Srebrnik, op. cit., fn 6, p ix.
84 See above discussion on statehood as per Principle vi of UN General Assembly Resolution 1541 this could be exercised through: '(a) Emergence as a sovereign independent State; (b) Free association with an independent State; or (c) Integration with an independent State', see Appendix 16.
85 For a complete discussion of the Bangladesh experience see Castellino, op. cit., fn 8, Chapter 5.
86 Bahcheli, Bartmann and Srebrnik, op. cit., fn 6, p ix.
87 Opinion No 1, Arbitration Commission, EC Conference on Yugoslavia: Badinter Chairman, 29 November 1991, 92 ILR 162.
88 Opinion No 1, ibid.
89 Opinion No 3, Arbitration Commission, EC Conference on Yugoslavia: Badinter Chairman, 11 January 1992, (1992) 92 ILR 170.
90 Bahcheli, Bartmann and Srebrnik, op. cit., fn 6, p ix.
91 Buchheit, op. cit., fn 26, p 17.
92 *Reference Re Secession of Quebec Judgment* [1998] 2 SCR 217, Supreme Court of Canada.
93 For an excellent discussion on the history of the secession movement in Quebec, see P Dumberry, 'Lessons Learned from the Quebec Secession Reference before the Supreme Court of Canada', in Kohen, op. cit., fn 75, pp 416–52.
94 Dumberry, ibid, para 126.
95 Dumberry, op. cit., fn 93, para 126.
96 Dumberry, op. cit., fn 93, para 126.
97 Dumberry, op. cit., fn 93, para 83.
98 Dumberry, op. cit., fn 93, para 111.
99 Dumberry, op. cit., fn 93, para 103.
100 Dumberry, op. cit., fn 93, para 130.
101 P Macklem, 'Militant Democracy, legal pluralism, and the paradox of self-determination', (2006) *International Journal of Constitutional Law* 488, p 504.
102 LS Eastwood, 'Secession: State Practice and International Law after the dissolution of the Soviet Union and Yugoslavia', (1993) 3 *Duke Journal of Comparative & International Law* 299.
103 Bahcheli, Bartmann and Srebrnik, op. cit., fn 6, p 13.
104 Bahcheli, Bartmann and Srebrnik, op. cit., fn 6, p 13.
105 See UN Doc A/C.3/48/L.17, November 1993. See also W Danspeckgruber (ed), *The Self-Determination of Peoples: Community, Nation and State in an Interdependent World* (Boulder, CO: Lynne Reinner, 2002), where the draft convention is reprinted together with legal commentaries.
106 W Kymlicka, 'The Internationalization of Minority Rights', (2008) *International Journal of Constitutional Law* 1, p 21.
107 C Warbrick, 'Kosovo: The Declaration of Independence', (2008) 57 ICLQ 675, p 676.
108 Cassese, op. cit., fn 9, pp 359–60.
109 The Secretary General's special representative for Kosovo.
110 S Breau, *Humanitarian Intervention; The United Nations and Collective Responsibility* (London: Cameron May, 2005), Chapter 4.
111 UN Security Council Resolution 1244 dated 10 June 1999.
112 B Coppieters and R Sakwa, *Contextualising Secession – Normative Studies in Comparative Perspective* (New York: Oxford University Press, 2003), p 124.
113 'Who has Recognized Kosovo as an Independent State', Ministry of Foreign Affairs of the Republic of Kosovo, 2009, available at <http://www.ks-gov.net/MPJ/Njohjet/tabid/93/Default.aspx> (accessed 5 April 2009).

114 Coppieters and Sakwa, op. cit., fn 112, p 123.
115 D Kumbaro, 'Final Report: The Kosovo Crisis in an International Law Perspective: Self-Determination, Territorial Integrity and the NATO Intervention', NATO Office of Information & Press, 2001, available at <http://www.nato.int/acad/fellow/99–01/kumbaro.pdf> (accessed 21 August 2009).
116 S Cvijic, 'Self-determination as a Challenge to the Legitimacy of Humanitarian Interventions: The Case of Kosovo', (2007) 8 *German Law Journal* 1, pp 57–79 and 71–72.
117 Kumbaro, op. cit., fn 115, pp 41–42 and 48.
118 *Reference Re Secession of Quebec*, above, fn 92, para 126.
119 'The Åland Islands Question, Report presented to the Council of the League by the commission of Rapporteurs', DOC.B.7.21/68/106, 1921, cited in BS Brown, 'Human-Rights, Sovereignty and the Final Status of Kosovo', (2005) 80 *Chicago-Kent Law Review* 295.
120 M Goodwin, 'Special Issue Introduction – What Future for Kosovo? – From Province to Protectorate to State? Speculation on the Impact of Kosovo's Genesis upon the Doctrines of International Law', (2007) 8 *German Law Journal* 1, pp 1–20 and 6.
121 *The Economist*, 'If Kosovo goes free', 2007, available at <http://www.economist.com/world/europe/displaystory.cfm?story_id=10225052> (accessed 21 August 2009).
122 *The Economist*, 'A year in the life of Kosovo', 2009, available at <http://www.economist.com/opinion/displaystory.cfm?story_id=13109697> (accessed 21 August 2009).
123 European Parliament Resolution of 5 February 2009 on Kosovo and the Role of the European Union (adopted by 424 votes to 133 against).
124 *The Economist*, above, fn 122.
125 *The Economist*, above, fn 121.
126 *The Economist*, above, fn 121.
127 *EurActiv.com*, 'Ahtisaari seeks compromise on Kosovo plan', 2007, available a <http://www.euractiv.com/en/enlargement/ahtisaari-seeks-compromise-kosovo-plan/article-161416> (accessed 5 April 2009). NB: European Commission spokesperson: 'our opinion is that Kosovo is a sui generis case and does not provide a blueprint for anyone else', see also Warbrick, op. cit., fn 107.
128 Warbrick, op. cit., fn 107, p 680.
129 Goodwin, op. cit., fn 120, p 19.
130 Russian News & Information Agency Novosti, 'Russia to support Abkhazia, South Ossetia if they are attacked', 2008, available at <http://en.rian.ru/russia/20080826/116296248.html> (accessed 5 April 2009).
131 Cvijic, op. cit., fn 116, p 60.
132 Cvijic, op. cit., fn 116, p 60.
133 Cvijic, op. cit., fn 116, p 79.
134 For a comprehensive discussion of this topic see the edited collection, Kohen, op. cit., fn 75.
135 Buchheit, op. cit , fn 26, p 6.
136 B Coppieters, 'Introduction', in Coppieters and Sakwa, op cit., fn 112, p 4.
137 M Kohen, 'Introduction', in M Kohen (ed), *Secession: International Law Perspectives* (Cambridge: Cambridge University Press, 2006), p 2.
138 Kohen, ibid, p 14.
139 M Dixon, *Textbook on International Law*, 6th edition (Oxford: Oxford University Press, 2007), p 118.
140 Raič, op. cit., fn 7, p 315.
141 A Buchanan, *Secession: The Morality of Political Divorce from Fort Sumter to Lithuania and Quebec* (Boulder, CO: Westview Press, 1991), p 61.
142 Buchanan, ibid, p 132.
143 Buchanan, op. cit., fn 141, p 132.
144 Kohen, op. cit., fn 137, p 14.

145　Opinion No 1, above, fn 87.
146　I Brownlie, *Principles of Public International Law*, 7th edition (Oxford: Oxford University Press, 2008), p 649.
147　A Zimmermann, 'Secession and the law of State Succession', in Kohen, op. cit., fn 137, p 209.
148　Opinion No 1, above, fn 87.
149　Zimmermann, op. cit., fn 147, p 211.
150　Zimmermann, op. cit., fn 147, p 211.
151　Opinion No 8, Arbitration Commission, EC Conference on Yugoslavia: Badinter Chairman, 4 July 1992, (1992) 31 ILM 1521.
152　Opinion No 3, above, fn 89, and see DM Ong, 'Australia and Indonesia Timor Gap Treaty', (2001) 31 *Netherlands Yearbook of International Law* 67, p 101 for discussion of definition of *uti possidetis*.
153　Council of Ministers of the European Commission, 16 December 1991, Guidelines on the Recognition of New States in Eastern Europe and in the Soviet Union.
154　J Dugard and D Raić, 'The role of recognition in the law and practice of secession', Kohen, op. cit., fn 75, p 112.
155　Vienna Convention on Succession of States in respect of State Property, Archives and Debts adopted 7 April 1983, not yet in force, see also the Vienna Convention on Succession of States in Respect of Treaties 1978, (1946) UNTS 3.
156　V Lowe, *International Law* (Oxford: Oxford University Press, 2007), Chapter 4.18.
157　Lowe, ibid, p 169.
158　Zimmermann, op. cit., fn 147, pp 213–14.
159　Brownlie, op. cit., fn 146, p 652, and *Peter Pázmány University Case*, (1933) PCIJ, Ser A/B, No 61, p 237.
160　Brownlie, op. cit., fn 146, p 653.
161　Brownlie, op. cit., fn 146, p 653.
162　Brownlie, op. cit., fn 146, p 653.
163　Brownlie, op. cit., fn 146, pp 653–54.
164　G Smith 'Mapping the Federal Condition: Ideology, Political Practice and Social Justice', in G Smith (ed), *Federalism: The Multiethnic Challenge* (London: Longman, 1995), p 1.
165　R Watts, *Comparing Federal Systems*, 2nd edition (Montreal: McGill-Queen's University Press, 1990), p 6.
166　Smith, op. cit., fn 164, p 4.
167　Smith, op. cit., fn 164, p 5.
168　M Burgess, 'Federalism and Federation: A Reappraisal', in M Burgess and A Gagnon, *Comparative Federalism and Federation* (London: Harvester, 1993), p 3.
169　Watts, op. cit., fn 165, p 7.
170　King, 'Federation and Representation, in Burgess and Gagnon, op. cit., fn 168, pp 94–101.
171　E Barendt, *An Introduction to Constitutional Law* (Oxford: Oxford University Press, 1998), pp 51–52.
172　Barendt, ibid, p 52.
173　Watts, op. cit., fn 165, p 3.
174　Watts, op. cit., fn 165, pp 1 and 8–13.
175　Watts, op. cit., fn 165, p 1.
176　Smith, op. cit., fn 164, p 2.
177　Barendt, op. cit., fn 171, p 55.
178　Watts, op. cit., fn 165, p 40.
179　Watts, op. cit., fn 165, p 55.
180　Smith, op. cit., fn 164, p 2.
181　Smith, op. cit., fn 164, p 3.
182　Smith, op. cit., fn 164, p 3.

183 King, op. cit., fn 170, p 97.
184 King, op. cit., fn 170, pp 95–96.
185 D Brancati, 'Can Federalism Stabilize Iraq?', (2004) 27 *The Washington Quarterly* 7, p 7.
186 Brancati, ibid, p 11.
187 For a discussion of the potential problems of an Iraqi Federation see, R Visser and G Stansfield (eds), *An Iraq of its Regions: Cornerstones of a Federal Democracy?* (London: Hurst & Company, 2007).
188 *Reference Re Secession of Quebec*, above fn 92.

Chapter 9

1 Report of the Special Rapporteur, Ms Asma Jahangir, 'Civil and Political Rights, including the Question of Disappearances and summary executions', submitted pursuant to Commission on Human Rights Resolution 2001/45, 18 December 2001, UN Doc E/CN.4/2002/74/Add.1, para 36.
2 Kerim Yildiz and Mark Muller, *The European Union and Turkish Accession: Human Rights and the Kurds* (London: Pluto Press, 2008), p 106.
3 In the First World War, 5 per cent of victims were civilians, in the Second World War they constituted 48 per cent, rising to 84 per cent in the Korean War and 90 per cent in the Vietnam War, cited in Ingrid Detter, *The Law of War*, 2nd edition (Cambridge: Cambridge University Press, 2000), p 286.
4 For example, a study by the World Organisation Against Torture and Human Rights Association in 2003 found that Kurdish IDPs suffered disproportionately high levels of psychological problems related to their experiences in the conflict, cited in Kurdish Human Rights Project (KHRP), *The Internally Displaced Kurds of Turkey: Ongoing Issues of Responsibility, Redress and Resettlement* (London: KHRP, September 2007), p 97.
5 Chandra Lekha Sriram, Olga Martin-Ortega and Johanna Herman, *War, Conflict and Human Rights* (London: Routledge, 2009), p 75.
6 As is noted earlier in the book, violations of Common Article III to the Geneva Conventions have not been regarded as 'grave breaches' in the majority of the jurisprudence.
7 *Armed Activities on the Territory of the Congo (Democratic Republic of the Congo v Uganda)*, Judgment of 19 December 2005, [2005] *ICJ Reports* 168.
8 Sriram, Martin-Ortega and Herman, op. cit., fn 5, p 114.
9 With the exception, as we see in Chapter 7, of the new context of alliances in the war on terrorism, where military assistance is sought for combating domestic terrorist threats, but the terrorism label prohibiting any further involvement of the international community as the proscription clauses prohibit engagement.
10 Michelle L Mack, 'Compliance with international humanitarian law by non state actors in non international armed conflicts', Harvard University, November 2003, available at <http://ihl.ihlresearch.org/index.cfm?pageId=2069>.
11 Yildiz and Muller, op. cit., fn 2, p 124.
12 Sadi Cayci (Branch Chief, International Law, Office of the Legal Advisor, Turkish General Staff), 'Countering Terrorism and the Law of Armed Conflict', in Harvey Langholtz, Boris Kondoch and Alan Wells (eds), *International Peacekeeping: The Yearbook of International Peace Operations*, Volume 8 (2003), p 333.
13 Oren Gross and Fionnuala Ní Aoláin, *Law in Times of Crisis, Emergency Powers in Theory and Practice* (Cambridge: Cambridge University Press, 2006), p 352.
14 *Wall Street Journal* (Nicholas Birch), 'Turkey Seeks End to Kurdish Conflict', 6 August 2009, available at <http://online.wsj.com/article/SB124950871809009061.html> (last accessed 26 October 2009).
15 *The Times* (Anthony Lloyd), 'PKK leader offers Turkey an olive branch to end war', 26 May 2009, available at <http://www.timesonline.co.uk/tol/news/world/europe/article6360955.ece>.

16 Andrew Clapham, *Human Rights Obligations of Non-State Actors* (Oxford: Oxford University Press, 2006).

17 Dr François Bugnion, Former Director of International Law and Cooperation, International Committee of the Red Cross, presentation at British Institute of International and Comparative Law seminar, 'The ICRC and the Geneva Conventions', 7 September 2009, available at <http://www.biicl.org/events/view/-/id/422/>.

18 Prime Minister Recep Tayyip Erdoğan refused to meet with Democratic Society Party (DTP) members after they were elected in 2007 on this basis, until August 2009 when he agreed to meet DTP members saying he regarded them as interlocutors for the Kurdish problem, available at <http://www.hurriyetdailynews.com/n.php?n=pm-meets-dtp-today-2009-08-04>.

19 *Today's Zaman*, 'Should the State Talk to PKK leader Öcalan?', 23 July 2009, available at <http://www.todayszaman.com/tz-web/columnists-181714-should-the-state-talk-to-pkk-leader-ocalan.html>, <http://www.upi.com/Top_News/2008/02/24/Gates-calls-on-Turkey-to-talk-with-PKK/UPI-76401203893959/>, <http://www.turkishweekly.net/news/86188/turkey-39-s-main-opposition-accuses-erdogan-of-talking-indirectly-with-pkk.html>.

20 As is stated in Chapter 3, any attack must be shown to be carried out for the specific purpose of 'military advantage' and not to terrorise or dislocate or injure civilians.

21 L Moir, *The Law of Internal Armed Conflict* (Cambridge: Cambridge University Press, 2002), p 36. See Chapter 2.

22 Additional Protocol I has 168 state parties and Additional Protocol II has 164 state parties.

23 Blog of the European Journal of International Law, 'Afghanistan accedes to Additional Protocols to Geneva Conventions: Will AP II govern the conflict in Afghanistan?', 30 June 2009, available at <http://www.ejiltalk.org/afghanistan-accedes-to-additional-protocols/>.

24 Koçak Cemil, 'Parliament membership during the single-party system in Turkey (1925–45)', Sabancı University Faculty of Arts and Social Sciences, available at <http://209.85.229.132/search?q=cache:rNDUb8WXRk8J:>, <, https://research.sabanciuniv.edu/27/1/3011800000203.pdf+Free+Republican+Party+dissolved+in+Turkey&cd=15&hl=en&ct=clnk&gl=uk> (accessed 19 November 2009).

25 See <http://www.faqs.org/minorities/Middle-East-and-North-Africa/Kurds.html> (accessed 20 November 2009).

26 Hukuki Net, 'Political Structure of Turkey', available at <http://en.hukuki.net/index.php?topic=58.0;wap2> (accessed 20 November 2009).

27 Michael M Gunter, 'Political Instability in Turkey during 1970s', *Conflict Quarterly*, available at <http://www.lib.unb.ca/Texts/JCS/CQ/vol009_1winter1989/gunter.pdf> (accessed 20 November 2009)

28 In Turkish, *Anavatan Partisi* (ANAP), founded in 1983.

29 Irina A Danilkina, 'TURKEY: The Party System from 1963 to 2000', available at <http://janda.org/ICPP/ICPP2000/Countries/7-MiddleEastNorthAfrica/78-Turkey/Turkey63–00.htm> (accessed 20 November 2009).

30 Jonathan Fryer, 'Turkey's Democratic Opening to the Kurds', 4 October 2009, available at <http://jonathanfryer.wordpress.com/2009/10/04/>.

31 On 27 April 2007, the Turkish Armed Forces issued a memorandum regarding the presidential nomination of Abdullah Gül, containing such thinly veiled threats as 'those who are opposed to Great Leader Mustafa Kemal Atatürk's understanding "How happy is the one who says I am a Turk" are enemies of the Republic of Turkey and will remain so. The Turkish Armed Forces maintain their sound determination to carry out their duties stemming from laws to protect the unchangeable characteristics of the Republic of Turkey. Their loyalty to this determination is absolute'. Further excerpts are available at <http://news.bbc.co.uk/1/hi/world/europe/6602775.stm> (accessed 29 October 2009).

32 A closure case against the AKP on grounds of being the 'centre of anti-secular activities' was filed on November 2007. The case against the AKP was defeated by a narrowly balanced Constitutional Court decision on 30 July 2008, but the Court nonetheless halved treasury funding to the party as a 'serious warning' over its supposed antisecular activities.

33 Aliza Marcus, *Blood and belief: the PKK and the Kurdish fight for independence* (New York, NY: New York University Press, 2007), p 250.

34 *Hurriyet*, 'Opposition Leader Sets Red Lines, Incurs Gov't Wrath', 9 August 2009, available at <http://www.hurriyetdailynews.com/h.php?news=opposition-leader-sets-red-lines-incurs-gov8217t-wrath-2009-08-09>.

35 *Eurasia Daily Monitor*, 'AKP's Kurdish Initiative Sparks Political Controversy in Turkey', Volume 6, Issue 157, available at <http://www.jamestown.org/single/?no_cache=1&tx_ttnews[tt_news]=35417>.

36 The Jamestown Foundation, AKP's Kurdish Initiative Sparks Political Controversy in Turkey, 14 August 2009 (originally published in Eurasia Daily Monitor, Vol 6: Issue 157), available at: http://www.jamestown.org/single/?no_cache=1&tx_ttnews [tt_news]=35417.

37 Turkish President Abdullah Gul, during his recent visit to the Kurdish city of Bitlis, referred to its Kurdish name (which was replaced with its Turkish name in 1990s), which received furious criticism from the Nationalist Action Party (MHP) The Jamestown Foundation, AKP's Kurdish Initiative Sparks Political Controversy in Turkey, 14 August 2009 (originally published in Eurasia Daily Monitor, Vol 6:Issue 157), available at: http://www.jamestown.org/single/?no_cache=1&tx_ttnews [tt_news]=35417.

38 *Today's Zaman*, 'MHP's Vural: "Turkey Forced to Deal with Fabricated Problems"', 3 August 2009, available at <http://www.todayszaman.com/tz-web/news-182827-mhps-vural-turkey-forced-to-deal-with-fabricated-problems.html>.

39 *Eurasia Daily Monitor*, 'The Turkish Military and the MHP: The End of a Platonic Love Affair?', Volume 5, Issue 24, available at <http://www.jamestown.org/single/?no_cache=1&tx_ttnews[tt_news]=33363>.

40 *Bianet*, 'MHP and CHP Should be Most Supportive of Kurdish Initiative', 12 August 2009, available at <http://bianet.org/english/english/116418-mhp-and-chp-should-be-most-supportive-of-kurdish-initiative>.

41 Sabri Sayari and Yilmaz Esmer (eds), *Politics, Parties and Elections in Turkey* (Boulder, CO: Lynne Reinner Publishers, 2002), p 30.

42 Article 33 of Turkey's 1983 Electoral Law (Law No 2839) states: 'In a general election parties may not win seats unless they obtain, nationally, more than 10% of the votes validly cast … An independent candidate standing for election on the list of a political party may be elected only if the list of the party concerned obtains sufficient votes to take it over the 10% national threshold'.

43 KHRP assisted case *Yumak and Sadak v Turkey*, Application No 10226/03, on behalf of applicants who had stood as candidates for the political party DEHAP (Democratic People's Party) in the province of Sirnak in the 2002 parliamentary elections. As a result of the ballot, DEHAP obtained approximately 45.95 per cent in the province, however, it did not secure 10 per cent of the national vote. Relying on Article 3 of Protocol No 1 to the European Convention on Human Rights (right to free elections), the applicants submitted that setting a threshold of 10 per cent of the vote in parliamentary elections interfered with the free expression of the opinion of the people in their choice of the legislature.

44 Article 81(a) states, 'Political parties shall not a) assert that there exist within the territory of the Turkish Republic any national minorities based on differences relating to national or religious culture, membership of a religious sect, race or language or (…); b) aim to destroy national unity by proposing, on the pretext of protecting, promoting or disseminating a non-Turkish language or culture, to

create minorities on the territory of the Turkish Republic or to engage in similar activities … '.

45 Article 81(c) of the Political Parties Law states, 'Political parties … (c) cannot use a language other than Turkish in writing and printing party statutes or programs, at congresses, indoors or outside; at demonstrations, and in propaganda; cannot use or distribute placards, pictures, phonograph records, voice and visual tapes, brochures and statements written in a language other than Turkish; cannot remain indifferent to these actions and acts committed by others. However, it is possible to translate party statutes and programs into foreign languages other than those forbidden by law'.

46 Article 78 states, 'Political parties (a) shall not aim, strive or incite third parties to change: the republican form of Turkish state; the … provisions concerning the abso-lute integrity of the Turkish State's territory, the absolute unity of its nation, its official language, its flag or its national anthem; … the principle that sovereignty resides unconditionally and unreservedly in the Turkish nation; … the provision that sover-eign power can not be transferred to an individual, a group or a social class … jeopardize the existence of the Turkish State and Republic, abolish fundamental rights and freedoms, introduce discrimination on grounds of language, race, colour, religion or membership of a religious sect, or establish, by any means, a system of government based on any such notion or concept … '.

47 *Sadak and Others v Turkey (No 1)*, Application Nos 29900/96, 29901/96, 29902/96 and 29903/96, Judgment of 17 July 2001, European Court of Human Rights, *Sadak and Others v Turkey (No 2)*, Application Nos 25144/94, 26149/95 to 26154/95, 27100/95 and 27101/95, Judgment of 11 June 2002, para 40, European Court of Human Rights, *Freedom and Democracy Party (ÖZDEP) v Turkey*, Application No 23885/94, Judgment of 8 December 1999, European Court of Human Rights.

48 *IPS*, 'TURKEY: Ruling Party Risks Closure', 20 March 2008, available at <http://ipsnews.net/news.asp?idnews=41670> (accessed 16 November 2009).

49 Jonathan Powell, *Great Hatred, Little Room: Making Peace in Northern Ireland* (London: The Bodley Head, 2008), p 4. Jonathan Powell was Tony Blair's Chief of Staff during his terms as Prime Minister and played a lead role in the Northern Ireland process.

50 'Peacemaking in Northern Ireland: A model for conflict resolution?', Speech by Peter Hain MP, Chatham House, 12 June 2007, available at <http://www.peterhain.org/default.asp?pageid=62&mpageid=61&groupid=2>.

51 John Bew, Martyn Frampton and Inigo Gurruchaga, *Talking to Terrorists* (London: Hurst & Company, 2009), p 22.

52 Paul Dixon, *Northern Ireland: the politics of war and peace* (Basingstoke: Palgrave, 2001), p 4.

53 J Whyte, 'How much discrimination was there under the unionist regime, 1921–68?', in T Gallagher and J O'Connell (eds), *Contemporary Irish Studies* (Manchester: Manchester University Press, 1983).

54 Dixon, op. cit., fn 52, p 69.

55 G Peatling, *The Failure of the Northern Ireland Peace Process* (Dublin: Irish Academic Press, 2004), p 29.

56 Dixon, op. cit., fn 52, p 118.

57 Dixon, op. cit., fn 52, p 11.

58 David McKittrick, et al, *Lost lives: the stories of the men, women and children who died as result of the Northern Ireland troubles* (London and Edinburgh: Mainstream, 1999), p 1473.

59 Peatling, op. cit., fn 55, pp 50–51.

60 McKittrick, op. cit., fn 58.

61 See, for example Chris Gilligan, 'Peace or pacification process? A brief critique of the peace process', in Chris Gilligan and Jon Tonge (eds), *Peace or war? Understanding the peace process in Northern Ireland* (Aldershot: Ashgate, 1997), p 30, and Peatling, op. cit., fn 55, pp 94–97.

62 Dixon, op. cit., fn 52, pp 273–74.

63 Peatling, op. cit., fn 55, p 72.

64 Department of Foreign Affairs Ireland, available at <http://www.dfa.ie/home/index.aspx?id=27210>.
65 Powell, op. cit., fn 49, p 322.
66 Dixon, op. cit., fn 52, p 120.
67 Powell, op. cit., fn 49, p 70.
68 Bew, Frampton and Gurruchaga, op. cit., fn 51, p 50.
69 Gilligan, op. cit., fn 61, p 25, and Powell, op. cit., fn 49, p 64.
70 Powell, op. cit., fn 49, p 73.
71 Gilligan, op. cit., fn 61, p 26.
72 Dean Pruitt, 'Negotiation with Terrorists', (2006) 11 *International Negotiation* 371–94, p 387.
73 Clive Walker, *The prevention of terrorism in British law* (Manchester: Manchester University Press, 1992), p 58.
74 *Bianet*, 'Party Leader Erdogan Finally to Meet Kurdish MPs', 4 August 2009, available at <http://bianet.org/english/minorities/116267-party-leader-erdogan-finally-to-meet-kurdish-mps>. The DTP states that it will not call the PKK a terrorist organisation, as the PKK has to be part of the solution to the Kurdish conflict, and therefore this would not be a productive approach.
75 Ibrahim Ferhad and Gürbey Gülistan (eds), *The Kurdish Conflict in Turkey* (London: Palgrave Macmillan, 2000), p 106, and Henri J Barkey and Graham E Fuller, *Turkey's Kurdish Question (Carnegie Commission on Preventing Deadly Conflict)* (New York, NY: Rowman & Littlefield, 1998), pp 50 and 53.
76 ÇANDAR, CENGİZ, *Sabah newspaper*, 'Turkish Press Scanner', 7 August 1996, available at <http://www.hurriyetdailynews.com/h.php?news=turkish-press-scanner-1996-08-07>.
77 *Hurriyet*, 'Trial draws to an end as Öcalan disowns PKK terror', 3 June 1999, available at <http://www.hurriyetdailynews.com/h.php?news=trial-draws-to-an-end-as-ocalan-disowns-pkk-terror-1999-06-03>.
78 *PKK/Kongra-Gel Terör Örgütü: Analiz Notları, Mücadele Metodları* [The PKK/Kongra-Gel Terror Organization: Analytic Notes and Combat Methods] (Ankara: Emniyet Genel Müdürlüğü İstihbarat Daire Başkanlığı, 2008), cited in Marlies Casier, Andy Hilton and Joost Jongerden, '"Road Maps" and Roadblocks in Turkey's Southeast', 30 October 2009, available at <http://www.merip.org/mero/mero103009.html>.
79 Gerry Adams, *Hope and history: making peace in Ireland* (County Kerry: Brandon, 2003), p 49.
80 Cited in Gilligan, op. cit., fn 61, p 28.
81 Gladys Ganiel, '"Preaching to the Choir?" An Analysis of DUP Discourses about the Northern Ireland Peace Process', (2007) 22(3) *Irish Political Studies* 305.
82 Henri Barkey, 'Preventing Conflict over Kurdistan', Carnegie Endowment for International Peace, 2009, available at <http://carnegieendowment.org/publications/index.cfm?fa=view&id=22725&prog=zgp&proj=zme>.
83 Hurriyet, 'AKP Keeping Kurdish Plan Secret says Baykal,' 6 August 2009, available at <http://www.hurriyetdailynews.com/h.php?news=akp8217s-kurdish-plan-is-secret-says-baykal-2009-08-06>.
84 *Today's Zaman*, 'MHP Warns Turkey may Turn into "Hell of Minorities"', 31 August 2009, available at <http://www.todayszaman.com/tz-web/news-185639-100-mhp-warns-turkey-may-turn-into-hell-of-minorities.html>.
85 Ed Moloney, *Paisley: from demagogue to democrat?* (Dublin: Poolbeg Press, 2008), pp 356–57.
86 Ganiel, op. cit., fn 81, p 310.
87 Ganicl, op. cit., fn 81, p 310.
88 Adams, op. cit., fn 79, p 317.
89 Powell, op. cit., fn 49, p 310.
90 Bew, Frampton and Gurruchaga, op. cit., fn 51, pp 109–12 and 246–47.

91 Brian Currin, 'Lessons learnt from peace processes in South Africa, Northern Ireland and the Basque Country', EUTCC paper, p 1 (on file with authors).

92 Currin, ibid, p 4.

93 Powell, op. cit., fn 49, p 66.

94 *Today's Zaman*, 'Erdogan makes emotional appeal for unity on Kurdish initiative', 12 August 2009, available at <http://www.todayszaman.com/tz-web/news-183728-erdogan-makes-emotional-appeal-for-unity-on-kurdish-initiative.html>.

95 *Today's Zaman*, 'Erdogan to Meet with Commanders', 3 September 2009, available at <http://www.todayszaman.com/tz-web/news-185998-turkey-press-scan.html>.

96 *The Times*, 'PKK Leader Offers Turkey and Olive Branch to End War', 26 May 2009, available at <http://www.timesonline.co.uk/tol/news/world/europe/article6360955.ece>.

97 BBC News, 'IRA 'Moved Slowly' to Disarmament', 26 September 2005, available at <http://news.bbc.co.uk/1/hi/northern_ireland/4282858.stm>.

98 Gilligan, op. cit., fn 61, p 24.

99 Brian Rowan, *The armed peace: life and death after the ceasefires* (Edinburgh: Mainstream Publishing, 2004), p 45.

100 Sinn Féin and the IRA were not coterminous organisations, although there was significant overlap in their membership and constituencies, and had significant influence upon each other throughout the negotiations.

101 BBC News, Provisional IRA: War, Ceasefire, Endgame?', available at <http://news.bbc.co.uk/hi/english/static/in_depth/northern_ireland/2001/provisional_ira/1981.stm>.

102 Pruitt, op. cit., fn 72, p 386.

103 Rowan, op. cit., fn 99, p 28.

104 BBC News, 'IRA Says Armed Campaign is Over', 28 July 2005, available at <http://news.bbc.co.uk/1/hi/northern_ireland/4720863.stm>.

105 Gilligan, op. cit., fn 61, p 26.

106 Moloney, op. cit., fn 85, p 517.

107 Rowan, op. cit., fn 99, p 16.

108 Rowan, op. cit., fn 99, p 10, and Irish Republican Army (IRA) Statement ending the Ceasefire, 9 February 1996, available at<http://cain.ulst.ac.uk/events/peace/docs/ira9296.htm>.

109 See <http://www.oxfordresearchgroup.org.uk/publications/briefing_papers/what_lies_beneath_hamas_rhetoric_what_west_needs_hear>, and Alex Glennie, *Building Bridges, Not Walls: Engaging with political Islamists in the Middle East and North Africa* (London: Institute for Public Policy Research, 2009), p 39.

110 Powell, op. cit., fn 49, p 109.

111 Adams, op. cit., fn 79, pp 360–61.

112 Dean Godson, *Himself alone: David Trimble and the ordeal of unionism* (London: HarperCollins, 2004), p 351.

113 BBC News, 'Timeline: Northern Ireland Assembly,' 14 March 2008, available at <http://news.bbc.co.uk/1/hi/northern_ireland/2952997.stm>.

114 *World Tribune*, 'Turkey Plans to Move 250,000 Troops to Iraqi Border', 25 April 2006, available at <http://www.worldtribune.com/worldtribune/WTARC/2006/me_turkey_04_25.html>.

115 BBC News, 'Rendezvous with PKK', 29 July 2008, available at <http://news.bbc.co.uk/1/low/world/europe/7530713.stm>.

116 Brian Currin, 'Negotiation: A Conflict Resolution Process', paper delivered at the British Irish Association Annual Conference 1999, on file with author, pp 3–5.

117 Powell, op. cit., fn 49, p 314.

118 Peatling, op. cit., fn 55, pp 94–97.

119 Bew, Frampton and Gurruchaga, op. cit., fn 51, pp 156–57, and Moloney, op. cit., fn 85, p 352.

120 Currin, above, fn 91, p 12, and Peter Gastrow, *Bargaining for Peace: South Africa and the National Peace Accord*, (Washington, DC: United States Institute of Peace Press, 1995).

121 Thania Pfaffenholz, Darren Kew and Anthony Wanis-St John, *Civil Society and Peace Negotiations: Why, Whether and how they could be involved*, Centre for Humanitarian Dialogue, available at <http://www.hdcentre.org/publications/civil-society-and-peace-negotiations-why-whether-and-how-they-could-be-involved>, p 73.

122 Pfaffenholz, Kew and Wanis-St John, ibid, p 68.

123 Feargal Cochrane and Seamus Dunn, *People Power: The Role of the Voluntary and Community Sector in the Northern Ireland Conflict* (Cork: Cork University Press, July 2002), pp 4–5.

124 Powell, op. cit., fn 49, p 138.

125 Rowan, op. cit., fn 99, pp 15–32.

126 Report of the International Body – Senator George J Mitchell (Chairman), General John de Chastelain – Mr Harri Holkeri, 22 January 1996, available at <http://www.dfa.ie/home/index.aspx?id=8741>.

127 Powell, op. cit., fn 49, p 87.

128 The Groote Schuur Minute, 4 May 1990, available at <http://www.anc.org.za/ancdocs/history/minutes.html>. The agreement also set up a working group on political prisoners and amnesty arrangements, and entailed a government pledge to review security legislation and the state of emergency.

129 Moloney, op. cit., fn 85, p 519.

130 Nineteenth Report of the Independent Monitoring Commission, Presented to the Houses of Parliament by the Secretary of State for Northern Ireland, 3 September 2008, available at <http://www.independentmonitoringcommission.org/publications.cfm?id=69> p 7

131 Nineteenth Report of the Independent Monitoring Commission, ibid, p 8.

132 Peatling, op. cit., fn 55, pp 13–14.

133 Gilligan, op. cit., fn 61, p 23.

134 The Independent International Commission on Decommissioning (IICD) was set up in 1997 and is still active, and due to end in 2010. It has a slightly different remit to that of the Independent Monitoring Commission (IMC) that was established in 2004. The IICD is an international body focusing on arms decommissioning, while the IMC monitors any continuing activity by paramilitary groups, on the normalisation of security measures in the province, and on claims by Assembly parties that other parties, or Ministers in a devolved Executive, are not living up to the standards required of them. See <http://www.nio.gov.uk/index/key-issues/decommissioning.htm>, and <http://www.independentmonitoringcommission.org/>.

135 Andrew J Wilson, *Irish America and the Ulster Conflict: 1968–1995* (Belfast: Blackstaff Press, 1995), pp 136–37.

136 Wilson, ibid, p 249.

137 USAID Overview of Internatinoal Fund for Ireland, available at <http://www.usaid.gov/locations/europe_eurasia/countries/ie/>.

138 Reports available at <http://ec.europa.eu/enlargement/candidate-countries/turkey/key-documents/index_en.htm>. The EU accession process has played a vital role in promoting reform in Turkey, but while the accession reports have noted violence in southeast Turkey, the reports have made only limited recommendation of reform, and have not addressed the armed conflict directly by calling for its lasting and peaceful resolution.

139 Paul Collier, VL Elliott, Havard Hegre, Anke Hoeffler, Marta Reynal-Querol and Nicholas Sambanis, *Breaking the conflict trap: civil war and development policy* (Washington, DC: World Bank, May 2003).

140 The Scotland Act, the Government of Wales Act and the Northern Ireland Act were passed by the UK Parliament in 1998.

141 Russell Deacon and Alan Sandry, *Devolution in the United Kingdom* (Edinburgh: Edinburgh University Press, 2007), p 5.

142 Dixon, op. cit., fn 52, p 48.

143 Christine F Collette and Keith Laybourn, *Modern Britain Since 1979: A Reader* (London: IB Tauris, 2003), pp 144–59.

144 Secondary legislation, otherwise known as delegated legislation, is delegated through an enabling act to a body or government minister and legislates the technicalities or implementation of primary legislation, which must be passed as an Act of Parliament.

145 Leading scholar of consociational theory, Arend Lijphart, defines consociations as possessing four main characteristics: proportionality, segmental authority, coalition between groups, and mutual veto. Arend Lijphart, *Democracy in Plural Societies: A Comparative Exploration* (New Haven, CT: Yale University Press, 1977). Consociational arrangements may allocate power at the executive or legislative level, or both.

146 The First Presidential Council established following constitutional ratification in Iraq consists of the President Jalal Talabani who is Kurdish, and Vice Presidents Adel Abdul Mahdi who is Shi'i and Tariq Al-Hashimi who is Sunni.

147 For example, for application of these arguments to Lebanon see Daniel L Byman, *Keeping the Peace: Lasting Solutions to Ethnic Conflicts* (Baltimore, MD: Johns Hopkins University Press, 2002), pp 141–42. The 1943 National Pact in Lebanon allocated parliamentary positions at a ratio of 6:5 for Christian and Muslim communities, in accordance with the demographics of the time. Since then the Muslim communities in Lebanon have grown much larger than Christian communities, and the Ta'if Accord of 1989, which ended the civil war in Lebanon and established equal representation of Muslims and Christians in the legislature, still gives significantly disproportionate weight to the Christian community in the Parliament relative to its demographic weight.

148 John McGarry and Brendan O'Leary, 'Consociational Theory, Northern Ireland's Conflict, and its Agreement, 2. What Critics of Consociation Can Learn from Northern Ireland', (2006) 41(2) *Government and Opposition* 249–77.

149 The Comprehensive Settlement of the Cyprus Problem (31 March 2004), available at <http://www.unficyp.org/nqcontent.cfm?a_id=1637>.

150 From the Northern Ireland Office, available at <http://www.nio.gov.uk/the-agreement>.

151 See <http://www.britishirishcouncil.org>.

152 George Anderson, *Federalism: An Introduction* (Oxford: Oxford University Press, 2008), p 1.

153 Article 3 of the Iraqi constitution, available at <http://www.krg.org/articles/detail.asp?lngnr=12&smap=04030000&rnr=107&anr=12329>.

154 Article 4 of the Iraqi constitution.

155 Articles 116–21 of the Iraqi constitution.

156 Article 110 of the Iraqi constitution.

157 Article 114 of the Iraqi constitution.

158 'Regions and governorates shall be allocated an equitable share of the national revenues sufficient to discharge their responsibilities and duties, but having regard to their resources, needs, and the percentage of their population', Article 121.

159 Article 47 of the Iraqi constitution.

160 Article 62 of the Iraqi constitution.

161 Article 117 of the Iraqi constitution.

162 *Time*, Vivienne Walt, 'Why Iraq's Oil Law Remains Deadlocked Three Years On', 10 October 2009, available at <http://www.time.com/time/world/article/0,8599,1929201,00.html>.

163 Articles 117–19 of the Iraqi constitution.

164 BBC News, 'Iraq Passes Regional Autonomy Law,' 11 October 2006, available at <http://news.bbc.co.uk/1/hi/world/middle_east/6041916.stm>.

165 Article 113.

166 KHRP FFM Report, *Kurdistan, Iraq: Gaps in the Human Rights Infrastructure* (London: KHRP, July 2008), p 35.

167 Michael Gunter, 'Federalism and the Kurds of Iraq', in Faleh A Jabar and Hocham Dawod (eds), *The Kurds: Nationalism and Politics* (London: Saqi Books, 2006), p 238.

168 *Today's Zaman*, 'Regional Administration's Draft Constitution Kirkuk is Kurdish', 8 September 2009, available at <http://www.todayszaman.com/tz-web/columnists-186472-regional-administrations-draft-constitution-kirkuk-is-kurdish.html>.

169 Adeed I Dawisha and Karen Dawisha, 'How to build a democratic Iraq', (2003) 83(3) *Foreign Affairs*.

170 Daniel J Elazar, *Federalism and the way to peace* (Kingston: Institute of Intergovernmental Relations, Queen's University, Kingston, 1994), pp 167–69, Jack Snyder, *From voting to violence: democratization and nationalist conflict* (New York, NY/London: WW Norton, 2000), and Rogers Brubaker, *Nationalism reframed: nationhood and the national question in the New Europe* (Cambridge: Cambridge University Press, 1996).

171 John McGarry, 'Canadian Lessons for Iraq', in Brendan O'Leary, John McGarry and Khaled Salih (eds), *The Future of Kurdistan in Iraq* (Philadelphia, PA: University of Pennsylvania Press, 2005), p 94.

172 In order to adhere to the principle of federal equality, income tax collection was offered to all provinces, but in the expectation that only Quebec would take this up. McGarry, ibid, p 100.

173 Constitution of the Principality of Andorra, Articles 43–49, available at <http://www.coe.int/t/e/legal_affairs/legal_co-operation/foreigners_and_citizens/nationality/documents/national_legislation/andorra-constitution-en.asp#P263_16526>.

174 Michael G Karnavas, 'Creating the Legal Framework of the Brčko District of Bosnia and Herzegovina: A Model for the Region and Other Postconflict Countries', (2003) 97(1) *The American Journal of International Law* 111–31.

175 The Arbitral Tribunal for the dispute over the Inter-Entity Boundary in the Brčko Area: Final Status Award, available at <http://www.ohr.int/ohr-offices/brcko/arbitration/default.asp?content_id=42738>.

176 The Arbitral Tribunal, ibid, note 6, para 36, available at <http://www.ohr.int/ohr-offices/brcko/arbitration/default.asp?content_id=42738>.

177 Markku Suksi, *Autonomy: Applications and Implications* (The Hague: Brill, 1998), p 160.

178 Rolf Steininger, *South Tyrol: A Minority Conflict of the Twentieth Century* (Edison, NJ: Transaction Publishers, 2003), p 144.

179 UN Human Rights Council, Report on the United Nations Fact Finding Mission on the Gaza Conflict, available at <http://www2.ohchr.org/english/bodies/hrcouncil/specialsession/9/FactFindingMission.htm>.

180 Human Rights Watch (HRW), 'Selling Justice Short: Why Accountability Matters for Peace', 7 July 2009, available at <http://www.hrw.org/node/84264>, p 6.

181 HRW, ibid, p 1.

182 *The Washington Post*, 'Justice Off Course in Darfur', 28 June 2008, available at <http://www.washingtonpost.com/wp-dyn/content/article/2008/06/27/AR2008062702632.html>.

183 BBC News, 'African Union in Reft with Court', 3 July 2009, available at <http://news.bbc.co.uk/1/hi/8133925.stm>. Nick Grono, Deputy President of the International Crisis Group, presentation at the Overseas Development Institute seminar, 'Peace versus Justice? Understanding transitional justice in fragile states', 9 October 2009, available at <http://www.odi.org.uk/events/details.asp?id=2043&title=peace-versus-justice-understanding-transitional-justice-fragile-states>.

184 Report from the Waki Commission into post-election violence, available at <http://www.dialoguekenya.org/docs/PEV%20Report.pdf>.

185 International Criminal Court Press Release, 'ICC Prosecutor Supports Three Pronged Approach to Justice in Kenya', 30 September 2009, available at <http://www.icc-cpi.int/menus/icc/structure%20of%20the%20court/office%20of%20the%20prosecutor/comm%20and%20ref/kenya/pr456>.

186 International Criminal Court. Rome Statute, available at <http://www.icc-cpi.int/NR/rdonlyres/EA9AEFF7–5752-4F84-BE94–0A655EB30E16/0/Rome_Statute_ English. pdf>, p 12.

187 International Center for Transitional Justice, 'What is Transitional Justice?', 2008, available at <http://www.ictj.org/en/tj/>.

188 International Center for Transitional Justice, ibid.

189 Grono, above, fn 183.

190 HRW, above, fn 180, p 4. Radovan Karadžić was finally captured in July 2008 after nearly 13 years on the run, and his trial before the ICTY began on 26 October 2009. Karadžić refused to attend the trial and the case was postponed until March 2010, to give an ICTY appointed counsel the opportunity to prepare the defence case should Karadžić continue to refuse to appear before the Court, available at <http://www.icty.org/sid/10262>.

191 Marieke Wierda, 'The Potential of Complementarity' (International Center for Transitional Justice, September 2009), available at <http://www.ictj.org/static/Publications/bp_wierda_complement_rev2.pdf>.

192 Sriram, Martin-Ortega and Herman, op. cit., fn 5, p 195.

193 See Chapter 3 for more details.

194 Article 13 (b) of the Rome Statute, available at <http://www.icc-cpi.int/NR/rdonlyres/EA9AEFF7-5752-4F84-BE94–0A655EB30E16/0/Rome_Statute_English.pdf>.

195 *The Situation in Darfur, Sudan, The Prosecutor v Omar Hassan Ahmed Al Bashir*, Case ICC–0–2/05–01/09, International Criminal Court, available at <http://www.icc-cpi.int/NR/rdonlyres/08B26814-F2B1–4195-8076-B4D4026099EC/280476/CISAlBashir ENG.pdf>.

196 Article 12(3) of the Rome Statute, available at <http://www.icc-cpi.int/NR/rdonlyres/EA9AEFF7-5752-4F84-BE94–0A655EB30E16/0/Rome_Statute_English.pdf>.

197 Article 11 of the Rome Statute, available at <http://www.icc-cpi.int/NR/rdonlyres/EA9AEFF7–5752-4F84-BE94–0A655EB30E16/0/Rome_Statute_English.pdf>.

198 Coalition for the International Criminal Court Press Release, 'Turkey: Urge the Government to ratify the Rome Statute of the International Criminal Court', available at <http://www.iccnow.org/?mod=urc0205>.

199 The four crimes within the jurisdiction of the ICC as set out in Articles 5, 6, 7 and 8 are crime of genocide, crimes against humanity, war crimes, and the crime of aggression, available at <http://www.icc-cpi.int/NR/rdonlyres/EA9AEFF7-5752-4F84-BE94–0A655EB30E16/0/Rome_Statute_English.pdf>, p 3. Turkey's amended penal code (2004) criminalised genocide and crimes against humanity in Articles 76 and 77. It has been reported that a working group is preparing an International Crimes Act to fully apply the Rome Statute in Turkey's law, but this has yet to be implemented.

200 A study by Amnesty International in September 2001 found that 125 out of 130 countries studied had universal jurisdiction over one or more of the crimes of genocide, crimes against humanity, war crimes, torture, extrajudicial executions and 'disappearance' in their national criminal law. In addition, the study found that since the Second World War Australia, Austria, Belgium, Canada, Denmark, France, Germany, Israel, Mexico, the Netherlands, Senegal, Spain, Switzerland, the United Kingdom and the United States have conducted investigations, commenced prosecutions and completed trials based on universal jurisdiction for the crimes or arrested people with a view to extraditing the persons to a state seeking to prosecute them. Amnesty International, 'Universal Jurisdiction', December 2001, available at <http://www.amnesty.org/en/library/info/IOR53/020/2001>.

201 Cordula Droege establishes the historical development of international jurisprudence and state practice in this regard in Cordula Droege, 'The Interplay between International Humanitarian Law and International Human Rights Law in Situations of Armed Conflict', (2007) 40(2) *Israel Law Review* 312–24.

202 *Legal Consequences of the Construction of a Wall in the Occupied Palestinian Territory*, Advisory Opinion of 9 July 2004, [2004] *ICJ Reports* 136, paras 101–6, available at <http://www.icj-cij.org/docket/index.php?p1=3&p2=4&k=5a&case=131&code=mwp&p3=4>.

203 Droege, op. cit., fn 201, p 321, and *Bamaca Velásquez v Guatemala*, Petition No 11.129/1993, Judgment of 25 November 2000.

204 Dr Liesbeth Zegveld, presentation at Harvard University Program on Humanitarian Policy and Conflict Research seminar, 'Human Rights in the Battlefield: Litigating violations in Iraq', 24 September 2009, available at <http://ihl.ihlresearch.org/index.cfm?fuseaction=page.viewPage&pageID=2109>.

205 *Issa and Others v Turkey*, Application No 31821/96, Judgment of 16 November 2004, brought on behalf of the applicants by the KHRP.

206 *Ababekir and Others v Turkey*, Application No 16838/08, brought on behalf of the applicants by the KHRP.

207 Professor Marco Sassòli, presentation at London School of Economics on 'IHL and International Human Rights Law in Non-International Armed Conflicts', 19 February 2009, available at <http://www2.lse.ac.uk/PublicEvents/events/2008/20081203t1519z001.aspx>.

208 Clapham, op. cit., fn 16, p 284.

209 The only exception being Article 5 of the Fourth Geneva Convention, Droege, op. cit., fn 201, p 336.

210 Droege, op. cit., fn 201, p 318.

211 Peter R Baehr, 'How to Come to Terms with the Past', in Edel Hughes, William A Schabas and Ramesh Thakur (eds), *Atrocities and International Accountability: Beyond Transitional Justice* (New York, NY: United Nations University Press, 2007), p 13.

212 Tim Murithi and Paula Murphy, 'Under the Acacia: Mediation and the dilemma of inclusion', Centre for Humanitarian Dialogue, 23 April 2007, available at <http://www.hdcentre.org/publications?page=5>.

213 Janet Love, Director, Legal Resources Centre (South Africa) presentation at the Overseas Development Institute seminar, 'Peace versus Justice? Understanding transitional justice in fragile states', 9 October 2009, available at <http://www.odi.org.uk/events/details.asp?id=2043&title=peace-versus-justice-understanding-transitional-justice-fragile-states>.

214 Howard Adelman, 'Rule-based reconciliation', in Elin Skaar, Siri Gloppen and Astri Suhrke, *Roads to Reconciliation* (London: Lexington Books, 2004), pp 296–97.

215 Priscilla B Hayner, 'Fifteen Truth Commissions – 1974–94: A Comparative Study', (1994) 16(4) *Human Rights Quarterly* 604.

216 Promotion of National Unity and Reconciliation Act 1995, available at <http://www.doj.gov.za/trc/legal/act9534.htm>.

217 Paul Van Zyl, 'Dilemmas of Transitional Justice: The Case of South Africa's Truth and Reconciliation Commission', (1999) 2(2) *Journal of International Affairs* 657.

218 Jorge Heine, 'All the Truth But Only Some of the Justice?', in Hughes, Schabas and Thakur, op. cit., fn 211, pp 75–6.

219 Richard Dowden, Director, Royal African Society presentation at the Overseas Development Institute seminar, 'Peace versus Justice? Understanding transitional justice in fragile states', 9 October 2009, available at <http://www.odi.org.uk/events/details.asp?id=2043&title=peace-versus-justice-understanding-transitional-justice-fragile-states>.

220 HRW, above, fn 180, p 8.

221 Love, above, fn 213.

222 International Center for Transitional Justice, 'Bilgi University Reaches Back to Advance Peace,' 26 February 2007, available at <http://www.ictj.org/en/news/coverage/article/1168.html>.

223 International Center for Transitional Justice, ibid.

224 Vicenç Fisas, School for a Culture of Peace, Universitat Autònoma de Barcelona, *2009 Yearbook on Peace Processes* (Barcelona: Icaria editorial/School for a Culture of Peace, Universitat Autònoma de Barcelona, 2009), p 223, available at <http://escolapau.uab.cat/img/programas/procesos/09anuarii.pdf>.

225 HRW, above, fn 180, p 6.

226 Formed in 1999, see <http://healingthroughremembering.info/>.

227 'Healing Through Remembering' Report, available at <http://healingthroughremembering.info/images/pdf/htrreport.pdf>.

228 Report of the Consultative Group on the Past, Presented to the Secretary of State for Northern Ireland, in accordance with the Terms of Reference given to the Consultative Group on the Past, 22 June 2007, available at <http://www.cgpni.org>.

229 Report of the Consultative Group on the Past, ibid, pp 134–59.

230 Submission by KHRP, *NGO Shadow Report for the Review of the Turkish Government Under the UN International Convention on the Elimination of All Forms of Racial Discrimination (CERD)*, February 2009, available at <http://www.khrp.org/component/option,com_docman/task,cat_view/gid,45/Itemid,47/limit,15/limitstart,0/order,date/dir,ASC/>.

231 European Stability Initiative, available at <http://www.esiweb.org/index.php?lang=en&id=281&story_ID=21&slide_ID=5>.

232 *Bianet*, 'New Constitution Must Be Pluralist', 24 August 2007, available at <http://www.bianet.org/english/diger/101346-new-constitution-must-be-pluralist-2>.

233 YNetNews, 'Turks Vote 'Yes' in Referendum on Electing Presidents By Popular Vote', 21 October 2007, available at <http://www.ynetnews.com/Ext/Comp/ArticleLayout/CdaArticlePrintPreview/1,2506,L-3462453,00.html>.

234 Love, above, fn 213.

235 Ergun Özbudun and Omer F Genckaya, *Democratization and the Politics of Constitution Making in Turkey* (Budapest: Central European University Press, 2009), pp 4–5.

236 Özbudun and Genckaya, ibid, p 18.

237 Hayner, op. cit., fn 215, p 16.

238 Rama Mani, 'Does Power Trump Morality?', in Hughes, Schabas and Thakur, op. cit., fn 211, p 36.

239 *Hurriyet*, 'Will the PKK Take Turkey's Olive Branch?', 16 August 2009, available at <http://www.hurriyetdailynews.com/n.php?n=will-the-pkk-take-turkey8217s-olive-branch-2009-08-15>.

240 United Nations Development Group, 'Post Conflict Needs Assessment', available at <http://www.undg.org/index.cfm?P=144>.

241 Joaquin M Chavez, 'Perspectives on Demobilisation, Reintegration and Weapons Control in the El Salvador Peace Process', in *Reflections on Guns, Fighters and Armed Violence in Peace Processes* (Geneva: Centre for Humanitarian Dialogue, 2008), pp 13–19.

242 *Jane's Defence Weekly*, 'Army modernisation hampered by PKK', 19 August 1998.

243 *Bianet*, 'Öcalan: Only Democratization Can Solve the Kurdish Question', 31 August 2009, available at <http://bianet.org/english/english/116740-ocalan-only-democratization-can-solve-the-kurdish-question>.

244 'A New Beginning: Policing in Northern Ireland', A Report of the Independent Commission on Policing in Northern Ireland, September 1999, available at <http://www.nio.gov.uk/a_new_beginning_in_policing_in_northern_ireland.pdf>.

245 HRW, above, fn 180, pp 4–5.

246 Ben Chigara, *Amnesty in international law: the legality under international law of national amnesty laws* (Harlow: Longman, 2002).

247 Vicenç Fisas, School for a Culture of Peace, op. cit., fn 224.
248 *Bianet*, 'Presentation of the "State Democracy Package" After 1 October', 1 September 2009, available at <http://bianet.org/english/minorities/116765-presentation-of-the-state-democracy-package-after-1-october>.
249 Camilla Waszink, 'Trends in Weapons Control and Disarmament in Peace Processes', in Cate Buchanan (ed), *Viewpoints: Negotiating Disarmament* (Geneva: Centre for Humanitarian Dialogue, March 2008), available at <http://www.hdcentre.org/files/Report%201%20Apr08.pdf>, p 10.
250 Waszink, ibid, p 10.
251 More information on the European Union's Assistance Mission Curbing Small Arms and Light Weapons in Cambodia is available at <http://www.eu-asac.org/>.
252 Leila Nadya Sadat, 'The Effect of Amnesties', in Hughes, Schabas and Thakur, op. cit., fn 211, p 239.

Appendix 1

Provisions in Geneva Convention III respecting the classification of prisoners of war

Article 43. Armed forces

1. The armed forces of a party to a conflict consist of all organised armed forces, groups and units which are under a command responsible to that party for the conduct of its subordinates, even if that party is represented by a government or an authority not recognised by an adverse party. Such armed forces shall bex subject to an internal disciplinary system which, inter alia, shall enforce compliance with the rules of international law applicable in armed conflict.

2. Members of the armed forces of a party to a conflict (other than medical personnel and chaplains covered by Article 33 of the Third Convention) are combatants, that is to say, they have the right to participate directly in hostilities.

3. Whenever a party to a conflict incorporates a paramilitary or armed law enforcement agency into its armed forces it shall so notify the other Parties to the conflict.

Article 44. Combatants and prisoners of war

1. Any combatant, as defined in Article 43, who falls into the power of an adverse party shall be a prisoner of war.

2. While all combatants are obliged to comply with the rules of international law applicable in armed conflict, violations of these rules shall not deprive a combatant of his right to be a combatant or, if he falls into the power of an adverse party, of his right to be a prisoner of war, except as provided in paragraphs 3 and 4.

3. In order to promote the protection of the civilian population from the effects of hostilities, combatants are obliged to distinguish themselves from the civilian population while they are engaged in an attack or in a military operation preparatory to an attack. Recognising, however, that there are situations in armed conflicts where, owing to the nature of the hostilities an armed combatant cannot so distinguish himself, he shall retain his status as a combatant, provided that, in such situations, he carries his arms openly:

(a)   During each military engagement, and

(b)   During such time as he is visible to the adversary while he is engaged in a military deployment preceding the launching of an attack in which he is to participate.

Acts which comply with the requirements of this paragraph shall not be considered as perfidious within the meaning of Article 37, paragraph 1 (c).

4. A combatant who falls into the power of an adverse party while failing to meet the requirements set forth in the second sentence of paragraph 3 shall forfeit his right to be a prisoner of war, but he shall, nevertheless, be given protections equivalent in all respects to those accorded to prisoners of war by the Third Convention and by this Protocol. This protection includes protections equivalent to those accorded to prisoners of war by the Third Convention in the case where such a person is tried and punished for any offences he has committed.

5. Any combatant who falls into the power of an adverse party while not engaged in an attack or in a military operation preparatory to an attack shall not forfeit his rights to be a combatant and a prisoner of war by virtue of his prior activities.

6. This Article is without prejudice to the right of any person to be a prisoner of war pursuant to Article 4 of the Third Convention.

7. This Article is not intended to change the generally accepted practice of States with respect to the wearing of the uniform by combatants assigned to the regular, uniformed armed units of a party to the conflict.

8. In addition to the categories of persons mentioned in Article 13 of the First and Second Conventions, all members of the armed forces of a party to the conflict, as defined in Article 43 of this Protocol, shall be entitled to protection under those Conventions if they are wounded or sick or, in the case of the Second Convention, shipwrecked at sea or in other waters.

Article 45. Protection of persons who have taken part in hostilities

1. A person who takes part in hostilities and falls into the power of an adverse party shall be presumed to be a prisoner of war, and therefore shall be protected by the Third Convention, if he claims the status of prisoner of war, or if he appears to be entitled to such status, or if the party on which he depends claims such status on his behalf by notification to the detaining Power or to the Protecting Power. Should any doubt arise as to whether any such person is entitled to the status of prisoner of war, he shall continue to have such status and, therefore, to be protected by the Third Convention and this Protocol until such time as his status has been determined by a competent tribunal.

2. If a person who has fallen into the power of an adverse party is not held as a prisoner of war and is to be tried by that party for an offence arising out of the hostilities, he shall have the right to assert his entitlement to prisoner-of-war status before a judicial tribunal and to have that question adjudicated. Whenever possible under the applicable procedure, this adjudication shall occur before the

trial for the offence. The representatives of the Protecting Power shall be entitled to attend the proceedings in which that question is adjudicated, unless, exceptionally, the proceedings are held in camera in the interest of state security. In such a case the detaining Power shall advise the Protecting Power accordingly.

3. Any person who has taken part in hostilities, who is not entitled to prisoner-of-war status and who does not benefit from more favourable treatment in accordance with the Fourth Convention shall have the right at all times to the protection of Article 75 of this Protocol. In occupied territory, an such person, unless he is held as a spy, shall also be entitled, notwithstanding Article 5 of the Fourth Convention, to his rights of communication under that Convention.

Article 46. Spies

1. Notwithstanding any other provision of the Conventions or of this Protocol, any member of the armed forces of a party to the conflict who falls into the power of an adverse party while engaging in espionage shall not have the right to the status of prisoner of war and may be treated as a spy ...

Article 47. Mercenaries

1. A mercenary shall not have the right to be a combatant or a prisoner of war.
2. A mercenary is any person who:

(a) Is specially recruited locally or abroad in order to fight in an armed conflict;
(b) Does, in fact, take a direct part in the hostilities;
(c) Is motivated to take part in the hostilities essentially by the desire for private gain and, in fact, is promised, by or on behalf of a party to the conflict, material compensation substantially in excess of that promised or paid to combatants of similar ranks and functions in the armed forces of that party;
(d) Is neither a national of a party to the conflict nor a resident of territory controlled by a party to the conflict;
(e) Is not a member of the armed forces of a party to the conflict; and
(f) Has not been sent by a state which is not a party to the conflict on official duty as a member of its armed forces.

Appendix 2

Terrorism Conventions

Convention on Offences and Certain Other Acts Committed On Board Aircraft

Signed at Tokyo on 14 September 1963
    Entered into force on 4 December 1969
    Status: 184 parties

- Applies to acts affecting in-flight safety
- Authorises the aircraft commander to impose reasonable measures, including restraint, on any person he or she has reason to believe has committed or is about to commit such an act, where necessary to protect the safety of the aircraft; and
- Requires contracting states to take custody of offenders and to return control of the aircraft to the lawful commander.

Convention for the Suppression of Unlawful Seizure of Aircraft

Signed at The Hague on 16 December 1970
    Entered into force on 14 October 1971
    Status: 183 parties

- Makes it an offence for any person on board an aircraft in flight to 'unlawfully, by force or threat thereof, or any other form of intimidation, [to] seize or exercise control of that aircraft' or to attempt to do so;
- Requires parties to the convention to make hijackings punishable by 'severe penalties';
- Requires parties that have custody of offenders to either extradite the offender or submit the case for prosecution; and
- Requires parties to assist each other in connection with criminal proceedings brought under the Convention.

Convention for the Suppression of Unlawful Acts Against the Safety of Civil Aviation

Signed at Montreal on 23 September 1971
  Entered into force on 26 January 1973
  Status: 187 parties

- Makes it an offence for any person unlawfully and intentionally to perform an act of violence against a person on board an aircraft in flight, if that act is likely to endanger the safety of the aircraft; to place an explosive device on an aircraft; to attempt such acts; or to be an accomplice of a person who performs or attempts to perform such acts;
- Requires parties to the Convention to make offences punishable by 'severe penalties'; and
- Requires parties that have custody of offenders to either extradite the offender or submit the case for prosecution.

Convention on the Prevention and Punishment of Crimes against Internationally Protected Persons, including Diplomatic Agents

Adopted at New York on 14 December 1973
  Entered into force on 20 February 1977
  Status: 171 parties

- Defines an 'internationally protected person' as a Head of State, Minister for Foreign Affairs, representative or official of a state or international organisation who is entitled to special protection in a foreign state, and his her family; and
- Requires parties to criminalise and make punishable 'by appropriate penalties which take into account their grave nature' the intentional murder, kidnapping or other attack upon the person or liberty of an internationally protected person, a violent attack upon the official premises, the private accommodations, or the means of transport of such person; a threat or attempt to commit such an attack; and an act 'constituting participation as an accomplice'.

International Convention Against the Taking of Hostages

Adopted at New York on 17 December 1979
  Entered into force on 3 June 1983
  Status: 166 parties

- Provides that 'any person who seizes or detains and threatens to kill, to injure, or to continue to detain another person in order to compel a third party, namely, a state, an international intergovernmental organization, a natural or juridical person, or a group of persons, to do or abstain from doing any act as an explicit or implicit condition for the release of the hostage commits the offence of taking of hostage within the meaning of this Convention'.

Convention on the Physical Protection of Nuclear Material

Signed at Vienna on 26 October 1979
  Entered into force on 8 February 1987
  Status: 139 parties

- Criminalises the unlawful possession, use, transfer or theft of nuclear material and threats to use nuclear material to cause death, serious injury or substantial property damage.

Amendments to the Convention on the Physical Protection of Nuclear Material

Signed at Vienna on 8 July 2005
  Status: 22 parties

- Makes it legally binding for states parties to protect nuclear facilities and material in peaceful domestic use, storage as well as transport; and
- Provides for expanded cooperation between and among states regarding rapid measures to locate and recover stolen or smuggled nuclear material, mitigate any radiological consequences or sabotage, and prevent and combat related offences.

Protocol for the Suppression of Unlawful Acts of Violence at Airports Serving International Civil Aviation, Supplementary to the Convention for the Suppression of Unlawful Acts against the Safety of Civil Aviation, done at Montreal on 23 September 1971

Signed at Montreal on 24 February 1988
  Entered into force on 6 August 1989
  Status: 167 parties

- Extends the provisions of the Montreal Convention (see Convention for the Suppression of Unlawful Acts Against the Safety of Civil Aviation, above) to encompass terrorist acts at airports serving international civil aviation.

Convention for the Suppression of Unlawful Acts Against the Safety of Maritime Navigation

Done at Rome on 10 March 1988
  Entered into force on 1 March 1992
  Status: 152 parties

- Establishes a legal regime applicable to acts against international maritime navigation that is similar to the regimes established for international aviation; and
- Makes it an offence for a person unlawfully and intentionally to seize or exercise control over a ship by force, threat, or intimidation; to perform an act of violence against a person on board a ship if that act is likely to endanger the safe navigation of the ship; to place a destructive device or substance aboard a ship; and other acts against the safety of ships.

Protocol to the Convention for the Suppression of Unlawful Acts Against the Safety of Maritime Navigation

Adopted at London on 14 October 2005
  Status: 8 parties

- Criminalises the use of a ship as a device to further an act of terrorism;
- Criminalises the transport on board a ship various materials knowing that it is intended to be used to cause, or in a threat to cause, death or serious injury or damage to further an act of terrorism;
- Criminalises the transporting on board a ship of persons who have committed an act of terrorism; and
- Introduces procedures for governing the boarding of a ship believed to have committed an offence under the Convention.

Protocol for the Suppression of Unlawful Acts Against the Safety of Fixed Platforms Located on the Continental Shelf

Done at Rome on 10 March 1988
  Entered into force on 1 March 1992
  Status: 140 parties

- Establishes a legal regime applicable to acts against fixed platforms on the continental shelf that is similar to the regimes established against international aviation.

Protocol to the Protocol for the Suppression of Unlawful Acts Against the Safety of Fixed Platforms Located on the Continental Shelf

Adopted at London on 14 October 2005
  Status: 6 parties

- Adapts the changes to the Convention for the Suppression of Unlawful Acts against the Safety of Maritime Navigation to the context of fixed platforms located on the continental shelf.

Convention on the Marking of Plastic Explosives for the Purpose of Detection

Done at Montreal on 1 March 1991
  Entered into force on 21 June 1998
  Status: 139 parties

- Designed to control and limit the use of unmarked and undetectable plastic explosives (negotiated in the aftermath of the 1988 Pan Am flight 103 bombing):
- Parties are obligated in their respective territories to ensure effective control over 'unmarked' plastic explosives, ie those that do not contain one of the detection agents described in the Technical Annex to the treaty; and
- Generally speaking, each party must, *inter alia*, take necessary and effective measures to prohibit and prevent the manufacture of unmarked plastic explosives; prevent the movement of unmarked plastic explosives into or out of its territory; exercise strict and effective control over possession and transfer of unmarked explosives made or imported prior to the entry into force of the Convention; ensure that all stocks of unmarked explosives not held by the military or police are destroyed, consumed, marked, or rendered permanently ineffective within 3 years; take necessary measures to ensure that unmarked plastic explosives held by the military or police are destroyed, consumed, marked or rendered permanently ineffective within 15 years; and, ensure the destruction, as soon as possible, of any unmarked explosives manufactured after the date of entry into force of the Convention for that state.

International Convention for the Suppression of Terrorist Bombings

Adopted at New York on 15 December 1997
  Entered into force on 23 May 2001
  Status: 161 parties

- Creates a regime of universal jurisdiction over the unlawful and intentional use of explosives and other lethal devices in, into, or against various defined public places with intent to kill or cause serious bodily injury, or with intent to cause extensive destruction of the public place.

International Convention for the Suppression of the Financing of Terrorism

Adopted at New York on 9 December 1999
  Entered into force on 10 April 2002
  Status: 167 parties

- Requires parties to take steps to prevent and counteract the financing of terrorists, whether direct or indirect, though groups claiming to have charitable, social or cultural goals or which also engage in illicit activities such as drug trafficking or gun running;
- Commits states to hold those who finance terrorism criminally, civilly or administratively liable for such acts; and
- Provides for the identification, freezing and seizure of funds allocated for terrorist activities, as well as for the sharing of the forfeited funds with other states on a case-by-case basis. Bank secrecy is no longer adequate justification for refusing to cooperate.

International Convention for the Suppression of Acts of Nuclear Terrorism

Adopted at New York on 13 April 2005
  Entered into force on 7 July 2007
  Status: 47 parties

- Covers a broad range of acts and possible targets, including nuclear power plants and nuclear reactors;
- Covers threats and attempts to commit such crimes or to participate in them, as an accomplice;
- Stipulates that offenders shall be either extradited or prosecuted;
- Encourages states to cooperate in preventing terrorist attacks by sharing information and assisting each other in connection with criminal investigations and extradition proceedings; and
- Deals with both crisis situations (assisting states to solve the situation) and post-crisis situations (rendering nuclear material safe through the International Atomic Energy Agency (IAEA)).

  Various possible definitions have been reviewed. There is one international instrument that includes a definition: the International Convention for the Suppression of the Financing of Terrorism, adopted by the General Assembly of the United Nations on 9 December 1999. Within this treaty there is one short provision on terrorism:

- (b) Any other act intended to cause death or serious bodily injury to a civilian, or to any other person not taking an active part in the hostilities in a situation of armed conflict, when the purpose of such act, by its nature or context, is to intimidate a population, or to compel a government or an international organization to do or to abstain from doing any act.

Treaties referred to in the Council of Europe Convention

1 Convention for the Suppression of Unlawful Seizure of Aircraft, signed at The Hague on 16 December 1970;

2 Convention for the Suppression of Unlawful Acts Against the Safety of Civil Aviation, concluded at Montreal on 23 September 1971;

3 Convention on the Prevention and Punishment of Crimes Against Internationally Protected Persons, Including Diplomatic Agents, adopted in New York on 14 December 1973;

4 International Convention Against the Taking of Hostages, adopted in New York on 17 December 1979;

5 Convention on the Physical Protection of Nuclear Material, adopted in Vienna on 3 March 1980;

6 Protocol for the Suppression of Unlawful Acts of Violence at Airports Serving International Civil Aviation, done at Montreal on 24 February 1988;

7 Convention for the Suppression of Unlawful Acts Against the Safety of Maritime Navigation, done at Rome on 10 March 1988;

8 Protocol for the Suppression of Unlawful Acts Against the Safety of Fixed Platforms Located on the Continental Shelf, done at Rome on 10 March 1988;

9 International Convention for the Suppression of Terrorist Bombings, adopted in New York on 15 December 1997;

10 International Convention for the Suppression of the Financing of Terrorism, adopted in New York on 9 December 1999.

Appendix 3
The Mitchell Principles

- To democratic and exclusively peaceful means of resolving political issues;
- To the total disarmament of all paramilitary organisations;
- To agree that such disarmament must be verifiable to the satisfaction of an independent commission;
- To renounce for themselves, and to oppose any effort by others, to use force, or threaten to use force, to influence the course or the outcome of all-party negotiations;
- To agree to abide by the terms of any agreement reached in all-party negotiations and to resort to democratic and exclusively peaceful methods in trying to alter any aspect of that outcome with which they may disagree; and,
- To urge that 'punishment' killings and beatings stop and to take effective steps to prevent such actions.

Bibliography

Adams, Gerry, *Hope and history: making peace in Ireland* (County Kerry: Brandon, 2003)

Adelman, Howard, 'Rule-based reconciliation', in Skaar, Elin, Gloppen, Siri and Suhrke, Astri (eds), *Roads to Reconciliation* (London: Lexington Books, 2004)

Ahmad, Feroz, *The Making of Modern Turkey* (London: Routledge, 1993)

Allawi, Ali A, *The occupation of Iraq: winning the war, losing the peace* (New Haven, CT: Yale University Press, 2007)

Anderson, George, *Federalism: An Introduction* (Oxford: Oxford University Press, 2008)

Baehr, Peter R, 'How to Come to Terms with the Past', in Hughes, Edel, Schabas, William A, and Thakur, Ramesh (eds), *Atrocities and International Accountability: Beyond Transitional Justice* (New York, NY: United Nations University Press, 2007)

Bahcheli, Tozun, Bartmann, Barry and Srebrnik, Henry (eds), *De Facto States: The Quest For Sovereignty* (New York, NY: Routledge, 2004)

Barendt, Eric, *An Introduction to Constitutional Law* (Oxford: Oxford University Press, 1998)

Barkey, Henri J and Fuller, Graham E, *Turkey's Kurdish Question* (New York, NY: Rowman and Littlefield, 1998)

Bassiouni, M Cherif (ed), *Legal Responses to International Terrorism* (Dordrecht: Martinus Nijhoff, 1988)

Bew, John, Frampton, Martyn and Gurruchaga, Inigo, *Talking to Terrorists* (London: C Hurst & Co Publishers, 2009)

Bobbitt, Philip, *Terror and Consent: The Wars for the Twenty-First Century* (London: Penguin Books, 2008)

Brancati, Dawn, 'Can Federalism Stabilize Iraq?', (2004) 27 *The Washington Quarterly* 7

Breau, Susan, *Humanitarian Intervention: The United Nations and Collective Responsibility* (London: Cameron May, 2005)

——, 'International Court of Justice Advisory Opinion on the Legal Consequences of the Construction of the Wall in the Occupied Palestinian Territory', (2005) 54 *International and Comparative Legal Quarterly* 1003

——, 'The Impact of the Responsibility to Protect on Peacekeeping', (2006) 11 *Journal of Conflict and Security Law* 429

Brownlie, Ian, *Principles of Public International Law*, 7th edition (Oxford: Oxford University Press, 2008)

Buchanan, Allen, M, *Secession: The Morality of Political Divorce from Fort Sumter to Lithuania and Quebec* (Boulder, CO: Westview Press, 1991)

Buchheit, Lee C, *Secession: The Legitimacy of Self-Determination* (London: Yale University Press, 1978)

Bullock, John and Morris, Harvey, *No Friends but the Mountains: The Tragic History of the Kurds* (Oxford: Oxford University Press, 1992)

Burgess, Michael, 'Federalism and Federation: A Reappraisal', in Burgess, Michael and Gagnon, Alain G, *Comparative Federalism and Federation* (London: Harvester, 1993)

Byman, Daniel L, *Keeping the Peace: Lasting Solutions to Ethnic Conflicts* (Baltimore, MD: Johns Hopkins University Press, 2002)

Cassese, Antonio, 'Political Self-Determination – Old Concepts and New Developments', in Cassese, Antonio (ed), *UN Law/Fundamental Rights: Two Topics in International Law* (Dordrecht: Martinus Nijhoff Publishers, 1979)

——, *Self-determination of Peoples* (Cambridge: Cambridge University Press, 1995)

——, 'The Helsinki Declaration and Self-Determination', in Buergenthal, Thomas and Hall, J (eds), *Human Rights, International Law and the Helsinki Accord* (New York, NY: Allenheld, 1977)

Castellino, Joshua, *International Law and Self-Determination* (The Hague: Martinus Nijhoff, 2000)

Chaliand, Gerard (ed), *A People without a Country: The Kurds and Kurdistan* (New York, NY: Olive Branch Press, 1993)

Chigara, Ben, *Amnesty in international law: the legality under international law of national amnesty laws* (Harlow: Longman, 2002)

Clapham, Andrew, 'Secession, terrorism and the right of self-determination', in Kohen, Marcelo G (ed), *Secession: International Law Perspectives* (Cambridge: Cambridge University Press, 2006)

Cleveland, William, L, *A history of the modern Middle East* (Boulder, CO: Westview Press, 2004)

Cline, Lawrence E, 'From Ocalan to Al Qaida: The Continuing Terrorist Threat in Turkey', (2004) 27 *Studies in Conflict & Terrorism* 321

Cochrane, Feargal and Dunn, Seamus, *People Power: The Role of the Voluntary and Community Sector in the Northern Ireland Conflict* (Cork: Cork University Press, July 2002)

Collette, Christine F and Laybourn, Keith, *Modern Britain Since 1979: A Reader* (London: IB Tauris, 2003)

Collier, Paul, Elliott, VL, Hegre, Havard, Hoeffler, Anke, Reynal-Querol, Marta and Sambanis, Nicholas, *Breaking the conflict trap: civil war and development policy* (New York, NY: World Bank, 2003)

Coppieters, Bruno and Sakwa, Richard, *Contextualising Secession – Normative Studies in Comparative Perspective* (New York, NY: Oxford University Press, 2003)

Crawford, Emily, 'Unequal before the Law: The Case for the Elimination of the Distinction between International and Non-international Armed Conflicts', (2007) 20 *Leiden Journal of International Law* 441

Crawford, James, *The Creation of States in International Law*, 2nd edition (Oxford: Oxford University Press, 2006)

——, *The International Law Commission's Articles on State Responsibility: Introduction, Text and Commentaries* (Cambridge: Cambridge University Press, 2002)

——, 'The Rights of Peoples: "Peoples" or "Governments"?', in Crawford, James (ed), *The Rights of Peoples* (Oxford: Clarendon Press, 1988)

Cullen, Anthony, 'Key Development Affecting the Scope of Internal Armed Conflict in International Humanitarian Law', (2005) 183 *Military Law Review* 66

Cutler, Lloyd N, 'The right to intervene', (1985–86) 64 *Foreign Affairs* 96

Cvijić, Srdan, 'Self-determination as a Challenge to the Legitimacy of Humanitarian Interventions: The Case of Kosovo', (2007) 8 *German Law Journal* 57

Dammers, Chris, 'Iraq', in Hampton, Janie (ed), *Internally Displaced People: A Global Survey* (London: Earthscan, 1998)

Danspeckgruber, Wolfgang (ed), *The Self-Determination of Peoples: Community, Nation and State in an Interdependent World* (Boulder, CO: Lynne Reinner, 2002)

Deacon, Russell and Sandry, Alan, *Devolution in the United Kingdom* (Edinburgh: Edinburgh University Press, 2007)

DeRouen, Karl and Heo, Uk (eds), *Civil Wars of the World: Major Conflicts since World War II* (Santa Barbara, CA: ABC-CLIO, 2007)

Dinstein, Yoram, *War, Aggression and Self-Defence*, 4th edition (Oxford: Oxford University Press, 2005)

Dixon, Paul, *Northern Ireland: the politics of war and peace* (Basingstoke: Palgrave, 2001)

Doswald-Beck, Louise, 'Military Intervention by Invitation of the Government' (1986) *British Yearbook of International Law* 197

Draper, Gerald, 'The status of combatants and the question of guerrilla warfare', (1971) *British Yearbook of International Law* 173

Droege, Cordula, 'The Interplay between International Humanitarian Law and International Human Rights Law in Situations of Armed Conflict', (2007) 40(2) *Israel Law Review* 312

Duffy, Helen, *The 'War on Terror' and the Framework of International Law* (Cambridge: Cambridge University Press, 2005)

Dugard, John, 'International Terrorism: Problems of Definition', (1974) 50 *International Affairs* 67

Eastwood, Lawrence, S, 'Secession: State Practice and International Law after the dissolution of the Soviet Union and Yugoslavia', (1993) 3 *Duke Journal of Comparative & International Law* 299

Farer, Tom, 'Humanitarian Law and Armed Conflicts: Towards the Definition of "International Armed Conflict"', (1971) 71 *Columbia Law Review* 37

Ganiel, Gladys '"Preaching to the Choir"' An Analysis of DUP Discourses about the Northern Ireland Peace Process', (2007) 22 *Irish Political Studies* 303

Gasser, Hans-Peter, 'Acts of Terror, Terrorism and International Humanitarian Law', (2002) 84 *International Review of the Red Cross* 547

——, 'International Humanitarian Law: an Introduction', in Haug, H (ed), *Humanity for All: the International Red Cross and Red Crescent Movement* (Berne: Paul Haupt Publishers, 1993)

Gastrow, Peter, *Bargaining for Peace: South Africa and the National Peace Accord* (Washington, DC: United States Institute of Peace Press, 1995)

Ghandi, M, 'Common Article 3 of the Geneva Conventions, 1949 In the Era of International Criminal Tribunals', [2001] *ISIL Year Book of International Humanitarian and Refugee Law* 11

Gilligan, Chris 'Peace or pacification process? A brief critique of the peace process', in Gilligan, Chris and Tonge, Jon (eds), *Peace or war?: understanding the peace process in Northern Ireland* (Aldershot: Ashgate, 1997)

Godson, Dean, *Himself alone: David Trimble and the ordeal of unionism* (London: HarperCollins, 2004)

Gomien, Donna, Harris, David and Zwaak, Leo, *Law and Practice of the European Convention on Human Rights and the European Social Charter* (Strasbourg: Council of Europe Publishing, 1996)

Goodwin, Morag, 'Special Issue Introduction – What Future for Kosovo? – From Province to Protectorate to State? Speculation on the Impact of Kosovo's Genesis upon the Doctrines of International Law', (2007) 8 *German Law Journal* 1

Gorelick, Robert E, 'Wars of National Liberation: *Jus Ad bellum*', (1979) 11 *Case Western Reserve Journal of International Law* 71

Gray, Christine, *International Law and the Use of Force*, 3rd edition (Oxford: Oxford University Press, 2008)

Greenwood, Christopher, *Essays on War in International Law* (London: Cameron May, 2006)

——, 'International Humanitarian Law and the Tadic Case', (1996) 7 *European Journal of International Law* 265

Gross, Oren and Ní Aoláin, Fionnuala, *Law in Times of Crisis, Emergency Powers in Theory and Practice* (Cambridge: Cambridge University Press, 2006)

Grotius, Hugo, *The Law of War and Peace*, F Kelsey Translation (Oxford: Oxford University Press, 1925)

Gunter, Michael, 'Federalism and the Kurds of Iraq', in Jabar, Faleh A and Dawod, Hocham (eds), *The Kurds: Nationalism and Politics* (London: Saqi Books, 2006)

——, *The Kurds in Turkey: A Political Dilemma* (Boulder, CO: Westview Press, 1990)

——, and Yavuz, M Hakan, 'Turkish Paradox: Progressive Islamists versus Reactionary Secularists', (2007) 16(3) *Middle East Critique* 289

Hampson, Francoise, 'Fundamental Guarantees' and 'Other Areas of Customary Law in relation to the Study', in Wilmshurst, Elizabeth and Breau, Susan, *Perspectives on the ICRC Study on Customary International Law* (Cambridge: Cambridge University Press, 2007)

Hannum, Hurst, *Autonomy, Sovereignty, and Self-Determination* (Philadelphia, PA: University of Pennsylvania Press, 1996)

——, 'Human Rights', in Joyner, C, *The United Nations and International Law* (Cambridge: Cambridge University Press, 1997)

Harris, David, J, *Cases & Materials on International Law*, 6th edition (London: Sweet & Maxwell, 2004)

Hayner, Priscilla B, 'Fifteen Truth Commissions – 1974–94: A Comparative Study', (1994) 16 *Human Rights Quarterly* 597

Heintze, Hans-Joachim, 'On the relationship between human rights law protection and international humanitarian law', (2004) 86 *International Review of the Red Cross* 789

Henckaerts, Jean Marie and Doswald-Beck, Louise, *Customary International Humanitarian Law, Volume 1: Rules* (Cambridge: Cambridge University Press, 2005)

Higgins, Rosalyn, 'Postmodern Tribalism and the Right to Secession, Comments', in Brölmann, Catherine, Zieck, Marjoleine and Lefeber, René (eds), *Peoples and Minorities in International Law* (Dordrecht: Martinus Nijhoff, 1993)

——, *Problems and Process: International Law and How We Use It* (Oxford: Oxford University Press, 1994)

——, 'The General Law of Terrorism', in Higgins, Rosalyn and Flory, Maurice (eds), *Terrorism and International Law* (London: Routledge, 1997)

Honoré, Tony, 'The Right to Rebel', (1988) 8 *Oxford Journal of Legal Studies* 34

Humphrey, John Peters, 'Political and Related Rights', in Meron, T (ed), *Human Rights in International Law: Legal and Policy Issues*, two volumes (Oxford: Clarendon Press, 1984)

Ibrahim, Ferhad and Gürbey, Gülistan (eds), *The Kurdish Conflict in Turkey* (London: Palgrave Macmillan, 2000)

Jachec-Neale, Agnieszka, 'Status and treatment of prisoners of war and other persons deprived of their liberty', in Wilmshurst, Elizabeth and Breau, Susan, *Perspectives on the ICRC Study on Customary International Law* (Cambridge: Cambridge University Press, 2007)

Kahraman, Ahmet, *Uprising, Suppression, Retribution: The Kurdish Struggle in Turkey in the Twentieth Century* (London: Garod Books Ltd, 2007)

Karnavas, Michael G, 'Creating the Legal Framework of the Brčko District of Bosnia and Herzegovina: A Model for the Region and Other Postconflict Countries', (2003) 97 *American Journal of International Law* 111

Khan, L Ali, 'A Legal Theory of Revolution' (1987) 5 *Boston University International Law Journal* 1

King, Preston, 'Federation and Representation', in Burgess, Michael and Gagnon, Alain G, *Comparative Federalism and Federation* (London: Harvester, 1993)

Kinzer, Stephen, *Crescent and Star: Turkey Between Two Worlds* (New York, NY: Farrar, Straus and Giroux, 2001)

Kohen, Marcelo (ed), *Secession: International Law Perspectives* (Cambridge: Cambridge University Press, 2006)

Kutner, Luis, 'Due Process of Rebellion', (1972–73) 7 *Valparaiso University Law Review* 1

Kymlicka, Will, 'The Internationalization of Minority Rights', (2008) *International Journal of Constitutional Law* 1

Lauterpacht, Hersch, *Recognition in International Law* (Cambridge: Cambridge University Press, 1947)

Lee, Martin A, *The Beast Reawakens: Fascism's resurgence from Hitler's Spymasters to Today's Neo-Nazi Groups and Right Wing Extremists* (London: Routledge, 1999)

Lewis, Bernard, *The Emergence of Modern Turkey* (Oxford: Oxford University Press, 2001)

Lillich, Richard, *The Human Rights of Aliens in Contemporary International Law* (Manchester: Manchester University Press, 1984)

Locke, John, *Two Treatises of Government* (1683) reprinted (Clark, NJ: The Lawbook Exchange Ltd, 2006)

Lootsteen, Yair M, 'The Concept of Belligerency in International Law', (2000) 166 *Military Law Review* 109

Lowe, Vaughan, *International Law* (Oxford: Oxford University Press, 2007)

Macklem, Patrick, 'Militant Democracy, legal pluralism, and the paradox of self-determination', (2006) *International Journal of Constitutional Law* 488

Malone, David, *The International Struggle over Iraq: Politics in the UN Security Council 1980–2005* (Oxford: Oxford University Press, 2006)

Manes, Aaron, *Profiles in Terror: The Guide to Middle East Terrorist Organizations* (Lanham, MD: Rowman & Littlefield, 2004)

Marcus, Aliza, *Blood and Belief: The PKK and the Kurdish Fight for Independence* (New York, NY: New York University Press, 2007)

McDowall, David, *A Modern History of the Kurds*, 3rd edition (London: IB Tauris, 2004)

——, *The Kurds: A Nation Denied* (London: Minority Rights Publication, 1992)

McGarry, John, 'Canadian Lessons for Iraq', in O'Leary, Brendan, McGarry, John and Salih, Khaled (eds), *The Future of Kurdistan in Iraq* (Philadelphia, PA: University of Pennsylvania Press, 2005)

——, and O'Leary, Brendan, 'Consociational Theory, Northern Ireland's Conflict, and its Agreement, 2. What Critics of Consociation Can Learn from Northern Ireland', (2006) 41 *Government and Opposition* 249

McKittrick, David, Kelters, Seamus, Feeney, Brian and Thornton, Chris, *Lost lives: the stories of the men, women and children who died as result of the Northern Ireland troubles* (London and Edinburgh: Mainstream, 1999)

Moir, Lindsay, *The Law of Internal Armed Conflict* (Cambridge: Cambridge University Press, 2002)

Moloney, Ed, *Paisley: from demagogue to democrat?* (Dublin: Poolbeg Press, 2008)

Muller, Mark, 'Terrorism, proscription and the right to resist in the age of conflict', (2008) 20 *Denning Law Journal* 111

Nanda, Ved, 'Self-Determination under International Law: Validity of Claims to Secede', (1981) 13 *Case Western Reserve Journal of International Law* 257

Oppenheim, Lassa, *International Law, Volume II* (London: Longmans, Green & Co, 1906)

Özbudun, Ergun and Genckaya, Omer F, *Democratization and the Politics of Constitution Making in Turkey* (Budapest: Central European University Press, 2009)

Peatling, Gary, *The Failure of the Northern Ireland Peace Process* (Dublin: Irish Academic Press, 2004)

Peijić, Jelena, 'Status of armed conflicts', in Wilmshurst, Elizabeth and Breau, Susan, *Perspectives on the ICRC Study on Customary International Law* (Cambridge: Cambridge University Press, 2007)

Pictet, Jean, *Commentary on the Geneva Convention for the Amelioration of the Condition of the Wounded and Sick in Armed Forces in the Field* (Geneva: International Committee of the Red Cross, 1952)

——, *Commentary IV Geneva Convention Relative to the Protection of Civilian Persons in Time of War* (Geneva: International Committee of the Red Cross, 1958)

Pope, Nicole and Pope, Hugh, *Turkey Unveiled: A History of Modern Turkey* (Woodstock, NY: Overlook Press, 2000)

Powell, Jonathan, *Great Hatred, Little Room: Making Peace in Northern Ireland* (London: The Bodley Head, 2008)

Prevost, René, *International Human Rights and Humanitarian Law* (Cambridge: Cambridge University Press, 2002)

Pruitt, Dean, 'Negotiation with Terrorists', (2006) *International Negotiation* 370

Quigley, John, 'David v. Goliath: Humanitarian and Human Rights Law in light of the Palestinian Right to Self-Determination and the Right to Recapture Territory Taken by Force', (1988–89) 21 *New York University Journal of International Law and Policy* 489

Raič, David, *Statehood & The Law of Self-Determination* (The Hague: Martinus Nijhoff, 2002)

Rehman, Javaid, *Islamic State Practices, International Law and the Threat from Terrorism: A Critique of the Clash of Civilizations in the New World Order* (Oxford: Hart Publishing, 2005)

Reinisch, August, 'The Action of the European Union to Combat International Terrorism', in Bianchi, Andrea, *Enforcing International Law Norms Against Terrorism* (Oxford: Hart Publishing, 2004)

Reisman, Michael, 'Coercion and Self-Determination: Construing Charter Article 2(4)', (1984) 78 *American Journal of International Law* 642

Roberts, Adam and Guelff, Robert (eds), *Documents on the Laws of War*, 3rd edition (Oxford: Oxford University Press, 2000)

Rogers, Anthony, 'Combatant Status', in Wilmshurst, Elizabeth and Breau, S (eds), *Perspectives on the ICRC Study on Customary International Humanitarian Law* (Cambridge: Cambridge University Press, 2007)

Rowan, Brian, *The armed peace: life and death after the ceasefires* (Edinburgh: Mainstream Publishing, 2004)

Ruys, Tom, 'A Legal Analysis of Turkey's Military Operations against the PKK in Northern Iraq', (2008) 9 *Melbourne Journal of International Law* 334

Saeedpour, Vera, *Meet the Kurds* (London: Cobblestone Publishing, 1999)

Sandoz, Yves (ed), *Commentary on the Additional Protocols of 8 June 1977 to the Geneva Conventions of 12 August 1949* (Geneva: International Committee of the Red Cross, 1987)

Saul, Ben, *Defining Terrorism in International Law* (Oxford: Oxford University Press, 2008)

Schindler, Dietrich, 'The Different Types of Armed Conflicts According to the Geneva Conventions and Protocols', (1979) 163(ii) *Recueil des cours* 117

Schindler, Dietrich and Toman, Jiri (eds), *The Laws of Armed Conflict*, 4th edition (Leiden: Martinus Nijhoff, 2004)

Schmitt, Michael, 'The Law of Targeting', in Wilmshurst, Elizabeth and Breau, Susan (eds), *Perspectives on the ICRC Study on Customary International Humanitarian Law* (Cambridge: Cambridge University Press, 2007)

——, Garraway, Charles and Dinstein, Yoram, 'The Manual on the Law of Non-International Armed Conflict With Commentary', in Dinstein, Yoram and Domb, Fania (eds), *Israel Yearbook of Human Rights (Special Supplement)*, Volume 36 (Dordrecht: Martinus Nijhoff, 2006)

Shaw, Malcolm, *International Law*, 6th edition (Cambridge: Cambridge University Press, 2008)

Sloan, Blaine, 'General Assembly Resolutions Revisited (Forty Years After)', (1987) 58 *British Yearbook of International Law* 39

Smith, Graham, 'Mapping the Federal Condition: Ideology, Political Practice and Social Justice', in Smith, Graham (ed), *Federalism: The Multiethnic Challenge* (London: Longman, 1995)

Stahn, Carsten, 'Enforcement of the Collective Will after Iraq', (2003) 97 *American Journal of International Law* 804

Stewart, James, 'Towards a single definition of armed conflict in international humanitarian law: A critique of internationalized armed conflict' (2003) 85 *International Review of the Red Cross* 315

Thornberry, Patrick, 'Self-Determination, Minorities, Human Rights: A Review of International Instruments', (1989) 38 ICLQ 867

——, 'The Principle of Self-determination', in Akehurst, Michael, Lowe, Vaughan and Warbrick, Colin (eds), *The United Nations & Principles of International Law* (London: Routledge, 1994)

Vattel, Emmerich, *Law of Nations*, Volume III (1758), English translation by CG Fenwick; reprinted (Dobbs Ferry, NY: Oceana Publications Inc, 1964)

Visser, Reidar and Stansfield, Gareth (eds), *An Iraq of its Regions: Cornerstones of a Federal Democracy?* (London: Hurst & Company, 2007)

Walker, Clive, *The prevention of terrorism in British law* (Manchester: Manchester University Press, 1992)

Warbrick, Colin, 'Kosovo: The Declaration of Independence', (2008) 57 ICLQ 675

Watts, Ronald, *Comparing Federal Systems*, 2nd edition (Montreal and Kingston: McGill-Queen's University Press, 1999)

Whyte, John, 'How much discrimination was there under the unionist regime, 1921–68?', in Gallagher, Tom and O'Connell, James (eds), *Contemporary Irish Studies* (Manchester: Manchester University Press, 1983)

Williams, Andrew, *EU Human Rights Policies, A Study in Irony* (Oxford: Oxford University Press, 2004)

Wilson, Andrew J, *Irish America and the Ulster Conflict: 1968–1995* (Belfast: Blackstaff Press, 1995)

Yildiz, Kerim, *The Kurds in Iraq: Past, Present and Future* (London: Pluto Press, 2004)

——, *The Kurds in Turkey* (London: Pluto Press, 2005)

——, and Muller, Mark, *The European Union and Turkish Accession: Human Rights and the Kurds* (London: Pluto Press, 2008)

Index